Sermons

of

Martin Luther

Sermons

of

Martin Luther

Edited by John Nicholas Lenker

Translated by John Nicholas Lenker and others

Volume 5

Sermons on Gospel Texts

for the 13th to 26th Sundays After Trinity

Baker Book House

Grand Rapids, Michigan 49506

Reprinted 1988
by Baker Book House Company

Eight-volume set
ISBN: 0-8010-5626-8

Volume 5 is a reproduction of
*The Precious and Sacred Writings
of Martin Luther*, volume 14
(Minneapolis: Lutherans in All Lands, 1905)

Printed in the United States of America

CONTENTS

PREFACE

Among the new features of this volume are the references at the head of each sermon to the page or column and volume of the Erlangen, Walch and St. Louis Walch editions in German, where each sermon in the original may be found. Erl. stands for Erlangen edition; W. for the Walch, and St. L. for the St. Louis edition. The c. and other letters referring to different editions of Luther's complete works are according to the Erlangen edition. The number 14 on the back of the book and on the first title page correspond with the number of the same volume in the Erlangen edition.

To the following colaborers grateful acknowledgment is hereby made: To Rev. J. Humberger, Steubenville, O., for translating the first sermons of the 13th, 14th, 18th, 19th, 22d and 24th Sundays after Trinity; Rev. S. E. Ochsenford, D. D., Professor of English, Muhlenberg College, Allentown, Pa., for the second sermons of the 16th and 24th Sundays; Rev. J. D. Severinghaus, D. D., Chicago, for the sermon of the 17th Sunday and the second sermon of the 23d Sunday; Rev. C. Huber, D. D., Richmond, Ind., for the second sermons of the 18th and 25th Sundays; Rev. John Sander, late professor of German in Gustavus Adolphus College, St. Peter, Minn., for the second sermon of the 19th and the sermon of the 26th Sunday, and to Prof. Hans Juergensen, of the German Department of the University of Minnesota, for assistance in proofreading. The other sermons and all the "Analyses" by Walch and "Summaries" by Bugenhagen were translated and the whole volume edited by the undersigned.

J. N. LENKER

THIRTEENTH SUNDAY AFTER TRINITY.

This sermon is not found in edition c. The second part under
the heading: "Of the Law and the Gospel" was published earlier
in the "Sermon von den Heilthumen." Compare the "Sermon on
the Day of the Exaltation of the Cross" in vol. 15. This is also
found in the collection of twelve sermons. Erl. 14, 1; W. 11, 2062;
St. L. 11, 1536.

*Text: Luke 10, 23-37. And turning to the disciples, he said
privately, Blessed are the eyes which see the things that ye see:
for I say unto you, that many prophets and kings desired to
see the things which ye see, and saw them not: and to hear the
things which ye hear, and heard them not.*

*And behold, a certain lawyer stood up and made trial of him,
saying, Teacher, what shall I do to inherit eternal life? And
he said unto him, What is written in the law? how readest
thou? And he answering said, Thou shalt love the Lord thy
God with all thy heart, and with all thy soul, and with all thy
strength, and with all thy mind; and thy neighbor as thyself.
And he said unto him, Thou hast answered right: this do, and
thou shalt live. But he, desiring to justify himself, said unto
Jesus, And who is my neighbor? Jesus made answer and said,
A certain man was going down from Jerusalem to Jericho;
and he fell among robbers, who both stripped him and beat him,
and departed, leaving him half dead. And by chance a certain
priest was going down that way: and when he saw him, he
passed by on the other side. And in like manner a Levite also,
when he came to the place, and saw him, passed by on the other
side. But a certain Samaritan, as he journeyed, came where
he was: and when he saw him, he was moved with compassion,
and came to him, and bound up his wounds, pouring on them
oil and wine; and he set him on his own beast, and brought
him to an inn, and took care of him. And on the morrow he*

*took out two shillings, and gave them to the host, and said,
Take care of him; and whatsoever thou spendest more, I, when
I come back again, will repay thee. Which of these three,
thinkest thou, proved neighbor unto him that fell among the
robbers? And he said, He that showed mercy on him. And
Jesus said unto him, Go, and do thou likewise.*

CONTENTS: A SERMON ON THE LAW AND THE GOSPEL,
OR THE TWO GREATEST COMMANDMENTS, AND THE
GOOD SAMARITAN.

I. A SERMON ON THE LAW.
* The sum of this Gospel. 1.
A. What Preceded This Sermon. 2 f.
* The difference between the
Apostles seeing Christ and the
Prophets seeing Him. 3-4.
B. The Oppertunity Given Christ to
Preach This Sermon. 4-5.
C. The Sermon Itself.
1. How Christ gives us a good
lecture in this sermon. 6.
2. This sermon contains the
greatest and most important
part of the teachings of Moses.
7f.
* The law claims the whole
man.
* The blindness of the Jews
in explaining the first commandment. 8-10.
* The form and ways of the
hypocrite. 11.
3. How Christ in this sermon
thoroughly puts to shame
work-righteousness. 12.
4. How this sermon teaches we
should love God.
1. With your whole heart.
13-14.
2. With your whole soul. 15.
3. With all your powers. 16.
4. With all your strength. 17.
5. How this sermon makes all
men sinners. 18-19.

II. A SERMON ON THE GOSPEL
THAT CHRIST DELIVERS TO
US IN A PARABLE.

1. The occasion given Christ for
uttering this parable. 20-21.
2. How this parable greatly puts

to shame the work-righteous
persons. 22-23.
* In what a Christian life consists. 24.
3. The sense and understanding
of this parable.
a. What is understood by the
Samaritan. 25-27.
b. What by the wounded and
the murderer. 28-29.
c. What by the Priest and
Levite. 30-31.
d. What by the oil, poured into the wounds by the Sa-
maritan. 32.
e. What by the wine the Samaritan poured into the
wounds. 33.
f. What by the Samaritan
placing the wounded one
upon his own beast. 34.
g. What by the inn and the
keeper of the inn. 35.
4. The summary of this parable.
36.
* In what does the office of a
true preacher and bishop
consist. 37.
* OF THE LAW AND THE
GOSPEL.
a. The difference between
them. 38.
b. No person can fulfill the
Law. 39-40.
c. To what the Law should
serve. 41.
d. The Sophists do not understand the Law. 42-43.
e. When, where and how
the Gospel shows it's
power. 44-46.

THE SUMMARY OF THIS GOSPEL: 1. The disciples saw and
heard with their eyes and ears, and also understood in their hearts
all that the prophets had desired to see and hear; both of which the
old sainted fathers did not experience, who desired to see and hear
in the body, what they knew before in the spirit; but the Pharisees

saw and heard it, but understood it not, as Is. 6, 9–10 prophesied; and the Lord himself cites this passage of Isaiah in Mat. 13, 14; John 12, 40; Acts 28, 26.

2. The people of the law require works; but the law requires the the love of the heart.

3. The law concerning love, both toward God and toward our neighbor, condemns us all.

4. Our neighbor is the one who needs our help and to him we can do favors.

5. From the passage in this Gospel: "Whatsoever thou spendest more, when I come again, I will repay thee," foolish interpreters wish to confirm human laws; but they will not succeed. The two pence or shillings are the wine and oil the Samaritan poured into the wounds of the unfortunate man, or the law and the Gospel. For what should he leave the servant by which to serve the rich but the very things he had himself used? One can also say that the two pence are faith and love, which are the only things one should preach and bear to the people. Our foolish bishops now wish to do more than is committed to and commanded them.

6. "What is more" does not mean to burden the sick with human commandments and institutions; for what would be more foolish. But it means to give him faithful counsel where there is no revealed and clear word of God, as St. Paul did when he said to the Corinthians, 1 Cor. 7, 25: "Now concerning virgins I have no commandment of the Lord; but I give my judgment." In like manner did Daniel, 4, 24, when he had no clear word nor commandment of God, he gave the king faithful counsel, etc.

I. A SERMON ON THE LAW.

1. I hope you thoroughly understand this Gospel lesson, inasmuch as it recurs every year. And since it annually returns in the Pericopes we are required to consider it; and this we will now gladly and briefly do. In the first place, the Evangelist relates how Christ our Lord led his disciples aside, and being alone with them rejoiced in his spirit, and earnestly and directly said to them:

"Blessed are the eyes which see the things that ye see; for I say unto you, that many prophets and kings desired to see the things that ye see, and saw them not: and to hear the things which ye hear, and heard them not."

2. This hearing and seeing must be understood simply and plainly as external seeing and hearing, namely, that they saw Christ and his office, heard his preaching, and witnessed the miracles he performed among the Jews. The Jews also beheld these things with their natural eyes and some of them indeed experienced them in part in their

hearts. But in fact they did not recognize him as the Christ, like the Apostles did, and like Peter, who representing all the others, confessed and said in Mat. 16, 16: "Thou art the Christ, the Son of the living God." We indeed admit, that even some of the Jews like the Apostles recognized him as the Christ; but since they were but few who did, Christ therefore takes his Apostles here to himself apart.

3. However, in spirit, many prophets and kings saw Christ, as Christ himself says to the Jews concerning Abraham in John 8, 56: "Your father Abraham rejoiced to see my day, and he saw it, and was glad." Then the Jews thought he spoke of natural seeing, but Christ spoke of spiritual seeing, as all pious Christian hearts saw him before he was born, and still daily see him. For if Abraham saw him, without doubt many more prophets in whom the Holy Spirit dwelt saw him. And although this seeing made the holy fathers and prophets blessed, yet they had a real heart-felt longing and desire to behold Christ the Lord in the flesh, as is intimated time and again in the prophets.

4. Therefore the Lord here says to his desciples who saw both with their natural and their spiritual eyes: "Blessed are the eyes which see the things that ye see." As though he would say: This is a blessed time, an acceptable year, a special season of grace. That which is now at hand is so precious that the eyes which see it are truly called blessed. For in the past ages the Gospel was never preached so publicly and clearly unto all men as at present; the Holy Spirit was not yet publicly poured out; but was still concealed, and had as yet accomplished little. But Christ began the office of the Holy Spirit, and afterwards the Apostles continued it in full earnest. Therefore he calls all those blessed, who see and hear such grace. Now when the Lord said this and was rejoicing in spirit, one presents himself, a lawyer, who acting as though he also amounted to something, tempted the Lord and said:

"Teacher, what shall I do to inherit eternal life?"

5. This lawyer was perhaps a wise man and well acquainted with the Scriptures, as his answer also suggests;

yet here he becomes a fool, and must first begin to learn from the Lord, when he is put to shame and disgrace. For Christ teaches him a good lesson, and with one word takes out of him all his self-conceit. For he was in the delusion that he had kept the law wholly and perfectly, and was therefore something extra, above others, which undoubtedly he was, and imagined, because he was so pious and learned, that he was of course worthy to talk with the Lord. But now what does the Lord do to ensnare him in a masterly manner? He does this: he permits him to judge himself. For the Evangelist proceeds thus:

"And he said unto him, What is written in the law? how readest thou? And he answering said: Thou shalt love the Lord thy God with all thy heart, and with all thy soul, and with all thy strength, and with all thy mind; and thy neighbor as thyself. And he said unto him, Thou hast answered right: this do, and thou shalt live."

6. I think the Lord gave this pious man a good lecture. Alas, it was not right, he should have spared him a little, he puts him to shame before all the world. For what good does it do him? Christ shows him that he has as yet done nothing, when he allowed himself to think he had done everything. He asks what he should do. I contend that he has enough to do now, if he is only able to do great things.

7. Now much might be said on these two commandments, and it is also really needed, had we the time, for these are the highest and greatest themes on which Moses wrote; yea, on these hang all the law and the prophets, as Christ himself says in Mat. 22, 40. Nevertheless, we will briefly consider some phases of them.

8. When we examine the laws of Moses, we find they all treat of love. For the commandment: "Thou shalt have no other Gods before me," I cannot explain or interpret otherwise than: Thou shalt love God alone. Thus Moses himself interprets it in Deut. 6, 4-5, where he says: "Hear, O Israel; Jehovah our God is one Jehovah; and thou shalt love Jehovah thy God with all thy heart, and with all thy soul, and with all thy might." From this passage the lawyer has

taken his answer. But the Jews understand this law to mean no more than that they should not set up idols and images to worship, and when they could say and confess with their lips that they have only one God and honor no other gods, they think they have kept this commandment. Thus this lawyer also understood it, but it was a false, erroneous knowledge of the law.

9. Now we must have high regard for the law. It says: "Thou shalt have no other gods before me." Thou, thou, it says, thou, and everything thou art; and especially does it mean the heart, the soul and all thy powers. It does not speak of the tongue, or the hands, or the knees; but it speaks of the whole body, and of all thou hast and art. If I am to have no other God, then I must surely possess the only true God with my heart, that is, I must in my heart be affectionate to him, evermore cleave to him, depend upon him, trust him, have my desire, love and joy in him, and always think of him. Just as we say at other times when we delight in something, that it tastes good in our very heart. And when one speaks or laughs and is not in earnest, and does not mean it from his heart, we say: You laugh, and your heart is not in it. The heart is quite a different thing than the lips. Therefore in the Scriptures the heart signifies the great and ardent love we should have for God. Those who serve God only with their lips, with their hands or with their knees, are hypocrites, and God cares nothing for them. For God does not want only a part, on the contrary he wants the whole man.

10. The Jews abstained outwardly from idolatry, and served God only with their lips; but their hearts were far from him, full of mistrust and unbelief. Outwardly they appeared beautiful, as though they meant it in all sincerity, but within they were full of idolatry. Therefore the Lord said unto them in Mat. 23, 27-28: "Woe unto you, scribes and Pharisees, hypocrites! for ye tithe mint and anise and cummin, and have left undone the weightier matters of the law, justice, mercy, and faith. For ye are like unto whited sepulchers, which outwardly appear beautiful, but

inwardly are full of dead men's bones and of all uncleanness. Even as ye also outwardly appear righteous unto men, but inwardly ye are full of hypocrisy and iniquity.''

11. They are really wicked people who become proud in external things, who desire to justify and make themselves pious by their works, as this lawyer here does. Behold, what a proud character he is, he presents himself in his own name, and thinks Christ will not rebuke him; yea, he allows himself to think that the Lord will extol and praise his life in the presence of all the people, and does not think of learning anything from the Lord, but only seeks his own praise. The ignorant pretender would have gladly heard a psalm of praise from the man whom the people esteemed, and at whom all men wondered. Thus all hypocrites do, who outwardly parade their excellent, great and noble works. They well say that they do not seek honor and praise, but inwardly in their hearts they are full of ambition, and desire all the world to know of their holiness, and smile very nicely when they hear men speak of it.

12. Yet the Lord does not serve this lawyer thus, but puts him to shame. This Christ is an unfriendly, ungracious man, he tells the people the truth, and well deserves that they should hate him. The pious, holy lawyer still does his utmost, and knows nothing but how to harvest great honors and obtain high renown for his precious life; he thinks he has perfectly fulfilled this commandment, and hopes for a favorable answer, that the Lord will say: Dear Sir, you have done it all. But Christ goes to work and first tells him: "Do this!" That is to say in good German: You are a rogue in the hide, you have not done this during your whole life; yea, you have not kept a single letter of the law; and thus shows him his wickedness. The poor fellow thinks he should sit in the first seat, that he is really pure and beautiful, and by rights should sit among the angels, rather than here among the people. What a wonderful Christ is this! The people regard this lawyer as pious and holy; but Christ says he shall first go and begin to fulfill the law. Be consistent with thyself!

13. Now these are the very fellows who most of all sin against the first commandment, and think no further than the words read: I must love God, and think they have fulfilled the law, while it remains hovering on their tongues and over their hearts, but never enters. This, however, is not enough, it must reach much farther, namely, that I so love God that for his sake I can forsake all creatures, and should he require it, also body and life; yea, that I should love him above all things. For God is a jealous God and cannot suffer us to love anything above himself. But to love anything beneath himself, he of course allows. Just as a husband can easily allow his wife to love the maid servants, the house and house utensils, cattle and other things; but to love with the love she should have for him, he will not suffer her to love anyone besides himself; yea, he desires her to forsake all things for his sake; and so again the wife also requires the same from her husband.

Thus God can also allow us to love his creatures; yea, they are created for this purpose and are good. The sun is an excellent creature; gold and silver and all things that are attractive and beautiful by nature cause us to love them. This God indeed permits us to do. But that I should cling to the creature and love it with the same love with which I love God the Creator, this he can and will not allow; yea, his will is that I should deny and forsake all things, should he desire and require it of me, and be satisfied should I nevermore behold the sun, my money and possessions. The love of the creature should stand far, far below our love to him; and as he is the chief good, his will is also to be loved in the highest degree, above all other good. If he will not allow me to love anything as much as I love him, much less will he allow me to love anything more than himself, though it be a creature of his own creation.

14. Now I think you understand what it is to love God with all the heart, with all the soul and with all the mind. To love God with all the heart is to love him above all creatures; that is, although many creatures are quite lovely, as they please me and I love them, nevertheless, I am to

despise and forsake all these for God's sake, whenever God my Lord desires it.

15. To love God with all the soul is to devote your entire bodily life to him that you can say when the love of any creature, or any persecution threatens to overpower you: All this I will give up, before I will forsake my God; let men cast me away, murder or drown me, let what God's will is happen to me, I will gladly lose all, before I will forsake thee, O Lord! unto thee will I cling more than to all thy creatures, or to anything that is not thyself. I will risk all things together with what I have and am that I may not forsake thee. The soul in the Scriptures signifies the life of the body, which acts through the five senses, eating, drinking, sleeping, waking, seeing, hearing, smelling, tasting and everything that the soul does through the body.

16. To love God with all our strength is to devote all our members and whatever we may be able to do through our bodies to the love of God, and sacrifice all rather than do anything contrary to his will.

17. To love God with all the mind is to take to nothing except that which is pleasing to God. By which is meant the self-conceit which man has that the same be directed to God and that all things be pleasing to him.

18. Thus you see what the commandment requires: "Thou shalt love God." Thou, thou wholly and fully, not thy hands, not thy lips, not thy knees. Those who do this, fulfil the commandment in the right sense. But there is not a man on earth who thus fulfils the law; yea, we all do just the opposite. Thus this law here makes us all sinners so that not the least letter of this commandment is fulfilled, even by the most holy persons in the world. For no one clings so firmly to God with all the heart, that he could forsake all things for God's sake. We have, God be praised, become so competent that we can almost not suffer the least word, yea, we will not let go of a nickel for the sake of God.

How is it possible for us to love God, as long as his will displeases us? For if I love God I love also his will. Now, when God sends us sickness, poverty, shame and disgrace, that is his will. But what do we do under such circumstances? We thunder, scold and growl, and bear it with great impatience. And this is the least part, for what would we do if we had to forsake body and life for God and Christ's sake? Then we would act quite differently. Yet in the meantime I act like this Pharisee and lawyer does, I lead a fine outward life, honor and serve God, fast, pray, and appear very pious and holy. But God does not want this. He wants us to accept his will with joy and love, and this we are too tardy in doing.

19. Therefore, what the Lord here says to this lawyer, he says to us all, namely, that we have not yet fulfilled the law, and still he requires us to do it. On this account all men are guilty of death, and are the devil's own property. "All men are liars," Ps. 116, 11, vain and offensive. What they pretend does not avail before God. In our own affairs we are shrewd; how to scrape together money and goods, how to speak well of God before the people, and how to push ourselves ahead in a masterly manner. But what does God care for this? His will is that we should love him with all our hearts. This no man can do, and the conclusion is that we are all sinners, and especially those who walk in a beautiful outward show. Therefore it is safer that we go and confess that we all are sinners, than that we have respect to our works and cling to our beautiful, glittering lives.

II. A SERMON ON THE GOSPEL IN A PARABLE.

20. The foregoing is the first part of our Gospel lesson, and it is a sermon on the law. The second part now follows, and it preaches the Gospel, how and whence we are to receive power to fulfill the Law. This the good Samaritan will teach us.

21. How does this lawyer act now after the Lord had thus turned him away? He goes ahead, the Evangelist says, and desires to justify himself and says to the Lord:

"And who is my neighbor?"

22. He does not ask: Who is my God? As though he would say: "I owe God nothing, with God I am in good

standing. I am also inclined to think that I am under obli-
gations to no man; yet, I would like to know who my
neighbor is? The Lord answers and tells him a very beautiful parable, by which he shows that we are all neighbors
among one another, both he who does another a kindness, as
well as he who is in need of a kindness. Although the text
reads as if Christ said that he is our neighbor who does
another a kindness. In this, however, the Scriptures make
no difference. Here they call him neighbor who does a kindness, and at other places him who receives the kindness.

23. By means of this parable the Lord concludes with the
words, "*Go, and do thou likewise,*" so that this lawyer did
not only sin against God, but also against his neighbor. He
not only failed to love God, but he did not love his neighbor,
and never did him a favor. By this the poor man falls into
such a sweat that he is only deceived from head to foot.
How could he be so mistaken, the highly learned and pious
man? His mistake came in this way; he led a Pharisaical,
feigned and hypocritical life. He did not look down to his
neighbor to help him with his life, but only sought thereby
his own vain glory and honor before the eyes of the people,
and with this he stared piously toward heaven.

24. Now you have often heard that a Christian life consists in acting before my God in faith and with a pure heart,
but toward my neighbor in right living and good works; and
not wait until my neighbor seeks a kindness of me, and asks
me for something, but approach and meet him with kindness
and freely offer it to him. Let us now see what the parable
in itself teaches.

25. This Samaritan of course is our Lord Jesus Christ
himself, who has shown his love toward God and his neighbor. Toward God, in that he was obedient to him, came
down from heaven and became man, and thus fulfilled the
will of his Father; toward his neighbor, in that he immediately after his baptism began to preach, to do wonders, to
heal the sick. And in short, he did no work that centered
in himself alone, but all his acts centered in his neighbor.
And this he did with all his powers, and thus he became our

servant, who could have well remained in heaven and been equal to God, Phil. 2, 6. But all this he did because he knew that this pleased God and was his Father's will.

26. When he entered upon that high mission to prove that he loved God with all his heart, he laid down his bodily life with all he had, and said: Father, here you have all, my bodily life, my glory and honor, which I had among the people; all this I give as it is for thy sake, that the world may know how I love thee. My Father, let my wisdom perish, so that the world may look upon me as most foolish. Let me be the most despised, who was heretofore praised by all the world. Now I am the worst murderer, who before was friendly, useful and serviceable to the whole world. Dear Father, all this I despise, only that I may not be disobedient to thee.

27. This is the Samaritan who came uninvited, and fulfilled the law with his whole heart. For only he fulfilled the law, and no one can deprive him of this honor. He alone merits it, and well maintains it all alone. Now this would be no special comfort for us; but that he has compassion on the poor wounded man, takes him under his care, binds his wounds, takes him into the inn and waits on him, this avails for us.

28. The man who here lies half dead, wounded and stripped of his clothing, is Adam and all mankind. The murderers are the devils who robbed and wounded us, and left us lying prostrate half dead. We still struggle a little for life; but there lies horse and man, we cannot help ourselves to our feet, and if we were left thus lying we would have to die by reason of our great anguish and lack of nourishment; maggots would grow in our wounds, followed by great misery and distress.

29. The parable stands in bold relief, and pictures us perfectly, what we are and can do with our boasted reason and free will. If the poor wounded man had desired to help himself, it would only have been worse for him, he would only have done harm to himself and irritated his wounds, and only prepared more misery and distress for himself.

Had he remained lying quiet, he would have had as much suffering. Thus it is when we are left to ourselves. We are always lost, we may lay hold where we will. Hitherto man has always acted thus, he has thought out many ways and methods how we might reform our lives and get to heaven. One found this way, another that, therefore so many kinds of orders arose: in like manner the letters of indulgence and crusades originated; but they have only made evil worse. Such is the world, and it is thus finely portrayed in this wounded man, it lies in sins over head and ears and cannot help itself.

30. But the Samaritan who has fulfilled the law and is perfectly healthy and sound, comes and does more than both priest and Levite. He binds up the sores of the wounded man, pours in oil and wine, lifts him upon his own beast, and brings him into the inn, takes good care of him, and when he departs he carefully commends him to the host, and besides leaves him a sufficient supply of money, while neither the priest nor Levite would do one of these kind acts. The priest signifies the dear sainted fathers before Moses; the Levite the priesthood of the Old Testament. All these however have accomplished nothing by their works, and have passed by on the other side like this priest and Levite.

31. Therefore, if I had for example all the good works of Noah, Abraham and of all the dear fathers, they would still be of no benefit to me. They have indeed beheld the wounded man lying helpless and half dead, but they could not help it. He who lay there half dead, saw it too, but what of it, he could make it no better. The dear sainted fathers saw very well that the people lay in their sins over their ears, and also felt the anguish of sin, but what could they do to remedy it? They could make it only worse, but not better. These were the preachers of the law, and showed what the world was, namely, full of deadly sins, and it lay there half dead, and could not help itself, notwithstanding all its powers, reason and free will. Go then, thou beautifully painted rogue, and boast of thy free will, of thy merits and holiness!

32. But Christ, the true Samaritan, takes the poor man to himself as his own, goes to him and does not require the helpless one to come to him; for here is no merit, but pure grace and mercy; and he binds up his wounds, cares for him and pours in oil and wine, this is the whole Gospel from beginning to end. He pours in oil when grace is preached, as when one says: Behold thou poor man, here is your unbelief, here is your condemnation, here you are wounded and sore. Wait! All this I will cure with the Gospel. Behold, here cling firmly to this Samaritan, to Christ the Savior, he will help you, and nothing else in heaven or on earth will. You know very well that oil softens, thus also the sweet, loving preaching of the Gospel gives me a soft, mild heart toward God and my neighbor, so that I risk my bodily life for the sake of Christ my Lord and his Gospel, if God and necessity require it.

33. But wine is sharp and signifies the holy cross that immediately follows. A Christian need not look for his cross, it is always on his back. For he thinks as St. Paul says, 2 Tim. 3, 12: "All that would live godly in Christ Jesus shall suffer persecution." This is the court-color in this kingdom. Whoever is ashamed of the color, does not belong to this king.

34. Then the Samaritan lifts the wounded man on his beast. This beast is Christ the Lord himself, he carries us, we lay upon his shoulders, neck and body. There is scarcely a more lovely picture in the entire Gospel, than where Christ the Lord compares himself to a shepherd, in Luke 15, who carries the lost sheep on his shoulders back to the fold. He still continually carries his lost sheep thus at the present day.

35. The stable or inn is Christianity, here in this world, where we must remain for a short time. The host is the preacher of the Word of God and of the Gospel, who is to nurse and care for us.

36. Now here we have the substance of the Gospel. The kingdom of Christ is a kingdom of mercy and grace, in which there is nothing but a continual carrying of the lost. Christ carries our infirmities and sicknesses, he takes our

sins upon himself and has patience when we fail. We still always lay about his neck, and yet he does not become weary of carrying us, which should be the greatest comfort for us when we are in conflict with sin.

37. Ministers in this kingdom are to comfort the consciences, deal gently with them and feed them with the Gospel, carry the weak, heal the sick, and know how to divide the Word rightly, and administer the same to every one according to his needs. This is the office of a true bishop and minister, and not to proceed with violence as our bishops do, who come threatening with stocks and the block, crying: "Ho! up there, up there, who will not, must!" This should not be, but a bishop or minister ought to resemble one who waits upon the sick, who treats them very gently, gives kind words, speaks very friendly to them and exercises all diligence in their behalf. Thus a bishop or minister should also do, and remember that his bishopric or parish is nothing but a hospital and an infirmary, where he has very many and various kinds of sick people for treatment. When Christ is thus preached faith and life meet together and fulfil the commandment of love.*

OF THE LAW AND THE GOSPEL.

38. I have often told you, dearly beloved, that the entire Scriptures consist of two parts, of the law and the Gospel. It is the law that teaches what we are required to do; the Gospel teaches where we shall receive what the law demands. For it is quite a different thing to know what we should have, and to know where to get it. Just as when I am given into the hands of the physicians, where it is quite a different art to tell what my disease is than to tell what medicine I must take so as to recover. Thus it is likewise here. The law discovers the disease, the Gospel ministers the medicine. This you clearly see in today's Gospel. The lawyer comes desiring eternal life, and inquires what he shall do to secure it? The law tells him, and says: "Thou shalt love the Lord

*The following Luther preached on another occasion. Translator.

thy God with all thy heart, and with all thy soul, with all
thy strength and with all thy mind; and thy neighbor as
thyself.''

39. He who reads this only superficially as this lawyer
here does, will not understand it. One must enter into it
and portray and even behold himself in it. For if I try to
love God with all my heart, I will soon see how far I fail.
So, with all the soul, that is, with the inner soul which I
feel in the flesh, that I love and experience love in all my
senses; for to love with the soul in the Scriptures means the
love that a gallant youth feels towards his beloved. Again,
with all thy strength, that is, with all thy members. Again,
with all thy mind, that is, all thy senses, thoughts and de-
lusions must be directed toward God. For if I am to love
God with all my heart, soul, strength and mind, then my
eyes dare not give one scornful glance, my tongue speak an
angry word, my feet, hands, ears must all be one, and give
forth no angry sign. That is to say: Thou shalt love God
with all thy heart, so that thy whole body from the crown of
the head to the soles of the feet, inwardly and outwardly,
goes forth in love, and rejoices in God and honors him.

40. Now find me a man who is chaste or otherwise pious
with a burning passion and love; there is none such on the
earth. We find ourselves much more inclined to anger,
hatred, envy, worldly pleasures, than to tender heartedness
and other virtues. And when I find in my inclination such a
spark, it is all false, the law is not satisfied. But I find not
only a spark in me, but a whole bakeoven full of the fire of
evil inclinations, for there is no love in the heart, nor in any
member of the body. Therefore I here see in the law as in a
mirror, that everything I have is condemned and cursed; for
not one jot of the law shall pass away but all must be fulfilled, as Christ says, Mat. 5, 18: ''For verily I say unto you,
Till heaven and earth pass away, one jot or one tittle shall
in no wise pass away from the law, till all things be accomplished.''

41. Now you do not find in yourself, that you do with all
your soul and with all your heart, with joy and pleasure,

what the law requires of you; therefore you are condemned and the child of satan; then know by this how to govern yourself in the future. Behold, you must first come to the knowledge to confess that you are the devil's own property. But if you would know no more than how you are to treat him to be freed from him, you would have to perish. To this end the law serveth, that we may learn that we are condemned, for this evil lust is found in us all, and yet we should not have a spark of it in us.

42. Our sophists failed to see this, and have taught, if a man does the best he can, God then gives him grace. They are blind guides, and themselves confess that man has little desire for the good; yet still, if he go and do it, even though disorderly, unwillingly, indolently, he is nevertheless in favor with God. Christ here teaches the contrary that we should go forth with a passion and love and do the law with a joyful and happy mind. Now, whom would you rather believe, Christ or the sophists? I leave this to you. From such false knowledge the cloisters later arose, into which men entered and contended that if a man were only in a cloister, and it matters not how unwillingly he was there, then he would be saved. So they taught. But now Christ's will is that man should do good works willingly and joyfully. Hence, if they are done with a troubled conscience and a heavy heart, it is sin. Therefore cease from all works that you do not perform with pleasure and love.

43. They therefore should have said: Man, do you see, you poor condemned creature, you should have delight in God's law, and you have no pleasure in it; hence show some delight and love, or you are God's enemy and the devil's friend. Thus the people would have bravely forsaken their own presumption and come to a knowledge of themselves and would have said: O God, now I am condemned. Yes, this is right. Here every one might soon know and conclude, that we all belong to satan, as long as we find within us displeasure in the law of God. Therefore, boldly cast away all works from you, then you will find delight in and love for God's law in your heart. I experience indeed that

God's law is holy, right and good, but it is my death. And if it could be, I would prefer that it did not exist. And thus all people are disposed in their hearts, as St. Paul very beautifully writes in the seventh chapter of Romans.

44. Had we now remained in this condemnation, we would have had to perish forever. Therefore another part is added, the Gospel, which speaks of consolation and teaches salvation, and whence we are to obtain it, so that the law may be satisfied. Now when I see by the law that I am condemned, lying even among murderers, half dead, the devil has stolen my soul and taken it captive in Adam and Eve, with all faith and righteousness, and has left nothing except my bodily life which will soon be extinguished; now here come the Levite and the priest, who render human satisfaction and teach this and that; but it does no good, they pass by.

45. However when the Samaritan comes, he helps, that is, when Christ comes and offers us his mercy, and says: Behold, you are indebted to love God with all your heart, but you have not done it; now believe in me, I will give you my sufferings: this will help me. Here he lifts me on his beast, that is, on himself, and takes me to the inn, that is, into the Christian Church. After this he comes and pours into me his grace, which is the oil, so that I feel I am lying on his shoulders, this gives me a very joyful conscience; moreover he pours into me wine, which is to devour and drown the old Adam. But even then I am not perfectly well. Health has indeed been poured into me and there is a turn for the better, but nevertheless I am not perfectly restored to health. Meantime Christ serves and purifies me by the grace he pours into me, so that day by day I become purer, chaster, milder, gentler and more believing until I die, when I shall be entirely perfect.

46. Thus when we now come before God the Father and are asked: whether we have also believed and loved God, and have wholly fulfilled the law; then the Samaritan will step forth, Christ the Lord, who carries us lying on his beast, and say: Alas, Father! although they have not wholly

fulfilled thy law, yet I have done so, let this be to their benefit because they believe in me.   Thus all saints must do, however holy and pious they may be, they must lay on Christ's shoulders.   If even the most holy people, as priests and Levites, could not satisfy the law, how shall we undertake to do so with our feigned works, bald pates and caps? O our wretched and corrupt nature!   Let this be sufficient for the present, and let us call on God for grace.

THIRTEENTH SUNDAY AFTER TRINITY.

Second Sermon.   Luke 10, 23-37.

The following sermon is found in place of the foregoing one in the c. edition. Erl. 14, 20; W. 11, 2086; St. L. 11, 1552.

CONTENTS: HOW CHRIST PRAISES THE TIME OF THE GOSPEL; PREACHES ON TRULY GOOD WORKS; AND HOW THE KINGDOM OF CHRIST IS REPRESENTED HERE IN A BEAUTIFUL PICTURE.

I. CHRIST PRAISES THE TIME OF THE REVELATION OF THE GOSPEL.
 * Summary of this Gospel. 1.
I. The Nature of this Praise. 2.
II. How this Praise Includes both an Admonition and a Lamentation.
 A. The Lamentation.
  1. The Lamentation in itself. 3-5.
  2. This Lamentation was also needed in the time of the reformation. 6-8.
   * The great punishment, that is visited upon the despisers of the Gospel. 8.
 B. The Admonition.
  1. Its foundation and aim. 9f.
   * The Gospel should be highly and worthily esteemed. 10-11.
  2. How this Admonition stirs us to continue faithful to Christ and the Gospel. 12.
II. THE SERMON OF CHRIST ON TRULY GOOD WORKS.
I. The Occasion of This Sermon. 13-14.
 * Hypocrites know of nothing but works. 14.
II. The Sermon Itself.
  1. How it contains the summary of all the commandments. 15f.
  2. How it presents the greatest wisdom and art; which can never be learned perfectly. 16-17.
   * It is shameful and unpleasant to have anything to do with work-righteous persons. 18.
  3. How a severe judgment is here passed upon all sophists and work-righteous persons. 19-21-.
  4. How this sermon makes all guilty, so that none can glory before God. 22-25.
  5. Whether the work-righteous persons do what this sermon teaches. 26-27.
III. THE REPRESENTATION OF THE KINGDOM OF CHRIST BY A BEAUTIFUL PICTURE.
I. The Occasion of This Representation. 27-29.
 * The shameful presumption of work-righteous people. 29.
II. The Representation.
  1. How this representation puts to shame all hypocrisy. 30-31.
   * The questions and disputes about the law are very harmful, where faith and the Gospel are not present. 31.
   * The work-righteous persons understand not the law, yea, no one understands the law without the power of the Holy Spirit. 32.
  2 How the interpretation by the Jews of our neighbor is to be rejected. 33-34f.
   * What is understood here by our neighbor. 35-36.
  3. How this representation teaches that those least belong to the Kingdom of Christ,

who in the eyes of the world are the holiest, wisest and mightiest. 37.

4. How Christ in this picture shows the kindness, help and consolation, we naturally expect from him and his Kingdom. 38-40.

* The preaching of the Gospel.

a. How it is pictured forth by the oil and wine. 41.

b. How and to what end Christ entrusted this to his church. 42.

c. Its power and working. 43-44.

d. Without the thought of this sermon the law can not be fulfilled. 44.

5. How to defend this representation against the false interpretation of the monks and the sophists.

A. The first false interpretation and its correction. 45-47.

B. The second false interpretation and its correction. 48-53.

I. HOW CHRIST PRAISES THE DISPENSATION OF THE GOSPEL.

1. This Pericope contains especially three lessons. First, that Christ praises the time when the Gospel was revealed and published, which is rightly and justly called the time of grace. Secondly, what truly good works are according to the command of God, which he pictures by the beautiful example or history of the Samaritan's actions to the one wounded by robbers. In the same history he sets forth as in a loving picture the third lesson, a portrayal of the kingdom of Christ, or of grace, which the preaching of the Gospel makes known. The first lesson is given in these words:

"Blessed are the eyes which see the things that ye see: for I say unto you, that many prophets and kings desired to see the things which ye see, and saw them not; and to hear the things which ye hear, and heard them not."

2. The Evangelist says Christ spoke these words especially to his disciples, and just at the time when he was greatly moved with joy in his soul or with spiritual delight, and therefore he thanked and praised his heavenly Father from his heart for the revelation of the Gospel. Here we see that he was especially anxious to speak thus with his disciples, since their own salvation also depended upon that revelation. And such words are nothing more than praise of the Gospel, that they lived in the time (and now hear and see) of the revelation of the Gospel, which brings to the

world deliverance and salvation from sin and all misery. And of this time or revelation the beloved prophets formerly prophesied in a glorious manner, and they longed and cried for it beyond measure in their very souls, as is manifest especially in the Psalms and in the Prophesy of Isaiah. Therefore, you are blessed and more than blessed; for you enjoy now the truly golden year, the pure kingdom of grace and the blessed time; therefore only see to it that you retain it and make good use of it.

3. For such praise is true admonition, yea, an earnest discourse of lamentation; for he exhorts to thanksgiving for such grace. And on the other hand he laments over the great ingratitude of the world, that there are so few people who know and receive this, while so many despise it, therefore he says Christ turned especially to the disciples and praised them; as if he wished to say: Yes, your eyes and ears are indeed blessed, which see and hear this; for, alas! on the other hand there are many eyes and ears that do not wish to see or hear it, although they have it right before their eyes and ears. Christ thus shows however great and superabundant the treasure is and however comforting the preaching of it may be, yet among the great mass of people it is only despised and persecuted.

4. And now the times are changing, since the beloved fathers and prophets in their day would have given their body and life had they been able to live to see it, and had they experienced it their hearts would have blossomed to fruit in their bodies because of joy and they would have thought they were walking where there were only roses. As the pious, aged Simeon, Luke 2, 28f., embraced in his arms the Savior while he as an infant could not yet speak nor walk, and with all joy entrusted his life to him, and no longer cared for this life nor for anything in it. Dear mother Eve also, Gen. 4, 1, earnestly prayed and longed for this salvation, and was glad when God gave her a firstborn son; for she thought he would be the Savior; but when her hope in him failed, she longed still more for it. And later the hearts of all the fathers clung to and sighed for the

same deliverer until he came and permitted himself to be seen and heard. Then the whole world should have received him at once with all joy and gloried in being saved; just as he himself praises this grace.

5. Joyfully and with his whole heart aglow pious David thanks God when he heard the first time from the Prophet Nathan God's promise, 2 Sam. 7, 12f., that he would establish not only a dynasty and a permanent kingdom with his descendants; but also that he would let Christ be born of his body and thus he would found an eternal kingdom of his grace and mercy. And because of this his great joy he did not know what he should say before God and how he should thank him, and hence he composed so many beautiful Psalms about it, especially the 89, and besides in his last words and testament he praises this kindness in the highest manner and says: "He hath made with me an everlasting covenant; ordered in all things and sure: for it is all my salvation and all my desire," etc. 2 Sam. 23. But now the dear, blessed time has come, and there is a change, I say, so that people live and appear who wish neither to see nor to hear, neither to know nor to tolerate this rich grace and this highest favor of God bestowed so gratuitously.

6. Just as we also see at present and easily understand how those who wish to be the Church and to be called Christians, the Pope and bishops with their followers, who should lift their hands to heaven and thank God for their deliverance from darkness and blindness that they have again the pure light of the Gospel; these bring fire and water, wet their sword and polish their weapons to exterminate from the earth those who teach and confess the pure Gospel, and there are so many unthankful, false Christians among us just like them, who despise this salvation in the most defiant manner. Formerly, when we were captives under the Pope's tyranny, burdened with the preaching of lies, relating to indulgences, purgatory and all the dreams of the monks, what a sighing and longing there was then in all the world for the true preaching of the Gospel. How gladly would one

then have given, labored and suffered all things possible to
secure true instruction and comfort, and to be delivered
with a good conscience from the fearful martyrdom of the
confessional and other oppressive burdens imposed by the
Pope! And how happy were many pious people at first
because of this deliverance who learned it and thanked God
for it! But now, how many are there who rejoice from
their hearts and acknowledge how blessed they are in that
they can see and hear this? How soon they took offense
at this blessed treasure and then sought something else,
when they forgot all they had received, and the world became again filled with fanaticism and false teachings.

7. Indeed it really depends upon seeing and hearing;
it is fully revealed and it stands forth clearly in the light
before our eyes and ears; but the great mass of the world
can not see nor understand it, even if it were stuck in
their eyes and continually rung and hammered into their
ears. For if they could hear and see a little of it, then it
would accomplish something among them and improve them,
so that they would become more reasonable and would not
thus oppose the truth.

8. What did it help all the Pharisees that Christ himself
preached the Gospel to them? And what would it help
all the fanatics and critics even if it were preached twice
as clearly, how we obtain the forgiveness of sins and true
consolation of the conscience, likewise how a Christian
should live in every calling of life and should know that
he pleases God. Of all this they heretofore knew and heard
nothing, so that they themselves acknowledged that the
teaching was indeed excellent, but at the same time they
remained stone-blind and it never entered their hearts that
they could walk and live in harmony with it, all is strange
to them that they hear, read or they themselves speak
concerning it. For they are too completely chilled and
choked with other thoughts of their own self-conceit
and pleasure about things dear to them, so that aside from
these they can neither see nor hear anything. Thus among
them it is fulfilled as the prophets and Christ spoke before

to the Jewish people and all like them, that with eyes to see they shall not see and with ears to hear they shall not hear, in order that they may change and be saved. This is the highest, the most horrible and the most fearful punishment they can bring upon themselves, and in addition be tormented in that they must daily see and hear the word and work of God, that is offered to all men for their salvation; and yet they have not the grace to receive it, Mat. 13, 14; but only hear and see in it their vexation and thus become so bitter against it that they would rather hear and see the devil from hell.

9. On the other hand it is great grace and a precious treasure for him who receives this teaching that he sees and hears it aright, so that we should indeed declare such a one saved. For the seeing and hearing that enter the heart bring and give a fulness and richness of possessions in understanding, enlightenment, comfort, strength and growth of spirit, joy and life, that we can never hear and see enough of it and prefer to hear, to learn and to know this above everything else that may be preached, taught, sung or said, that it should help to our salvation. Yea, it lets all other things pass as if it heard and saw them not, although in civil government and life it must see and hear much, yet it clings alone to this light and knowledge, which is so great that it completely fills the eyes and heart, and darkens and blinds everything else.

10. In like manner the sun at its rising so completely fills the world with light that the moon and stars are no longer seen or thought of, although they give their light every night. Just so let those, who can, give light also here, be they learned, wise, holy people, even Moses, the Prophets, the fathers, or St. John the Baptist himself; yet they all should yield to Christ, yea, bear witness that he alone is the light, by whom all men are to be enlightened and that they themselves must become partakers of that light, and that in Christendom all light, wisdom and teaching aside from Christ must cease, or be found alone in him.

11. In the same manner should the beautiful sound and

the lovely music of the Gospel of Christ so engage and fill our ears, that we may hear nothing else, as when a great bell or a kettledrum and trumpet sound and resound, the air is so full that whatever else is spoken, sung or cried cannot be heard. So should Christ's words constantly in all our lives and actions have the upper hand in our hearts through faith, and know of comfort, righteousness and salvation from none other. These would indeed be blessed eyes and ears that could thus make use of the blessed time or dispensation of the Gospel, and know what God has given them in it; for such eyes and ears God himself esteems as an excellent and precious treasure and a sacred and holy possession, which could not be purchased by the whole world even if it had many more and brighter lights and suns.

II. THE SERMON OF CHRIST ON TRULY GOOD WORKS.

12. This is an admonition of Christ to his dear disciples, yea, a consolation and encouragment heartily to stand by the Gospel, since he esteems and praises it to be so precious.

13. But how it is esteemed by others who are not true disciples of Christ, but are much smarter and holier themselves than that they should need his teaching, the lawyer shows, who stands by (as they were all together with Christ wherever he came, and they heard whatever he spoke); he had heard that Christ speaks earnestly to his disciples that they hear and see what was never seen nor heard before. This lawyer could no longer retain his great skill and wisdom, he had to step forward and let himself be heard, and try if he could not put him to shame, and carry off the glory, that Christ was nothing, but he was the highly educated Rabbi, in that he propounds to him a much higher theme. Hence he steps forward and proposes to him this question:

"Teacher, what shall I do to inherit eternal life?"

14. That these are not the eyes and ears of one who hears and sees what Christ is, he himself makes manifest by his own words, as all must do, if they in the most perfect

way prove themselves to be such. For he hereby confesses he
knows nothing more nor higher than the doctrine that treats
of our own doings and works; of God's grace, Christ's office
and work he knows nothing, he has as yet never understood
anything about them, although he had heard Christ speak
of them; he at once imagines he knows much better than
Christ can teach him; he wished to say like our fanatics
and critics: that which I have hitherto heard from you, is
common; you must ascend much higher to interest us. Dear
sir, teach the people once to do something, by which man
is saved. But Christ lets such a tempter rush ahead and
gives him a good handle by which he in a masterly manner
ensnares himself in his own words, bids him to report and
answer himself, since he wishes to be so learned and clever,
and says:

"What is written in the law? how readest thou?"

15. As if he would say: I hear indeed that you profess
to have higher wisdom than I. Come, deliver yourself, I
will be a pupil of your discourse and consider you a teacher.
In his answer Christ however forces him into the Scriptures,
when he says: "How readest thou?" For it is not Christ's
pleasure for people to propound and preach their own
arrogance; and hereby he shows this lawyer (as he later
draws from him through his own confession with the question, who is his neighbor etc.), that he does not understand
the Scriptures, even in that part where they speak of our
own works; therefore much less does he understand the other
higher teachings. Here he must not and cannot answer
differently than as Moses in Deut. 6, 5 comprehended in the
shortest form the summary of all God's commandments, how
we should live in our relations both to God and men.

"Thou shalt love the Lord thy God with all thy heart, and with
all thy soul, and with all thy strength, and with all thy mind;
and thy neighbor as thyself."

16. That is teaching truly of high order; yea, the greatest
thing that can be required of a man; as Christ himself
confesses and confirms, when he says: "Thou hast answered
right; this do, and thou shalt live." But it is nevertheless

a teaching that is common, that is well known to all the
Jews as to the words, although they did not rightly understand them, and the disciples of Christ had also certainly
heard them. Hence this critic should have indeed known
that Christ spoke of another, a higher theme, since he said
his disciples were especially blessed in that they see and hear
what others did not. But all such hypocrites and fanatics
must prove that they esteem Christ and his Gospel as
nothing, and let themselves imagine they know everything
much better.

17. Now, this commandment has often been explained
and there is still much to be said about it; for it is indeed
the highest art and wisdom, it is never learned perfectly,
much less perfectly fulfiled and lived; so that God's Son
had therefore to come from heaven, shed his blood and give
us the Gospel, so that this commandment might be kept.
Although here in this life it makes only a little beginning
among Christians; yet in the life beyond we will constantly
and forever have it in our eyes and hearts, and live it.
In short, it is far too high above the mind, heart and sense
of all mortals what the words mean, to love God with all
thy heart, with all thy strength, with all thy soul and with
all thy mind. For as yet no one experiences it, except those
a little, who have the Gospel and embrace Christ by faith,
and receive the comfort and power of it in times of need,
temptation and prayer, and thus experience a taste of it;
yet these persons themselves feel and lament, like all the
saints and Paul himself, that they are still far from it and
their flesh and blood feel nothing but sin and death; which
of course would not be the case if this commandment had
gone fully into practice and life.

18. Therefore such proud, godless spirits are shameless
and troublesome, as this lawyer who went forward so boldly, that they esteem nothing at all, neither the high and
earnest command of God nor do they wish to hear and know
the doctrine of the Gospel: they imagine, it is enough if they
have heard and can say the words: "Thou shalt love the
Lord thy God with all thy heart and thy neighbor as thy-

self." They do not perceive that God wants such doctrines not only heard and spoken, but put into practice, and where one does not esteem this, it will bring upon him higher and unbearable condemnation, as Christ says in Luke 12, 47: "And that servant, who knew his Lord's will, and made not ready nor did according to his will, shall be beaten with many stripes," etc. Therefore Christ gave this lawyer no other reply than this:

"Thou hast answered right; this do and thou shalt live."

19. That means, preaching the law aright and delivering a good strong lecture, yea, snaring him with his own words and taking hold of him at the right place, to show him where he was lacking. The doctrine he says is precious and true; but, dear sir, do it also; I would gladly see the doer of the law, then be a master and let your work of art be exhibited; for you all have spoken, written and known it; and you need nothing more; but just here you and others are lacking, that you do not do what you profess, but imagine it is enough to speak and think the words. No, in this way no one will live or be saved. The commandments must be kept and done, or the wrath of God and eternal death instead of life will abide upon you.

20. Such is the judgment upon the critics, who wish to know so much and teach everybody the way of salvation, yet they know nothing more than their own doings and works, and despise the teaching of the Gospel; so that such talk is nothing but mere empty, wicked and vain nonsense, since nothing follows from it; as St. Paul says of these doctrines of the law and of works in Gal. 6, 13: "For not even they who receive circumcision do themselves keep the law." Hence one may justly say to them, as Christ here says to this lawyer: Dear Teacher! Do yourself what you tell and teach others; and also as St. Paul, Rom. 2, 19-23, says: "Thou art confident that thou thyself art a guide of the blind," etc. "Thou therefore that teachest another, teachest thou not thyself?" "Thou who gloriest in the law, through thy transgression of the law dishonorest thou God?"

21. Thus one sees in the papal sophists, fanatics and all

who are not of the pure Gospel teaching, what great and
excellent works they profess and how they adorn themselves
in the highest degree with them, as the saintly monks do;
and yet they accomplish nothing. Yea, they only transgress
God's law and oppose it; as is proved in their case and
Christ shows in the following parable that no persons are
more unmerciful, more unpleasant and of course more un-
loving to their neighbor, more destitute of love to God, than
such hypocrites.

22. Yea, "this do" are the words of Christ, the eternal
lesson and sermon that is here spoken and preached to all
men, also to the saints, and it accuses them, that they cannot and dare not glory before God on account of their
works, merits and sanctity. But they must, if they would
know themselves aright and stand before God, condemn themselves and their manner of life; so that here no
saint has ever been able to stand upon this foundation,
neither in the Old nor in the New Testament. They must
all be mirrored in these words, "this do," which mean
nothing more than: See, you have not yet done this, nor
fulfilled it. Like Moses himself, who had the honor of being
faithful in all the things of God, and God called him his
friend, with whom he spake by word of mouth and face to
face; yet he had to say to God, Ex. 34, 6-7: "Oh, Lord God
of all spirits and of all flesh! Thou art merciful and
gracious, slow to anger, and abundant in loving kindness,
thou forgivest iniquity, transgression and sin, and before
thee none is guiltless. Here he casts away both his own
holiness and that of all men and pleads guilty before God."

23. In like manner the prophet Isaiah, Is. 6, 5-6, when he
stands before God and sees his glory confesses that he is
unclean, and must be comforted by an angel that his sins
are forgiven him, etc. And Jeremiah, when he prayed before
God and gloried in opposing his persecutors, Jer. 17, 16-17:
"Lord, thou knowest: That which came out of my lips was
before thy face"; here he is holy and happy; and yet soon
after he turns and says: "Be not a terror unto me; thou
art my refuge in the day of evil." Likewise, Jer. 10, 24:

"Oh, Jehovah, correct me, but with measure", that is, with grace; "not in thine anger, lest thou bring me to nothing." Where is here the pious and holy man with whom the Lord is never angry? Why then does he fear that he will bring him to naught?

24. Thus also Daniel confessed his own sin and the sin of all his people and said in Dan. 9, 18: "We do not present our supplications before thee for our righteousness, but for thy great mercies' sake." And David himself, when he received the forgiveness of his sins and sure consolation, that he had a gracious God, often glories, especially in Ps. 119, 97f., how he did what is right and pleasing to God; and God himself bears witness of this concerning him, 1 Sam. 13, 14, that he had found a man after his own heart. Yet he prays and sings Psalms of the greatest fear and anxiety: "O Jehovah, rebuke me not in thine anger, neither chasten me in thy hot displeasure," etc. Ps. 6, 1. Likewise Ps. 143, 2: "O Jehovah, enter not into judgment with thy servant; for in thy sight no man living is righteous."

25. In the same manner also St. Peter opens his mouth boldly in Acts 15, 10 and says of the whole law: "Now therefore why make ye trial of God, that ye should put a yoke upon the neck of the disciples which neither our fathers nor we were able to bear?" This he says of all saints, fathers, prophets, apostles and he should in this manner exclude all from heaven; as must have happened on account of the law and their doings, had they not remained under the heaven of grace, as he in verse 11 further says: "But we believe that we shall be saved through the grace of the Lord Jesus, in like manner as they." And St. Paul in Acts 13, 38-39: "Through this man is proclaimed unto you remission of sins; and by him every one that believeth is justified from all things, from which ye could not be justified by the law of Moses."

26. Now if the saints must confess this, who still have grace and the Holy Spirit, how will or dare the other blind, poor spirits presume and imagine that they have kept the commandments of God, when they form human thoughts

and dream they love God and their neighbor. And yet they
are so far from it that they do not understand nor know
what God's commandment requires and how it is kept. This
they prove when they are put to the test, when they are
to exhibit in a becoming manner love to their God and their
neighbor. As when they are required to suffer anything
for God's sake, as injury and disgrace, either from men or
when God himself visits them with his rod; then one sees
that the thoughts springing from their own brain are really
nothing, yea, they work only the opposite, they rage, murmur, curse and blaspheme against God, as if God did them
an injustice, etc. In like manner they act to their neighbors.
Where they know not how to enjoy a neighbor or to secure
some advantage and honor from him, but should serve him
gratuitously and help the poor, as this Samaritan did the
wounded one by the wayside, or expect also harm and ingratitude for extending the helping hand; then there is not
only no spark of love, but at once they seek revenge, turn
the people over to satan and think they do right in this and
are under no obligation to love such persons.

III.   A BEAUTIFUL PICTURE OF THE KINGDOM OF CHRIST.

27. Even this blind hypocrite is of the same mind, he
never thinks and speaks of what he owes his neighbor, and
yet he wants to be considered saintly and holy, because
he is a lawyer and knows how to speak of the law. And
although he was indeed reproved by Christ, and he surely
knows he was hit and was told he did not keep the law;
yet notwithstanding he is so bold and impudent as to despise
God's word, so that he beautifully adorns himself and shines
brightly and begins to ask:

"And who is my neighbor?"

28. He feels that he made a mistake in speaking and that
he opened his mouth too wide against himself. He is now
caught and taken captive by the Lord's answer, and he
drives a pin before his tongue so that he is not able to take

it back. Yet he was not so pious that he did Christ and God
the honor to humble himself and confess the truth, that
he did not keep these commandments etc.; but he forges
ahead and desires to be viewed as having done all, especially
all that is due to God. Hence he does not even think of
asking if he is indebted more to God, but desires no more
than that Christ shows him who his neighbor is, to whom
he should still be indebted anything and he has not performed it.

29. It is shameless presumption on the part of such saints
of satan, that they are so very certain in their knowledge
when God judges them: and even when they have been
moved by the law, and it is sufficiently proved to them
that they did not keep the law, they are not changed by
it until they once meet the judgment and the wrath of
God in their severity, so that they are compelled to feel them.
However the lies and shame of such hypocrites are hereby
sufficiently uncovered; although they will not be ashamed;
nor turn red for it, so that they must show by their own
confession that they do not yet understand what Moses and
the law require; because those who still wish to be masters
of the Scriptures prove themselves to be guilty in that they
do not know or do not appreciate who their neighbor is,
as he is clearly enough set forth by Moses and in this commandment. Therefore Christ also shows the same to this
lawyer clearly and plainly enough; not from the Scriptures,
but by means of a plain parable and picture, so that he
himself must seize it and let fall upon him the judgment
to his own shame that he did not wish to know or understand it.

*"A certain man was going down from Jerusalem to Jericho;
and he fell among robbers,"* etc.

30. Now the lawyer hears for the first time the appropriate text that puts him and all hypocrites like him to
shame, and publicly he is convinced that he never kept the
law, yea, that he did not understand it, even in the smallest
point referring to his neighbor, because he still doubts and
does not know, whom to consider as his neighbor, otherwise

he is inclined to love his neighbor. But thus it serves them right, who wish to master this man Christ and his word. And because they are very anxious to approach Christ with the law and plan to present it to him in a high and sharp manner, so they find also sharp opposition and they are obliged to depart in shame, and they see that he also knows something to say about the law, and that he lays hold of it and has Moses in his eye in a different way than they.

31. In brief, Christ shows here that he will not and cannot be caught by questions and debates relating to the law, and it is hurtful to no one but to those who let themselves fall into such questions and become entangled by them so that they can never get out again. For this surely happens to all, who deal with the law independent of faith and the right understanding of the Gospel. For where Moses alone with his shining light and rays, which are the horns going forth from his countenance, strikes us in our eyes, no one can stand before him. In short, whoever allows himself to be driven to Moses and will deal with the law, is lost; so that here even Christians must battle until they get out and are again wrapped up and enclosed in Christ, concerning which I have said more elsewhere.

32. Now in their folly and blindness all hypocritical saints resemble this lawyer, in that they not only fail to keep an iota of the law, however high they praise it; but as to its fundamental meaning they understand nothing about it; nor do they know how to make the right use of it, unless they learn to repeat its words like crows. As St. Paul also says of them in 1 Tim. 1, 7: "Desiring to be teachers of the law, though they understand neither what they say, nor whereof they confidently affirm." Yea, verily it is true that no man on earth knows, except by the Spirit of Christ, either what God is, how he should honor and thank him, or who his neighbor is. For just as all the world make their own gods and never happen to produce the true God, but is divided into innumerable idolatries; so is the world also blind here in that it never meets its neighbor, whom it sees ever before its eyes; passes by him, lets him suffer in distress and

hunger, whom it should serve and help, since it in other ways gives very much and does many great works.

33. And especially are the Jewish hypocritical interpretations hereby reproved and rejected, which paint and polish their neighbor according to their own fancy, consider him a neighbor whom they like, that is, he who is a friend, who has well merited and is worthy of a kindness and of love, whom they have enjoyed or hope yet to enjoy; they imagine they are not indebted to serve and help the stranger, the unacquainted, the unworthy, unthankful enemies, etc.

34. Against such hypocrisy Christ answers with the history of this poor, wounded man, who fell among robbers and was lying half dead, whom the Samaritan alone receives, serves and helps, and whom both the priest and the Levite pass by and leave lying helpless. Here the lawyer himself must answer that neither the priest nor the Levite was a neighbor to this man, but he who extended to him a kind helping hand was. The hypocrite did not dare to mention the Samaritan by name; for the Jews were bitter enemies to the Samaritans their neighbors, considered them to be the worst people, like we look upon heretics or fallen Christians. By this, without any praise to himself, yea, against his own will, he is obliged to confess and say, who is a neighbor to another.

35. And truly it sounds strange that he should be called a neighbor who does a good act and loves another, since otherwise (to speak after the manner of the Scriptures and of this commandment) he is called a neighbor who needs a favor or should be served and shown love; but both belong together and both are comprehended as in the predicate of relationship (praedicamento relationis) and they bind us all together so that every one is a neighbor to another. However to be such neighbors among one another is twofold: the first only in name and with words, the other in deed and with works of love.

36. In this sense the Samaritan was neighbor to the wounded man, not the priest nor Levite, who by right should have been and were under obligation to be. For in this

respect all men are debtors to one another and have the same commandment: "Thou shalt love thy neighbor", etc. Hence there is no difference, and in brief the meaning of this example is as Christ forces this hypocrite to confess, according to the common understanding of men, that they are neighbors, who before God belong together, where one needs help and another can give it, and here no one is excused nor free, be he priest or Levite.

37. And Christ is here especially sarcastic and vexed so that he attacks the priest and Levite, the most holy persons and the commissioned servants of God, and accuses, shames and scorns them by the example of the Samaritan, before whom they had a horror and an aversion as before a condemned criminal. But by this he shows that those who are the greatest and boast most of keeping God's commandments and teaching others, and should go ahead with good examples, in brief, those who are considered to be the high, the wise, the influential, and the best, have the least neighbor love; especially to the poor, forsaken, persecuted Christians, who suffer for the sake of God and his Word. For with their eyes centered constantly on their own sanctity, wisdom, and great talents they imagine every person is obligated to serve them, they do not think, that which they have is given by God only for the purpose that they might let their righteousness, wisdom, honor and possessions serve the needy, ignorant, sinful and despised. Hence this Samaritan is justly praised to the everlasting shame of the priests, the Jewish saints and also this hypocrite, for he showed such kindness and love to this stranger and wounded man, who was doubtless a Jew; while his own priest, Levite and scribes left him lying in his misery and wretchedness and as far as they were concerned, dying and perishing.

38. But by Christ making the Samaritan a neighbor of him who had fallen among the robbers, is meant especially to prove that he himself is and desires to be neighbor, who fulfils the law in the right sense and shows his love to the poor, wretched, and before God wounded and perishing consciences and hearts of all men. And by this he also is an

example that his Christians should do as he does, who is considered as a Samaritan before the whole world and especially in the eyes of the great saints, his own Jewish countrymen; that they do the same, since other people do it not, also that they take to themselves the need of the poor, forsaken and helpless, and know what they do to them they do to Christ as their neighbor.

39. Now here in this Samaritan Christ pictures and makes known the kindness, help and comfort, which he ministers in his kingdom through the Gospel; which is the same of which he spoke to his disciples at the beginning: "Blessed are the eyes which see the things that ye see", etc. He paints in the most comforting manner what faith possesses in him, and how far his Gospel differs from the doctrine of the law of the priests and Levites; concerning which I have said so much heretofore. We see in this picture how we, who have fallen in sin against God, lie under the wrath of God and must die the eternal death, are again rescued only by him, in that we receive God's grace and comfort, and a quickening of conscience, and we begin to keep the law.

40. This is the principal article of the doctrine of faith, that says we cannot save ourselves, neither can anything we do nor the doctrines of the law; but he must begin faith in us, who does not force the law upon our attention, when we feel our sins and misery; for that is the work of the secure spirits like this lawyer, who resent being reproved as sinners. But he has tender mercy upon us, besides is friendly and consoling through his Word, and himself binds up the sores of the wounded, places him on his own beast, nurses and looks after him. For he had to accomplish our redemption alone and take our place, bear in his own body our sins and need; he himself publishes this and gives us the comforting word, by which our wounds are bound up and healed.

41. This is called pouring wine and oil into the wounds, both of which are good medicines for the injured. The wine preserves the flesh clean and fresh that the wounds may

not corrupt or fester; likewise this balsam is especially given to the land of the Jews, namely, the noble, precious oil, that is, the best remedy known for all kinds of injuries. It is the preaching of the holy Gospel, which does both; it keeps the penitent conscience in the knowledge of its sins and' wickedness, that it neither becomes secure nor ceases to long for grace, and besides he comforts the conscience by grace and forgiveness, and thus ever makes man better until he is again well and begins again to do the work of a healthy man.

42. And to this end he now makes use of the office and service of the Church, as Christ commands her to expect and take care of such by means of the same office and spirit, which he bestows, and asks her to be faithful in everything that ministers to their strength and improvement, to comfort, admonish, restrain, chastise, etc.; and assures her what she does and sacrifices in such cases, he will reward.

43. Behold, this is the doctrine and the power of the Gospel and the treasure by which we are saved; which brings us to the point that we also begin to fulfill the law. For where the great unfathomable love and favor of Christ are known and believed, thence flows forth also love both to God and to our neighbor. For by means of such knowledge and consolation the Holy Spirit moves the heart to love God, and gladly does what it should to his praise and thanks, guards against sin and disobedience and willingly offers itself to serve and help everybody, and where it still feels its weakness it battles against the flesh and satan by calling upon God, etc. And thus while ever rising in faith it holds to Christ, where it does not do enough in keeping the law, its comfort is that Christ fulfills the law and bestows and imparts his fulness and strength, and thus he remains always our righteousness, salvation, sanctification, etc.

44. This is the right way to secure the observance of the law, of which our blind critics know nothing; but Christ beautifully shows by this, that one must hear the Gospel and believe in Christ before he can fulfill the law; otherwise there is nothing but hypocrisy and nothing but pure

boasting and talking about the law without any heart and life in it all.

45. Here we should also answer those, who misuse to-day's Gospel to support their blasphemous doctrine, when Christ says of the Samaritan, he commended the sick to his host, and when he gives him the half dollar, says to him: "Whatsoever thou spendest more, I, when I come back again, will repay thee." For the monks and sophists have invented from these words their lies about works which they call the works of supererogation, works in excess or more than are required, when one does more than God commands him, which he is otherwise not obligated to do. And such lies they confirmed by other blasphemies in making rules from the sermon of Christ in which he explained the ten commandments, Mat. 5, 21f.; and later applied them to their monastic life as if the monks were the greatest saints, for whom it was too insignificant a thing to keep God's commandments. As if they did on a higher plane many and great excessive works in their orders; for which God was obliged to give much more than heaven not only to themselves, but to other people to whom they wished to impart their works of supererogation, namely, to sell their lies and blasphemies for money. Their god the pope confirmed this and canonized and exalted these his saints as those who hereby strengthened his godhead and influence also over the dead in purgatory.

46. This blasphemy is however entirely too base and shameless, far above the blindness and presumption of this lawyer and those like him; for they do not only wish to be praised for keeping God's commandments, none of which they understand, nor think of keeping the least one in earnest. But they wish to be considered as having done much higher and many more works than all the saints whom God himself praises in the Scriptures; all of whom nevertheless confess that they have not kept the law for themselves, and must therefore, because they did not fulfill the law, seek and pray for grace and forgiveness with Christ.

47. What a shame! that people in the Church of Christ

dare speak of works and spheres of influence which should
be superfluous, and they be said to have done more than
God's command required; and still Christ said publicly of
the lives of all men in Luke 17, 10: "Even so ye also, when
ye shall have done all the things that are commanded you,
say, We are unprofitable servants; we have done that which
it was our duty to do." Thus you hear that it is purely a
debt and a duty, even if one should reach the point, which
no saint on earth can, that he had done all, and he would
then have nothing of which to boast, and for which God
would be obliged to thank him. Still what better and higher
work will one find or name that should have been commanded by God? For although they have now for a long
time driveled about virginity, I ask if such work can be better than what God calls here to love God with the whole
heart, yea, if independent of this command it can succeed
or be done, should it be good and well pleasing to God in a
different or extraordinary way? How is it then possible to
have an excess of good works or do anything better than God
has commanded? For what good can you do that you do not
do either to God or to man out of love, which you are indebted to do by reason of your eternal condemnation. What
can father and mother do more for their child, yea, what
more can God himself and Christ do for us, than to love us.
What does it mean then to advance such shameless lies and
foolishness about certain works, which are an excess over
those that are commanded when no one has as yet fully
attained to the measure of the ten commandments here upon earth?

48. It is true the Papists are now ashamed of such
slabbering, with which they have poured all their books
full, but yet they cannot quit their blasphemy. Since they see
now that this lie will not stand, they fall upon another interpretation that is just as blasphemous as the first; they turn
the words, "Whatsoever thou spendest more", from the life
and works to the doctrine, and say we must do not only
what the Scriptures teach, but hear also what the Church
teaches and decrees concerning the same. For the Apostles

and bishops are commanded to add more to the two shillings, namely, to the Old and New Testaments.

49. Yet see how the devil juggles and distorts himself by his sophistry and blind tricks in that he adorns and colors his lies. They have heard and learned something of us that in this parable the two shillings apply to the office of the ministry in the Church. For Christ is speaking of the office that should attend and care for the sick, and is administered for their relief and recovery. Hence, the two shillings are the Holy Scriptures or rather the pound as Christ calls them in another place, that is, the understanding of the Scriptures in the measure and the gifts of the Spirit, given to each one; all which is still the one and the same understanding without one having it in a richer degree than another. These sophists wish now to cite these words to support the foundation of their lies, that in Christendom we must teach, believe and hold as essential for salvation more than Christ has given and commanded us to teach. They are blind, mad, perverted persons who always seek something different and more, both to do and teach, than God's Word require, and yet they do not do it nor teach it, but let that be realized which they wish to have taught and practiced.

50. Therefore we tell you here again as before: Beloved, what can you do or what do you know that is better and more necessary to teach, than what Christ taught or commanded to teach? And what do we need more, to minister to the consciences in every thing that is necessary for them, to instruct, admonish, comfort, strengthen, correct and in short to do all that is necessary for salvation, than the doctrine of the Scriptures, namely, both of the law and of the Gospel? as St. Paul also shows in 2 Tim. 3, 16-17: "Every scripture inspired of God is also profitable for teaching, for reproof, for correction, for instruction which is in righteousness: that the man of God may be complete, furnished completely unto every good work." In these words you hear that the Scriptures richly contain and offer everything that serves to right living and good works; why will you then feign or seek something different that is to be

taught above or along side of the Scriptures? Beloved, first
explain the two shillings Christ gives and practice well the
doctrine they teach, then we will see later what more you
are able to explain or teach.

51. For this excess or explanation of the two shillings
we may without danger and in harmony with the meaning
of the Scriptures also interpret as the growth and exercise
in the true doctrine and the understanding of it; as St. Paul
admonishes in 1 Tim. 4, 13-15: "Give heed to reading, to
exhortation, to teaching, neglect not the gift that is in
thee," etc. "Be diligent in these things; give thyself wholly
to them; that thy progress may be manifest unto all." For
the more one practices and exercises himself in the doctrines
of the Scriptures, the more learned, gifted and powerful
he becomes in them, as is the case in other arts. Therefore
the explanation of this excess is, where one practices this
doctrine among the people, as every one is bound to do, and
according to his faithfulness in doing it he is either weak
or strong, and needs more comfort, admonition, etc., than
another.

52. But it is not the intention and the zeal of these sophists
to be so faithful and diligent that they correctly explain the
two shillings, that is, that they teach diligently what Christ
commanded, since they do not wish to do or to know
this, for they shun the Scriptures like they shun satan, they
neither understand the teaching of the law nor of the
Gospel. But they fill the Church with their prattle and
human doctrines, pervert and counterfeit God's Word, as
the devil advocates that this explanation of the two shillings
must teach them something different than the Gospel teaches; as they do nothing but propagate another and contrary
doctrine of their cursed lying prattle against the faith of
Christ among the people.

53. The summary is, since Christ himself and the Apostles
everywhere forbid the introduction of other doctrines, it
cannot stand the test that one should desire to confirm a
different doctrine by this parable or allegory; so Christ will
not expect of such sick persons anything different than

he himself gives to them; and that which can be further
explained must not be anything different, but be in harmony
with that which Christ himself has given.   However it is
possible that one should study a doctrine more and harder
than another and thus he explains more; as St. Paul says
of himself in 1 Cor. 15, 10, that he labored more and accomplished more than all the other Apostles.   And St. Ambrose
also applies this explanation to himself and says: He did
with his sermons and writings, which indeed are nothing
more than Christ commanded him to teach, fill his measure
to overflowing and he accomplished thereby more than
others; but of himself and other preachers he says: God
grant that we might make use of and compute what we
have received of Christ.

FOURTEENTH SUNDAY AFTER TRINITY.

In 1521 Luther published a sermon in pamphlet form on "The Ten Lepers," of which the following is a part. The sermon here given is found in all editions of Luther's Church Postil. The rest of the sermon of 1521 is printed in Luther's miscellaneous sermons. Erl. 14, 41; W. 11, 2113; St. L. 11, 1572.

Text: Luke 17, 11-19. And it came to pass, as they were on the way to Jerusalem, that he was passing along the borders of Samaria and Galilee. And as he entered into a certain village, there met him ten men that were lepers, who stood afar off: and they lifted up their voices, saying, Jesus, Master, have mercy on us. And when he saw them, he said unto them, Go and show yourselves unto the priests. And it came to pass, as they went, they were cleansed. And one of them, when he saw that he was healed, turned back, with a loud voice glorifying God; and he fell upon his face at his feet, giving him thanks: and he was a Samaritan. And Jesus, answering said, Were not the ten cleansed? but where are the nine? Were there none found that returned to give glory to God, save this stranger? And he said unto him, Arise, and go thy way; thy faith hath made thee whole.

CONTENTS: THE MIRACLE OF CLEANSING THE TEN LEPERS, IN WHICH IS PORTRAYED THE WHOLE CHRISTIAN LIFE, WITH ALL ITS INCIDENTS AND SUFFERINGS.

I. THE PORTRAYAL OF THE BEGINNING OF THE CHRISTIAN LIFE.

Here there are two principal parts. The order Luke followed in describing the journeys of Christ. 1-3.

I. These Two Parts In General. 4.

II. These Two Parts In Detail. 5-30.

A. Of Faith.
  1. Faith and its attributes.
    a. The first characteristic and attribute of faith, and how they are discovered in the lepers. 5-9.
    b. The second characteristic and attribute of faith, and how they are seen in the ten lepers. 10-11.
    c. The third characteristic and attribute of faith, and how they appear in the ten lepers. 12-14.
  1. Incentives to faith. 15-17.
B. Of Love.
  1. How Christ requires this love of his followers. 18f.

2. This love and faith compose the whole Christian life. 19-20.
3. This love is a mark of true Faith and of the friendship of God. 21-23.
4. How Christ teaches us the works of love by his example.
   a. The first work. 24-25.
   b. The second work. 26-27.
   c. The third work. 28-30.

II. THE DEVELOPMENT AND GROWTH OF THE CHRISTIAN LIFE.

I. The Necessity of This Development and Growth. 31.
II. The Foundation and Cause of This Development and Growth. 32f.
   * The Temptations to which faith is subject.
   1. It can easily cause your fall. 33.
   Because of it faith should increase and grow firmer. 34-35.
   3. It continues as long as man lives. 36.
     * Where God appears to be the farthest away he is the nearest. 37-38.
     * The great harm that follows where one loses his faith. 39.
     * Faith and Works.
   1. Faith cannot fail. 40.
   2. Faith and not works makes us pleasing to God. 41-43.
   3. Faith is not idle, but ever active. 42.
   4. The works of faith are spontaneous. 43.

III. How this Growth and Progress are Taught in the Example of the Samaritan.

A. In his returning to give thanks.
   1. How it shows his great love. 44.
   2. Why the other nine did not return with the Samaritan. 45f.
   3. The barriers laid in the way of returning.
     a. The first barrier. 45-49.
     b. The second barrier. 50.

* Of the temptation of faith.
   (1) The first form of temptation. 51.
   (2) The second form. 52.
   (3) The third form. 53.
   (4) How one should conduct himself in these temptations. 54-55.
4. How his return shows the excellent faith of the Samaritan. 56.
* What answer we are to give the Papists, when they say we must hear them, because the lepers were directed to the priests. 57-58.

B. In his knowledge of the kindness shown him and in the praise and gratitude he offers to God.
   1. Why the Evangelist ascribes to the Samaritan a knowledge of the help with the praise of it and denies it to the others. 59-61.
   2. How this knowledge and praise teach what is the true divine worship. 62-63.
   3. How this knowledge and praise compared with the returning of the Samaritan. 64f.
   4. The nature of this knowledge and praise. 65-67.
     * Of the hatred, which the Christians must suffer for the sake of Christ. 67-68.
     * Of the praise of God. 69-71.
     * The Christian life far surpasses the natural life. 72.
   5. Why the Evangelist in the narrative of this knowledge and praise adds the nature of the person in whom it is to be found. 73f.
     * Of the two kinds of people God serves. 73-75.
   6. Christ's conduct in the presence of this knowledge and praise.
     a. His conduct in itself. 76.
     b. How Christ here comforts his own. 77.
     c. How his conduct teaches us several good lessons. 78-80.
     * Concerning faith, love and hope. 81-83.

SUMMARY OF THIS GOSPEL: 1. The Papists, contrary to God and the Scriptures, use this Gospel lesson to enforce the compulsory confession of sin, just as if we were Jews and priests, descendants of the Levites. These lepers were not commanded that they should show their leprosy, but that they were cleansed and should do it according to the law. They were not cleansed by the priests, but in that they go to the priest according to the word and command of Christ, they became cleansed. Therefore they were cleansed through the command of Christ while on the way, and not by showing themselves to the priests; as Christ said to the one who returned and gave thanks. The others were not praised, but only the Samaritan who returned and ascribed all to the true priest. Consequently those, who wish to establish from this the Romish confession, show that they are blasphemers and perverters of the Word of God, who, since they have no argument in their favor, seek everywhere to maintain their tyranny with might and force.

2. Here you have a difference between those who are helped by the evangelical Word. Some acknowledge the grace, but some trust in the works of the law, and return not again to Christ; therefore outwardly they are considered clean and healthy.

I. THE PORTRAYAL OF THE BEGINNING OF THE CHRISTIAN LIFE OR CHARACTER.

1. St. Luke excels the other Evangelists in that he not only describes Christ's work and doctrine like they, but also observes the order of his journeys and circuits. His Gospel to the thirteenth chapter shows how Christ began at Capernaum to preach and do wonders, whither he moved from Nazareth and where he made his home, so that Capernaum is called his city in the Gospel. From there he went out everywhere, into cities and villages, preaching and working miracles. After he had accomplished all his work and had preached over the whole country, he prepared to go up to Jerusalem. This journey to Jerusalem he describes from the end of the ninth chapter to the close of his Gospel, how Christ during this journey preached and worked miracles. For this is Christ's last journey, and was finished in his last year at the close of his life. This is what he means here when he says: "And it came to pass, as they were on the way to Jerusalem, that he was passing along the borders of Samaria and Galilee." That is to say, this miracle he performed during his last journey to Jerusalem.

2. Now this was not the direct road from Capernaum to Jerusalem. For Galilee is north of Jerusalem, and Samaria is south of Galilee, and Capernaum is in Galilee. The Evangelist with special pains desires to show that he did not journey on the usual road, as he mentions Samaria and Galilee, and adds that he went through between them, and

not across their borders the nearest way. Christ journeyed from Capernaum eastward to the Jordan and southward from Galilee to Jerusalem, which was a tiresome, far and circuitous route, in doing which he took his own leisure and time. For he did not journey thus for his own sake, but in order to preach as much as possible and be of service to many. Therefore he journeyed on the borders of these lands to appear publicly, that people might come to him from all sides to hear him and obtain his help. For he was sent to offer his services to every one, that all might freely enjoy his favor and grace. Thus the Evangelist now describes the miracle and says:

"And as he entered into a certain village, there met him ten men that were lepers, who stood afar off; and they lifted up their voices, saying, Jesus, Master, have mercy on us."

3. One might ask the Evangelist how these lepers could stand afar off and lift up their voices, as lepers could not as a rule speak loud, and therefore they had to make a noise by rattling or clapping something? Of course he would answer they did not stand a mile away, only that they were not as near to him as those following him; and that all lepers are not so entirely voiceless that they cannot be heard even at a distance. However, the Evangelist, according to the custom of Holy Writ, desires hereby to indicate the great earnestness of their desire, that the voice of their heart was great that compelled them to cry out bodily as loud as they could.

4. This entire Gospel, however, is a plain, simple history or transaction, which requires little explanation. Yet as plain as it is, great is the example it presents to us. In the leper it teaches us faith, in Christ it teaches us love. Now, as I have often said, faith and love constitute the whole character of the Christian. Faith receives, love gives. Faith brings man to God, love brings man to his fellow. Through faith he permits God to do him good, through love he does good to his brother man. For whoever believes has every thing from God, and is happy and rich. Therefore he needs henceforth nothing more, but all he lives and does,

he orders for the good and benefit of his neighbor, and
through love he does to his neighbor as God did to him
through faith. Thus he reaps good from above through
faith, and gives good below through love. Against this
kind of life workrighteous persons with their merits and
good works terribly contend for they do works only to serve
themselves, they live only unto themselves, and do good
without faith. These two principles, faith and love, we will
now consider as they appear in the lepers and in Christ.

5. In the first place it is a characteristic of faith to presume to trust God's grace, and it forms a bright vision and
refuge in God, doubting nothing it thinks God will have
regard for his faith, and not forsake it. For where there
is no such vision and confidence, there is no true faith, and
there is also no true prayer nor any seeking after God.
But where it exists it makes man bold and anxious freely to
bring his troubles unto God, and earnestly to pray for help.

6. Therefore it is not enough for you to believe there is
a God, and pray many words as the wretched custom now is.
But observe here in the leper how faith is constituted, how
without any teacher at all it teaches us how our prayers
may be truly fruitful. You here observe how they had a
good opinion of and a comforting assurance in Christ, and
firmly thought he would be gracious to them. This thought
made them bold and anxious to bring their troubles to him,
and to cry for help with great earnestness and a loud voice.
For if they had not previously possessed this fancy and
expectation, they would undoubtedly have remained at
home, or would not have gone forth to meet him, nor would
they with raised voices have cried to him, but their doubt
would have advised them thus: What shall we do? Who
knows whether he would like to have us ask him? Perhaps
he will not notice us!

7. O such wavering and doubt offer sluggish prayers, it
does not raise the voice nor go forward to meet Christ! It
indeed murmurs many words and chants many songs very
unwillingly. But it does not pray, and only desires first to
be sure it will be heard, which is nothing else than to tempt

God. But true faith does not doubt the good and gracious will of God. Wherefore its prayer is strong and firm like faith itself. St. Luke does not relate three things of them in vain; first, that they went to meet him; second, they stood; third, they lifted up their voices. By these three things their strong faith is commended and presented to us as an example.

8. The going forth to meet him is the boldness excited by comforting assurance. The standing is the firmness and sincerity against doubt. The lifting up the voice is the great earnestness in prayer, growing out of such confidence. But powerless doubt does not go forth, nor stand, nor call, but turns and twists and hangs the head, grasps it in the hands, opens the mouth wide and stammers forth perpetually: Who knows? Who knows? If it were certain? How if it would fail? and similar faint-hearted expressions. For it has no favorable conception or thought of God, expects nothing of him, and hence will receive nothing, as James says, 1, 6-7: "But let him ask in faith, nothing doubting; for he that doubteth is like the surge of the sea driven by the wind and tossed. For let not that man think that he shall receive anything of the Lord." Afterwards they come like the foolish virgins who spilt their oil, with their empty lamps, that is with their works, and think God should hear them knock and open to them. But he will not.

9. Behold this good inclination or comforting trust, or free presumption toward God, or whatever you may call it, in the Scriptures is called Christian faith and a good conscience, which man must have if he desires to be saved. But it is not obtained by human works and precepts, as we shall see in this example, and without such a heart no work is good. Therefore be on your guard, there are many lecturers who want to teach faith and conscience, and know less about them than a common blockhead. They think it is a sleepy, lazy thing in the soul, that it is enough for the heart to believe that God is God. But here you observe what a thoroughly living and powerful thing faith is. It creates wholly a new heart, a new man, who expects all grace from

God. Therefore it urges to walk, to stand, makes bold to cry and pray in every time of trouble.

10. The second characteristic of faith is that it does not desire to know, nor first to be assured whether it is worthy of grace and will be heard, like the doubters, who grasp after God and tempt him. Just as a blind man runs against a wall, so they also plunge against God, and would first gladly feel and be assured that he can not escape out of their hands. The Epistle to the Hebrews says, 11, 1: "Now faith is assurance of things hoped for, a conviction of things not seen." This clearly means faith holds fast to what it does not see, feel or experience, either in body or soul, but as it has firm trust in God it commits itself to and relies upon it without any doubt but its hope will be realized. Thus it will also certainly be realized, and the feeling and experience will come to it unsought and unsolicited, even in and through such hope or faith.

11. For tell me, who had given these lepers a letter and seal that Christ would hear them? Where is there any experince and feeling of his grace? Where is the information, knowledge or certainty of his goodness? Nothing of the kind is here. What then is here? A free resignation and joyful venture on his imperceptible, untried and unknown goodness. Here there is no trace in which they might discover what he would do, but his mere goodness alone is kept in view, which fills them with such courage and venture to believe he would not forsake them. Whence, however, did they receive such knowledge of his goodness, for they must have known of it before, be they ever so inexperienced and insensible of it? Without doubt from the good reports and words they had heard about him, which they had never yet experienced. For God's goodness must be proclaimed through his Word, and thus we must build upon it untried and inexperienced, as will hereafter appear.

12. The third characteristic of faith is, that it allows of no merit, will not purchase the grace of God with works, like the doubters and hypocrites do, but brings with it pure unworthiness, clings to and depends wholly on the mere

unmerited favor of God, for faith will not tolerate works and merit in its company, so entirely does it surrender, venture and raise itself into the goodness for which it hopes, that for its sake it cannot consider either good works or merit. Yea, it sees that this goodness is so great, that all good works compared with it are nothing but sin. Therefore it finds only unworthiness in self, that it is more worthy of wrath than of grace; and it does this without any dissimulation, for he sees how in reality and in truth it cannot be otherwise

13. These lepers here prove this clearly, who hope for the grace of Christ without the least merit. What good had they ever done to him before? They had never seen him, how then could they have served him? Besides they were lepers, whom he could justly have avoided according to the law, Levit. 13, and kept himself free from them as was just and right. For in reality and truth there was unworthiness, and reason why he should have nothing to do with them nor they with him. For this cause they also stand far off, like those who well knew their unworthiness. Thus faith also stands far from God, and yet it goes to meet him and cries out, for it knows itself in the reality of truth to be unworthy of his goodness, and has nothing on which to depend, except his highly renowned and loudly praised goodness. And such a soul also seeks Christ's favor, while it stands far off and is empty; for it cannot in the least tolerate in its company our merit and work, and comes freely like Christ into this village to the lepers, in order that its praise may be free and pure.

14. Observe how everything agrees perfectly that God's love gives its favor freely, does not take nor seek anything for it, and how faith also receives quite freely and pays nothing for it, and thus the rich and the poor meet together, as the Psalms say, To this their words also testify when they say: Have mercy on us! He who seeks mercy of course neither buys nor sells anything, but seeks pure grace and mercy, as one unworthy of it, and evidently having greatly deserved the contrary.

15. Behold, here is a good, real, living and true example of Christian faith, that sufficiently teaches us how we must be disposed if we would find grace, piety and salvation. Now, in addition to this doctrine follows the incentive or inducement to faith, that we should gladly believe as we are at present taught to believe. This incentive, however, consists in that we observe how such faith never fails, that as it believes so it comes to pass, and that it is certainly heard and answered.

For Luke describes how graciously and willingly Christ beheld and heard the lepers, and says:

"And when he saw them, he said unto them, Go and show yourselves unto the priests."

16. How very friendly and lovingly the Lord invites all hearts to himself in this example, and stirs them to believe in him! For there is no doubt that he desires to do for all what he here does for these lepers, if we only freely surrender ourselves to him for all his favor and grace. Just as true faith and a Christian heart should do and delight to do; so these lepers also do and teach us to do. For how earnestly the Lord desires that we should joyfully and freely venture to build on his favor before we experience or feel it, he has here sufficiently testified that he hears them willingly, without any hesitation, that he does not first say he will do it, but as though it were already done, he did as they wished. For he does not say: Yes, I will have mercy on you, ye shall be cleansed; but merely: "Go and show yourselves unto the priests." As though he would say: There is no use of asking, your faith has already acquired and obtained it, before you began to ask; you were already cleansed in my sight when you began to expect such things of me; it is no longer necessary, only go and show your purity to the priests; as I consider you and as you believe, so you are and shall be. For he would not have sent them to the priests, if he had not considered them clean, and so wished to deal thus with them, as those who had become cleansed.

17. Behold, so powerful is faith, to obtain all it wants of

God, that God considers it done before the asking. Of this Isaiah says, 65, 24: "And it shall come to pass that, before they call, I will answer; and while they are yet speaking, I will hear." Not as though faith or we were worthy of it, but in order that he might show his unspeakable goodness and willing grace, thereby to stir us to believe in him, and comfortingly look to him for every good thing, with joyful and unwavering consciences, which do not stumble after him nor tempt him. So now you also see that Christ hears these lepers before they call, and before they cry out he is prepared to do all their hearts desire. "Go," he says, I will not add a word, for it has succeeded in your case farther, no promise or consent is necessary; take what you ask and go. Are not these strong incentives that make the heart joyful and eager? Behold, then his grace permits itself to be felt and grasped, yea it grasps and satisfies us. This has been said on the first part, namely, faith.

18. Now we must also examine the other part of this example of the nature of Christianity, love. The lepers have instructed us how to believe; Christ teaches us to love. Love does to our neighbor as it sees Christ has done to us, as he says in John 13, 15: "For I have given you an example, that ye also should do as I have done to you." And immediately afterwards he says in verse 34: "A new commandment I give unto you, that ye love one another; even as I have loved you, that ye also love one another. By this shall all men know that ye are my disciples, if ye have love one to another." What else does this mean than to say: Through me in faith you now have everything that I am and have; I am your own, you are now rich and satisfied through me; for all I do and love I do and love not for my but only for your sake, and I only think how to be useful and helpful to you, and accomplish whatever you need and should have. Therefore consider this example, to do to each other as I have done to you, and only consider how to be useful to your neighbor, and do what is useful and necessary for him. Your faith has enough in my love and grace; so your love shall also give enough to others.

19. Behold, this is a Christian life, and in brief it does not need much doctrine nor many books, it is wholly contained in faith and love. Thus also says St. Paul, Gal. 6, 2: "Bear ye one another's burdens, and so fulfill the Law of Christ." And to the Phil. 2, 4 he says: "Not looking each of you to his own things, but each of you also to the things of others." And there he gives us Christ as an example, v. 6: "Who existing in the form of God, counted not the being on an equality with God a thing to be grasped." Who, although he was true God, yet became our servant and served us, and died a scandalous death for us. This Christian, free and joyful life has the evil spirit as its enemy, who with nothing else does such great injury as with the doctrines of men, as we shall hear. For truly the manner of a Christian's life is briefly marked out in the words, have a good heart toward God and a good will toward your fellow man, here it consists entirely within us.

20. His good heart and faith naturally teach him how to pray. Yea, what is such faith, but pure prayer? It continually looks for divine grace, and if it looks for it, it also desires it with all the heart. And this desire is really the true prayer, that Christ teaches and God requires, which also obtains and accomplishes all things. And because it does not trust or seek comfort in self, its works or worthiness, but builds upon God's pure grace, therefore whatever he believes, desires, hopes and prays, also comes to pass; so that the holy Prophet Zechariah justly calls the Spirit a Spirit of grace and of prayer, where God says, Zech. 12, 10: "And I will pour upon the house of David, and upon the inhabitants of Jerusalem, the Spirit of grace and supplication." Because faith recognizes and desires God's favor without any intermission.

21. Again, love naturally teaches him how to do good works. For they alone are good works which serve your neighbor and are good. Yea, what is such love but only good deeds continually shown toward your neighbor, so that our work is called love, our faith is called prayer? Thus Christ speaks in John 15, 12-13: "This is my command-

ment, that ye love one another, even as I have loved you. Greater love hath no man than this, that a man lay down his life for his friends." As though he would say: So completely have I done all my works for your benefit, that I also gave my life for you, which is the greatest of all love, that is, the greatest work of love. If I had known a greater love, I would have manifested it to and for you. Therefore you should also love each other, and do all good deeds to one another. I require no more of you. I do not say you are to build for me churches, make pilgrimages, fast, sing, become monks or priests, or that you are to enter into this order or rank; but you do my will and service when you do good to each other, and no one cares for himself but for others, on this all entirely depends.

22. And these he calls "friends." By this he does not mean that we should not love our enemies. For he says clearly: "Who lays down his life for his friends." "His friends" are more than mere "friends." It may come to pass that you are my friend, and yet I am not your friend, or I may love you and receive you as a friend and offer you my friendship, and yet you may hate me and remain my enemy. Just as Christ says to Judas in the garden: "Friend, do that for which thou art come." Mat. 27, 50. Judas was his friend, but Christ was Judas' enemy, for Judas considered him his enemy and hated him. Christ loved Judas and esteemed him as his friend. It must be a free, perfect love and kindness toward every one.

23. See, this is what James means when he says, 2, 26: "Faith apart from works is dead." For as the body without the soul is dead, so is faith without works. Not that faith is in man and does not work, which is impossible. For faith is a living, active thing. But in order that men may not deceive themselves and think they have faith when they have not, they are to examine their works, whether they also love their neighbors and do good to them. If they do this, it is a sign that they have the true faith. If they do not do this, they only have the sound of faith, and it is with them as the one who sees himself in the glass and when he

leaves it and sees himself no more, but sees other things, forgets the face in the glass, as James says in his first chapter, verses 23-24.

[This passage in James deceivers and blind masters have spun out so far, that they have demolished faith and established only works, as though righteousness and salvation did not rest on faith, but on our works. To this great darkness they afterwards added still more, and taught only good works which are no benefit to your neighbor, as fasting, repeating many prayers, observing festival days; not to eat meat, butter, eggs and milk; to build churches, cloisters, chapels, altars; to institute masses, vigils, hours; to wear gray, white and black clothes; to be spiritual; and innumerable things of the same kind, from which no man has any benefit or enjoyment; all which God condemns, and that justly. But St. James means that a Christian life is nothing but faith and love. Love is only being kind and useful to all men, to friends and enemies. And where faith is right, it also certainly loves, and does to another in love as Christ did to him in faith. Thus everyone should beware lest he has in his heart a dream and fancy instead of faith, and thus deceives himself. This he will not learn anywhere as well as in doing the works of love. As Christ also gives the same sign and says: "By this shall all men know that ye are my disciples, if ye have love one to another." John 13, 35. Therefore St. James means to say: Beware, if your life is not in the service of others, and you live for yourself, and care nothing for your neighbor, then your faith is certainly nothing; for it does not do what Christ has done for him. Yea, he does not believe that Christ has done good to him, or he would not omit to do good to his neighbor.

This St. Paul also requires, 1 Cor. 13, 2: "If I have all faith, so as to remove mountains, but have not love, I am nothing." This explains the whole matter, not that faith is insufficient to make us pious, but that a Christian life must embrace and never separate these two, faith and love. But the presumptuous undertake to separate them, they want only to believe and not to love, they despise their neighbor, and yet pretend to have Christ. This is false and must fail.

Thus we say, too, that faith is everything and it saves us, that a man needs no more for his salvation.   Yet he is on this account not idle, but labors much, all however for the benefit of his neighbor, and not for himself; for he does not need it, he has enough in Christ. If, however, he does not do this, he is certainly not right. And this his work is his love. But the blind guides want to teach that works are necessary, that the worker needs them for his salvation. This is the chief perversion, the error of all errors, for by this they destroy both faith and love, the entire Christian nature and example. They take the work from the neighbor, and give it to the person himself doing it, as though he needed it. Here faith cannot live, for he knows that his work is not necessary and helpful for himself, but only for his neighbor. Thus they are opposed to each other; faith casts the works from itself on the neighbor through love; but the blind teachers tear them from the neighbor, and apply them to their own persons, and thus choke and dampen both love and faith, and cause man only to love himself and to seek only his own salvation and trust in his own works. From this evil must follow dull consciences and much self-chosen work, building churches, much praying, the saints' fasting and the like, which are beneficial to no one, and all misery and misfortune must follow, as is at present evident in the cloisters, monasteries and high schools.]

24. Now let us observe the works of the love of Christ in this example of the ten lepers. But what is in Christ besides pure love? Everyone can easily find out for himself. First, why is it necessary for him to travel between Samaria and Galilee? Or who paid him anything for doing this? Or who requested him to do so? Is it not manifest, that he does all this freely, willingly, without receiving anything for it, and comes of himself uninvited, that no one can say that he deserved such a visitation or acquired it by prayer. Thus we see here that he does nothing whatever for himself or for his own sake, but all for the sake of others, unrequested and altogether freely, out of mere grace and love.

25. In like manner, that he had just gone into this village, why did he need to do this? Who asked him to do so? Who paid him anything for it? Is it not true that he came before any merit was possible, any prayer could be said; and offers his love and kindness freely and gratuitously, and seeks nothing of his own in it but only serves others thereby, so that he might draw all hearts unto himself to believe in him? Behold, such virtue has love, that it does only good and lives for the benefit of others, seeks nothing with selfish motives, does all freely and gratuitously, and surprises everyone. Such life and work you must observe and direct your life accordingly, if you would be a Christian, and banish all such works and power from your view that are not of this nature, even if they be so great as to remove mountains, like the Apostle says, 1 Cor. 13, 2.

26. Note in the second place how Christ does good without harm to others, yea, by preventing harm to others. For there are some who do good in a way that is harmful to others, as the proverb runs, they offer our lady a penny and steal her horse. So they who give alms from ill-gotten goods, as God says in Is. 61, 8: "For I,. Jehovah, love justice, I hate robbery for burnt offering." Of this nature are nearly all monasteries and cloisters that devour the sweat and blood of the people, and then pay God with masses, vigils, rosaries, or monasteries and holidays, and at times they also give an alm. This is to love with the goods of others, and to serve God in prosperous days and in the fullness of wealth with an all sufficiency. This disgraceful welldoing is indeed a far reaching plague. But here Christ does no one harm, but prevents injury rather, and directs the lepers to the priests, so that they may be deprived of none of their rights.

27. Thus he bestows his kind deeds upon the lepers, as though he went into this village for this purpose; he looks upon them graciously and willingly, and gladly helps them. Besides he thereby also prevents any disadvantage to the priests, although he is under no obligation to them. For as he cleansed the lepers in a supernatural manner without the

priests doing anything, he was indeed not obliged to direct them to them, and could say: Inasmuch as you have not performed your office toward these according to the law, therefore you should also not have the emoluments of the office, which is just and right. But love does not look on what is right nor does it contend, it is present only to do good, and so it does even more than it is obliged to do, and goes beyond what is right.

Therefore St. Paul says in 1 Cor. 6, 1, that among Christians there should be no lawsuits at court, because love does not seek or demand its rights, nor cares anything for them, but is bent only on doing good. Although he says at another place, 1 Cor. 13, 1: "If I speak with the tongues of men and of angels, but have not love, I am become sounding brass, or a clanging cymbal." Thus are truly the learned of our day, who teach much about rights, which is only unchristian and opposed to love. I do not speak of those who are forced to contend for their rights; for as right is preferred by some unchristian people, they must be present and defend the right so that nothing worse occurs. It is not Christian, to hang or to crush under the wheel; but in order to restrain murderers, such things must also be done. It is not Christian to eat and drink, nevertheless man is compelled to do both. These are all necessary works, which do not concern the inner nature of Christianity. Therefore a person should not be satisfied in doing them, as though the doing of them made a Christian. The work in the married state is not distinctively Christian, yet it is necessary to avoid evil. Other examples might be given.

28. Thirdly, Christ shows love is still greater, in that he exercises it where it is lost and receives ingratitude from the majority; ten lepers were cleansed and only one thanks him, on the nine his love is lost. If he would have made use of justice here instead of love, as men are accustomed to do and nature teaches, he would have made them all lepers again. But he lets them go and enjoy his love and kind deed, although they return to him enmity instead of thanks. Nor did he prevent the priests from enjoying their own, but

gave them their honor and rights, although without any need and obligation to do so. And the priests thank Christ by alienating from him the lepers, so that they believed Christ did not cleanse them, but their offering and obedience to the law did it. And thus they destroy the faith in the lepers, and cause Christ to be despised and hated by them, as though he had taken to himself an office that did not belong to him.

29. That the priests had examined these lepers one may readily believe, and this the text also suggests. Therefore they must have trumpeted into these lepers many wicked words against Christ, and highly praised the works and offerings of the law, so that they might root out of them their great and noble faith, and establish themselves in place of Christ in their heart. And the lepers accepted this, and regarded Christ as the priests told them, so that they became his enemies, and ascribed their purification to God as obtained by virtue of their offerings and merit, and not by Christ and his pure grace. And while they were thus released from bodily leprosy, they thereby fell into spiritual leprosy, which is a thousand times worse. But Christ permits both parties to go and enjoy his goodness, is silent about his rights, receives hatred and displeasure for praise and thanks; that we may hereby learn how we often pray, and that it were better for us if our prayers were not answered. It would have been better for these lepers if they had remained unclean than that by their bodily cleansing they should become diseased with a more dangerous spiritual leprosy.

30. Now study this example and incite your life that you may do your good works not only without harm to others, but also to their advantage, and not only to friends and the good, but consider that the greater portion will be lost, and that you will receive ingratitude and hatred as your reward. Then you will walk the right road in the footprints of Christ your Lord. Until you have accomplished this, you should not regard yourself a true, perfect Christian, it matters not whether you wear ten hairy shirts and fast every day, or celebrate mass every day, and pray the psalter, make pil-

grimages, and establish churches or yearly festivals. For Christ wishes to have such works done, if they are done in the right spirit. Behold, this is truly a Christian life.

[But now you see whither Christ's works tend. Therefore attend to this with all diligence, and view your own life aright. If you find a work of yours, which you need or think you need for your salvation, stamp it under your feet, guard yourself as in the presence of all the devils, and never rest until you are delivered from such a spirit or work, and strive that your life may be useful and serviceable not to your, but only to your neighbor's need. Cursed be he who lives and works only for himself, for Christ did not wish to do his own will nor live for himself! For your own works will certainly lead you away from love and faith. You have no other work that is necessary and useful for thy salvation than to believe, and daily to exercise yourself in this faith, and see to it that you continue steadfast in it, and not allow the priests to deprive you of it, as they did these nine lepers, for they have slick tongues and a beautiful color. Only let all other works go in one bundle, be they lost or well applied, let that not trouble you; you remain in the faith Christ gives you, here you have many times enough; and in love, which gives you to your neighbor, you will have enough to do, for which you will find yourself many times deficient. For what you do in this is nothing, even if you should possess all the works of the saints. Hear what St. Paul says, 1 Cor. 13, 3: "And if I bestow all my goods to feed the poor, and if I give my body to be burned, but have not love, it profiteth me nothing." It is not enough to help the poor and torment yourself, you must love your enemy and cast your goods with yourself into the waste heap, and not choose one rather than another to whom to do good.

Here you might say: Alas, what will now become of the spiritual orders, the priests, the monks and the nuns? Are they of service to no one, and do they perform only their own works? Answer: Why do you ask about priests and monks? Has not Christ ordered you to follow him, and not priests and monks? If their works are not done in the sense

before mentioned, that one should serve the other and cling
to faith, you are never to doubt that they are opposed to
Christ, and are as the foolish virgins with their empty, dark
lamps. For their sake another Christ will not come. Of
this St. Peter prophesies, 2 Pet. 2, 1: "There shall be false
teachers among you, they will bring forth destructive sects,"
that is, spiritual orders and ranks, in which souls will only
be condemned. And St. Paul, in 2 Thess. 2, 10-11: "Because
they received not the love of the truth, that they might be
saved. And for this cause God sendeth them a working of
error, that they should believe a lie, that they all might be
judged who believed not the truth, but had pleasure in unrighteousness." In these words the spiritual orders and
ranks are set forth, how they are constituted and whence
they come. For they pretend to be something extraordinary and better than other callings and stations in the Christian life, while they are farther from the Christian life than
any other calling or any other people on earth, and need
more to bring them to the true Christian life. Some of these
callings and their governments are well ordered, for there
are wife and child and subject, who exercise and give occasion for love, and likewise insist that you must not live or
work for yourself, but are compelled to work only for the
good of others. If you only know the faith and really live
according to it, you then have no work of your own and you
will have so much to do that you will be obliged to forget
your own work. For in that you fast, labor, eat, drink, sleep,
take a wife, in short do everything for the needs of your body
and estate, is all done that you may live here and support the
body in order that you may serve others. Behold, this is
truly a Christian life. Therefore St. Paul says, in Rom. 13, 8:
"Owe no man anything, save to love one another," and in
love to serve each other. From this you may know why
all the world is full of spiritual orders, that is, dens of hell
and murder, but no one knows any longer what a Christian
life is, not to mention that one should find an example of it.
This is all the fault of the Pope and his cursed law, which

has given us God's wrath for our masters, as St. Peter and St. Paul have declared.]

This is enough on the first part of our Gospel, let us now examine its second part. The Evangelist says:

II. A PICTURE OF THE CHRISTIAN CHARACTER IN ITS DEVELOPMENT AND GROWTH.

"And it came to pass, as they went, they were cleansed."

31. Thus far we have learned how faith works, its nature, whence it comes, what its beginning is, what it brings, and how acceptable it is before God. All this is said of the beginning of a Christian life. But it is not enough to begin, we must increase and continue steadfast, for Christ says, Mat. 24, 13: "But he that endureth to the end shall be saved." And Luke 9, 62: "No man, having put his hand to the plow, and looking back, is fit for the kingdom of God." Therefore this second part treats of the increase and perfection of faith.

32. The faith or confidence of the heart in God is a very tender and sensitive thing indeed, and it may very easily be injured, so that it begins to tremble and despair, when it is scarcely yet exercised and established. And thus it has countless attacks and dangers from sin, from nature, from reason and self-conceit, from human doctrine, from the examples of the saints and from devils. In short, it is attacked without intermission from all sides, in front and in the rear, so that it trembles and despairs, or falls to trusting in good works. Hence St. Peter truly says, 1 Pet. 4, 18: "The righteous is scarcely saved." And the Prophet Zechariah compares the righteous to a brand plucked from the fire, that he may not be entirely consumed; and Amos the Prophet to a sheep's ear that the shepherd delivered from the jaws of the wolf. So malignantly temptations rage about a believing heart.

Therefore St. Paul says to the Corinthians, 1 Cor. 10, 12: "Wherefore let him that thinketh he standeth take heed lest he fall." And in all places he teaches how we should walk

with watchfulness and fear, and always take good care of
our faith, for, as he says in 2 Cor. 4, 7: ''We have this treasure in earthen vessels,'' which are very easily broken if God
does not preserve us.

33. Therefore we should not be secure but stand in the
fear of God and pray with Jeremiah, 17, 17, that God might
protect our faith, and not permit us to tremble or be frightened in the presence of our faith. This Gospel also sufficiently
shows this danger by a terrible example, that among these
ten lepers who believed, nine fell away, and in the end only
one stands and continues steadfast. It is here as with a beautiful tree in full bloom, that we think cannot bear all its
fruit; but later so many blossoms are destroyed by storms,
the fruit becomes wormeaten and falls, that scarcely one-
tenth of it ripens. So there are many who receive the Word
and begin to believe; but as the Lord says, Mat. 13, 10-21,
the soil is stony and not deep enough, or faith stands among
thorns and thistles; that is, by reason of temptations and en-
ticements they fall and continue not steadfast. For as soon
as things go wrong with them and God afflicts them, they
forget his goodness and see only his anger. Hence faith
vanishes, and there remains a wavering, discouraged and
frightened conscience, that flees from God, not to mention
that it should go to meet him, as indeed it did at first.

34.* Thus we see here that the lepers began to believe, and
expected help from Christ, who then further awakens their
faith and tries it, does not immediately make them well, but
speaks a word to them, to show themselves to the priests.
If there had been no faith in them their reason and natural
fancy would have spoken thus and immediately murmured:
What is this? we expected great kindness from him, and
heartily believed in him, that he would help us; but now he
does not touch us, as is his custom, and as he did to others,
but only looks at us and passes on. Perhaps he despises us,
besides he neither promises nor denies whether he will
cleanse us or not, but leaves us in doubt, and says no more
than that we should show ourselves to the priests. Why

* § 34 to § 39 is found in Edition c and pamphlets.

should we show ourselves to them, they already know we are lepers?

We see that nature would thus become angry and luke-warm against him, because he does not immediately do her bidding, and he does not with certainty tell what he will do. But here is faith, that strengthens itself and only increases through such temptation, and cares naught how unkind or uncertain the actions and words of Christ sound, but clings fast to his goodness, and does not permit itself to be fright-ened away. And of a truth, there was in them a strong, rich faith, that upon his word they promptly went forth; for had they doubted they certainly would not have gone, and yet they had here no clear promise.

35. And this is the method God employs with us all to strengthen and prove our faith, and he treats us so that we know not what he will do with us. This he does for the reason, that man is to commend himself to him and rely on his mere goodness, and not doubt that he will give what we desire or something better. So also these lepers thought: Very well, we will go as he commands, and although he does not tell us whether he will cleanse us or not, this shall not influence us to esteem him any the less than before. Yea, we will only esteem him so much the more and higher, and joyfully wait, if he will not cleanse us, he will do still better for us than if we were cleansed, and we will not on that account despair of mercy and favor. Behold, this is the true increase of faith.

36. Such trials continue as long as we live, therefore we must also continue to grow just as long. For when he tries us in one instance in which he makes us uncertain how he will treat us, he afterwards always takes another and con-tinually enlarges our faith and confidence, if we only re-main unmovably steadfast.

Behold, this is what St. Peter calls growth in Christ when he says, 1 Pet. 2, 2: "As newborn babes, long for the spiritual milk which is without guile, that ye may grow thereby unto salvation." Again in the latter part of 2 Peter, verse 18: "But grow in the grace and knowledge of our

Lord and Savior Jesus Christ." And St. Paul in all places desires we should increase, continue and become rich in the knowledge of God and Jesus Christ. This is nothing else than in this manner to become strong in faith, when God conceals his kindness and appears as Christ does here to the lepers, so that we do not know what to expect of him. For faith must be (argumentum non apparentium) an argument not an appearance, and be certain and not doubt in the things that are concealed and are not experienced. Heb. 11, 1.

37. Therefore observe that when God appears to be farthest away he is nearest. This word of Christ reads as though we cannot know what he will do, he does not refuse nor promise anything, so that the lepers, who previously certainly relied on his kindness for all things, might have become offended at it, and begun to doubt, and taken quite a different sense of it than Christ meant. Christ speaks it out of an overflowing kindness that he thinks it unnecessary to tell them that they have already obtained what they want. But as the sense was not clear to them they might have thought he was entirely of a different opinion, and farther from them than before.

38. Thus are all his superabundant kindnesses, works and words, that we may think that he was previously more kind and gracious than afterwards, when he first had anything to do with us.

Thus it also happened to the people of Israel in the desert, they thought God did not bring them out of Egypt, upon whom nevertheless they called and they knew while in Egypt that he would help them. But all this is done that we may not remain in weakness when we first begin to believe, but grow and ever increase until we be able to take the strong nourishment and become satisfied and full of the Spirit, that we may not only despise and triumph over riches, honor and friends, but also over death and hell.

39. Hence it is with the faithless and unbelieving as with unfortunate mine workers, who begin to prospect with great confidence, and dig extensively. But when they are

about to strike the treasure, which would have taken but a little more labor, they give up, and look at what they did as in vain, and think, there is nothing in it. Then comes another worthy of the task, who had never yet made a beginning, but he strikes away boldly and finds what the former hunted and dug for him. Thus it is also with the grace of God; he who begins to believe and will not continually grow and increase, from him grace will be taken and given to another who begins with it; if he, too, will not continue it will be taken also from him and given to another. It only wants to be believed. And here our high schools speak wholly blind, mad, and poisonous things about faith, when they teach that the beginning of faith is enough for salvation, and is only a small degree or step from it.

40. So these words of the text, "And it came to pass, as they went, they were cleansed," would say: It is impossible for faith to fail, it must take place as it believes. For if these lepers had not believed and remained steadfast, of course they would not have gone. Therefore, not for the sake of their going, but on account of their faith they became cleansed, because of which they also went.

41. All this I say in order that some blind teacher may not come to this text and stick his eyes into good works without seeing the faith; and afterwards pretend that works make us acceptable and save us, because these lepers went forth and thus became cleansed. This error must be opposed, that one may rightly see the faith of these lepers, and thus it will appear that their work of going did not obtain the cleansing, but faith did. [So also the Lord opposes the same error in that he cleanses them before they accomplish the work assigned them. For he did not only command them to go, but to show themselves to the priests. Now they evidently became cleansed before they arrived at the priests and before they had finished the work. If they had first become cleansed after they had arrived and brought the offering, the priests might have had ground for the prtense that they were cleansed by their offering and works, as they even did, and misled the poor people.]

42. Now I have often said that works are twofold; some before and without faith, others come out of and after faith. For as little as nature without faith can be idle and inactive, so much less also can faith be idle. And as nature's works do not precede or make nature, but nature must first be present and do the works out of and by virtue of herself; so also the works of faith do not make faith, but they follow and spring from faith. So there must be works, but they have no merit nor saving power, but all salvation and merit must first be present in faith.

43. This is also the reason that the works of faith are free and spontaneous, and not premeditated. For these lepers were also free, and if Christ had commanded them to do something else, they would have done it. And if they had been asked whether they went in order to be cleansed, they would have replied, no. This must have been so, if the cleansing took place because of their works. Just as if you should ask the hypocrites whether they work in order to be saved, they would say: Yes, and without works they would not want to be saved. [But these lepers would not speak thus, they hope he will cleanse them out of pure kindness, without considering their work of going, which they do only because he wills it to satisfy the law, although unnecessary. For all lepers might also go to the priests, and yet they would not on that account be cleansed, which nevertheless must be, if the work were necessary and useful for the cleansing. Just as the workrighteous persons think, that he who works will be saved; so it must also be here, he who goes will be cleansed. But now as the cleansing takes place only because of the presence of faith, so salvation comes also on account of faith alone.] But as the lepers must go not for their own sakes, but for the sake of the priests, that they might be satisfied, although they were not obliged to go to them; so all believers must work, not for their own sake, but for the sake of others, to serve them. Although they owe them nothing, but freely do good as Christ has done to them, about which enough has been said above in the first part.

There follows further in the text:

"And one of them, when he saw that he was healed, turned back, with a loud voice glorifying God."

44. The returning of one must have taken place after he and the others had shown themselves to the priests. But the Evangelist is silent as to how they came to the priests and what took place there. However, from the return and thankfulness of this one, he gives us to understand how it went. He without doubt very unwillingly returned alone, for as with all his heart he thanks Christ and is kind to him, the conclusion is clear how he persevered, admonished, urged, prayed and did his utmost for the others that they should go with him and acknowledge the great kindness; and no doubt it grieved him that he could not prevail upon the nine and had to leave them with tears and grief. All these and similar things force us to think of the love he had for Christ, that leaves nothing unattempted, fears no one, regards no one, if they only worthily honor and praise Christ.

45. What kind of a tempest visited the nine, that they so firmly separated from the one; as we have heard they all made a good beginning and grew in the faith of Christ? Of their own accord they would not have fallen so completely; some one must have first overthrown their faith, so that the honor which they previously gave Christ so freely and honestly, they now divert from him and rob him of this honor, and turn their friendship into enmity. Nor was it a weak falling away, that so severely offends and opposes the one leper with all his admonitions and regrets. Behold, the priests did this, they could not bear that the honor be given to Christ; hence they no doubt preached a strong sermon against him to root out their faith.

46. But what might they have said to them? Because they fought against Christ and the faith it is easy to think what they said and did, namely, what is contrary to faith; that is, they heralded into these poor lepers that they should not believe that Christ cleansed them, but should thank God, who had regard to their offering and the prayers of the priests, and heard them, and on this account cleansed them; and whatever else they said to draw away the hearts of the

lepers. But the one leper did not permit himself to be drawn from Christ; he remained steadfast and overcame all the assaults of faith.

47.* Therefore with two strong assaults their hearts were changed. First, to cleanse one from leprosy is impossible for a creature, and it is certainly only the work of God, therefore it cannot be in any way attributed to Christ, whom they saw and regarded as a man and not as God; therefore they should beware by no means to blaspheme God, and make a god out of a mere creature. O what a fine pretense and powerful stroke this was! What a great faith must be there to stand, when it is opposed by God himself, by his honor and work, with which one is threatened not to deny God! What heart does not think, that it would be the very best to yield to a temptation like this?

48. The next stroke was to bring forth the law of Moses, where it was commanded to hearken unto the priests at the risk of death, what they judged according to the law, Deut. 17, 12. As the priests here judged the cleansing was from God and not from Christ, they powerfully caught their consciences, and crushed faith to powder in the nine, for to act against the law, is also to act against God.

49. Here observe what a terrible opposition this was, when bodily and eternal death is placed in opposition to the conscience, together with the anger of God and man, the highest and greatest sins, with the greatest punishment. What heart would not fall before such terrors, or never tremble, especially when the law of God is offered as the signal of truth? With this these nine fell, and had sooner denied ten Christs than offend God and transgress the Law, and thought they did well by doing so.

50. Then an ugly contention arose first of all concerning the one, who alone stood opposed to the priests; while all his companions fall and join his opponents. Then they also exercised diligence, prayed and threatened, that he should by no means offend God, believe the priests, nor despise the law of Moses, and beware that he be not put to death as a

    * §§ 47 to 72 are found only in edition c. and pamphlets.

blasphemer. Here the poor child must be a fool or insensible, so good he has it, or a heretic and apostate; he has become cleansed, but he must on that account risk body and life, goods and honor, friends and companions; and besides had to allow them the name that they were pious, did good and honored God, while he must be a sinner and dishonors God. And because he was a Samaritan they esteemed him perhaps the less, and thought: Let him go, he is but a Samaritan, a man lost and not of Israel; or they had mercy on him, as a man mad and possessed. See, this is the last and greatest opposition to faith. But he who continues steadfast, abides indeed forever, for here is overcome the fear of death and hell with all their terrors, in this world and in the world to come.

51. Thus the name of God must at all times do the greatest evil and be a cover for the greatest scandal through its misuse by the devil and wicked men. For as they know that man does not fear and honor anything so much as God's name and glory, especially among good hearted people; therefore they take just such a one and bring him to their mind, that what they pretend is God; then the poor crowd follows that thinks nothing else than that a man must fear and accept all this, by which God's name or Word is presented. Therefore an extensive knowledge is necessary in such opposition, that a man may not err, although he be threatened by the name of God. For idols have even assumed the name and honor of God. Thus the Pope always employs the name of God for every sin and shame, and all his disciples and false teachers follow him, and especially the priests who pretend that their unchristian, unbelieving orders and works are divine and Christian.

52. But it is still harder when the evil spirit torments the conscience in the throes of death, and pretends God is angry and does not care for you; of this David says, Ps. 3, 2: "Many there are that say of my soul, There is no help for him in God." Or as the Jews spoke to Christ while on the cross, Mat. 27, 43: "He trusted on God; let him deliver him now, if he desireth him: for he said, I am the Son of God."

As though they would say: It is impossible for God to help him, he is wholly lost.

53. Or when God himself thus tries and forsakes a man, so that he feels nothing else in his conscience than that God has forsaken him, and will never welcome him, as David says, Ps. 31, 23: "I said in my haste, I am cut off from before thine eyes." This also tempted Abraham, Gen. 15, 12; and Jacob, Gen. 32, 24.

Here faith suffers its greatest distress, and is in the pangs of hell. Here it is necessary to hold fast and not suffer yourself to err, when God himself is pictured before you. Behold, this is the last and greatest trial of faith; he who remains firm here abides firm forever, for here is overcome the fear of death and hell with all the terrors in this world and the world to come. They are the strongest Christians and the greatest spirits, who resist this temptation.

54. All this I say that we may learn to hold fast to faith, in which we have begun, and ever remain in the same firm conviction that looks to God for every good thing, and not permit ourselves to be forced or driven from it by man, the devil, sin, the law, the name of God or God himself, which we will be able to do if we only abide in the true nature of faith, as St. Paul says, Heb. 11, 1: "Faith is assurance of things hoped for, a conviction of things not seen;" but not the substance of things fleeing away, nor the evidence of things seen; that is, the nature of faith is, that it relies on the goodness of God and thinks of nothing else than to hope for and desire it. The contrary of this is to flee from it, which is terrible, and that is not an example of faith, but of assault and temptation; for God has not built our faith or good conscience, or confidence on wrath, but on grace, therefore all his promises are lovely and gracious; on the contrary his threats are terrible and bitter, which we must also believe; but on his threats Christian faith cannot build, it must have before it only that which is good.

55. Secondly, man should possess assurance. The good for which faith looks and on which it depends, must not be seen or experienced. Therefore everything a person feels, whether

of pleasure or pain, he must know it is not that which he is to believe, but it is the opposition and temptation, over which he must leap and jump, close his eyes and all his senses, and cling only to the good which he neither sees nor hears, until the contention ceases. Just as Elijah wrapped his face in a mantle, when the great earthquake, wind and fire passed by.

56. The blows and assaults against this leper were much greater, besides he was left alone; but he stood firm. So far is his faith greater and more perfect, and was quite ripe. Without doubt it is an example for us, that we, too, may not permit ourselves to be influenced by like priests and saints, even though the great crowd of all the world go with them. It was indeed a great sight, that the priests withstood him, whose duty it was to teach other people the right way, and who should by rights have been the most learned.

57. And here we learn a good answer for the Pope, the priests and the wise, when they appear with their power, government, office and dignity, and pretend that we must believe them, and only hear what they say; who know well enough what it is, when Christ directs the lepers to the priests, but appear as though they could not see how this lonely man, who was not a priest but a common layman, nor was he even an Israelite, but a Samaritan, and yet he pronounces judgment on the priests' doctrine and opinion, and is more learned than they all put together; nor does he worry about being alone, and the crowd being on their side. Now, if this had been sufficient, as our Papists say, that they are the priests, the learned, the rulers and the power, and besides they have the multitude with them, and that a man should not oppose what the government, dignity, power and multitude offer, then this Samaritan did what was not right. But God preserve us! For this Gospel here teaches that scarcely no one is so accustomed to err and go astray as just these very priests, the clergy, the most learned, the rulers, the most dignified and the greatest crowd, wherefore we are scarcely to avoid any one more than just these very ones.

58. But since Christ directs the lepers to the priests, he gives them to understand it is not their office, but the misuse

of their office that is to be avoided, and draws the line how far we are to believe and follow them, namely, when they teach according to the law we are to hear them, as Moses, Deut. 17, 11, 12, clearly declares, that the priests shall judge according to the law, and then, whoever will not hear is to be stoned; but when they without law offer their own doctrine, we shall regard neither their office nor power, and abide alone with the Scriptures. Of course the people say, that no one writes false things except the scribe; so no one preaches false doctrine except the preachers; and again as the common saying runs: The learned are the perverted! If then the priests who are placed in their offices by divine order to teach God's Law, often and most grievously err; what shall our popes, cardinals and bishops do, who are not placed in their offices by God nor man, but by themselves, who neither preach nor study, and produce nothing but human doctrine and their own dreams? Therefore neither their office nor doctrine is any good here, they are nothing but error from head to foot, that is only to be avoided, for little of their doctrine and character is subject to controversy; for they are not the priests referred to here, as we shall hear.

59. But why does St. Luke say that this single person saw that he was cleansed; did not the others see it too, as all ten were surely cleansed? So the nine, as we have heard, with the priests, also praised God, and held him in high esteem, so that they would not give the honor to Christ as to a creature; why then does he say that this one only greatly praised God with a loud voice?

60. In the first place this is said by Luke according to a general custom, as when one says of the unthankful: he does not see the kindness done him; that is, he will not see it nor take it to heart, nor think that he ought to be thankful, but acts as though he knew nothing about it, he despises it and regards it not. Thus these nine did not want to see and consider the kindness of Christ, and despised him as though he did nothing for them. On the contrary he who is thankful will and cannot forget, and does not cease to recognize and

acknowledge his benefactor and kindness. With such eyes did this Samaritan see his cleansing.

61. On the other hand, the nine also praised God, but with their tongues, and at the same time blasphemed him in Christ. It would not have been punishable, if even at that time they had not regarded Christ as God; for he was not yet glorified, as St. John says, 7, 39. And this one also, perhaps, still held him as a mere man. But they wanted Christ to be looked upon as a sinful man and a blasphemer, and to be regarded with the utmost contempt. Such was the poison they brewed into the nine. Christ at that time sought nothing more than that they should receive him as sent to them from God, and that they should believe that God dwelt, spoke and worked in him. This they did not wish, and would not allow others to receive him thus; but he was to be looked upon as coming from the devil, and speaking and working through the devils. And such faith the nine permitted to be driven into them.

But this one remained firm in spite of them, that God must be with Christ, who spoke, worked and dwelt through and in him. Therefore his praise and thanks are mentioned and the praise of the others ignored. Through what strife and opposition he remained in his faith, we have heard above. It was a great faith that held so firmly to him who was despised, condemned and blasphemed by the priests, the learned, the rulers, the best, the greatest and the largest number among all the people. Who dare thus hold Christ at present, when the Pope, the bishops, doctors, monks, priests, princes, with all their host, have condemned him, and issued a bull against him, as we see they publicly do?

62. And here this Gospel teaches what works tried and experienced faith produces, and what is the true worship and honor man may give to God. Some build churches for him, some arrange masses, some ring bells for him, some light candles for him that he may see; and act no differently than as though he were a child, who is in need of our gifts and services. Although the building of churches and holding of masses at first arose from the Christians coming to-

gether to conduct the true worship; afterwards the same
worship disappeared and was entirely omitted. Since then
we have continued to cling to charitable foundations, build-
ings, singing, ringing, lighting, clothing, smoking, and as
many more such preparations as there are for worship, that
we have come to consider such preparations as the chief
divine worship, and know nothing of any other. And we do
wisely, as he who builds a house anl spends all his money
on the scaffolding, and during his whole life should get no
further, not even to lay a single stone for the foundation.
Pray tell, where will he dwell at last, when the scaffolding is
torn down?

63. But the true worship is to return and praise God with
a loud voice. This is our greatest work in heaven and on
earth, besides it is the only worship we may bring to God;
for he needs none of the other kind, and is not capable for
it: he will be only loved and praised by us. Concerning this
Psalm 50, 12-14 speaks: "For the world is mine and the fulness thereof. Offer unto God the sacrifices of thanksgiving,
and pay thy vows unto the Most High." Do you think God
would drink the blood of goats, or eat the flesh of bulls?
Thus he might also say now to the founders of charitable
institutions, smokers, singers, ringers and candle lighters:
Do you think that I am blind and deaf, or that I have no
house for shelter? You shall love and praise me, this is the
incense you are to burn to me and the bells you are to ring
for me.

64. The returning means, to bring home again to God the
grace and goods received, not to keep them, not to boast of
them or exalt self above others, or praise self on their account, not to reap honor thereby nor wish to be better than
others, not to be satisfied with self, not to have joy in them,
but to have all such joy, pleasure, honor and praise, only
in him who has given them, and stand there willing and
quite composed, when he shall again take them from you,
and none the less just then to love and praise him. O how
few there are who thus return, of course scarcely one among
ten. If one has more beautiful hair than another, he delights

in himself because of it above others; what then will he do with the great gifts of reason, spirit, etc.? These are the ravens of Noah that flew out of the ark, and did not return, Gen. 8, 7. To sum up all: To return embraces these two thoughts: not to cling to God's gifts, but only to himself, who gives them.

65. Thus the great praise of God includes two parts: The first is to esteem him highly in the heart, and to have a lovely disposition toward him, so that we taste and experience how sweet the Lord is, of which St. Peter speaks, 1 Pet. 2, 3, and Psalm 34, 8: "O taste and see that Jehovah is good." All this faith, that has been tried, teaches and brings us at the end of the conflict. For as long as the strife and conflict endure, faith is in labor, and all is painful and bitter, it experiences and tastes no sweetness in God. But as soon as the evil hour is past, if we persevere and remain firm, then the sweetness of God will be ours. God will become so lovely, satisfactory and sweet to the heart, that it will desire nothing more than to battle and to seek to try his faith, and now as it were thirsts and longs for suffering and misfortune, which all the world fears, and which he also himself previously feared, of which Psalm 26, 2 speaks: "Examine me, O Jehovah, and prove me; try my heart and my mind." Out of this valiant faith comes quite a different man with a different taste, so that henceforth he does not feel well without suffering, and as it were lives contrary to all the world, so that he rejoices where the world mourns, and mourns where the world rejoices, until he becomes an enemy of this whole life and becomes eager for death.

66. This is what St. Paul means when he says, Gal. 6, 14: "Through which the world hath been crucified unto me, and I unto the world." That is, my joy and life are the suffering and death of the world, and her joy and life are my suffering and death. Therefore he says again, Phil. 1, 23: "Having the desire to depart and be with Christ." To this taste and knowledge no hypocrite can come, for conflict and suffering they do not want, and so they must remain faithless and wholly unexperienced in spiritual things.

67. The other part is to break forth with the voice, and to confess before the world what the heart within believes of God. This is nothing else than to bring down upon one's self the enmity of the world, and to send many messengers after death and the cross. For he who would praise and honor God with his voice, must condemn all the praise and honor of the world and say that all the works and words of man are nothing, with all the honor they have from them, and that God's work and Word alone are worthy of praise and honor. But you see that the world cannot tolerate this, and so you must bear the brunt and be a heretic, a deceiver, a blasphemer, while you promise many good works and a spiritual life in all your divine services. Then they will command your silence, or make it hot for you. And it is not possible for them to suffer it from you, for their pet affairs they will not allow you to reject. So is it also impossible for you to cease and be still, but with loud voice like this leper you rather confess God's praise and honor alone in his works and words; and thus you then go to pieces and become ashes. Then the Pope goes to work and enlarges his almanac with red ink, and makes them saints in heaven, and blots you out of the book of life, and casts you four thousand miles on the other side of hell, and you are now a rotten member cut off from holy Christendom, that you may not infect the holy church with the poison of your foul odor and your satanic doctrines.

68. Christ speaks of this in Mat. 24, 9: "Ye shall be hated of all the nations for my name's sake." Why for my name's sake? They would and might not tolerate the name, praise and honor of God, for then they and their whole cause would be put to shame. And if God alone were wise, good, just, faithful and strong, then they would be fools, wicked, unjust, liars, false and impotent. Who would bear this great injustice, the devilish heresy, that so much divine service and godly life should for God's sake be abolished and changed as a foolish, unjust, false and impotent thing? Not so, it must not be God, but the devil who pretends this. Behold, upon the highways all the prophets are murdered

and Christ himself. The world does not want to be a fool nor to be unjust. But God will not suffer this from it, and hence he sends his messengers to punish it. And thus the saints must then shed their blood on account of it. Therefore it is a great act to praise God and to raise a free and loud voice before the world.

69. However, the false saints and murderers of Christ also now praise and extol with a loud voice God and his works, yea, they preach and cry more about God than the true saints do. As we even now see every corner full of preachers, who highly extol and praise God, that he alone is worthy of praise and honor, and use the very same voice and Word which the true preachers use. Why then is it not valid? Or what is the matter with it? Without doubt nothing else than that they with this leper do not fall down at the feet of Christ to thank him, but want Christ to fall down at their feet and thank them. For the Jews give all honor to God, but of Christ they will know nothing. So it is with these; as long as we leave their cause alone and do not reject it they cry and praise us very highly. But if one also judges them by their doctrine, and their own cry falls upon them, that they are nothing and their whole cause nothing but falsehood and foolishness; then their praise and cry are gone, and their false heart breaks forth and is revealed, so that they praise and honor God only with the mouth and themselves with the heart.

70. It is not enough that you loudly call and cry that God does all things and our work is nothing; you must also suffer such things to be said of you and your affairs. You can agree that Christ's and your enemy is nothing, and all he does is rejected, and you think it is right and well done; for his cause is not from God, but against God. But you do not wish to be rejected with him. Your cause is to be God himself and unrejected; how then is it possible that you should tolerate the rejected Christ, not to mention falling at his feet and regarding yourself as unworthy, when with him you would be rejected? Now as God has concealed himself in the despised man Christ, and will dwell there,

you must not undertake to find him anywhere else, except in contempt; yea, you must reach the point to rejoice that you are found worthy to be despised, and must also fall at his feet and thank him for the contempt, which will not suffer your cause to be anything, so that it be not words but deeds; that you say: God alone is to be praised and not man, such instruction is first to be proved by you, you suffer such things just for the sake of his doctrine, and you consider yourself unworthy of all this.

71. Thus Christ also taught the same and praised God's name alone; and also suffered first and most of all, that he became as nothing, so that no one can be compared to him in this. O this is a rich, great example, of which much might be said. But now it is sufficient that we may see a little how great a cause it is to prove God's praise by our actions, and fall upon our faces at the feet of Christ, the man despised; as the Apostles were glad, Acts 5, 4, that they were worthy to suffer dishonor for the Name, of which it is said, Ps. 72, 9, that the enemies of Christ are to bow before him, and lick the dust from his footprints. That is as St. Paul also says, they shall boast in his sufferings and cross, that shall come upon them on account of the praise of God and the punishment of men. For as Christ himself thus suffered, suffering has become so precious that no one is worthy of it, and it is to be regarded and esteemed as great grace.

72. From this we see how far a Christian life is above the natural life. First, it despises self; secondly, it loves and thirsts for contempt; thirdly, it punishes everything that is unwilling to be despised, by which it resigns itself to all misfortune; fourthly it is also despised and persecuted on account of such contempt and punishment; fifthly, it does not think itself worthy to suffer such persecution. Now from the very first part the world and nature flee, when then will they come to the last? But there is still another and a greater behind it, concerning the falling at the feet of Christ, which the priests neither understand nor want;

for not every faith is sufficient for it, but the faith of Christ must be there, that truly humiliates us. Of this we will treat later under the spiritual interpretation.

"And he was a Samaritan."

73. Why was it necessary for the Evangelist to write, rather than something else, that this one leper was a Samaritan? By this he opens our eyes and warns us that God has two kinds of people who serve him. One, that has the appearance and name of having a great, spiritual, holy life, is employed almost wholly in it, and yet it is all in vain. They are nothing more than ravenous wolves in sheep's clothing. Yet they have the honor of it, and are regarded by every one as the true worshipers of God; therefore goods, honor, friendship flow to them, and everything the world has, for God's sake; for they think he is there, and he who thinks differently is worse than a heathen, heretic and an apostate.

74. The others are without any show and name, yea, they are of the opposite appearance, as though no one were less God's people than they, and in short, they are thorough Samaritans; a word that sounds as badly among the Jews, as if at present you should revile one as a Turk, Jew, heathen or heretic. For the Jews alone had the name of being God's people, and they alone had God and his worship for themselves in preference to all other people on the earth. And they hated the Samaritans above all nations, for they too claimed to be God's people along with the Jews; therefore a Samaritan was to them as an apostate Christian is among us. And although it be true that the Samaritans did not rightly believe, and that the Jews had the true law of God, it was according to human custom that they boasted alone of Judaism and despised the Samaritans, who were less Jews and worse Samaritans, than the natural Samaritans. But now, as God loves the truth and is an enemy of hypocrisy with all its boasting, he turns it round and accepts the Samaritans and lets the Jews go. Thus it occurs that they are not his people who still have the name, the appearance and honor of his people. Again, those who are

his people and have the name and appearance, are **heretics,** apostates and the devil's children.

75. So it is even at the present time. The clergy, **priests** and monks call themselves and are regarded as the **servants** of God, and no one is a Christian who does not believe as they believe, whereas no one is less a Christian and God's people than just those who thus turn up and boast themselves among them. Again, those whom they hold are heretics, many of whom they have also burned and exiled, like John Huss and his followers they dare not be Christians, although they alone are the true Christians. Here then this Gospel is so powerful that no one returns, no one exalts God with a loud voice, no one falls on his face at the feet of Christ, except the Samaritans, the despised, the condemned, the accursed, who must be heretics, apostates, errorists and satan's own children. Therefore let us guard against everything that makes only a show, it certainly is deceiving; and let us not reject what does not make a display, so that we do not go and reject Christ and God, as the Jews did. This Christ also desires when he says:

"And Jesus answering said, Were not the ten cleansed? but where are the nine? Were there none found that returned to give glory to God, save this stranger?"

76. The stranger does it, he sincerely gives God all the glory. O, what a terrible example is this! Among ten only one, and he among the least and most worthless. How entirely does God indeed overlook that which is great, wise, spiritual and honorable! And yet such people have no fear, but become hardened and petrified in their nature. It is also terrible that the Lord knows ten of them were cleansed, of this they did not think. To it he is not silent, he inquires after and seeks them: Where are the nine? O, what a frightful thing it will be when they at some future time will feel this inquiry and must answer whither they went, that they did not give God the glory. Then they will say: Well, we have nevertheless praised and thanked God, and thus our priests have taught us! Then it will appear whether it will help us to follow the doctrines of men in

the name of God, and to forsake the doctrine and will of God. We are sufficiently warned in the Gospel, therefore no excuse will help us if we allow ourselves to be deceived. In Baptism we have all vowed to follow Christ and his doctrine; no one has vowed to follow the Pope, the bishops and clergy. Thus Christ has thoroughly rejected and forbidden the doctrines of men.

77. However, Christ here comforts his poor Samaritans, who for his name's sake must risk their lives with the priests and Jews, and strengthens their hope with the sentence and judgment that he demands the nine and judges them as God's thieves, who steal God's glory, and justifies the Samaritan. For this hope gives them strong courage, that their cause before God will be rightly maintained and will stand, but the opposite cause will be condemned and will not stand, it matters not how great they were and what right they had on earth.

78. Therefore observe, before Christ justifies the Samaritan, he judges the nine, that we should be certain not to hasten or desire revenge, but leave it only to him, and go our way. For he is in himself so careful to defend the right and punish the wrong, that he first takes up the latter before he rewards his Samaritans.

79. Besides, he uses many more words in this sentence than to the Samaritan; so that we see how greatly he is concerned about it, and he by no means forgets their wrongs and our rights. Nor does he wait long to have them accused before him, but of his own free will summons them, so that without doubt the cause of the unbelievers influences him more and sooner than it strikes or harms us. Of this God speaks in Moses, Deut. 32, 35: "Vengeance is mine, and recompense." And St. Paul says to the Romans, 12, 19: "Avenge not yourselves, beloved, but give place unto wrath." Now the words which the Lord says to the Samaritan, when he adjusts his affairs, are the following:

"And he said unto him, Arise, and go thy way; thy faith hath made thee whole."

80. Behold, is not this a wonderful expression, that he

attributes his cleansing to faith? This is opposed to the
judgment of the priests who told the nine that their offering
and obedience to the law had cleansed them. But Christ's
judgment stands and triumphs, that they were not cleansed
because they went to the priests, nor because of their offering, but alone on account of their faith. Therefore, as said
above, faith will not tolerate any work, that it should help
man to be justified and saved. For this faith more than
all other things must and will do it alone, and he employs
his works elsewhere, namely, to help his neighbor, as Christ
has helped him.

81. And in conclusion we observe that this Gospel sufficiently teaches and represents the entire Christian life with
all its events and sufferings; for the two chief things are
faith and love. Faith receives the good; love gives the
good. Faith offers us God as our own; love gives us to our
neighbor as his own. Now when such life begins, God goes
to work and improves it by trials and conflicts, through
which a man increases more and more in faith and love,
that through his own experience God becomes to him so
heartily dear and precious, and he no longer fears anything.

Then hope grows which is certain that God will not forsake her, of which St. Paul speaks, Rom. 5, 3-5: "We also
rejoice in our tribulations: knowing that tribulation worketh
steadfastness; and steadfastness, approvedness; and approvedness, hope; and hope putteth not to shame." And Paul
always treats of these three principles in his Epistles. To
the Collossians he speaks thus, 1, 3-5: "We give thanks
to God the Father of our Lord Jesus Christ, praying always
for you, having heard of your faith in Christ Jesus, and of
the love which ye have toward all the saints, because of the
hope which is laid up for you in the heavens." And still
more beautiful he says to the Thessalonians, 1, 2, 3: "We
give thanks to God always for you all, making mention of
you in our prayers; remembering without ceasing your work
of faith and labor of love and patience of hope in our Lord
Jesus Christ, before our God and Father."

82. How beautifully he divides the three principles, that

faith goes forth in trusting, love in laboring, and hope in patience and suffering. As though he would say: Your faith is not a dream nor a fancy, but it is life and action; and your love is not passive nor is it idle, but it serves well for your neighbor. All this takes place in prosperous days, while your hope is exercised in suffering and patience, and all this in Christ; for there is no faith, nor love, nor hope outside of Christ, as I said above. Thus a Christian life goes through good and evil until the end, and yet it does not seek revenge, and only grows more and more in faith, love and hope.

83. And love, which naturally follows faith, is divided into two parts: it loves God, who does so much for her through Christ in faith; it loves its neighbor, and does to him, as God does to her. Therefore, all the works of such a man go to his neighbor for God's sake who loved him, and he does no work relating to God except to love and to praise, and he confesses this freely before the world. For God does not need other works. Thus, all worship is with the mouth; although that is also called a service of God which is done to our neighbor. But I speak now only of the service rendered to God, in which the one part man can take is to love and to praise; but in this he must resign himself wholly and entirely in all adversity. Behold, what more would you know as to how to be a Christian? Have faith and love, continue in these, then you have and can do all things; the rest will all be taught and given to you without any exertion on your part: This Gospel of the Ten Lepers is further expounded in a special book or postil, which examine for additional information. There you will also find the allegorical interpretation or the spiritual meaning of it.*

---

* See the miscellaneous sermons of Luther.

FIFTEENTH SUNDAY AFTER TRINITY.

This sermon is found in all editions of the Church Postil, but in edition c. it is some different. Hence we add the extra matter in the second sermon. Erl. 14, 87; W. 11, 2168; St. L. 11, 1614.

Text: Mat. 6, 24-34. No man can serve two masters: for either he will hate the one, and love the other; or else he will hold to one, and despise the other. Ye cannot serve God and mammon. Therefore I say unto you, Be not anxious for your life, what ye shall eat, or what ye shall drink; nor yet for your body, what ye shall put on. Is not the life more than the food, and the body than the raiment? Behold the birds of the heaven, that they sow not, neither do they reap, nor gather into barns; and your heavenly Father feedeth them. Are not ye of much more value than they? And which of you by being anxious can add one cubit unto the measure of his life? And why are ye anxious concerning raiment? Consider the lilies of the field, how they grow; they toil not, neither do they spin: yet I say unto you, that even Solomon in all his glory was not arrayed like one of these. But if God doth so clothe the grass of the field, which to-day is, and to-morrow is cast into the oven, shall he not much more clothe you, O ye of little faith? Be not therefore anxious, saying, What shall we eat? or, What shall we drink? or, Wherewithal shall we be clothed? For after all these things do the Gentiles seek; for your heavenly Father knoweth that ye have need of all these things. But seek ye first his kingdom, and his righteousness; and all these things shall be added unto you. Be not therefore anxious for the morrow; for the morrow will be anxious for itself. Sufficient unto the day is the evil thereof.

CONTENTS: GOD OR MAMMON. EXHORTATION AGAINST AVARICE AND ANXIETY FOR TEMPORAL THINGS, AND AN INCENTIVE TO FAITH.

I. THE EXHORTATION.

I. This Exhortation in General.
  1. How Christ here at once ex-
     hibits the difference between
     his kingdom and that of the
     world. 1.
  2. The character of the persons
     addressed. 2.

II. This Exhortation in Detail.

A. The time, sense and understanding of this exhortation. 3-4f.
   * Of avarice and mammon.
  1. There are very few persons,
     who are free from mammon
     worship. 5-8.
  2. How and why those who are
     given to avarice, esteem God
     and his Word so little. 9.
  3. Why avarice is called idolatry.
     10f.
  4. It is great and horrible stupid-
     ity to worship mammon. 10-13.
  5. Avarice is the worst of evils.
     13-14.
  6. How we are to conduct our-
     selves toward mammon, if we
     are not to be injured by it.
     15-19.

B. The motives attached to this exhortation.

1. The first motive in general
   springs from the thought that
   one should not be over-anxious
   for food and raiment. 20-27.
   * Concerning work and an-
     xiety.
   a. Anxiety is forbidden, but
      not work. 21.
   b. God does not give his bless-
      ing without work. 22.
   c. The reply to those who wish
      to justify their anxiety by
      the Scriptures. 23-24.
   d. The labor and worry in
      educational and domestic
      life. 25-26.
   e. Man should labor and let
      the care and worry with
      God. 27.
2. The second motive emphasizes
   that one should not worry
   about securing his daily food.
   28-30.
3. The third motive emphasizes
   that one should not worry
   about securing his raiment.
   a. The nature of this motive.
      31-32.
   b. This motive is very power-
      ful and puts men to shame.
      32-34.
   * The summary of this Gos-
     pel. 35.

SUMMARY OF THIS GOSPEL: 1. Man cannot serve God and
Mammon; for as Paul says: "But they that are minded to be rich
fall into a temptation and a snare and many foolish and hurtful
lusts, such as drown men in destruction and perdition." 1 Tim. 6, 9.
2. We should labor, but let the worry with God; just as the
farmer, when he has done all, still expects the fruit and harvest
from God. But in this we all are tried and tempted.
3. Since God clothes and feeds the creatures he created, much
more will he clothe and feed us, whose father he also is, besides
being our creator.
4. They are heathen and not Christians, who do not trust God,
but depend upon and trust in their own wisdom and foresight.
5. We should ask God in prayer only that we may be his children
through faith, then temporal blessings enough will be added and
given us by our heavenly Father. Children do not care for themselves, but their father cares for them. This is a great promise
and invitation.

1. In this Gospel we see how God distinguishes Christians
from heathen. For the Lord does not deliver these teachings to the heathen, for they could not receive them, but to
his Christians. However, he does not consider those Christians, who only hear his Word, so as to learn it and be able

to repeat it, as the nuns do the Psalter. In this way satan also hears the Gospel and the Word of God, yea, he knows it far better than we do, and he could preach it as well as we, if he only wanted to; but the Gospel is a doctrine that should become a living power and be put into practice; it should strengthen and comfort the people, and make them courageous and aggressive.

2. Therefore they, who only thus hear the Gospel, so that they may know it and be able to speak about the wisdom of God, are not worthy to be classed among Christians; but they, who do as the Gospel teaches, are true Christians. However, very few of these are found; we see many hearers, but all are not doers of the Gospel. We wish now to examine more closely what kind of doctrine the Lord teaches in this Gospel. First, he begins with a plain, natural example, so that we all must confess it is true; experience also teaches the same to everybody. He says:

"No man can serve two masters: for either he will hate the one, and love the other: or else he will hold to one, and despise the other."

3. Now he, who tries to serve two masters, will do it in a way that cannot be called serving at all; for it will certainly be as the Lord here says. One can indeed compel a servant to do a certain work against his will and he may grieve while doing it; but no one can compel him to do it cheerfully, and mean it from the bottom of his heart. He of course does the work as long as his master is present, but when he is absent, he hurrys away from his task, and does nothing well. Hence the Lord desires our service to be done out of love and cheerfully, and where it is not done thus, it is no service to him: for even people are not pleased when one does anything for them unwillingly. This is natural, and we experience daily that it is so. Now, if it be the case among human beings that no one can serve two masters, how much more is it true in the service of God, that our service cannot be divided; but it must be done unto God alone, willingly and from the heart; therefore the Lord adds:

"Ye cannot serve God and mammon."

4. God cannot allow us to have another Lord besides himself. He is a jealous God, as he says, and cannot suffer us to serve him and his enemy. Only mine, he says, or not at all. Behold now how beautifully Christ here introduces the example: "No man," he says, "can serve two masters; for either he will hate the one, and love the other; or else he will hold to one and despise the other. Ye cannot serve God and mammon." As if to say: as it is here in man's relations to his fellows, so it is also before God.

5. We find very few, who do not sin against the Gospel. The Lord passes a severe judgment and it is terrible to hear that he should say this of us, and yet no one will confess, yea, no one will suffer it to be said that we hate and despise God and that we are his enemies. There is no one, when asked if he loves God and cleaves to him? would not reply, yes, I love God. But see how the text closes, that we all hate and despise God, and love mammon and cleave to it. But God suffers us to do this until his time; he watches the time and some day he will strike into our midst with all violence, before we can turn around. It is impossible for one, who loves gold and earthly possessions and cleaves to them, not to hate God. For God here contrasts these two as enemies to one another, and concludes, if you love and cleave to one of these two, then you must hate and despise the other. Therefore, however nicely and genteely one lives here upon earth and cleaves to riches, it cannot be otherwise than that he must hate God; and on the other hand, whoever does not cleave to gold and worldly goods, loves God. This is certainly true.

6. But who are they that love God, and cleave not to gold and worldly possessions? Take a good look at the whole world, also the Christians, and see if they despise gold and riches. It requires an effort to hear the Gospel and to live according to it. God be praised, we have the Gospel; that no one can deny, but what do we do with it? We are concerned only about learning and knowing it, and nothing more; we think it is enough to know it, and do not care

whether we ever live according to it. However, on the other hand, one is very anxious when he leaves lying in the window or in the room a dollar or two, yea, even a dime, then he worries and fears lest the money be stolen; but the same person can do without the Gospel through a whole year. And such characters still wish to be considered as Evangelical.

7. Here we see what and who we are. If we were Christians, we would despise riches and be concerned about the Gospel that we some day might live in it and prove it by our deeds. We see few such Christians; therefore we must hear the judgment that we are despisers of God and hate God for the sake of riches and worldly possessions. Alas! That is fine praise! We should be ashamed of ourselves in our inmost souls; there is no hope for us! What a fine condition we are in now! That means, I think, our names are blotted out. What spoiled children we are!

8. Now the world cannot conceal its unbelief in its coarse, outward sins, for I see it loves a dollar more than Christ; more than all the Apostles, even if they themselves were present and preached to it. I can hear the Gospel daily, but it does not profit me every day; it may indeed happen, if I have heard it a whole year, the Holy Spirit may have been given to me only one hour. Now when I enjoyed this hour I obtained not only five hundred dollars, but also the riches of the whole world; for what have I not, when I have the Gospel? I received God, who made the silver and the gold, and all that is upon the earth; for I acquired the Spirit by which I know that I will be kept by him forever; that is much more than if I had the church full of money. Examine now and see, if our heart is not a rogue, full of wickedness and unbelief. If I were a true Christian, I would say: The hour the Gospel is received, there comes to me a hundred thousand dollars, and much more. For if I possess this treasure, I have all that is in heaven and upon earth. But one must serve this treasure only, for no man can serve God and mammon. Either you must love God and hate money;

or you must hate God and love money; this and nothing more.

9. The master uses here the Hebrew, which we do not. "Mammon" means goods or riches, and such goods as one does not need, but holds as a treasure, and it is gold and possessions that one deposits as stock and storage provisions. This Christians do not do, they gather no treasures; but they ask God for their daily bread. However, others are not satisfied with this, they gather a great store upon which they may depend, in case our God should die to-day or to-morrow, they might then know a way out. Therefore St. Paul says, in Eph. 5, 5 and Col. 3, 5, riches and covetousness are the god of this world and are idolatry, with this Christ here agrees and calls it serving mammon.

10. Now, how does it come that the Gospel and St. Paul call especially covetousness and not other sins idolatry; since uncleanness, fornication, lust, base desires, unchastity and other vices are more opposed to God? It is done to our great shame, because gold is our god, that we serve, in that we trust and rely upon it, and it can neither sustain nor save us, yea, it can neither stand nor walk, it neither hears nor sees, it has no strength nor power, with it there is neither comfort nor help. For if one had the riches of the whole world, he would not be secure for one moment before death.

11. Of what help are his great treasures and riches to the Emperor when the hour of death arrives and he is called to die? They are a shameful, loathsome, powerless god, that cannot cure a sore, yea, it cannot keep and take care of itself, there it lies in the chest, and lets it's devotees wait, yea, one must watch it as a helpless, powerless, weak thing. The lord who has this god must watch day and night lest thieves steal it; this helpless god can aid no one. You should have contempt for this lifeless god that cannot help in the least, and is yet so scrupulous and precious; it lets its devotees wait in the grandest style and protects itself with strong chests and castles, its lord must wait and be in anxiety every hour, lest it perishes by fire or otherwise experiences

some misfortune. Does this treasure or god consist in clothing, then one must be careful and on his guard against the smallest little insects, against the moth, lest they ruin or devour it.

12. The walls of our rooms should spit upon us in contempt that we trust more in the god the moth eat and the rust corrupt, than in the God, who creates and gives all things, yea, who holds in his hand heaven and earth, and all that in them is. Is it not a foolish thing on the part of the world to turn from the true God and trust in base and low mammon, in the poor, miserable god, who cannot protect himself against rust. Oh, what a disgraceful thing this is on the part of the world! God visits gold and worldly possessions with many kinds of enemies, to bring us to see and confess our unbelief and godless character, that we thus trust in a powerless and frail god, we who could at once so easily approach and cleave to the true, powerful and strong God, who gives us everything, money, goods, fruit and all we need; yet we are so foolish and make gods out of his gifts. Shame on thee, thou cursed unbelief.

13. Other sins give us a little pleasure, we receive some enjoyment from them, as in the case of eating and drinking; in unchastity one has pleasure for a little while; likewise anger satisfies its desire, and other vices more so. Only in this vice one must incessantly be in slavery, hounded and martyred, and in it no one has any pleasure or joy whatever. There the money lies on a pile and commands you to serve it; in spite of it letting any one draw from it a thimble full of wine there comes rust and devours it, and yet he dares not attack it, lest he angers his god. And when his servants have protected their god a long time they have no more than any poor beggar. I have nothing, yet I eat and drink as heartily as any one who has a large supply of mammon. When he dies he takes just as much along with him as I do. And it is certainly the case that these people never live as well nor as richly as the poor people often do. Who arranges this thus? God, the Lord, does it. Here some have a certain affliction of the body that they have no appetite; there

others are internally unsound and never relish what they eat; here their stomach is out of order; there their lungs and liver are diseased; here is this, and there is that sickness; here they are weak and afflicted at one point, there at another, and they never have an enjoyable hour to relish what they eat or drink.

14. Thus it is with those who serve this god, mammon. The true God is still of some use, he serves the people, but mammon does not, it lies quiet and lets others serve it. And for this reason the New Testament calls covetousness idolatry, since it thus desires to be served. However, to love and not to enjoy may well vex the devil. This all now experience who love the god, mammon, and serve him. Whoever has now no sense of shame and does not turn red, has a brazen face.

15. Thus now it is with the word, "serve." For it is not forbidden to have money and possessions, as we cannot get along without them. Abraham, Lot, David, Solomon and others had great possessions and much gold, and at the present day there are many wealthy persons who are pious, in spite of their riches. But it is one thing to have possessions and another to serve them; to have mammon, and to make a god out of it. Job also was wealthy, he had great possessions and was more powerful than all who lived in the East, as we read in the first part of the book of Job: yet he says, in Job 31, 24-25: "If I have made gold my hope, and said to the fine gold, Thou art my confidence; have I rejoiced because my wealth was great, and because my hand had gotten much?"

16. The sum of all is, it is God's will that we serve not gold and riches, and that we be not overanxious for our life; but that we labor and commend our anxiety to him. Whoever possesses riches is lord of the riches. Whoever serves them, is their slave and does not possess them, but they possess him; for he dare not make use of them when he desires, and cannot serve others with them; yea, he is not bold enough to dare to touch it. However, is he lord over his riches, then they serve him, and he does not serve them; then he

dare use them, as Abraham, David, Job and other rich persons, and he casts his care only upon God, as St. Paul teaches in 1 Cor. 7, 32. Hence he aids the poor with his wealth and gives to those who have nothing. When he sees a person without a coat, he says to his money: Go out, Messrs. Dollars, there is a poor, naked man, who has no coat, you must be of service to him! There lies one sick, who has no medicine. Go forth, Squires Anneberger and Joachinesthaler, you must hasten and help him! Those, who act thus with their riches, are their lords; and all true Christians surely do this. But those who save piles of money, and ever scheme to make their heap larger instead of smaller, are servants and slaves of mammon.

17. He is a lord of mammon who lays hold of and uses it for the sake of those who need it and lets God rule, who says in Luke 6, 38: Give, and it shall be given unto you; have you nothing more, you surely have me still, and I have still enough, yea, I have more than I have given away and more than can ever be given away. We see here and there many pious poor people only for the purpose that the wealthy may help and serve them with their riches. If you do it not, you have the sure proof that you hate God. He, whom the sentence does not terrify, that he will hear on the day of judgment, can be moved by nothing. For he will hear then from God: Behold, thou hast hated me and loved that which could not protect itself against rust and moth. Ay, how firmly you will then stand!

18. Hence the sense is, we must own some possessions, but are not to cleave to them with our hearts; as Ps. 62, 10 says: "If riches increase, set not your heart thereon." We are to labor; but we are not to be anxious about our existence. This the Master says here in our Gospel in plain and clear words, when he thus concludes:

"Be not anxious for your life, what ye shall eat, or what ye shall drink: nor yet for your body, what ye shall put on."

19. And he now uses a reasonable and natural form of speech, by which to close, that they are not to be anxious for the nourishment of their lives; for reason must conclude

and yield that it is as Christ says, when he gives the ground and reason of his discourse by asking:

"Is not the life more than the food, and the body than the raiment?"

20. As if he would say: You turn it just around, the food should serve your life and not your life the food. The same is true in respect to raiment; the clothing should serve the body, thus the body serves the clothing. The world is so blind that it cannot see this.

21. Now we must here have a high esteem for the words of the Lord. He says, "Be not anxious;" he does not say, Labor not. Anxiety is forbidden, but not labor; yea, it is commanded and made obligatory upon us to labor until the sweat rolls down our faces. It is not God's pleasure for man to tramp around idly; therefore he says to Adam in Gen. 3, 19: "In the sweat of thy face shalt thou eat bread, till thou return unto the ground; for out of it wast thou taken." And as Ps. 104, 22-23 says: "The sun ariseth, man goeth forth unto his work and to his labor until the evening." We are not to be anxious, this is forbidden; for we have a rich God who promises us food and clothing; for he knows what we lack, before we are concerned and begin to pray.

22. Why then does he not give us what we need without our labor? Because it is thus pleasing to him; he tells us to labor and then he gives it; not because of our work, but out of kindness and grace. This we see before our eyes; for although we labor every year in the field, yet God gives one year more than another. Therefore, we are fools, yea, we act contrary to God's will, when we are worried as to how to scrape together gold and riches, since God gratuitously and richly promises that he will give us all and will abundantly provide for our every want.

23. However, one may say: Does not St. Paul tell us to be diligent, as in Rom. 12, 8: "He that ruleth, with diligence," and there immediately follows verse 11, "In diligence, not slothful?" In like manner to the Phillipians 2, 20, he says of Timothy: "For I have no man likeminded,

who will care truly for your state." And Paul himself in
2 Cor. 11, 28 boasts that anxiety for all the churches presses
upon him. Here you see how we are nevertheless to be
anxious. Answer: Our life and a Christian character consist of two parts, of faith and of love. The first points us to
God, the other to our neighbor. The first, namely faith, is
not visible, God alone sees that; the other is visible, and is
love, that we are to manifest to our neighbor. Now the
anxiety that springs from love is commanded, but that
which accompanies faith is forbidden. If I believe that I
have a God, then I cannot be anxious about my welfare; for
if I know that God cares for me as a father for his child,
why should I fear? Why need I to be anxious, I simply say:
Art thou my Father, then I know that no evil will befall me,
as Ps. 16, 8 says: "I have set Jehovah always before me: because he is at my right hand, I shall not be moved." Thus
he has all things in his hand; therefore I shall want nothing,
he will care for me. If I rush ahead and try to care for myself, that is always contrary to faith; therefore God forbids
this kind of anxiety. But it is his pleasure to maintain the
anxious care of love, that we may help others, and share our
possessions and gifts with them. Am I a ruler, I am to care
for my subjects; am I a housefather, I must take care of the
members of my family, and so forth, according as each one
has received his gifts from God. God cares for all, and his
is the care that pertains to faith. We are also to be interested in one another and this is the care of love, namely,
when something is given to me, that I be diligent so that
others may also receive it.

24. Here we must be guarded, lest we make a gloss, instead of understanding simply the words as they read: Be
not anxious for your life. God says: Labor, and if you accomplish nothing, I will give what is needed; does he give
then see that you rightly distribute it. Do not be anxious
to get, but see to it that your domestics and others also receive of that which God has given to you, and that your
domestics labor and receive a Christian training.

25. Am I a preacher, my anxiety should not be where to

receive what I am to preach; for if I have nothing, I can give nothing. Christ says in Luke 21, 15: "I will give you a mouth and wisdom, which all your adversaries shall not be able to withstand or to gainsay." But if I have that I ought to be anxious for others to receive it from me, and that I endeavor to impart it to them in the best form possible, to teach the ignorant, to admonish and restrain those who know it, rightly to comfort the oppressed consciences, to awaken the negligent and sleepy, and put them on their guard, and the like, as St. Paul did (1 Tim. 4; 2 Tim. 3, Tit. 3) and commanded his disciples Timothy and Titus to do. My anxiety should be how others are to receive something from me; but I am to study and pray to God. Studying is my labor, this is the work he desires me to do, and when it is his pleasure he will give. It can indeed happen that I may study a long time and he gives nothing, a year or more, and when it is his pleasure, he gives as long as it is pleasing to him. Then he gives copiously and to overflowing, suddenly in an hour.

26. Thus a housefather also does, he attends only to that which is commanded him, and lets our Lord God arrange as to how he will give. When he gives, then man is concerned how to impart it to his family, and he sees that they have no need as to the body and the soul. This is what the Lord means, when he says we are not to be anxious for our food and raiment; but he certainly requires us to labor. For thou must be a long time behind the oven until something is given to thee if thou dost not till the soil and work. True it is, God can easily nourish thee without thy work, he could easily have roasted and boiled corn and wine grow on thy table; but he does not do it, it is his will that thou shouldst labor and in doing so to use thy reason.

27. In like manner it is with preaching and all our affairs. God gives us the wool, that he grows on the sheep; but it is not at once cloth, we must labor and make it into cloth; when it is cloth, it does not at once become a coat, the tailor must first work with the cloth before it is a coat; and so God does with all things, he cares for us, but we must toil and

work. We have plenty examples of this before our eyes, and God relates especially two here that should really make us blush with shame, namely, those of the birds and the lilies in the field. Pointing to the birds he says:

"Behold the birds of the heaven, that they sow not, neither do they reap, nor gather into barns; and your heavenly Father feedeth them."

28. As if the Lord would say: You have never yet seen a bird with a sickle, with which it harvested and gathered into barns; yea, the birds do not labor like we; and still they are nourished. By this the Lord does not however teach that we are to be idle; but he tries by this example to take all anxiety from us. For a bird cannot do the work of a farmer as we do; yet, it is not free from labor, but it does the work for which it was created, namely, it bears its young, feeds them and sings to our Lord God a little song for the privilege of doing this. Had God imposed more labor upon it, then it would have done more. Early in the morning it rises, sits upon a twig and sings a song it has learned, while it knows not where to obtain its food, and yet it is not worried as to where to get its breakfast. Later, when it is hungry, it flies away and seeks a grain of corn, where God stored one away for it, of which it never thought while singing, when it had cause enough to be anxious about its food. Ay, shame on you now, that the little birds are more pious and believing than you; they are happy and sing with joy and know not whether they have anything to eat.

29. This parable is constantly taught to our great and burning shame, that we cannot do as much as the birds. A Christian should be ashamed before a little bird that knows an art it never acquired from a teacher. When in the spring of the year, while the birds sing the most beautifully, you say to one: How canst thou sing so joyfully, thou hast not yet any grain in thy barn? It would thus mock you. It is a powerful example and should truly give offense to us and stir us to trust God more than we do. Therefore he concludes with a penetrating passage, and asks:

"Are not ye of much more value than they?"

30. Is it not a great shame that the Lord makes and presents to us the birds as our teachers, that we should first learn from them? Shame on thee, thou loathsome, infamous unbelief! The birds do what they are required to do; but we not. In Genesis 1, 28 we have a command that we are to be lords over all God's creatures; and the birds are here our lords in teaching us wisdom. Away with godless unbelief! God makes us to be fools and places the birds before us, to be our teachers and rule us, in that they only point out how we serve mammon and forsake the true and faithful God. Now follows the other example of the flowers in the field, by which the Lord encourages us not to worry about our raiment; and it reads thus:

"And which of you by being anxious can add one cubit unto the measure of his life? And why are ye anxious concerning raiment? Consider the lilies of the field, how they grow: they toil not, neither do they spin: yet I say unto you, that even Solomon in all his glory was not arrayed like one of these. But if God doth so clothe the grass of the field, which to-day is, and to-morrow is cast into the oven, shall he not much more clothe you, O ye of little faith?"

31. As if to say, your life is not yours, nor is your body, you cannot make it one cubit longer or shorter; neither be anxious as to how you are to clothe yourself. Behold the flowers of the field how they are adorned and clothed, neither do they anything to that end; they neither spin nor work, yet they are beautifully clothed.

32. By this illustration the Lord again does not wish to have us cease to sew and work, but we should labor, spin and sew, and not be overanxious and worry. The evil we have is our toil; will we in addition worry, then we do like the fools; for it is enough that each day has its own evil. It seems to me, this is disdain that is commanded, that the flowers stand there and make us blush and become our teachers. Thank you, flowers, you, who are to be devoured by the cows! God has exalted you very highly, that you become our masters and teachers. Shame, that this earth bears us! Is it an honor for us? I do not know. We must here

confess that the most insignificant flower, that the cattle
tread under foot, should become our teacher, are we not fine
people? I think so. Now Christ places alongside of this the
richest and most powerful king, Solomon, who was clothed
in the most costly manner in purple and gold, whose glory
was not to be compared with that of the flowers, 1 Kings
10. Is it not remarkable that the adornment of the flowers
in the field should be esteemed higher than all the precious
stones, gold and silver?

33. However, we are so blind that we do not see what God
designs thereby and what he means. The flower stands
there that we should see it, it strikes us and says: If thou
hadst the adornment of the whole world even then thou
wouldst not be equal to me, who stand here, and am not the
least worried whence this adornment comes to me. I do not
however concern myself about that, here I stand alone and
do nothing and although thou art beautifully adorned, thou
art still sickly and servest impotent mammon; I however am
fresh and beautiful and serve the true and righteous God.
Behold, what a loathsome, vicious thing is unbelief!

34. These are two fine and powerful examples of the birds
and the lilies. The birds teach us a lesson as to our daily
food; the flowers as to our raiment. And in the whole New
Testament our shame is no where so disclosed and held to
view, as just in this Gospel. But they are few who understand it. From these examples and parables the Lord now
concludes and says:

"Be not therefore anxious, saying, What shall we eat? or,
What shall we drink? or, Wherewithal shall we be clothed?
For after all these things do the Gentiles seek; for your heavenly
Father knoweth that ye have need of all these things. But seek
ye first his kingdom and his righteousness; and all these things
shall be added unto you. Be not therefore anxious for the
morrow; for the morrow will be anxious for itself. Sufficient
unto the day is the evil thereof."

35. Now the sum of this Gospel is: Christians should
not worry about what they are to eat; God provides for
them before they think of their need; but they are to labor,

that is commanded them. But what the kingdom of God and his righteousness are, would require too much time to discuss, you have often heard about them, if you have been attentive. This is now enough on to-day's Gospel. May God grant us grace that some day we may also even put it into practice! May the Gospel remain not only in our ears and on our tongues, but come into our hearts and break forth fresh into loving deeds!

36. (We follow the paragraphs of the St. Louis Walch here which has 35 instead of 36 as in old Walch.)

FIFTEENTH SUNDAY AFTER TRINITY.

Second Sermon. Mat. 6, 24-34.

The following sermon appears in the c. edition. Erl. 14, 103;. St. L. 11, 1628.

CHRISTIANS SHOULD NOT BE ANXIOUS FOR THINGS OF THIS LIFE, BUT SEEK THE KINGDOM OF GOD.

1. This Gospel is a part of the long sermon Christ delivered to his disciples on the mount, in which among other things he especially warned and admonished his disciples against the infamous vice of avarice and anxiety for daily bread, the legitimate fruit and proof of our unbelief. This does great harm in Christendom when it takes possession of those in the office of the ministry, who should be occupied by nothing except teaching the Word of God and faith aright, and chastising the error and sin of the world; or when it possesses these it should confess God's Words before all persons and be prepared to serve everybody for the sake of God, even if they be obliged on that account to lose their riches, honor, body and life.

2. Christ wishes also to teach here how he desires to have his kingdom distinguished from the civil life and government, that he will not govern his Christendom upon earth so that it be conceived and vested as a government where Christians are first of all to be amply provided with

temporal goods, riches and power, and who need not fear
any need or danger; but he wishes to provide them with
spiritual treasures and what their souls need, so that they
may have his Word, the consolation of his grace, and the
power and strength of the Holy Spirit against sin and death
unto everlasting life. Moreover whatever they need of temporal things for this life and the necessaries for present
wants they are to expect also from him, and they are not to
be terrified if they do not see this before their eyes and have
it prepared for the future, and are tempted by want and
need. On the other hand they are to know that their God
and Father will care for them and will surely give them all
if they with firm faith are only anxious about and seek how
they may continue faithful to his word and in his kingdom,
and serve him there.

3. Therefore Christ makes a distinction in this sermon,
by which he separates his Christians from the heathen and
unbelievers. For he does not deliver this doctrine to the
heathen as they do not accept it, but to those who are already Christians. He does not however consider those
Christians, who only hear his word and can repeat it, like
the nuns do the Psalter. In this way satan also hears the
Gospel and the Word of God, yea, he knows it better than
we, and can preach it just as well as we, if he only wished
to do so. But the Gospel is doctrine that is to be a living
power and put into practice; it should strengthen and comfort the people and make us courageous and aggressive.
Therefore they who only hear the Gospel thus, so that they
know and can speak about it, are not to be classed among
Christians; but those who believe and do as the Gospel
teaches are righteous.

*"No man can serve two masters: for either he will hate the
one, and love the other: or else he will hold to one and despise
the other."*

4. Now he, who tries to serve two masters, will do it in a
way that cannot be called serving at all; for it will certainly
be as the Lord here says. One can indeed compel a servant
to do a certain work against his will and he may grieve

while doing it; but no one can compel him to do it cheerfully, and mean it from the bottom of his heart. He of
course does the work as long as his master is present, but
when he is absent, he hurries away from his task, and does
nothing well. Hence the Lord desires our service to be done
out of love and cheerfully, and where it is not done thus, it
is no service to him: for even people are not pleased when
one does anything for them unwillingly. This is natural,
and we experience daily that it is so. Now, if it be the case
among human beings that no one can serve two masters,
how much more is it true in the service of God, that our
service cannot be divided; but it must be done unto God
alone, willingly and from the heart; hence the Lord adds:
"Ye cannot serve God and mammon."

5. God cannot allow us to have another Lord besides
himself. He is a jealous God, as he says, and cannot suffer
us to serve him and his enemy. We find very few, who do
not sin against the Gospel. The Lord passes a severe judgment and it is terrible to hear, that he should say this of us;
and yet no one will confess, yea, no one will suffer it to be
said that we hate and despise God, and that we are his
enemies. There is no one, when asked if he loves God and
cleaves to him, who would not reply: Dost thou take me to be
such a desperate character as to be an enemy of God? But
see how the text here closes, that we all hate and despise
God, and love and cleave to mammon. For it is impossible
that he, who loves gold and riches and cleaves to them,
should not hate God. Christ here holds the two opposed to
one another and as enemies, and says: If you love one of
these two and cleave to the same, then you must hate and
despise the other. However well a man may live here upon
the earth, if he clings to riches it cannot be otherwise than
that he must hate God. And whoever does not trust in gold
and worldly riches, loves God. This is certain. 6-36.*

---

* 6–36 paragraphs inclusive are the same as paragraphs 6–36 in
the preceding sermon as will appear from a critical examina-
tion. The paragraphing is a little different, but the matter is the
same and it is not necessary, but rather confusing to repeat it here.

*"Be not therefore anxious, saying, What shall we eat? or,
What shall we drink? or, Wherewithal shall we be clothed?
For after all these things do the Gentiles seek; for your
heavenly Father knoweth that ye have need of all these things."*

37. As I said at the beginning Christ delivered this sermon to his Christians, especially to those in the office of the
ministry or to those who otherwise either had nothing or
never could acquire and gather for themselves riches and
mammon, as the rest of the world does; in order that they
might know, from what source they could nourish and support themselves and their families. Yea, they are compelled to live in the danger of being robbed of the little
earthly goods God gave them and thus they are without
the least doubt compelled to live entirely upon the help
that God sends them and they expect from him, since the
world gives them nothing.

38. This is indeed painful to flesh and blood, and is very
burdensome to them, yea, no one can bear or do it, unless
he is a believing Christian. For the world is so disposed
that it will not take the least risk in temporal matters for
the future; but it must be sure of them, order beforehand
and have in store and ready for use whatever it needs, as
food, peace, protection and insurance, so that it can live and
depend upon neither God nor the people; but as it is evident
that the world enriches no one because of his faith and
piety, they think they must act and live as others do, in order
that they may nevertheless have also something.

39. Against this he herewith comforts and strengthens his
Christians, and again repeats: They shall therefore not
worry nor doubt nor wriggle in such unbelief, saying: Oh,
what is to become of us? Who is going to give us anything? Where in this world are we Christians to get food,
protection, peace? But they must know that their heavenly
Father provides for this, and will also give it to them, he
who for this very reason is called their Father (not the unbelievers', although he feeds all the world, and gives everything), in order to show that he will also not leave his
children. He leads them into God's high work of the whole

creation, that they may see how he nourishes and supports all things which he creates, after having ordered and regulated each one,—also all the birds in the air, which, as you know, do not fret about their food nor know beforehand whither they shall take it. Aye, especially also the little flowers does he so deck and adorn that such beauty and finery might more fittingly be supplied elsewhere; for does it not seem quite useless, since they only bloom for perchance a day? Must he not therefore much more think and care for his Christians, how they may be fed and clad, and where they might dwell and stay as long as they have to live on earth?

40. This he admonishes them to believe; and to impress them most strongly with it, not by many but by earnest words, he suddenly breaks off after having held up to them the examples from daily life and God's work among his creatures; and closes with these words: Shall he not much more do such things for you, O ye of little faith? He wishes to say: Well, you ought to be ashamed of yourselves, if you are Christians and know that you have a Father in heaven, to let me do so much preaching about this! Yes, ashamed you ought to be, and not permit that such things be said of you. But must I not say it, that ye are so small and have so little faith, and that ye so little confide without doubt and care in the living God, who gives you his Word and promise and has chosen you as his children—that he would nourish and support your body and life? How then will ye stand without shame and disgrace, not alone before God but before all his creatures, if that is to be said of you, and you yourselves by your own confession must testify that you, having so plentifully God's word and grace, so little trust him with caring for your miserable maggot-sack and stinking belly?

41. Still more strongly does he speak to them by saying: "After all these things do the Gentiles seek" etc. This ought surely to deter a Christian, when he hears the public and terrible verdict spoken that those who worry and hanker after mammon are heathen, that is, people who really have

no God; who, instead of God, serve mammon, in which there
is only God's name and naught but lies and vanity; who
therefore are wholly cut off from God, deprived of all
divine knowledge, comfort, grace and bliss.   These are none
other than the most miserable, most unfortunate, condemned
people, who have never any salvation or comfort to hope for.

42. Here you see the world pictured, what sort of a thing
it is, namely the big, mighty crowd—excepting a very few
Christians—who, as soon as they have grown up, turn altogether away from God and serve mammon, the god of lies.
Him do they hold as the great, aye, the only god, because
the crowd that follows him is so great; nevertheless he is
nothing, a mere powerless name.   So a Christian should
truly be horrified and shocked, when thinking of such blindness and misery of the world; he should with sighs and
tears strive and work for it to be far removed from such
shameful practices, and run from it, as run he can, as it were
out of a fire, aye, out of the midst of hell.

43. Thirdly, in order in the most loving and comforting
way to entice us to believe he again says: "Your heavenly Father knoweth that ye have need of all these things."
Is he not your father, and only your father—not the
birds', the geese' or ducks', nor the godless heathens'
father!   Then trust him to be so loving that he will as a
father care for you and neither forget nor leave you; aye,
that he has long before known what he should give you, and
has provided therefor ere you yourselves think of it or feel
your wants.   For who but he has before known or thought
what you would be or need, ere you were born into this
world?   Therefore honor him so far as to believe that he
sees and knows such things and, knowing them, will act with
you as a father.

*"But seek ye first his kingdom and his righteousness; and all
these things shall be added unto you."*

44. That is the chief passage in this sermon, and states
the right rule and manner how we are to proceed in order to
get both the divine or eternal gift, and what we need for this
life.   Would you rightly and well take care whereof it be-

hooves you to take care, then let this be the first, aye, indeed, your only care, that you strive according to God's Word to do your duty, to serve him in his kingdom as his Word teaches you—for in this consists the righteousness belonging to this kingdom—and to prize this more highly than all pertaining unto this temporal life.

If you do this you have done and provided well and need not take any further burdens upon you nor cherish any cares in your heart; indeed, it should be much too small a thing for you to care for so slight a matter as the wants of your belly, and therefore to aggrieve yourselves. Rather do this for the honor of God, and furthermore for your own use and benefit, that you strive after the great and eternal good; which if you attain and keep, the rest will surely take care of itself. Neither can you in any better way arrive at obtaining it from God, than in this wise that you first seek and ask of him the great things.

45. For this is to his liking, that we ask great things of him, and that he be able to give great and many things. And for the reason that he gladly gives great things, he will also not stint the small things, but throw them to boot into the bargain. This God has constantly caused many pious people to experience, who, following this rule and precept, have striven to help in building God's kingdom, have served the church, furthered God's Word, and given thereto of their means. He then on the other hand has richly blessed them with goods, honor, etc. This is evidenced by the old examples not only of the Scriptures, but also by the history of some of our pious kings and princes, who, first having given plentifully for parishes and pulpits, for the support of the holy ministry and for schools, have thereby not become poorer, but were much more richly blessed and endowed by God, so that they have reigned in good peace, with victory and good fortune.

46. This he would gladly still do, if the world could or would haply for its own good follow the well-meant advice which he here gives, and not with unbelief, greed and unchristianlike scheming rage against his Word, to its own

harm and ruin. So must he turn this Word with her and prove the contrary; that he who will not strive after God's kingdom and his righteousness, but despises the same and reckons to provide for himself, against God's will, by means of his own wisdom and plotting, must be deprived both of the eternal and of the temporal, and either not obtain the temporal or at least not be satisfied and happy with it.

"Be not therefore anxious for the morrow; for the morrow will be anxious for itself. Sufficient unto the day is the evil thereof."

47. The world is always anxious about the future, and therewith thinks to assure its fate and to bring this much about that it may be removed from danger, protect and support itself. They see not the vanity thereof, and that their projects go wrong; that it be true, and experience testifies, as Christ here says, that each day brings its own misfortune and evil. Thus it comes to pass that, with such plottings and prudence of their own, whereby they mean to ensure themselves and to forestall all coming danger, the world only causes the more woe and harm. For whenever they see that things do not go as they expected, or that an accident happens, then they begin to despond, think of one remedy and another, and imagine they must, wherever and as best they can, look for help, protection and safety; thus they patch for themselves and think to help matters by all sorts of strange craftiness and practices, whereunto they are driven by unbelief, against God and their conscience, thus to carry out what they have in mind, albeit they see that God does not prosper such things. Hence springs so much misfortune, misery, murder, war, and all mischief and misdoing of the wicked world. Each one means to carry out his affairs without God, to oppress and choke whosoever would hinder him, and rather to throw all things higgledy-piggledy on a heap than to desist from his mind. Thereby in all affairs and governments all good things perish and naught but evil grows; as all history and daily experience more than amply show.

48. Against this Christ would caution his believers, that

they may not waver nor stake their affairs on that which is uncertain, vainly caring for the future, but at all times and daily do that which is right; that they may not worry how things will come out, nor permit themselves to be swerved by future and uncertain good or evil things; but rather commend care to God, and then take everything that occurs to them in good part and overcome it with faith and patience. For it cannot be on earth otherwise than that each one daily in his office, estate and calling meet with other things than he gladly welcomes, which causes him much trouble and labor. Hence does also Christ call this life daily evil or misfortune, that is to say, all sorts of misfortune, resistance, hindrance; that we may know it and be prepared for it, so as not to be frightened by any of them from doing good, neither yet to hanker after the world and become partakers in its unrighteous and evil affairs,— thereby leading ourselves and others into ruin and damnation.

SIXTEENTH SUNDAY AFTER TRINITY.

This sermon is not found in the c. edition. Erl. 14, 119; W. 11, 2195; St. L. 11, 1646.

Text: Luke 7, 11-17. And it came to pass soon afterwards, that he went to a city called Nain; and his disciples went with him, and a great multitude. Now when he drew near to the gate of the city, behold, there was carried out one that was dead, the only son of his mother, and she was a widow: and much people of the city was with her. And when the Lord saw her, he had compassion on her, and said unto her, Weep not. And he came nigh and touched the bier: and the bearers stood still. And he said, Young man, I say unto thee, Arise. And he that was dead sat up, and began to speak. And he gave him to his mother. And fear took hold on all: and they glorified God, saying, A great prophet is arisen among us: and, God hath visited his people. And this report went forth concerning him in the whole of Judœa, and all the region round about.

CONTENTS: THE MIRACLE OF CHRIST IN RAISING THE SON OF THE WIDOW OF NAIN FROM THE DEAD.

I. THE MIRACLE IN ITSELF.

1. How this miracle should move us to lift our hearts to God. 1.
2. How it teaches that God gives his great blessings out of pure grace, without our merit. 2f.
   * Of the blessings of God.
   a. They are given to man without his merit, out of pure grace. 3-5.
   b. Why man does not esteem but misuses them. 4-6.
   c. God's blessings are richly exhibited in all the creatures of God. 6.
   d. The way God seeks to bring us highly to appreciate his blessings. 7-8.
3. How this miracle teaches us to know what God is, what he thinks of us and what we should think of him. 8f.
   * To what end God bestows his gifts and blessings, and permits misfortune to visit men. 9-11.
4. How God's great power is made known by this miracle. 12f.
   * Of the miracles of God.
   a. How and why God's miracles are considered impossible in our eyes. 12.
   b. To what end should the miracles of God serve us. 12-15.

II. THE SPIRITUAL SIGNIFICANCE OF THIS MIRACLE.

1. That the young man was dead as to his body. 16-19.

SUMMARY OF THIS GOSPEL: Love is of such a nature
that it forgets itself, and takes upon itself the distress and need
of its neighbor.   Thus Christ also does here, he winds himself into
the distress of the widow and looks upon her misery as his own.

THE SPIRITUAL INTERPRETATION.   The lust we have inherited from Adam carries us on hour by hour to tne grave and constantly holds us in the grip of death.   There is no help or counsel
for us, except in the mercy of Christ.   When he, however, stirs our
hearts the violence of lust is allayed.   For by his voice, that is, by
the preaching of his Word, which moves the heart so powerfully,
we who were dead are made alive again to his praise and glory.

I. THE MIRACLE ITSELF.

1. In this Gospel you see how the Evangelist again presents to us a divine miracle, by which he desires to move us
to lift our hearts to God, in which is the same state of things
as at the time existed in this woman; for to-day's lesson was
not written for the sake of this widow, but for the instruction and help of all who should hear this Gospel until the
end of the world, among whom we also have been reckoned.

2. In the first place notice what lovingkindness and grace
were shown to this woman by Christ.   We must truly confess
she did not merit them; for she is going out of the city with
her friends, where there is nothing but crying and weeping.
The good woman thought of nothing as little as that she
should again lead back her son into the city alive, and for
this reason she does not desire it, nor does she ask it, much
less has she deserved it.   She never thought of such a thing
that Christ should come hither; yea, she did not at the time
know Christ nor did she know anything of his helping the
people.   Here all merit and preparations for meeting him
are out of the question.

3. Now all this has been written to the end that just as
here this deed of mercy befell this widow freely and
entirely of grace, only because it solicited Christ's sympathy,

so from this we can draw the general rule that applies to all the merciful deeds of God, that they all overtake us without our merits, even before we seek them. He lays the foundation and makes the beginning. But why does he pity us? In this way it continues to be the grace of God. Otherwise, if we deserved it, it would not be grace. And if it be of grace, then we can say to him: Thou art a gracious God, thou doest good also to them who deserve it not.

4. This sermon seems easy to us, but where are they who mean it with their heart? If we believed that everything comes to us from God's grace and mercy, we would daily run and rejoice, our hearts would continually rise and dwell in heaven. When we once get to heaven we will see that this is true. Now no one believes it. The god of this world, the devil, has such great power on earth that we do not see the work of God nor know it. 2 Cor. 4, 4. Therefore we do not appreciate it, we misuse God's mercies, and are entirely unthankful to him.

5. If I only kept in mind that he gave me eyes, truly a very great treasure, it would be no wonder if shame caused my death, because of my ingratitude in that I never yet thanked him for the blessing of sight. But we do not see his noble treasures and gifts; they are too common. But when a blind babe happens to be born, then we see what a painful thing the lack of sight is, and what a precious thing even one eye is, and what a divine blessing a healthy, bright countenance is; it serves us during our whole life, and without it one would rather be dead; and yet no one thanks God for it. Examine the entire body, and you will everywhere see traces of God's grace and goodness.

Hence Psalm 33, 5 says: "The earth is full of the goodness of the Lord." He had pure eyes and could see far, that the whole world was full of the goodness and lovingkindness of God. From whom, however, has this goodness come? Have we deserved it? No, but it pleased God to cast his gifts thus promiscuously into the world, which the unthankful receive almost as freely as the thankful. We are

grieved when we are obliged to throw away one or two
dollars, or less, or even to give them to the poor; how much
does God daily cast away of his goods into the world and
no one thanks him for anything? Yes, who even acknowledges their receipt?

6. Thus we may observe all creatures and become convinced of God's goodness in them. Christ says in Mat. 5,
45: "He maketh his sun to rise on the evil and on the good,
and sendeth rain on the just and on the unjust." As though
he would say: I give it to the whole crowd; but who thanks
me a single time for it? He enlightens my and your
eyes, but no one acknowledges that it is God's blessing. If
some morning the sun should not rise, or rise three hours
late, what distress and loss would that cause? How we
would open our mouths and eyes? Then everyone would
say: God be praised and thanked, who has given us such a
light! But since it occurs daily, that the sun rises and
shines at the appointed time, no one considers it a blessing.

So it is with the rain from heaven, with the grain in the
field and with all God's creatures. They exist in such
abundance, and we are daily so overwhelmed by their abundance that we fail to see them.

7. At times God permits some man to fall into anxiety
and need, into pain and distress, so that the world seems
as though it had no God, and it makes a person blind, lame,
dropsical, and lets anyone die, as here the widow's son; for
they are his creatures, he can do with them what he will.
Now, why does he do this? He does it in such an abundance
only that we may continually experience his lovingkindness.

Therefore as the disciples in John 9, 2 asked the Lord
concerning the man blind from his birth, whether he or his
parents sinned, the Lord answered and said: "Neither hath
this man sinned, nor his parents; but that the works of God
should be made manifest in him." As though he would
say: God desires to be praised in this blind person, for
he sees that the treasures of the whole world do not move
us, wherefore he floods us with his goodness out of pure

grace, that he may present a blind person before our eyes, for us to see what a costly treasure we have in the blessing of our sight, although we cannot recognize his grace and kindness in our fortune, that we at least might know and identify them then in our misfortune. Therefore this man had to be blind in order that the others might know themselves, and say: Alas thou good God, what a precious gift I have, what a good thing a healthy body is and a bright countenance! But no one takes it to heart! Yea, it is true we say: have not the cows eyes also! Now, if you were blind you would of course feel the loss, which you do not now feel, because you are well and overshowered with God's blessings.

8. So it was in the case of this widow, in whom God lets himself be known, as to what kind of a God he is, what he thinks of us, and what we must think of him. This woman has two misfortunes around her neck. First, she is a widow. This is misfortune enough for one woman, that she is forsaken and alone, and has no one to whom she dare look for comfort. And therefore God in the Scriptures is often mentioned as the Father of the widow and orphans, as in Ps. 68, 6 and 146, 9: "God setteth the solitary in families. The Lord preserveth the strangers and orphans, he delivers the widow." Again: she has an only son about to die, who should have been her comfort. Now, God comes and takes away her husband and son. She had much better have lost house and home, yes, her own life, than her son and husband. But the Lord turns it around. While the husband lived the woman did not appreciate what a blessing a husband was; but when he died she first became aware of it. When he lived, she thought: O, other women have husbands, too! And thought her husband was like other husbands. But afterwards when he was dead, she became aware what kind of a man she had lost.

So, too, when her son was bright and well, she did not appreciate the blessing of God, but as soon as he died, she then first saw what a treasure she had lost. Before she did not desire to spend on him; but now, since he is dead, she spends all she has and even herself upon him. And thus it is also with us. There are many of you who do not expend ten dollars that your child may be reared better; if the child dies the parents wish and say: O would to God he were alive, I would give many hundred dollars! Why did you not give something before that he might have learned a little? What is the reason you do not appreciate the grace and blessings of God? In short, the world remains world, and it will not change into anything else.

9. Now, the woman went ahead and did not know what God had given her; but she was soon obliged to experience it. For before she turns around, and she thinks she is the safest, God comes, tries the wife a little and teaches her certain things, takes her husband and her son. This all has been written for us that we might have an example and learn to acknowledge God when he blesses us with a healthy body, a bright countenance, and bestows upon us other blessings. He does not give them to the end that you should rejoice in them; but that you may know what to think of him. When he takes a member out of your family, permits your wife to die, or destroys one of your eyes, all this is done that you may see what you have enjoyed from him.

10. And this is now the common teaching through all the Gospels, that we may see what kind of a God we have. It is also shown us here in this Gospel that God will forsake no one; therefore he permits the wife to see in a new light what kind of a God she has. For when she was forsaken and had neither son nor husband, then Christ manifests himself to her and says: Learn to believe, trust God, know him to whom death and life are alike: have a good heart, be of good courage, weep not, there is no need of it. He then goes and awakens the dead, and gives him again to his mother.

11. This and like miracles God does that the heart may learn how it should be disposed to him and what it may expect from him. As now this wife was fully convinced that there was no hope for her son, that it was impossible for

her to receive him back alive again; yea, if one had said to her: Before an hour your son will be alive again, she would have regarded it as impossible and said: It is more possible for the heavens to fall than for my son to live again. Behold, here comes God before she looks around, and does what she never dared to ask of him, as it is impossible, and he restores her son alive to her again.

But why does God do this? He permits man to fall so deeply into danger and anxiety, until no help or advice is within reach, and still he desires that we should not doubt, but trust in him who out of an impossible thing can make something possible, and make something out of nothing. If you are so deep in sin that your heart denies you all grace and the mercy of God and makes you think there is no hope for you, as many consciences are ensnared by such anxiety and distress; then turn about and look here how friendly and graciously God allows himself to be pictured by Christ in this Gospel; that you may observe that he means it well with you from his heart; and that he is not here either to condemn or excommunicate you, but to preserve your soul forever. For this purpose such miracles and wonderful works are held before our eyes, and they also serve to the end, that we may see. As God here helps this widow in a temporal way through Christ, so he will help us not only bodily, but much more spiritually, and our soul forever, if we only put our hope in him.

12. But all miracles and works of God are considered impossible in our eyes, and they are also impossible for the natural man to grasp; and this is to the end that God may be confessed to be an almighty Creator, who from something impossible can create something possible, and can make something out of nothing. It is impossible after I am dead that I should live again; and even if I should pray to all the angels and all the saints for it; nothing will result from such prayers; what then can the free will accomplish? Nevertheless in death I should say: I shall live, not through myself, but because I know that my God is so skillful that he can make something, not out of wood that lies

before my eyes, but it is his nature and way to make a thing possible here from something impossible; and create something out of nothing; otherwise he were not the true and real God.

13. Therefore, if death be present and I can no longer live, I must still know enough to say: Yet I live, and will live; so that death, that is all about me, is like a spark of fire, and life is as great as the sea. Now reason cannot grasp how this takes place. But whoever believes, knows for a certainty that to him death will be like a spark of fire in the midst of the ocean, that is extinguished in a moment. God is almighty, he who believes is in God, therefore he is in life, and though he were in the midst of death. So too a poor person who believes, thinks like this one here in death: O! poverty is a spark of fire, and wealth is as abundant as water in the sea; now a moment only is needed for poverty to sink, and I will be rich; for by faith God has entirely changed him who now has all things in his power. So also with shame; when one's good name and reputation go down, people think they will never again be regained; if you believe and hold to God, it is a matter only of a moment, and you are again in great honor. For our God knows the art that from invincible poverty he can create great riches, from great shame unexpressable honor. So it is also with sin, if you believe. Thus sin compared with righteousness, is as a spark of fire compared with the whole sea of water.

14. This you see beautifully illustrated in the case of this woman. She is overwhelmed by exceedingly great pain and anguish, so that she thinks God, heaven, earth and all things are opposed to her. And since she looks into this with the eyes of sense, sees it as it is before her natural eyes, she must conclude it is impossible for her to be delivered from her great anxiety. But when her son was raised from the dead for her, she was as though the whole heaven and earth, wood and stone, and everything laughed and rejoiced with her; then she forgot all pain and suffering, this wholly disappeared just like a spark of fire is extinguished when it falls into the sea. Therefore it is written in the prophet Isaiah

54, 6-8: "For Jehovah hath called thee as a wife forsaken and grieved in spirit, even a wife of youth when she is cast off, saith thy God. For a small moment have I forsaken thee; but with great mercies will I gather thee. In overflowing wrath I hid my face from thee for a moment; but with everlasting lovingkindness will I have mercy on thee, saith Jehovah thy Redeemer."

But this I do not see, I think this moment is an eternal something before God; but it is in truth only a moment; and much joy follows as Psalm 8, 5 also says: "For thou hast made him but little lower than God, and crownest him with glory and honor." But this is still all hid from us, and we do not see it as this wife does. Her departed son is in the midst of life, for God has him in his bosom, and intends to wake him. There is a spark of death there that surrounds him, which no one saw. But now when he became alive that was revealed which before was hidden from the whole world.

15. Thus God certainly deals also with us. Here we should learn the kind of God we have, namely, he who surrounds us and is about us in our very greatest dangers and troubles. Therefore, if one is poor, sticks deep in sin, lies in death, is in sorrows and other afflictions, he thinks: it is a transition state, it is a drop and a spark; for God has surrounded him on all sides with pure wealth, righteousness, life and joy, only he does not permit him to see it. But it is a matter of only a little time when we shall see and enjoy it. Thus you have here an example, not of faith, but of the pure grace and lovingkindness of God. Now we must also say a little on the spiritual understanding or the allegorical interpretation of to-day's Gospel.

II. THE SPIRITUAL INTERPRETATION OF THIS MIRACLE.

16. All works and miracles that Christ does visibly and publicly should be interpreted to the end that they may show forth the works which he does among men unseen and

spiritually or within them. Therefore this bodily death signifies the spiritual death of the soul, which man must believe. For no one can see into the soul of another while we live; but when we are dead, we then have other eyes, then we see that the whole world is dead. Therefore the Lord spoke to a Pharisee, Mat. 8, 22, who first wanted to go and bury his father: "Follow me, and leave the dead to bury their own dead."

17. This youth who is here being borne to his grave is bodily dead. But there are also some inwardly dead before God who still live here in the body. The soul is dead that does not believe in God and cleave to him. And even though he be in the midst of death, yet he lives, as I said above.

18. This spiritual death occurs in a twofold manner: some are dead in their soul, but no one sees that death as we see bodily death, and this woman herself neither sees nor feels it. So the whole world is dead, but it realizes it not. Therefore some are also spiritually dead, who feel it well enough, as those whom the law has terribly punished. We do not here speak of those who care nothing for spiritual death; but of those who feel that they are dead and that their heart trembles, and who feel in their conscience that they have an unbelieving heart. He is dead quite otherwise than he who does not feel it, and yet always lives in wantonness. Now the one who does not experience their unbelief cannot be helped, for he does not know his sickness, and lives on, cares nothing for God nor the world. But he who feels this death, suffers misery and distress, there is struggling and despair, the world becomes too confined for him, he seeks assistance and advice, he despises neither stone nor wood, when they can afford him counsel, not to say that he should hear anything of man, even of the most insignificant person.

19. Who now gives him this feeling. The law does it, in that it reveals sin. The law says: "Thou shalt have no other gods." When I hear this, I must and should do it, but I cannot. Then I quickly conclude that I am condemned. When I act thus, death comes immediately and there is such

a struggle in my heart, that if I should receive no help I would have to remain forever in this death and struggle. This then is the death of the only son, who lies in the bier, the pallbearers are continually carrying him into hell.

20. The pallbearers are the preachers of the law, who do nothing else than plunge mankind ever deeper and deeper into death; as those here hasten to the grave with the dead they are the more terrified and driven the deeper into perdition. It never becomes better with mankind, yea, it is ever growing worse.

21. This we have thoroughly experienced under the Pope, in our confession of and in our making satisfaction for sin. We allowed ourselves to think we would atone for our sins by good works; but it was only an anxiety of the conscience. Thus we ever sank deeper toward hell. Hence, when you have people, who fear sin and condemnation, they are already dead, you dare not preach to these much more of the law, you must show them the way of salvation and preach to them the Gospel. When our Papists meet such troubled souls, they refer them to rosaries, to pilgrimages, to this and that work; but one helps like the other.

22. The pallbearers would have still moved on and laid the deceased in his grave and buried him, had Christ not come, so Christ must come also here with his Word and grace. And this now is that other office of the Gospel, which does not teach what you are to do; but whence you are to receive help, that you may do it; as Christ does here. He asks not, what is here? or how do you do this? do you wish to have the youth restored to life again, and the like? He asks none of these things; but he has mercy on the mother, goes to her, touches the bier, and the bearers soon stand still. That is, when man preaches the goodness of God, and when Christ presents us with his merits and works, then the hand is laid upon the coffin, and the bearers stand still, that is, you no longer hear the preachers of the law, you no longer believe them; but you say: preach works here, preach works there, we have a different sermon. While our hands are on the coffin they accomplished nothing; the

dead does not come to life again; but when Christ's hand
touches the coffin the mighty work is done. For when men
hear that Christ's work does it, and that his works are
presented to us, he says: What need we to do beside?
For here our doing is useless and in vain.

23. But the dead will not be raised to life so quickly.
The Word of God is of course preached to us, the goodness
of God and whatever is given us through Christ; but this
is not yet sufficient, this is only first touching the coffin.
The voice of Christ in the heart must also be added, that
we may believe the Word, that it is really as we preach.
The youth does not immediately arise after he is touched,
but when the Lord spoke: "Young man, I say unto thee,
Arise!" This voice stirred the heart and caused the dead
to rise to life. When I in like manner hear the Word, and
allow human traditions to move me, men still bear me ever
on and I ever remain in distress, it helps me little. I must
besides the external sermon also hear this voice in the heart:
"Young man, I say unto thee, Arise:" that is, I must believe
this sermon, cleave to it with my heart, trust in it, and let
neither sin, death, devil, nor hell draw me from it.

24. Thus we have two sermons. One lays the hand on the
bier. This does not yet accomplish anything. But the
other, when the hand is laid on the coffin and the voice follows in the heart, this accomplishes all. The first proclaims
to us the works of Christ, how they are done for us and
given to us. But when the voice is heard in the heart, then
the one who was before dead begins to speak and to confess the faith with his mouth which he believes and feels
in his heart. That is, when the heart believes, the work of
love follows, namely, that you speak, that is, preach to
others and thank God for the blessing and faith he has
shown and given unto you.

25. From this follows great joy and thanksgiving, by
which God is praised and exalted; just as here a great report about Christ went over the entire land of the Jews and
into all the neighboring countries. Thus a Christian can
lead many unto faith. Therefore man should not make a

work of jugglery out of miracles and wonders, as the Papists have done.

26. This is said on to-day's Gospel, in which we see how God helps and saves us, moved by pure grace and loving-kindness, without any merit or worthiness whatever on our part, yea, before we seek or request help from him. God grant that we may believe this!

SIXTEENTH SUNDAY AFTER TRINITY.

Second Sermon: Luke 7, 11-17.

This sermon, which is found only in Edition c, is composed by uniting two sermons, the first of which (§§ 1–13) appeared in 1534 under the title: "A short sermon on the Gospel of Luke 7 chapter, the widow whose son had died, 1534, Dr. Martin Luther." The other sermon (§§ 14–40) Cruciger embodied evidently from his own copy into the Postil and is also found in the little book issued by him: "Some comforting writings and sermons for those visited by death and other distress and temptations. Dr. Martin Luther, 1545."—At the end of the book are these words:,"Printed at Wittenberg, by Hans Luft, 1544." A second edition appeared at Wittenberg in 1548. Its title in this collection of sermons is: "A Sermon on Death and Life, on the Gospel of Luke 7 chapter, the widow's son raised from the dead." Erl. 14, 131; W. 11, 2211; St. L. 11, 1658.

CONTENTS: THE RESURRECTION OF THE WIDOW'S SON, THE YOUNG MAN OF NAIN.

I. THIS RESURRECTION IN GENERAL. How it praises the grace, work and power of God in the kingdom of Christ. 1.

* The conduct of flesh and blood in time of need and misery. 2.

II. THIS RESURRECTION IN DETAIL.

A. How it opposes the false notions, which human nature forms of God in the time of trouble, and awakens us to serve God. 3-5.
* The punishment of God in our temptations.
1. God permits the punishment for a time to pass upon the wicked and the pious. 6.
2. Why God permits punishment to pass upon the godly. 7.
3. How and why believers should not take offense at chastisement and temptation. 8f.
4. The thoughts believers should cherish under. chastisement and temptation. 8-12.
* A Christian should be strong in faith and praise God. 13.

B. How this resurrection paints before our eyes the true picture of Christ.

1. What is the true and characteristic work of Christ. 14.
2. How it is set forth in this resurrection. 15f.
* Of death and life.

in the time of death as well as of life. 16-17.
b. The thoughts reason has of death. 18-19.
c. The doctrine Christ teaches of death. 20-21.
d. No human wisdom and power can prevent death, and restore life. 22-24.
e. How without our works we must come to life through Christ.
(1) The nature, sense and understanding of this. 25-27.
(2) A picture of this. 28-32.
f. The essence of the whole world is nothing but a picture of death and a daily journey to death. 33-34.
g. In Christ we have a comforting picture of life. 35-38.
h. With what should a Christian comfort himself in time of death. 39-40.

1. This portion of the Gospel teaches us to know the grace, work and power of God in the kingdom of Christ, our Lord, and to praise and thank him, as well as cheerfully to serve and obey him. For this miracle and act of mercy are related in order that we may recognize him as our helper in all times of need; and then, when we acknowledge him as our helper, that we love him, thank him for his benefits, and willingly suffer and endure whatever he allows to befall us, especially since we know with certainty that he does not permit anything to happen to us in order to destroy us, but only to try our faith, to see whether our trust and refuge securely rest in him, or in something else.

2. It is the nature of flesh and blood always to seek help and comfort from other sources than God, where they should only be sought, and at last, when all other help fails, to come to God for aid; if, indeed, things turn out so well that they do not wholly despair of God, and rush to satan; for many, when no other help avails, give themselves over to the devil. This results from the fact that they do not know God, and think that he has forgotten them, if he permits some small misfortune to happen to them.

3. Overagainst such thoughts, this Gospel presents a picture of how the Lord Jesus Christ acted toward the poor widow in the time of her greatest need, at the death of her son. On earth no greater need can arise than that caused by death, when the world and everything else have an end. In this greatest extremity he helped her, and raised the dead to life, as an example for us who hear it. For this was done not merely for the sake of the widow and her son, but, as St. John, 20, 31, says: "But these things are done and written, that ye may believe." In this way he impresses upon the hearts of all this and his other miracles performed by the blessed Lord Jesus, as if he meant to say: Behold, now you hear how this widow's son was raised from the dead; let this be preached into your heart, in order that you may accept it, and in this learn what God can and will do, that he can and will help you in all times of need, no matter how great they may be. And if it should happen that your

needs should press heavily upon you and you realize
that earthly counsel and help are unavailing, that then you
do not despair but let this example strengthen your heart,
so that you may look to the Lord Jesus for the best that he
can give.

4. This was, indeed, no jest in the life of the widow.
First, she lost her husband, and then her only son, whom she
loved, died. Among those people it was regarded a great
misfortune, if parents could not leave a name or children.
They regarded this as a great disfavor of God. Hence this
widow, who after the death of her husband, placed all her
hope and comfort in her only son, must have had great
sorrow when her son was torn from her and she had nothing
left on earth. Under such circumstances the thoughts were
undoubtedly forced upon her: Behold, you are also one of
the cursed women to whom God is such an enemy that they
must pass from the earth without leaving an offspring.
For thus it is written in the Psalms and the Prophets, that
God threatens the ungodly, that he will destroy them root
and branch, exactly as when one so entirely destroys a tree
that neither leaf nor twig remains. This was regarded as
the greatest curse and punishment, as may be seen in the
lives of many emperors, kings and princes, who were so
completely destroyed that nothing is known of them. This
has the appearance as if it were the utmost disfavor.

5. Therefore this woman had great sorrow, not only because she had been robbed of her husband and afterwards
of her son and thereby the family destroyed before her eyes;
but, what seemed far more serious, because she was forced
to think: Now I see that God is unfavorable to me and I
am cursed; for this punishment has been executed upon me
because God in the Psalms and the Prophets has threatened
the ungodly to destroy them root and branch. This has
happened to me. Therefore the miracle the Lord Jesus
wrought in her behalf seemed to her altogether impossible;
and if some one had then said to her: Thy son shall live
again before your eyes, she would undoubtedly have said:
Alas! do not mock me in my deep sorrow. Grant me at least

so much that I may bewail my great misery, and do not add
to it by your mockery. This would undoubtedly have been
her answer, for she was greatly distressed, both by reason
of the loss she had sustained as well as on account of her
scruples of conscience.

6. But all this is portrayed here in order that we might
learn that with God nothing is impossible, whether it be
misfortune, calamity, anger, or whatever it may be, and that
he sometimes allows misfortune to come upon the good as
well as upon the wicked. Yea, that he even permits the ungodly to sit at ease, as in a garden of roses, and meet with
success in all their undertakings, while, on the other hand,
he appears to the pious as if he were angry with them and
unfavorable to them; as, for example, it happened to the
godly Job, all whose children were sadly destroyed in one
day, who was robbed of his cattle and land, and his body
most terribly tormented. He was an innocent man and yet
he was compelled to endure a punishment such as no ungodly person had suffered, so that at last even his friends
said to him: "You must undoubtedly rest under a great
and secret sin, since this has happened to you." While
attempting to comfort him, they added to his misery. But
he answered, saying: "I have done nothing and hence am
not an ungodly person, whom God often allows to live in
rioting and to go unpunished."

7. So also, it was undoubtedly a serious problem to the
widow that the Lord our God punishes the good and evil
alike. But to the godly this does not come as a mark of
God's anger or disfavor; while to the ungodly it comes truly
as a mark of anger, in order that they may be destroyed.
For God does not trifle with them, but is truly in earnest.
As to the God-fearing, who have not merited punishment, he
tries to see if they will remain steadfast. If they endure the
test and think: "My God, though thou triest me, yet thou wilt
not forsake me," he will come again and pour out his blessings as richly upon them as he did in the case of Job, who
received twice as much as he had lost, both in property and
children. The widow found all her joy in her son while he

lived. God tried her and took her son from her. When she wept and cried he came again and gave her tenfold more joy than she had had before; for she rejoiced more for her son in that one hour than she had done throughout her entire previous life. So richly does our Lord God give again, if only men endure and do not doubt him.

8. Therefore learn from this, whoever can learn: If we are pious and the trials come, which God sends upon us, let us cherish the thought that he means it well with us, and let us not be offended when he permits the wicked, the Pope, bishops and all others to do as they please. These think they have deserved this at the hands of our Lord God and try to justify themselves, if punished on account of their sins. But, dear friends, let us freely confess and say: Lord, thou doest right, even though thou dost punish us; for before thee, Lord, we have no right. But we hope that thou wilt punish graciously and in thine own good time cease. If we do thus, all distress will be removed, no matter how impossible help may seem to be.

9. Flesh and blood, when under trial, say, all is lost. For when our Lord God makes an attack, he does it in such a manner that we know not where to turn; and hence, no matter how we think or plan, we can find no way out, but are hemmed in on every side, as Job says, 3, 23: "As a man, whom the Lord has surrounded with darkness," as when one is in darkness and does not know which way to turn. If the trial does not go thus far it is no real trial. He who in hunger still knows of a supply of gold or grain, is not yet in real darkness; but when one is utterly helpless and without counsel he may be said to be really punished. As the widow's way was so hemmed in on every side that she was compelled to conclude: I am cursed, God is against me; so she was in the midst of darkness, where there was neither a way nor an opening, and knew not where to turn.

10. All this is presented to us as an example, that we may learn to remain steadfast in faith and regard God in no other light than that of a merciful God who, indeed, may permit us to be tempted, as if he were angry with us and

were laughing at us with the world; but let us guard ourselves against such laughter and not become terrified at the
anger, with which he attacks his people. It may appear as
if at times he were on the side of the wicked and persecuted
the godly without mercy; yet it does no harm and it depends only upon a glance. But it is a blind and spiritual
glance, which we must give with blind eyes, that is, with
the eyes of faith, which sees nothing; For faith is invisible.
Faith lays hold of things that are not seen and of things
that are not matters of experience, Heb. 11, 1.

11. Philosophers have an art that deals with visible
things, which can be experienced and comprehended; but a
Christian deals with invisible, unsubstantial, spiritual
things, that cannot be seen, nor comprehended, so that one
can hardly think they are possible. In this state Sarah
was with reference to her son. There was nothing but the
simple word. Her womb was not fit for that because of
her age and her natural condition that she was barren, and
her son Isaac was indeed invisible and as nothing. So this
widow, with reference to her son, did not see that he lived,
but saw only that he was dead; but Christ knew that he
lived and brought the dead son to life, and so made the invisible visible.

12. All this happened, as I have often said, for us to learn
to trust our Lord God and believe in him in all our need, and
not become terrified when we do not fare well, nor be
offended if the wicked prosper. For our Lord God is one
who tries, who allows his own to be tried and to suffer, so
that they may truly perceive and learn to know that he is a
gracious God, even though he at times hides his grace so
deeply that it cannot be seen. Afterwards, if men persevere,
it is only a matter of a single word and the necessary assistance is rendered; as in this Gospel, only a word was necessary and the dead son was restored to life. By this he desires to show that what is impossible with us, is so easy for
him that it requires only one little word: "Arise." It is
easily spoken, and yet is has power to restore the dead to

life. We should learn to know that he can and will help us out of all our needs.

13. He who desires to be a Christian should be strong in faith and praise God and his Word, and should say: "I will acknowledge, praise and serve that God, and gladly do and suffer what he wills, who can so readily and easily help." Thus, this and other miracles of Christ should serve to comfort us and make us better, and urge us on to believe in him and serve him, as no other god, for no other god manifests himself as our dear Lord Jesus has manifested himself. Therefore, we praise and magnify him daily, and daily bring others to him that they may also do the same. May God continue his help more and more. This is the teaching of the Gospel as presented in the example of the widow.

14. This narrative still further exhibits the true nature of Christ's work, showing why he came and reigns, namely, that he might destroy death and in its stead give life, as the prophet Isaiah, 25, 8, says: "He will swallow up death forever;" and St. Paul, 1 Cor. 15, 24-26, says that Christ must reign until he has destroyed the last enemy, death, for his Christians, and thus give them eternal life; after that he shall deliver up the kingdom to the Father, when he shall have abolished all rule and all authority and power. This is the work he will accomplish among his people and has already begun in faith before bodily death takes place. Afterwards, however, when he shall have brought all his own together he will complete his work in them at the last day.

15. Signs and types, yea, testimonies of the same are found in this and other narratives, that record the raising of people from the dead. But these form only the prelude to the work he will finally accomplish among all Christians. The pictures of both life and death are here placed over against each other, and it is shown where both originate and oppose each other, and how Christ manifests his power and authority over death.

16. For, first, when you hear the Scriptures speaking of death, you must think not only of the grave and the coffin,

and of the horrible manner in which life is separated from the body and how the body is destroyed and brought to naught, but you must think of the cause by which man is brought to death and without which death and that which accompanies it, would be impossible. This cause Scripture points out and teaches, namely, that it is sin and the wrath of God on account of sin. This cause brings death, always sticks in it, appears from it, and works and draws after it all the misery and misfortune on earth, and in addition banishes man from God and from all his grace and joy.

17. Likewise, on the contrary, when the Scriptures speak of life you must also conceive the cause that brings and gives life; that must be the righteousness by which man is acceptable to God and by which he also finds in God his pleasure, delight and joy, and receives thus from God every good thing he may desire through all eternity.

18. Both these things you may see in this picture, two sorts of persons and processions: the deceased with those who carry him out of the town, and Christ who comes to meet him. All men know very well that they must die and that all of us go the same way, and see death before us, by our side and behind us. Even the learned among the heathen have complained of this misery of the human race; but they have not been able to perceive the cause of death. Most of them think death is a matter of chance, that we die like the brute, and that man is so created that he must die.

19. Others, seeing that so much misfortune, misery and sorrow pass over the human race, that so many die before their time and many are miserably destroyed, things which could happen only by chance, have searched for the cause and have been surprised that such misfortunes befall man, who, alone among all living creatures, is the noblest and should be better situated, and guarded against injury, but they have not been able to ascertain the cause of the evil, except in so far that they have seen how many men, through their own malignity or wilfulness, have brought death and other misfortunes on themselves. But this in itself is a mat-

ter of great wonder how a man can be so wicked that he
can wilfully cast himself into trouble and misery.

20. Here Scripture teaches us, in the first place, that death
originated in paradise, as the result of the eating of the forbidden fruit, that is, from the disobedience of our first
parents, and since then has come upon all men on account
of their sins. For if sin did not exist, there would be no
death. By this we mean not only gross sins, such as
adultery, murder, and the like; but they also die who neither
commit, nor can commit these, as children in the cradle; yea,
even the great and holy Prophets, John the Baptist, all
must die.

21. Therefore some greater and different sins than murder and similar public crimes, which the executioner punishes with death, must be meant, why the whole human race
is subject to death. This is the sin which we have inherited
from Adam and Eve, and from our fathers and mothers,
which is innate in all men born according to the common
course of nature. This exists and remains, as it did in Adam
and Eve, after they had committed sin, had been banished
from the presence of God, full of evil lusts and disobedience
to God and his will. Hence all under the wrath of God are
condemned to death, and must be forever separated from
God. In this way God manifests his strong and terrible
wrath against all men, which we bring upon us through sin,
so that all of us must be overcome by death; because we are
born of flesh and blood and in consequence must bear the
guilt of our parents, and thus have become sinners and
worthy of death. Psalm 90, 7 teaches us: "For we are consumed in thine anger, and in thy wrath are we troubled."
It is the wrath of God, he says; hence it is not an accidental
thing, or because man has been so created by God; but it is
our fault that we commit sin. For since there is wrath, there
must also be guilt, which causes such wrath. This wrath is
not a mere ordinary thing, but such a serious affair that no
one can endure it, and under which all must succumb; and
yet the world is so blind that it does not see nor regard this
wrath of God; yea, even the pious do not sufficiently com-

prehend it. The Psalmist says, 90, 11: "Who knoweth the power of thine anger, and thy wrath according to the fear that is due unto thee?"

22. Much less can the world understand how one may be freed from all this misery, nor can it accomplish this by its own wisdom and power; even as in its blindness it attempts to do, when it hears of the wrath of God and seeks by its works and life to be reconciled to God and merit life. For since all men are by birth sinners and, under the wrath of God, subject to death, how shall we be able by our own works to free ourselves from death? Alas! when death is considered or how to escape death, there is neither comfort nor hope for any one, as St. Paul says, I. Thess. 4, 13: "That ye sorrow not, even as the rest who have no hope."

23. For neither do these know that it is possible for a single individual to be raised from death to life, and hence they conclude: "He who is dead, must remain dead forever and must be annihilated." Others, as the Jews, Turks, Papists, even though they hear that there is to be a resurrection, are nevertheless ignorant of the fact how they may take part in the resurrection of the righteous and the saved, think that they can merit eternal life by their own efforts; as we monks have hitherto believed and taught: that if we strictly observed the rules of our orders, prayed much, read mass, etc., God would have respect for such a holy life and in consequence help not only us, but others also, to escape death.

24. This, however, is nothing but a vain human comfort and hope, without any authority of the Word of God; for such power and authority to help ourselves cannot exist within us. Since on account of sin we have become subject to death, so that we cannot even delay bodily death, much less can we save ourselves or work ourselves free from eternal death. This we ourselves have been compelled to experience and testify to by our monkery and work-righteousness. For although we have had to do with these for a long time and comforted ourselves with them, yet at last we found them useless. When once the straits of conscience

were concerned, when we had to struggle and stand before
the judgment of God, all this comfort left the heart and
nothing remained but vain terrified doubts, yea, even con-
vulsions and tremblings on account of the thought: Alas!
I did not live a sufficiently holy life. How shall I be able to
stand before the judgment of God? For it must finally come
to this, that man must feel and become conscious of that
which all the Saints have experienced and confessed, namely,
that no one can stand in the judgment of God on the basis
of his own life, no matter how good it may have been. Of
this the prophet Isaiah speaks, 49, 24: "Shall the prey be
taken from the mighty, or the lawful captives be delivered?"
The "mighty" he calls the power of death, that strangles
and carries away all men and whom no one can resist or rob
of its prey; but by the "lawful captives" he means the law
with its judgment, which is God's judgment and which
rightly holds all men captive, so that no one can free himself
or others from it, but all must, as far as in them be, remain
forever captive under it; for they themselves have merited
such captivity through sin and disobedience, and have fallen
into the righteous and eternal wrath of God.

25. Therefore there is no help from any creature against
this. God himself had to have compassion on our misery
and to conceive a plan for our deliverance, as he said in the
prophecy of Isaiah, 49, 25: "Even the captives of the
mighty shall be taken away, and the prey of the terrible
shall be delivered." This had to be done by Christ, the Son
of God himself, and he therefore became man, that is, took
upon himself death and its cause, sin and the wrath of
God, in order that he might free us from these and bring us
to life and righteousness. For, as by one man both sin and
death came upon all of us; so also by one man must victory
over death, righteousness and life be given to us, as St. Paul
says, Rom. 5, 17.

26. Therefore this work of life has been accomplished in
such a manner that without our effort or work we attain it,
just as we became subject to death without our effort and
work. And in like manner as we did not bring death upon

ourselves, except in so far as we were born of Adam and through the sin of another our flesh and blood became corrupt, so that we also must die; so also can we much less work out and merit redemption from sin and death, that is, righteousness and life, but must be brought to it through the righteousness and life of another one. Therefore, since sin is born in us through Adam and has now become our own; so also must the righteousness and life of Christ become our own, so that this same power of righteousness and life may work in us, as if it had been born in us through him. For it is in him not only his personal, but an actual and powerful righteousness and life; yea, a fountain that gushes forth and overflows for all who have become partakers of him, in like manner as sin and death have gushed into human nature from Adam. It means, therefore, that now all men can be delivered from sin and death and be made alive, not by nor through their own efforts, but apart from themselves through the righteousness and life of this Lord Jesus Christ, namely, if he touches them with his hand and through his Word imparts to them his work and power to destroy sin and death, and provided they believe his Word.

27. For this reason we are called Christians, that is, righteous, living and holy people, because we have this Lord and have become partakers of him through the faith of his Word and Sacrament, who is the true sin-destroyer and death-devourer (I say of our sin and death, which have strangled and devoured us) by virtue of his own power and authority. He did both these things in his own person, inasmuch as he took upon himself our sin and death. But since he was not only without sin and the guilt of death, but in himself was perfect and eternal righteousness, and sin and death had no hold on him, they were condemned and destroyed by him, and pure righteousness and life presented to us in place of sin and death. For after his victorious death and resurrection he established a kingdom in Christendom, in which he now continually until death and the grave destroys sin in his Christians through forgiveness and the power of his Spirit, and begins life in them through

faith, until he can bring them all together on one day, when he will bestow on their perfect righteousness and life, both in body and soul.

28. All this you may see clearly and lovingly presented in this narrative: This youth died, not because he had been a murderer, adulterer or open sinner who had to be punished because of his misdeeds; but before he could have become guilty of sins which those commit who have grown to maturity, and become old, death carried him away only by reason of the sin in which he was born. His mother might well bemoan her own sin, by reason of which she lost her son, who had inherited sin and death from her.

29. But now that he has died, where may counsel or comfort and help be found? Certainly not through the mother's sorrow and tears, which must have been unlimited. If human work and effort could in this case have been of any avail or be meritorious, surely the tears of the widow would have accomplished much more; for they certainly came from a most anxious heart, as of a sorrowing and miserable mother, whose heart was broken by reason of her love for her son, and who would willingly have done and suffered anything, even her own death, in order to have saved her son. And now, that he was dead, she doubtless cherished the secret wish and longing: Ah! if it could be the will of God that my son might still be alive or could again be restored to life. This was so deeply concealed in her heart, that she could not see it herself, yea, she dared not even think of petitioning the Lord for it, and yet her heart was filled with the thought. If she had been asked and had confessed what her greatest desire was and what she would ask of God, she could have said nothing else than: Alas! what should I desire or ask more on earth than that my son might live. And this is a more earnest and heart-felt prayer than any one can express, for it proceeds from a purely inexpressible longing.

30. And yet this is useless both for her as well as all others, and she must cast it aside and remain in doubt; for had she not sighed, wept and prayed most earnestly before

her son died, that she might retain him alive? But since all this was of no avail and her son had died, how much less could she draw hope or comfort from his suffering; she saw clearly that he could not be brought back by sighs and tears. If this were possible, other mothers would have or would still do it.

31. In a word, unbelief fought against her prayer and made it unavailing; and hence contrary to all human thought, hope and effort, her son was restored to her, alone for the reason that the Lord met and had compassion on the poor widow, as the text says, and comforted her not only with friendly words, but also with his power and authority restored her son alive to her; so that she was compelled to say that it was not her merit or that of any human being, but the pure grace and gift of the Lord, and that he was a Lord who is able to do and give "exceeding abundantly above all that we can ask or think," as the Epistle for to-day says, Eph. 3, 20. For this is his way that he always manifests himself towards his saints in a wonderful manner, as Psalm 4, 3 says, and in their distresses hears, delivers and saves them, not according to their own thoughts, hopes and faith, but according to his own divine and almighty power, when human counsel fails and is despaired of.

32. Behold, how the Lord exhibits his work against death when it comes into his presence, and thereby typifies or indicates for our comfort what he will also do for all his people, when, like this youth, they are seized by death. For here you see two processions or companies meeting each other; the one, the poor widow with the dead youth and the people following him to the grave; the other, Christ and those who went with him into the city. The first picture shows what we are and what we can bring to Christ; for this is the picture of the whole world and the way of man on the earth. There is a crowd all of whom must follow death out of the city, and Christ, when he comes, finds nothing else than that which has to do with death.

33. This is the whole essence of human life on the earth, if we look at it in the proper light. There is nothing

but the image and work of death, and constant and daily
approaching death until the last day, since one after another
dies and the rest have to do only with the horrible affair
how one may carry the other to the grave, and others follow daily. They render this service to the dead, in order
that to-day or to-morrow some one else may follow them
also to their graves. Wherefore Christ speaks of the character and order of our earthly life to those whom he calls
into his kingdom, Mat. 8, 22: "Leave the dead to bury their
own dead."

34. Thus you see on this side and in this crowd of the whole
world and of the human race nothing but death. We bring
this with us and with it drag ourselves from our mother's
womb, and all at the same time travel the same road with
one another, only that one precedes or is carried before the
others, and the rest follow after until the last one dies.
Nor is there any deliverance or help for this from any creature, for death rules over them all, as St. Paul says, Rom. 5,
14, and drags all of them along, without the ability to resist.
Yea, with such demonstration and pomp does death do this
that when he overcomes one he defies all the rest who are
alive and carries the dead to the grave, and shows them that
he has them also in his clutches and under his power and
may seize them whenever he will.

35. But on the other hand, you see here also a comforting
counterpart of life, and a glorious and joyous procession of
the Lord Jesus, who does not go out of the city with the
dead, but meets death on his way into the city; not however
as those who return home from the grave, only until they
shall carry another one out. For the Lord does not come
with such thoughts of death, as if he had to fear death
and come under its power; but steps into his presence
and opposes him as the one who has power and authority
over death; first he comforts the poor widow, whose heart
is filled only with death, and tells her to sorrow and weep
no more, speaks other words which no one else can utter,
steps up to the bier, lays his hands on it, requests the bearers
to stand still, and immediately follows with a word and

says: "Young man, I say unto thee, Arise." These words are instantly followed by such power and efficacy that the dead man did not lie as before, but sat up, bound and covered as he was, began to speak and showed that he was no longer dead, but alive.

36. This was a wonderful and quick change from death to life, on the part of the young man. Where the spark of life had long been extinguished and there was truly no sign of life, there are instantly and fully restored breath, blood, sensibility, movement, thought, speech and everything else that belongs to life; and Christ, with one word, turned the sad and sorrowing procession, and the carrying of the dead from the gate of the city, into a joyous, lovely and beautiful procession of life, in which both the youth, who was being carried by four or more to be buried under ground, together with his sorrowing mother, joyously follow the Lord Jesus, accompanied by the whole crowd into the city, forgetting death, the bier and the grave, and speaking joyously and thankfully only of life.

37. But the glory and honor of this work belong only to the Lord Jesus, through whose power and authority alone death can be removed and life brought forth from it, as he also proves. Hence the fame and report concerning Christ, of which this Gospel speaks, saying that it went forth throughout the whole country, is recorded for our consolation and joy overagainst the fear and dread of death, in order that we may know what kind of a Savior we have in Christ. For he so manifested himself on earth in his ministry, office and form of a servant, that he can be known as the Lord both of death and life, to destroy the former and bring the latter to light; that although he often met death and fought with it, as in the case of the daughter of Jairus, and again in that of Lazarus, and at last in his own person, he nevertheless finally overcame and destroyed it.

38. Christ also desires to prove in our death and that of all Christians, since death casts every one of us under the ground and it thinks it has completely swallowed all; as Christ promised and confirmed by his own mouth and word

in John 11, 25: "I am the resurrection and the life; he that believeth in me, though he die, yet shall he live." Again, John 5, 28 says: "The hour cometh in which all that are in the tombs shall hear his voice, and shall come forth." Then only the work, which he has portrayed in this example, shall really begin, which he has put off until that time, since he wishes to complete it not only in cne or a few, but at one time in all, in order to destroy death with one blow, as Isaiah 25, 8 says, so that no one shall forever afterwards be overcome or taken captive by it. This shall then form a truly joyous and glorious procession, when he shall bring together, in a moment of time, all who have died, calling them forth with one word from the earth, dust and ashes, air, water and all other places. and, as St. Paul says, 1 Thess. 4, 14, will bring with himself, as the Head, in an innumerable company all believers, having freed all from death and given them eternal life, and, as Isaiah 25, 8 says, having wiped away all tears from their eyes, so that they may forever and without ceasing praise and glorify their Lord, with everlasting joy, praise and honor.

39. We should also learn to believe this and comfort ourselves in the hour of death and in all other distresses, so that, although we may come to such straits that we neither see nor feel anything else than death and destruction, as in the case of this poor widow, because of her son, yea, even though we may be in the clutches of death, as her son on the bier and on the way to the tomb; yet that we may nevertheless firmly conclude that in Christ we have obtained victory over death and life. For faith in Christ must be so disposed, as the Epistle to the Hebrews, 11, 1, teaches, that it can grasp and hold fast those things that can not, yea those things of which only the antithesis can be seen, as in this case, Christ wants this widow to believe in and hope for life, when he says, "Weep not;" although such faith was indeed weak and small in her, as it also is in us, since she and all the world had in their minds feelings and thoughts that despaired of life.

40. For he desires to teach us that also in our experience

there is nothing in us or apart from us, except **only** corruption and death; but from him and in him only life, which shall swallow up both our sin and death. Yea, the more misery and death are in us, the more and the more richly shall we find comfort and life in him, provided we hold fast to him by faith, to which he spurs us on and admonishes us both through his Word and such examples as the one before us. Amen.

SEVENTEENTH SUNDAY AFTER TRINITY.

This sermon is found in all editions of the Church Postil. Erl. 14, 150; W. 11, 2233; St. L. 11, 1674.

Text: Luke 14, 1-11. And it came to pass, when he went into the house of one of the rulers of the Pharisees on a sabbath to eat bread, that they were watching him. And behold, there was before him a certain man that had the dropsy. And Jesus answering spake unto the lawyers and Pharisees, saying, Is it lawful to heal on the sabbath, or not? But they held their peace. And he took him, and healed him and let him go. And he said unto them, Which of you shall have an ass or an ox fallen into a well, and will not straightway draw him up on a sabbath day? And they could not answer again unto these things.

And he spake a parable unto those that were bidden, when he marked how they chose out the chief seats; saying unto them, When thou art bidden of any man to a marriage feast, sit not down in the chief seat; lest haply a more honorable man than thou be bidden of him, and he that bade thee and him shall come and say to thee, Give this man place; and then thou shalt begin with shame to take the lowest place. But when thou art bidden, go and sit down in the lowest place; that when he that hath bidden thee cometh, he may say to thee, Friend, go up higher; then shalt thou have glory in the presence of all that sit at meat with thee. For every one that exalteth himself shall be humbled; and he that humbleth himself shall be exalted.

CONTENTS: CHRIST HEALS THE DROPSICAL MAN, OR FAITH AND LOVE, THE LAW AND THE RIGHT USE OF THE LAW, AND HUMILITY.

2. All laws bind no farther than love goes. 8f.

3. How and why all laws should be interpreted according to love and our need. 9-11.

4. Love and need abolish all laws. 12-15.

5. How the prophets of the Old Testament explained the law according to the spirit of love and had to suffer much on account of it. 16.

6. Where the laws do not serve love, we should quickly abandon them. 17f.

   * Where a vow conflicts with love, it should be abolished. 17-19.

7. A Christian has power to dispense with all laws. 20.

III. INSTRUCTION IN HUMILITY.

1. What moved Christ to give this instruction. 21.

2. The way and means, by which Christ gave this instruction. 22f.

3. How to defend this instruction against the false interpretation of the Papists. 23-26.

4. An opinion of the interpretation Augustine gives on this instruction. 27.

   * Love and need conquer all laws. 28.

SUMMARY OF THIS GOSPEL: 1. Here you see faith and love together. The heart of the man with the dropsy was right toward Christ; that is faith. Christ had mercy upon him and healed him, that is love.

2. Good works are to serve one's neighbor.

3. Love dispenses with and suspends the public command of God; but the Pharisees did not believe this.

4. The outward Sabbath denotes the inner Sabbath, when we are quiet before God, and let his will be pleasing to us, and he does with us as he pleases. Of this Isaiah and the Epistle to the Hebrews speak.

5. We are all invited to divine grace; but the Pharisees sit high in their pride; because of their pharisaical hypocritical holiness.

1. This Gospel offers us two leading thoughts; one is general and is found in all our Gospel lessons, the other is peculiar to this one. First, in its general character, it shows who the Lord Jesus is and what we may expect of him, and in this is exhibited both faith and love.

2. Faith is here set forth in that this man, sick with the dropsy, looks to Christ and firmly believes he will help him. This faith he had as the result of his previous acquaintance with Jesus. He knows him as a kind, friendly and sympathetic man who always helps everyone and lets none go away uncomforted. Had he not heard such reports about the Lord he would not have followed him, even into the house. He must indeed have had some gospel knowledge and believed the wonderful things spoken about him.

3. And this is the Gospel, as I said, that must be preached and heard before there can be faith. We must know that God is kindly disposed toward us and has sent his Son from

heaven to help us. This the conscience must hear and believe; for if God were unfriendly and unmerciful toward us,
it would avail little to know that all his creatures sympa-
thize with us. If God is satisfied with us, no creature can
do us any harm, as St. Paul says in Rom. 8, 31: "If God is
for us, who is against us?" Let death, devil, hell and all
creation rage; we are safe. Therefore it is the Gospel that
must present to us the God-man as merciful. This is the
fountain from which our heart can draw faith and a friendly
confidence toward God that he will help both the dying and
the living in every distress.

4. We notice this here in the man afflicted with dropsy.
He had heard of the kindness of Jesus to others and
now believes that he will show the same to him. Had
he not believed, it would have been impossible to help him.
The Gospel resounds in all the world, but it is not heard by
everybody. The Pharisees also sat there; they saw these
things with their own eyes and failed not to notice what a
friendly man Jesus was, but they believed not; hence the
Gospel could neither reform them nor give them help and
comfort. Thus the Gospel is very universal, but the true
laying hold of it is very rare. So much in regard to faith.

5. Later we have here pictured to us also the love in Christ
that goes forth and bears fruit, not for itself but for others,
as is the nature of true love to do. This is now said on the
first part of to-day's Gospel.

6. However, this Pericope especially teaches us in the second place a necessary doctrine we must possess, if we are to
make use of the laws that order the outward and temporal
matters and affairs, which the church is to observe. Here
we must act wisely and gently, if we wish to do the right
thing, especially when weak and timid consciences are concerned. For there is nothing more tender in heaven and on
earth, and nothing can bear less trifling, than the conscience.
The eye is spoken of as a sensitive member, but conscience
is much more sensitive. Hence we notice how gently the
Apostles dealt with conscience in divers matters, lest it be
burdened with human ordinances.

7. But as we cannot live without law and order, and as it is dangerous to deal with law since it is too apt to ensnare the conscience, we must say a little about human laws and ordinances and how far they are to be observed. The proverb says: "Everything depends upon having a good interpreter." That is particularly true here where human ordinances are concerned. Where there is no one to interpret and explain the law rightly it is difficult and dangerous to have anything to do with it. Take, for example, a ruler who acts like a tyrant and abuses his authority. If he makes a law and urgently insists on the law being executed, he treats conscience as if he had a sword in his hand and were intent on killing. We have experienced this in the tyrannical laws of popery, how consciences were tormented and hurled into hell and damnation. Yea, there is great danger where one does not know how to temper and apply the laws.

8. Therefore we conclude that all law, divine and human, treating of outward conduct, should not bind any further than love goes. Love is to be the interpreter of law. Where there is no love, these things are meaningless, and law begins to do harm; as is also written in the Pope's book: "If a law or ordinance runs counter to love, it will soon come to an end." This is in brief spoken of divine and human laws. The reason for enacting all laws and ordinances is only to establish love, as Paul says, Rom. 13, 10: "Love therefore is the fulfilment of the law." Likewise verse 8: "Owe no man anything, save to love one another." For if I love my neighbor, I help him, protect him, hold him in honor, and do what I would have done to me.

9. Since then all law exists to promote love, law must soon cease where it is in conflict with love. Therefore, everything depends upon a good leader or ruler to direct and interpret the law in accordance with love.

Take the example of the priests and monks. They have drawn up laws that they will say mass and do their praying and juggle with God in other ways at given hours according to the clock. If now a poor man should call and ask for a service at an hour when they were to hold mass or repeat their prayers, they might say: "Go your way; I must now read mass, must attend to my prayers," and thus they would fail to serve the poor man, even if he should die. In this manner the most sanctimonious monks and Carthusians act; they observe their rules and statutes so rigorously that, although they saw a poor man breathing his last breath and could help him so easily, yet they will not do it. But the good people, if they were Christians, ought to explain the laws and statutes in harmony with love, and say: Let the mass go, let the sacraments, prayers, and the ordinances all go; I will dispense with works, I will serve my neighbor; love put in practice in serving my neighbor is golden in comparison with such human works.

10. And thus we should apply every law, even as love suggests, that it be executed where it is helpful to a fellow-man, and dispensed with where it does harm. Take a common illustration: If there were a housekeeper who made the rule in his home to serve now fish, then meat, now wine, then beer, even as it suits him; but perchance some one of his household took sick and could not drink beer or wine, nor eat meat or fish, and the housekeeper would not give him anything else, but say: No, my rules and regulations prescribe thus; I cannot give you anything else: what kind of a housekeeper would such an one be? One ought to give him sneeze-wort to purge his brain. For if he were a sensible man he would say: It is indeed true that my rules and regulations prescribe meat or fish for the table to-day, yet since this diet does not agree with you, you may eat what you like. See how a housekeeper may adjust his own rules and make them conform to the love he entertains for his household. Thus all law must be applied as love toward a fellow-man may dictate.

11. Therefore, since the Mosaic law was not understood nor modified by love in the Old Testament, God promised the people through Moses that he would raise up a prophet who should interpret the law to them. For thus Moses says in Deut. 18, 25: "Jehovah thy God will raise up unto thee a prophet from the midst of thee, of thy brethren, like

unto me; unto him ye shall harken." God raised up prophets from time to time to explain the law and apply it, not in its rigor, but in love. Of this Moses himself is an example. He led the children of Israel out of Egypt for forty years hither and thither through the desert. Abraham had been commanded in Gen. 17, 12, to circumcise every male on the eighth day. This commandment was plain enough that all had to observe it, yet Moses neglected it and circumcised no one the whole forty years.

12. Now, who authorized Moses to violate this commandment, given to Abraham by God himself? His authority was vested in his knowledge of the law's spirit; he knew how to interpret and apply it in brotherly love, namely, that the law was to be serviceable to the people, and not the reverse. For, if during their journey they had to be ready day by day for warfare, circumcision would have hindered them, and he therefore omitted it, saying in effect: Although this law is given and should be observed, yet we will apply it in the spirit of love, and suspend its operation until we come to the end of our journey. Likewise should all laws be interpreted and applied as love and necessity may demand. Hence the importance of a good interpreter.

13. It was the same in the case of David when he partook of the consecrated bread, which was not lawful for anyone to eat, except the priest, Sam. 21, 6; as Christ himself makes use of this example in Mat. 12, 3. David was not consecrated, nor were his servants. When he was hungry he went to Ahimelech and asked for himself and men something to eat. Ahimelech answered: I have indeed nothing to give; the shew-bread of the tabernacle is for holy use. Then David and his men helped themselves and ate freely of it. Did David sin in the face of God's ordinance? No. Why not? Because necessity compelled him, seeing there was nothing else to eat. It is in this way that necessity and love may override law.

14. That is what Christ also does in our Gospel, when he heals the suffering man on the Sabbath, although he well knew how strictly the Old Testament required the observ-

ance of the Sabbath. But see what the Pharisees do! They stand by watching the Lord. They would not have helped the sick man with a spoonful of wine, even if they could have done so. But Christ handles the law even at the risk of violating it, freely helps the poor man sick with the dropsy and gives the public a reason for his action, when he says, in effect: It is indeed commanded to keep the Sabbath day, yet where love requires it, there the law may be set aside. This he follows up with an illustration from everyday life, then dismisses them in a way they must commend, and they answer him not a word. He says:

"Which of you shall have an ox or an ass fallen into a well and will not straightway draw him up on the Sabbath day?"

15. As if to say: Ye fools, are ye not mad and stupid! If you act thus in the case of saving an ox or an ass which may perhaps be valued at a few dollars, how much rather should one do the same to a neighbor, helping him to his health, whether it be the Sabbath or not! For the Sabbath, as he says elsewhere, was made for man, and not man for the Sabbath. So that the son of man is lord even of the Sabbath, Mark 2, 27.

16. Among the Jews there was a rigorous enforcement of the law, even their kings insisted on its strict observance. When the prophets came and explained the law in the spirit of love, saying: This is what Moses means, thus the law is to be understood, then there were false prophets at hand to side with the kings, insisting on the literal text and saying: There, so it is written; it is God's Word; one must not interpret it otherwise. Thereupon the kings proceeded to kill one prophet after another. In the same way the Papists, priests and monks act now. If anyone says: We need not observe their laws literally, but we should rather interpret them in love; then they immediately cry, Heretic! Heretic!! and if they could they would kill him; yea, they do so already quite lustily.

17. As Christ here treats of the law relating to the Sabbath and makes it subserve the needs of man, so we should treat laws of that kind and keep them only so far as they

accord with love. If laws do not serve love, they may be annulled at once, be they God's or man's commands. Take an illustration from our former darkness and sorrow under the Papacy. Suppose someone had vowed to visit St. Jacob, and he remembers the words: "Pay that which thou vowest," Eccl. 5, 4. He may have a wife, children or household to care for. What should such an one do? Should he proceed to St. Jacob, or remain at home and support his family? There, decide for yourselves which would be most needful and what harmonizes best with the spirit of love. I regard it best for him to remain home at work and attend to the care of his family. For his pilgrimage to St. Jacob, even if that were not idolatrous and wrong in itself, would be of little profit to him, yea, he would spend and lose more than he could gain.

18. Another example. A mother is about to bear a child, who vowed to eat no flesh on Wednesdays, as many foolish women do. And perhaps because of this vow the mother may injure her offspring and her own body. Then the foolish confessional fathers come and say: Dear daughter, it is written in the Scriptures, what one vows, that must be kept; it is God's command and thou must at any peril keep thy vow. Thus the good woman is soon taken captive and chained by her conscience, goes and fulfils her vow, and does harm both to herself and her offspring. Hence both have sinned, those who taught her thus, and the woman in that she did not esteem her love more than her vow, by which she neither served nor pleased God; yea, more than this, she thus provoked God to anger by keeping her vow. Therefore we should say to such a foolish mother: Behold, thou art about to bear a child, and thou must serve it and desist from this foolish thing, so that great harm may not spring from it; for all laws find their end in love.

19. We should act in like manner toward the false priests, monks and nuns. When they say: Yea, we have vowed so and so, and it is written: "Vow, and pay unto Jehovah your God," Ps. 76, 11, then say to them: Look, there is also a command: "Thou shalt love thy neighbor as thyself."

But in your vocation it is impossible to serve your neighbor, nor can you continue in it without sin. Therefore, forsake it openly and enter a state in which you are not so apt to sin, but where you may serve your fellow-man, help and counsel him; and do not bother about a vow which you did not give to God your Lord, but to the devil; not for the salvation of souls and blessedness, but for damnation and ruin of both soul and body.

20. If you are a Christian you have power to dispense with all commandments so far as they hinder you in the practice of love, even as Christ here teaches. He goes right on, although it is the Sabbath day, helps this sick man and gives a satisfactory and clear reason for his Sabbath work.

21. There is yet another thought in this Gospel about taking a prominent seat at feasts, which we must consider. When the Lord noticed how the guests, the Pharisees, chose to sit in the first seats, he gave them the following parable to ponder:

"When thou art bidden of any man to a marriage feast, sit not down in the chief seat; lest haply a more honorable man than thou be bidden of him, and he that bade thee and him shall come and say to thee, Give this man place; and then thou shalt begin with shame to take the lower place. But when thou art bidden, go and sit down in the lowest place; that when he that hath bidden thee cometh, he may say to thee, Friend, go up higher. Then shalt thou have glory in the presence of all that sit at meat with thee."

22. This parable is aimed at the laws and precepts of the Pharisees and scribes which provide that honor should be paid to the great and powerful, giving them the preference and allowing them to sit at the head. Christ here reverses the order and says: "He that would be the greatest, let him take the lowest seat." Not that a peasant should be placed above a prince; that is not what Christ means, nor would that be proper. But our Lord does not speak here of worldly, but of spiritual things, where humility is specially commended. Let rulers follow the custom of occupying the uppermost seats at festive boards, we have to do here with

matters of the heart. Christ does not appoint burgomasters, judges, princes, lords; these stations in life he ignores as subject to civil order and and the dictates of reason. There must be rulers and to them honors are due because of their position; but the spiritual government requires that its participants humble themselves, in order that they may be exalted.

23. Therefore the Lord said to his disciples when they disputed as to who should be the greatest among them: "The kings of the Gentiles have lordship over them, and they that have authority over them are called Benefactors. But ye shall not be so; but he that is the greater among you, let him become as the younger; and he that is chief, as he that doth serve," Luke 22, 25-27. He then speaks of himself as an illustration, asking: "For which is the greater, he that sitteth at meat, or he that serveth? is not he that sitteth at meat? But I am in the midst of you as he that serveth." And in another place, Mat. 20, 26-28, he said: "Whosoever would become great among you shall be your minister; and whosoever would be first among you shall be your servant: even as the Son of man came not to be ministered unto, but to minister, and to give his life a ransom for many."

24. The Papists have commented on these verses in their own way and twisted this Gospel, saying: Yea, the Pope is to be the least or youngest, sitting at the foot and serving others; but that is to take place in the heart. They pretended to sit at the foot and to serve others as the humblest; but withal they lorded it over all emperors, kings and princes, yea, trampled them in the dust; just as if emperors, kings, princes and rulers should not also possess in their hearts the humility of which the Lord here treats. They thus put on airs and make a show of their carnal interpretation. If they had any humility in their hearts their lives would bear testimony to it. Christ speaks here not of outward humility alone, for the inner is the source of the outer; if it is not in the heart it will hardly be manifest in the body.

25. Therefore the Gospel aims at making all of us humble,

whatever and whoever we may be, that none may exalt himself, unless urged and elevated by regular authority. That is what the Lord wants to inculcate by this parable, directing it to all, be they high or low. In this spirit he reproves the Pharisees and others who desire high places and are ambitious to get ahead of others. They may accept honors when regularly elected and forced to accept high places. I make these remarks to contravene and discredit their false spiritual interpretations.

26. But now they go and mingle and confuse spiritual and worldly things, and claim it is enough if they be humble in heart when they strive for the chief seats. Nay, dear friends, heart-humility must manifest itself in outer conduct, or it is false. All should therefore be willing to take a lower seat, even to throw themselves at the feet of others, and not move up higher, until urged to do so. Anyone who regards this rule, will do well; but he who disregards it will come to grief by so doing. That is what our Lord desires to impress upon his hearers as he closes this parable.

"For every one that exalteth himself shall be humbled; and he that humbleth himself shall be exalted."

27. St. Augustine adds a comment here which I wish he had not made, for it savors of vanity, when he says: "A ruler must not abase himself too much, lest his authority be weakened thereby." This is heathenish and worldly, not Christian; but we can pardon it in such a man, for even the saints on earth are not yet entirely perfect.

28. The sum of this Gospel then is: Love and necessity control all law; and there should be no law that cannot be enforced and applied in love. If it cannot, then let it be done away with, even though an angel from heaven had promulgated it. All this is intended to help and strengthen our hearts and consciences. In this way our Lord himself teaches us how we should humble ourselves and be subject one to another. [However concerning this virtue, what true humility is, I have said enough in former Postils c.] Let this suffice on to-day's Gospel.

EIGHTEENTH SUNDAY AFTER TRINITY.

This sermon is not found in the c. edition. Erl. 14, 163; W. 11, 2249; St. L. 11, 1686.

Text: Mat. 22, 34-46. But the Pharisees, when they heard that he had put the Sadducees to silence, gathered themselves together. And one of them, a lawyer, asked him a question, trying him: Teacher, which is the great commandment in the law? And he said unto him, Thou shalt love the Lord thy God with all thy heart, and with all thy soul, and with all thy mind. This is the great and first commandment. And a second like unto it is this, Thou shalt love thy neighbor as thyself. On these two commandments the whole law hangeth, and the prophets.

Now while the Pharisees were gathered together, Jesus asked them a question, saying, What think ye of the Christ? whose son is he? They say unto him, The son of David. He said unto them, How then doth David in the Spirit call him Lord, saying, The Lord said unto my Lord, Sit thou on my right hand, Till I put thine enemies underneath thy feet? If David then calleth him Lord, how is he his son? And no one was able to answer him a word, neither durst any man from that day forth ask him any more questions.

CONTENTS: OF THE LAW AND THE GOSPEL; OR THE TWO GREATEST COMMANDMENTS AND HOW CHRIST IS DAVID'S SON AND DAVID'S LORD.

about their ceremonies. 16-
17.
* A judgment on the state of
the priests and monks. 18.
5. There are but few persons who
understand the law. 19.
6. Whether nature and reason
can understand and fulfil the
law. 20-21.
7. When and how the law is correctly preached. 22.
8. There is no person who fulfils the law of God. 23-26.

* All people are alike in the
inner wickedness of their
hearts. 27.
II. OF THE GOSPEL.
1. The Gospel frees us of an evil
conscience. 28.
2. How the Gospel teaches us to
become free from the law. 29-
31.
* Faith and works. 32.
* To what extent Christ can
be called the son of David.
33-34.

SUMMARY OF THIS GOSPEL: 1. The two commands in this
Gospel, of the love of God and of our neighbor, condemn us all,
not to say anything then that the law justifies us.

2. The Spirit of God alone fulfills the commandment. Therefore
all that pertains to us is against and contrary to the law of God,
as St. Paul says in the third chapter of Romans.

3. Seeing all depends upon love, works do not justify, but faith
alone. Blessed is he who has faith.

4. Christ is both God and man, and David's son and David's
Lord; therefore he is also the only mediator between God and
man, as St. Paul says to Timothy, 1 Tim. 2, 5.

1. This Gospel consists of two questions. In the first the
lawyer on behalf of the other Pharisees asks Christ: Which
is the great commandment in the law? In the second the
Lord asks the Pharisees and the lawyer: Whose son is
David? These two questions concern every Christian; for
he who wishes to be a Christian must thoroughly understand
them. First, what the law is, and the purpose it serves; and
secondly, who Christ is, and what we may expect from him.

2. Christ explains here to the Pharisees the law, telling
them what the sum of the whole law is, so that they are
completely silenced both at his speech and his question, and
know less than nothing of what the law is and who Christ
is. From this it follows, that although unbelief may appear
as wisdom and holiness before the world, it is nevertheless
folly and unrighteousness before God, especially where the
knowledge of the two questions mentioned above is wanting.

For he who does not know how he stands before the law,
and what he may expect from Christ, surely has not the
wisdom of God, no matter how wise and prudent he may
pretend to be. Let us therefore consider the first question,

namely: What the law is; what it commands and how it is to be spiritually interpreted.

3. When the lawyer asked Christ, which was the great commandment in the law, the Lord said to him:

"Thou shalt love the Lord thy God with all thy heart, and with all thy soul, and with all thy mind. This is the great and first commandment. And a second like unto it is this, Thou shalt love thy neighbor as thyself. On these two commandments the whole law hangeth, and the prophets."

4. As if the Lord would say: He who possesses love to God, and love to his neighbor, has all things, and therefore fulfils the law; for the whole law and all the prophets point to these two themes, namely: how God and our neighbor are to be loved.

5. Now one may wish to ask: How can you harmonize this statement, that all things are to be comprehended in these two commandments, since there was given to the Jews circumcision and many other commandments? To answer this, let us see in the first place how Christ explains the law, namely, that it must be kept with the heart. In other words, the law must be spiritually comprehended; for he who does not lay hold of the law with the heart and with the Spirit, will certainly not fulfil it. Therefore the Lord here gives to the lawyer the ground and real substance of the law, and says that these are the greatest commandments, to love God with the heart and our neighbor as ourselves.

From this it follows that he, who is not circumcised, who does not fast nor pray, is not doing it from the heart; even though he may perform external acts, he nevertheless does nothing before God, for God looketh on the heart, and not on our acts, 1 Sam. 16, 7. It will not profit a man at all, no matter what work he may perform, if his heart is not in it.

6. From this arises another question: Since works are of no profit to a man, why then did God give so many commandments to the Jews? To this I answer, these commandments were given to the end that we might become conscious whether we really love God with all our heart, and

with all our soul, and with all our strength, and in addition our neighbor as ourselves; for St. Paul says in Rom. 7, 7 (3, 20), that the law is nothing but a consciousness and a revelation of sin. What would I know of sin, if there were no law to reveal it to me?

Here now is the law that saith: Thou shalt love God with thy heart, and thy neighbor as thyself. This we fulfil if we do all that the law requires; but we are not doing it. Hence he shows us where we are lacking, and that, while we ought really to do something, we are doing nothing.

7. That the Jews had to practice circumcision was indeed a foolish ceremony, yea, a command offensive to reason, even though it were given by God still to-day. What service was it to God, to burden his people with this grievous commandment? What good was it to him, or what service to a neighbor? Yea, and it did not profit the Jew, who was circumcised. Why then did God give the command? In order that this commandment and law might show them whether they really loved God with all their heart, with all their soul, and with all their mind, and whether they did it willingly or not. For if there were a devout heart, it would say: I verily do not know why God gave me circumcision, inasmuch as it does not profit any one, neither God, nor me, nor my neighbor; but since it is well pleasing to God, I will nevertheless do it, even though it be considered a trifling and despised act. Hence, circumcision was an exercise of the commandment, Thou shalt love God with all thy heart.

8. It was also a foolish command God gave to Abraham, to slay his son, Gen. 22, 2. For if reason had been the judge in this, both it and all mankind would have come to no other conclusion than this: It is an unfriendly and hostile command, how can it be from God, since God himself said to Abraham that he would multiply his seed through this son, and it would become as innumerable as the stars of the firmament and as the sand by the sea. Therefore it was a foolish commandment, a grievous, hard and unbearable commandment. But what did Abraham do? He closes his

senses, takes his reason captive, and obeys the voice of God, goes, and does as God commanded him.

By this he proved that he obeyed from the heart; otherwise, even if he had put his son to death a hundred times, God would not have cared for it; but God was pleased that the deed came from his heart and was done in true love to God; yea, it came from a heart that must have thought: Even if my son dies, God is almighty and faithful, he will keep his word, he will find ways and means beyond that which I am able to devise; only obey, there is no danger. Had he not had this boldness and this faith, how could his fatherheart have killed his only and well beloved son?

9. The Jews later wanted to follow this example and, like Abraham, offered their children unto God, hoping thereby to perform a service well-pleasing to God; but it was far from it. These poor people came to the conclusion: The service of Abraham was pleasing to God, therefore will ours also be, and consequently they killed one child after another. O, how many healthy, noble and beautiful children perished! The prophets protested against this service, they preached, warned and wrote against it, telling the people that it was deception, but all was in vain. Yea, many a prophet lost his life because of this, as the history in the books of the kings shows.

10. But why was this service of the Jews displeasing to God? For the reason that it did not come from their heart, and was not done out of love to God; but they simply looked upon the service, and did it without the command and word of God; but God saith: My dear sirs, I was not concerned about the fact that Abraham offered up his son, but that he proved by this act that he loved me with his whole heart. There must be first love in the heart, then follows the service that will be pleasing to God; for all the works of the law tend to the end thereby to prove our love to God, which is in the heart; which love the law requires, and will have above everything else.

11. We are also to notice here that all the works of the law are not commanded merely for the purpose that we

simply just perform them; no, no; for if God had given even
more commandments, he would not want us to keep them
to the injury and destruction of love. Yea, if these commandments oppose the love of our neighbor, he wants us to
renounce and annul them. Take the example of this, I recently gave you: Moses brought the children of Israel out
of Egypt, leading them for forty years through the wilderness, and not one of them was circumcised, although it was
commanded them. Where was their obedience to the commandment? Was God not angry with them because they
did not obey his commandment? No, there was a higher
commandment in force at that time, namely, that they
were to obey God who commanded them to come out of
Egypt in haste to the promised land. By their marching
they daily obeyed God, and God accepted it as obedience;
otherwise he would have been angry, in that they did not
keep his commandments. Both the need and the love were
at hand, which set aside all commandments, for it would
have been unbearable to endure the pain of circumcision
and at the same time the burden of the journey. Therefore
love took the place of the commandment of circumcision, and
thus should all commandments be kept in love, or not at all.

12. In like manner Christ excused his disciples, as is recorded in Matthew 12, 3-4, when the Jews accused them of
transgressing the law, of doing on the Sabbath that which
was not lawful to do on the Sabbath day, when they plucked
the ears of corn and ate them. Then the Lord gave them to
understand that they were doing no wrong, as if to say:
Here is no Sabbath; for the body needs food, necessity demands it; we must eat, even though it be on the Sabbath.
Therefore the Lord cited the example of David, which he
laid before the Jews, and said, "Have ye not read what
David did; he and they that were with him, when he was
an hungered, how he went into the house of God and ate
the shew bread which was not lawful to eat, nor for those
that were with him, excepting for the priests?" 1 Samuel 21,
3f. Then David ate the bread, though he was not a priest,
because hunger pressed him to do it. Neither did Ahimelech

the priest violate the law in giving the bread to David, for love was present and urged him to give it. Thus even the whole law would have had to serve David in his need.

13. Therefore, when the law impels one against love, it ceases and should no longer be a law; but where no obstacle is in the way, the keeping of the law is a proof of love, which lies hidden in the heart. Therefore ye have need of the law, that love may be manifested; but if it cannot be kept without injury to our neighbor, God wants us to suspend and ignore the law.

14. Thus you are to regulate your life and conduct. There are in our day many customs, many orders and ceremonies, by which we falsely think to merit heaven; and yet there is only this one principle, namely: the love to our neighbor, that includes in it all good works. I will give you an example we recently heard. Here is a priest or monk, who is to read his prayers or the rules of his order, or to hold mass, or say penance. At this moment there comes a poor man or woman to him who has need of his help and counsel. What shall this priest or monk do? Shall he perform his service, or shall he assist the poor man? He should therefore act prudently and think: True, I am required to read my prayers, hold mass, or say penance; but now on the other hand, a poor man is here; he needs my help and I should come to his rescue. God commanded me to do this; but the others man devised and instituted. I will let the mandates of men go, and will serve my neighbor according to God's commandment.

15. However, very seldom do we think that the precious service of holding mass and reading prayers should be put in the background; and such a humble service, as you regard it, should have the preference. But what is the reason? The reason is that these dream-preachers, who have nothing to present to us but the ordinances of men, have made us so timid and fearful that we came to the conclusion, if we did not regulate ourselves in everything according to their preaching, heaven itself would fall. Yea, they would rather let ten poor people starve than fail to say one mass.

We find even to-day many monks or priests who rather let a poor man freeze, than violate their statutes and ordinances. So lamentably and miserably have they been deceived by their godless preachers and teachers, and by their superiors, who with their statutes and devilish ordinances have drawn, and are still drawing, them away more and more from the law of God to our own notions.

16. These are the principal fruits of unbelief and godlessness, which, as the Scriptures declare, provoke God. Should not God be angry with me, if he commands me to show my neighbor love, and I go and follow my own or other people's dreams? It is as if a master said to his servant: Go and work in the field, and the servant went and desired to wash the dishes. Should not the master rightly be angry with such a servant? Thus it is also with God. He wants us to keep his commandments, and to regard them more than the commandments of men, and all the commandments to be subservient to love, so that all be comprehended in these two commandments, of which the Lord here speaks in this Gospel: "Thou shalt love the Lord thy God with all thy heart, with all thy soul and with all thy mind, and thy neighbor as thyself."

17. Do you want to do something pleasing to God, then do it out of genuine love. That the Jews practiced circumcision, fasted much, prayed much, and performed other like services, was not pleasing to God, for it did not come from the heart, as this commandment requires: Thou shalt love God with all thy heart. Thus it will be also with you, even though you should belong to the Carthusian friars, or to a still more exacting order; all would avail nothing, if you had not the love of God. From this you are to conclude, all works are nothing, that do not originate in love, or are against love. No commandments should be in force, except those in which the law of love can be exercised.

18. From this it now appears what a misleading calling that of the monks and priests is, in that they wish to merit heaven through their works alone, and they also bind the people to do good works, in order that they may thereby

merit heaven, which is a cursed and godless service. Hence, as already stated, the law is to be only an exercise to prove our love; otherwise, aside from love, God never inquires about works, no matter how excellent they are.

19. You can now see how many people know what the law means: Thou shalt love the Lord thy God with all thy heart, and thy neighbor as thyself. Surely they are few who know it, and fewer still who keep it. How can they keep that which they do not know? We are blind and our nature is totally blind, and so is also human reason. It knows nothing so imperfectly as that which the law of God requires.

20. Now here Christ shows the Pharisees and the Scribes a twofold kindness. In the first place, he dispels their blindness and teaches them what the law is. In the second place, he teaches them how impossible it is for them to keep the law. Their blindness he dispels, in that he teaches them what the law is, namely: that love is the law. Human reason cannot comprehend this nowadays any more than the Jews did then, for if it had been possible for human reason to comprehend it, the Pharisees and Scribes, who at that time were the best and wisest of the people, could have understood it; but they thought it consisted alone in performing the external works of the law; in giving to God, whether it be done willingly or unwillingly; but their inward blindness, their covetousness, and their hardened heart they could not see, and thought they thoroughly understood the law and were fine fellows, holy and pious people; but they stood in their own light. For no one is able to keep the law unless his nature is thoroughly renewed.

21. Therefore consider it an established fact that reason can never understand and fulfil the law, even though it knows the meaning of the law. When do you do to another what you want him to do to you? Who loves his enemy from his heart? Who loves to die? Who willingly suffers disgrace and shame? Dear sir, point me to a man who enjoys to have a bad reputation or to live in poverty! For nature and human reason flee entirely from this, are afraid, terrified

and shocked; and if it were possible, as far as it were in their power, they would never suffer such misfortune. Human nature alone will never be able to accomplish what God in this commandment requires, namely, that we surrender our will to the will of God, so that we renounce our reason, our will, our might and power, and say from the heart: Thy will be done. And indeed, nowhere will you find a person who loves God with his whole heart and his neighbor as himself. It may indeed happen that two companions live friendly together; but even there hypocrisy is hidden, which continues until you are wounded by him; then you will see how you love him, and whether you are flesh or spirit. This commandment therefore requires me to be friendly with all my heart to him who has offended me; but when do I do this?

22. Thus Christ desires to show us that we preach the law rightly, only when we learn from it that we are unable to fufil it, and that we are the property of the devil. This we learn from experience, and it is shown now and then in the Scriptures, especially by St. Paul when he says in Romans 8, 7-8: "Because the mind of the flesh is enmity against God, for it is not subject to the law of God, neither indeed can be," and it follows, that they who are in the flesh cannot please God.

23. Hence, take to thyself this commandment: Thou shalt love the Lord thy God with all thy heart, and think upon it, contemplate it, and search what kind of a law it is; how far you are from fulfiling it, yea, how you have not yet even made a beginning to suffer and to do from the heart what God demands of you. It is pure hypocrisy, if anyone wants to creep into a hiding-place and think: Oh I will love God. Oh, how I do love him, he is my Father! How gracious he is to me! and the like. Yes, when God does our pleasure, then we can easily say such things; but when he sends misfortune and adversity, we no longer regard him as our God, nor as our Father.

24. True love to God does not act in this way, but in the heart it thinks and with the lips says: Lord God, I am thy

creature; do with me as thou wilt; it matters not to me. I am ever thine, that I know; and if thou desirest, I will die this very hour or suffer any great misfortune; I will cheerfully do so from my heart. I will not regard my life, honor and goods and all I have, higher and greater than thy will, which shall be my pleasure all my days. But you will never find a person who will constantly regulate himself according to this commandment; for the whole life you are living in the body, in the five senses, and whatever you do in your body, should all be so regulated as to be done to the glory of God, according to the regulations of this commandment, which saith, "Thou shalt love the Lord thy God with all thy heart, with all thy soul, with all thy mind." As if Christ said: If you love God with all your heart, with all your soul, and with all your mind, then nothing will be lacking; you shall experience it in your daily life, namely: when everything you do, whether you wake or sleep, whether you labor or stand idle, whether you eat or drink, is directed and done out of love to God from the heart. In like manner your mind and thoughts will also be directed wholly and entirely to God, so that you will approve of nothing you are not certain is pleasing to God. Yea, where are those who do this?

25. And this part where he says, "With all thy mind," argues powerfully against the writings and teachings of man, upon which he especially depends, and thinks thereby to obtain a merciful God and merit heaven. Such imagination of the human reason draws us in a wonderful manner from this commandment, so that we do not love God with all the mind; as has been done hitherto, and is still done at the present day. For these priests and monks think nothing else than that God is moved by the mass and by other human inventions; but he abhors it and does not desire it, as is said in Isaiah 29, 13: "In vain do they serve me, because they are teaching such doctrines which are only the commandments of men." Mat. 15, 8-9. The commandment here requires you to consider nothing good that is against God and against everything he has commanded or

forbidden. It thus requires, you to give yourself wholly and entirely to him in all your life and conduct.

26. From this you can conclude, there is no human being who is not condemned, inasmuch as no one has kept this commandment, and God wants everyone to keep it. There we stand in the midst of fear and distress, unable to help ourselves, and the first knowledge of the law is, that we see our human nature is unable to keep the law; for it wants the heart, and if it is not done with the heart, it avails nothing before God. You may indeed do the works outwardly, but God is not thus satisfied, when they are not done from the heart, out of love; and this is never done except man is born anew through the Holy Spirit. Therefore God aims to accomplish through the law nothing more than that we should in this way be forced to acknowledge our inability, fraility and disease, and that with our best efforts we are unable to fulfil a letter of the law. When you realize this, the law has accomplished its work. This is what Paul means when he says in Romans 3, 20, "Through the law is the knowledge of sin."

27. From this it appears clearly that we are all alike, and are one in the inner wickedness of the heart, which the law reveals, when we look into it rightly. Therefore we might well say, If one is good, then all are good. Therefore no one should accuse another. It is indeed true that in public and gross sins there sticks a deeper sin; but the heart is alike bad, unless it be renewed by the Holy Ghost. But what shall I do when I once recognize my sin? What does it profit me? It helps me very much, for when I have come thus far, I am not far from the kingdom; as Christ says to a scribe in Mark 12, 34, who also knew that the works of the law were nothing without love.

28. But what shall we do to get rid of our bad conscience? Here follows now the other part of this Gospel, namely, who Christ is and what we can expect of him. From him we must receive and secure freedom from a wicked conscience, or we shall remain in our sins eternally, because for this purpose is Christ made known and given by the Father, in order

that he might deliver us from sin, death, from a wicked conscience, and from the law.

29. We have now heard what the law is, and how through the law we come to the knowledge of sin; but this is not enough, another has a work to do here, whose name is Christ Jesus; although the first, the law, must indeed remain; yea, it is necessary. For if I have no sense of my sins, I will never inquire for Christ; as the Pharisees and scribes do here, who thought they had done everything the law commanded and were ready to do yet more; but of Christ they knew nothing. Therefore, first of all, when the law is known and sin revealed through the law, it is then necessary that we know who Christ is; otherwise the knowledge of sin profits us nothing.

30. But the law is known, when I learn from it that I am condemned, and see that there is neither hope nor comfort anywhere for me, and I cannot even help myself, but must have another one to deliver me. Then it is time that I look around for him who can help, and he is Christ Jesus, who for this purpose became man, and became like unto us, in order that he might help us out of the mire into which we are fallen. He loved God with all his heart and his neighbor as himself, and submitted his will to the will of his Father, fulfiled the law in every respect; this I could not do and yet I was required to do it. Therefore, he accepts him; and that which he fulfiled in the law, he offers me. He freely gives me his life with all his works, so that I can appropriate them to myself as a possession that is my own and is bestowed upon me as a free gift. He delivers us from the law, for when the law says, Love God with all thy heart, and thy neighbor as thyself, or thou wilt be damned, then I say, I cannot do it. Then Christ says: Come to me, take me and cling to me by faith; then you shall be rid of the law.

31. Now this is accomplished in the following manner: Christ has through his death secured for us the Holy Spirit; and he fulfils the law in us, and not we. For that Spirit, whom God sends into your heart for the sake of his Son, makes an entirely new man out of you, who does with joy

and love from the heart everything the law requires, which
before would have been impossible for you to do. This new
man despises the present life, and desires to die, rejoices in
all adversity, and submits himself wholly and entirely to the
will of God. Whatever God does with him, is well pleasing
to him. This Spirit you cannot merit yourself, but Christ
has secured and merited it. When I believe from the heart
that Christ did this for me, I receive also the same Holy
Spirit that makes me an entirely new man. Then everything God commands is sweet, lovely and agreeable, and I
do everything he desires of me; not in my own strength, but
by the strength of him that is in me, as Paul says in Philip-
pians, 4, 13: "I can do all things through Christ that
strengtheneth me."

32. But you must take heed, that you do not undertake to
secure this faith in Jesus Christ by your own works or
power, or that you think lightly about this matter; for it
is impossible for the natural man; but the Holy Spirit must
do it. Therefore beware of the preachers of selfrighteous-
ness, who simply blabber and say: We must do good works
in order to be saved. But we say that faith alone is sufficient
to this end. Our good works are for another purpose,
namely, to prove our faith, as you have already frequently
heard from me.

33. Now this is the purpose of the question the Lord put
to the Pharisees: What think ye of Christ; who is he and
whose Son is he? But their answer, in that they say, He is
the son of David, the Lord rejects and obscures their answer
and refers to a passage from the Psalm, in order to leave
them in doubt; so that no one is able to answer him a word.

34. However, when David calls Christ his Lord, in that
he says in Psalm 110, "But the lord said unto my Lord,
'Sit thou on my right hand until I make thine enemies thy
footstool,' " it is to be understood that David speaks of him
both as God and man, for according to the flesh alone he
was the son of David. Paul also joins these two when he
says in Romans 1, 1-4: "I am called to be an apostle, separated unto the Gospel of God, which he promised afore

through his prophets in the Holy Scriptures, concerning his Son, who was born of the seed of David according to the flesh; who was declared to be the Son of God with power, according to the Spirit of holiness, by the resurrection from the dead.'' But it is something to know that Christ is Lord; for this has might and power and is especially comforting in the time of affliction. But concerning this I have said more elsewhere and will therefore now close, and pray God for grace.

EIGHTEENTH SUNDAY AFTER TRINITY.

Second Sermon: Mat. 22, 34-46.

This sermon appeared instead of the preceding one in the c edition, and in two pamphlet editions printed at Wittenberg in 1537, titled: "A beautiful sermon on the law and the Gospel." Erl. 14, 178; W. 11, 2268; St. L. 11, 1700.

CONTENTS: THE DOCTRINE CONCERNING THE LAW AND THE GOSPEL; OR THE GREATEST COMMANDMENT AND CHRIST.

I. IN GENERAL.

   1. How and why the doctrine of the law and the Gospel should not be separated from one another. 1-2.

   2. How and why God ordained these doctrines from the beginning that they should remain together. 2.

II. IN DETAIL.

A. The Doctrine of the Law.

   1. Why God gave this doctrine. 2-3.

   2. What one is to think of persons who wish to abolish this doctrine. 4-5.

B. The Doctrine of the Gospel.

   1. Its necessity. 6f.

   2. This doctrine will continue to the day of judgment. 7-8.

   3. The comforting contents of this doctrine. 9f.

   4. Whether this doctrine of the law is abolished by the preaching of the Gospel. 10-12.
     * Of the beginning and completion of the sanctification of believers. 12-13.

III. IN GENERAL THERE WILL BE A NEW TREATMENT OF THE LAW AND THE GOSPEL.

   1. How and why the doctrine of the law and the Gospel must always go together. 14-15.

   2. How and why the doctrine of the law and Gospel must be faithfully enforced in Christendom. 16f.

   3. This doctrine both of the law and of the Gospel have become entirely extinct in the Papacy. 17-18.

   4. In what way these doctrines are to be united with one another. 19f.
     * The two parts of help, which Christ gives us. 20-21.

   5. The doctrine of the law is not sufficient for salvation, the doctrine of the Gospel must come to its help. 22-25.
     * Christ alone aids to salvation. 26.

1. In this Gospel Christ answers the question the Pharisees put to him: Which is the greatest commandment in the Law? and in turn asks them the question: What think ye of the Christ, whose son is he? Thus this Gospel presents to us that

which we continually hear and should hear, so that these
two sermons must continue to be preached in Christendom,
namely: the first, the teaching of the Law or of the ten commandments, and the second, the doctrine concering the grace
of Christ. For if either of these fall it pulls the other
with it; while on the other hand, wherever the one remains steadfast and is faithfully put into practice, it brings
the other with it.

2. And God has ordained that these two themes shall be
preached forever in the Christian Church, yea, they have always since the beginning of the world accompanied one another; they were given to our father Adam, while he was still
in Paradise, and were later confirmed through Abraham,
Moses and the Prophets.

For they are required by the needs of humanity, fallen as
it is under the power of satan, so that we live and move in
sin and are worthy of eternal death. Adam felt and
lamented sin and its injuries; but later the sense of sin soon
weakened and was disregarded, so that the heathen did not
consider it sin although they indeed felt evil lust and desire
in their bodies; but they imagined all that belonged to the
character and nature of man. Yet they taught man should
restrain such lust and desires and not allow them to go too
far; but this nature in itself they did not condemn.

3. Therefore God gave this one simple teaching that reveals what man is, what he has been, and what he should
again become. This is the doctrine of the Law, which Christ
here cites: "Thou shalt love God with all thy heart, etc."
As if to say: Thus thou hast been, and thus thou shalt still be
and become. In Paradise you were in possesssion of the treasure, and were thus created that you loved God with all your
heart; this you have lost; but now you must again become
as you were, or you will never enter the Kingdom of God.
In like manner he speaks clearly and plainly in other places,
Mat. 19, 17: "If thou wouldst enter into life, keep the commandments." Likewise, Luke 10, 28: "This do and thou
shalt live, etc." This must in short be kept; and that we
wish to dispute so much about it amounts to nothing, as if

one might be saved without it, namely, without that which is called loving God with the whole heart and your neighbor as yourself. This divine law must be fulfilled by you as purely and completely as the angels in heaven fulfil it.

4. Therefore it is wrong and not to be allowed, as some in ancient times said and as some stupid spirits now say: Although you do not keep the commandment, and do not love God and your neighbor, yea, although you are even an adulterer, that makes no difference, if you only believe, then you will be saved. No, dear mortal, that amounts to nothing; you will never thus gain heaven; it must come to the point that you keep the commandments, and abide in love toward God and your neighbor. For there it stands briefly determined; "If thou wouldst enter into life, keep the commandments." Again, to the Galatians, 5, 19-21: "Now the works of the flesh are manifest, of which I forewarn you, even as I did forewarn you, that those who practice such things, shall not inherit the Kingdom of Heaven, etc."

5. And Christ wishes this doctrine to be observed by the Christians so that they may know what they have been, what they are still lacking and what they should again become, that they continue not in the misery and filth in which they find themselves now; for if they do, they must be lost.

Christ speaks right out plainly in Mat. 5, 17-18: "Think not that I came to destroy the Law or the Prophets; I am not come to destroy, but to fulfil. For verily I say unto you, the Law must be so taught and observed that not the smallest letter or one tittle of it shall in any wise pass away, till all things be accomplished." Again, Christ says further in Mat. 12, 36: "And I say unto you, that every idle word that men shall speak, they shall give account thereof on the day of judgment." And St. Paul in Rom. 8, 4: "God sent his Son in the flesh that the righteousness, required by the Law, might be fulfilled in us." And in Rom 3, 31: "Do we then make the Law of none effect if we teach man is justified through faith, and not through works. That is far from us; nay, we establish the Law." That is, for this very reason we teach faith, by which the law is fulfilled.

6. For this is indeed a glorious doctrine that teaches what we are to become; but that it may also be realized and not continue to be preached in vain, the other doctrine must be added, namely, how and through what means we may again return to our former state. We return when we hear what we lost in Paradise; when Adam lived in full love to God, and in pure love to his neighbor, and in perfect obedience without evil lust, and that had he remained thus we would still be so; but now, since through sin he fell from this command, we also lie in the same misery, full of sin and disobedience, under God's wrath and curse, and fall from one sin to another, and the Law stands there, holds us guilty, urges and requires us to be pious and obedient to God.

7. What shall we then do here, since the Law continually commands and drives us, and we are powerless? For here my own conscience argues ever against me: Since I am to love God with my whole heart and my neighbor as myself, and I do not do it, I must therefore be condemned and God approves and confirms the sentence of condemnation. Who will counsel me in this instance? I do not know what to counsel you, says the Law; but it decrees and demands plainly that you be obedient.

Here the Prophets come now, and preach Christ, and say: One is coming who will give counsel how man may regain what he lost and again enter the state from which he fell, to which the Law points him. This is the other sermon that should and must be preached until the day of judgment, namely, the help from sin, death and satan, and restoration of our bodies and souls, so that we may come into the state that we love God and our neighbor from our hearts. This is to be done fully and perfectly in the future life, but here in this life it should be commenced.

8. For in the life beyond there will be no longer any faith, but perfect love, and all the Law demands we will do with our whole heart. Therefore we must now preach what we should become and should forever continue to be, namely, that we are to love God and our neighbor with our whole heart. This I will commence, says Christ, and complete, not

alone as to my own person, but I will aid you to make a beginning, and to continue ever in it, until you come where you will also fulfil it perfectly.

9. Now this will come to pass thus. Since we are unable to keep the Law and it is impossible for the natural man to do so, Christ came and stepped between the Father and us, and prays for us: Beloved Father, be gracious unto them and forgive them their sins. I will take upon me their transgressions and bear them; I love thee with my whole heart, and in addition the entire human race, and this I will prove by shedding my blood for mankind. Moreover, I have fulfilled the Law and I did it for their welfare in order that they may partake of my fulfilling the Law and thereby come to grace.

10. Thus there is first given us through Christ the sense that we do not fulfil the Law and that sin is fully and completely forgiven: however, this is not bestowed in a way or to the end, that we in the future need not keep the Law, and may forever continue to sin, or that we should teach, if we have faith then we need no longer to love God and our neighbor. But there is bestowed upon us the sense that the fulfilling of the Law may now for the first time be successfully attempted and perfectly realized, and this is the eternal, fixed and unchangeable will of God. To this end it is necessary to preach grace, that man may find counsel and help to come to a perfect life.

11. But the help offered us is, that Christ prays the Father to forgive us our sins against this Law, and not to impute what we are still indebted. Then he promises also to give the Holy Spirit, by whose aid the heart begins to love God and to keep his commandments. For God is not gracious and merciful to sinners to the end that they might not keep his Law, nor that they should remain as they were before they received grace and mercy; but he condones and forgives both sin and death for the sake of Christ, who has fulfilled the whole Law in order thereby to make the heart sweet and through the Holy Spirit to kindle and move the heart to begin again to love from day to day more and more.

12. Thus begins in us not only love, but also truth, that is, a true character, as the Law requires; like St. John says in 1, 17, that Christ is full of grace and truth, and through him grace and truth grow in us, which neither Moses nor the law can give us. For the Law is not abolished thus by grace, that the truth is to be overlooked, and that we should not love God; but through him we experience that we do not as perfectly keep the Law as we ought in the kingdom of forgiveness or of grace. But besides the Holy Spirit is given us, who kindles a new flame or fire in us, namely, love and desire to do God's commandments. In the kingdom of grace this should begin and ever grow until the day of judgment, when it shall no longer be called grace or forgiveness, but pure truth and perfect obedience. In the meantime he continues to give, forgive, to bear and forbear, until we are laid in our graves.

13. Now if we thus continue in faith, that is, in what the Holy Spirit gives and forgives, in what he begins and ends, then the fire on the judgment day, by which the whole world is to be consumed, will cleanse and purify us, so that we will no longer need this giving and forgiving, as if there were something unclean and sinful in us, as there really is at present; we will certainly be as the brightness of the dear sun, without spot and defect, full of love, as Adam was at the beginning in Paradise.

Thus will it then be truly said, the Law is established and fulfilled, Rom. 3, 31. For it will then no longer blame and rebuke us; but the Law shall be considered satisfied, and the debt paid, even by ourselves; since all is now fulfilled, not through us, and yet by it we are freed and saved, so that we creep under Christ's mantle and wings, that he makes satisfaction for us until we lie under the earth and then come again out of the grave with a beautiful, glorified body that will be nothing but holiness and purity, with a cleansed soul full of the love of God. Then we will no longer be in need of his mantle and of his prayers, but we will all be there perfect and complete, as we should be. Now, since I believe in him, my sins are forgiven and I am called a child of grace. And moreover, the truth also should arise in me, that is, a new righteous character, that shall continue until it perfects me; since Christ, the truth, has come, not to destroy the Law, but to establish it, not only in himself, which was done long ago. but in me and in all Christians.

14. These are the two doctrines that should accompany one another, since they belong together or the one is in the other, and they must always go together as long as we live here, by which the Law or God's commandment may begin to work in Christians, so that the wicked, disobedient persons of the world may be restrained and punished. Since they will not fear and love God like Christians and believers, they are obliged to fear eternal fire, perdition and other punishments. Others, however, will be taught by it from what they have fallen and how sorely and fully they have inherited sin.

15. For when I compare my life with the Law I see and experience always the contrary of what the Law enjoins. I shall entrust to God my body and soul, and love him with my whole heart; yet, I would rather have a dollar in my chest than ten gods in my heart, and I am happier when I know how to make ten dollars, than when I hear the whole Gospel. Let a prince give a person a castle or several thousand dollars, what a jumping and rejoicing it creates! On the other hand, let a person be baptized or receive the communion which is a heavenly, eternal treasure, there is not one-tenth as much rejoicing. Thus we are by nature; there is none whc so heartily rejoices over God's gifts and grace as over money and earthly possessions; what does that mean but that we do not love God as we ought? For if we trusted and loved him, we would rejoice more that he gave us the sense of sight than if we possessed the whole world. And the word of consolation he speaks to me through the Gospel ought to give me higher joy than the favor, money, wealth and honor of the whole world. But that it is not so and ten thousand dollars can make people happier than all the grace and possessions of God, proves what kind of fruit we are, and what a distressing and horrible fall it is in which

we lie. And yet we would not see nor realize it, if it were not revealed to us through the Law, and we would have to remain forever in it and be lost, if we were not again helped out of it through Christ. Therefore the Law and the Gospel are given to the end that we may learn to know both how guilty we are and to what we should again return.

16. This now is the Christian teaching and preaching, which, God be praised, we know and possess, and it is not necessary at present to develop it further, but only to offer the admonition that it be maintained in Christendom with all diligence. For satan has continually attacked it hard and strong from the beginning until the present, and gladly would he completely extinguish it and tread it under foot. For he cannot endure that the people continue in it and conduct themselves uprightly and he seeks a hundred thousand arts and wiles only to crush it. Therefore I so gladly preach it, as it is greatly needed; for until the present it has never been heard nor known in the Papacy.

17. For I myself was a learned doctor of theology and yet I never understood the ten commandments rightly. Yea, there were many highly celebrated doctors who did not know whether there were nine, ten or eleven commandments, and much less did we know the Gospel and Christ. But the only thing that was taught and advocated was: Invoke the Virgin Mary and other saints as your mediators and intercessors; fast often and pray much; make pilgrimages, enter cloisters and become monks, or pay for the saying of many masses and like works. And thus we imagined when we did these things we had merited heaven.

18. That was the time of blindness when we knew nothing of God's Word, but led ourselves and others into misery by our own idle talk and dreams. And I was one of those who indeed bathed in this sweat or in this bath of anxiety. Therefore let us give heed that we may thoroughly grasp and retain this doctrine, if other fanatics and false spirits wish to attack it, so that we may be fore-armed and learn, while we have the time and the beloved sun again enlightens us, and buy while the market is at our door. For it will come to this

when once these lights, which God now gives, have departed, satan will not take a furlough until he raises up other fanatical spirits to do harm; as he has already commenced to do in many places during our generation.   What will take place after we are gone?

19. Therefore learn, who can learn, and learn well, so that we may know, first the ten commandments, what we owe to God.   For if we do not know this, then we know nothing and we will not inquire about Christ in the least. Just like we monks did who either held Christ to be an angry judge or despised him entirely in the face of our imaginary holiness.   We fancied we were not in sin, which the ten commandments show and punish; but we had the natural light of reason and free will, and if we lived according to that, as much as we were able, then God would have to bestow upon us his grace, etc.   But now, if we are to know Christ as our helper and Savior, then we must first know, out of what he can help us, not out of fire or water, or other bodily need and danger, but out of sin and the hatred of God.   But whence do I know that I lie drowned in misery? From no other source than from the Law, that must show me what my loss and disease are, or I will never inquire for the physician and his help.

20. Thus we have both parts of the help of Christ: the one, that he must represent us over against God and be a cloak to cover our shame, as the one who takes upon himself our sins and disgrace; a cloak, I say, for us, as the one who takes our sins and shame upon himself, but before God a throne of grace in whom there is no sin or shame; but only virtue and honor.   And like a hen he spreads out his wings against the buzzard, the devil with his sin and death, so that God for his sake forgives all, and to us he can do no harm. But on the condition that you only remain under these wings.   For while you are under his mantle and protection and do not come out from under it, sin that is still in you must not be sin for the sake of him who covers you with his righteousness.

21. Then in the second place Christ does not only thus

cover and protect us, but he will also nourish and feed us as the hen does her little chickens, that is, he gives us the Holy Spirit and strength, to begin to love God and to keep his commandments. And this shall continue to the last day when faith and this cloak of shame will cease, so that we will behold the Father without any medium or covering, and we ourselves stand before him, and there will be no longer any sin in us to be forgiven; but all will be again restored and brought back or perfected, as St. Paul says in Acts 3, 21, purified and perfect, what satan from the beginning disturbed and ruined.

22. Now Christ wishes to teach this by his answer and the question, with which he in reply upbraided the Pharisees. As if he should say, you know nothing more than to speak of the Law, which teaches you that you should love God and your neighbor and yet you do not understand it; for you imagine you have fulfilled it, though you are still far from doing so. Just like the one in Mat. 19, 20-21, who boasts he had kept all the commandments from his youth; but Christ says to him: "If thou wouldst be perfect, go sell that which thou hast, and give to the poor." This is as much as to say: Whoever will love God aright and keep his commandments, must be able to sacrifice his possessions, body and life. Therefore another thing is necessary, Christ will say, for you to know, namely, that you know and possess the man called Christ, who helps us to the end that this doctrine of the Law may be established and perfected in you.

23. But what does it mean to know Christ aright? This the Pharisees and scribes do not know; for they do not consider him more than David's son, that is, he who is to sit on David's throne (as born from his flesh and blood) and is lord and king, also greater and mightier than David was, and yet only to be a temporal ruler to make his people the lords of the world and bring all heathen under his rule, etc. But that they should need him in their lost state, to help them out of sin and death, of that they knew nothing. Therefore the Holy Spirit must teach that he was not only

David's son, but also God's Son, as was taught after his resurrection.

24. Now here Christ does not explain this, but he only broaches that David in Ps. 110, 1, called Christ his Lord: "How then," he says, "doth David in the Spirit call him Lord?" It does not sound right and it is against nature for a father to call his son lord, and to be subject to him and serve him. Now David calls Christ his Lord, and a Lord, to whom Jehovah himself says: "Sit thou at my right hand until I make thine enemies thy footstool," that is, be like me, acknowledge and worshipped as the right and true God; for it becometh none other to sit at his right hand; he is indeed so jealous that he allows no one aside from himself to sit equal to him, as he says in the prophesy of Isaiah 48, 11, "My glory will I not give to another." Since Jehovah now places Christ equal with himself, he must be more than all creatures. Therefore he proposes to them a great question, but lets them thus stick; for they did not understand it and it was not yet the time to make this known public. But the meaning is as our articles of faith teach us to believe; that Christ was both David's true natural son of his blood and flesh and also David's Lord, whom David himself must worship and hold as God. However it was impossible to make these statements harmonize, as it is still impossible for human reason, where the Holy Spirit does not reveal it, how the two should be at the same time in the one Christ, both that he was truly David's seed and God's Son by nature.

25. Now Christ propounded this question to teach it is not enough to have the Law which is the only thing that shows from what state we have fallen; but whoever will return again to it and become renewed, that Christ must do through a knowledge of him, who is indeed born of David and is his flesh and blood, but not born in sin, as David and all men are born, but had to be born without man of a drop of the pure blood of a virgin, sanctified by the Holy Spirit, that he was born a real and true man without any sin.

26. He is the only man that has been able to keep and ful-

fill the Law; like all other men by nature, and yet not in the same guilt, but reared without sin and God's wrath. This one had to intercede in our behalf before God and be our right hand and protection, be to us what the hen is to her little chickens, in whom we have forgiveness of sins and deliverance from God's anger and hell. And not only this, but he also gives us the Holy Ghost to follow him, and here begins to extinguish and slay sin, until we come to him and be like him without any sin and in perfect righteousness; for he was raised from the dead to the right hand of the Father to totally abolish sin, death and hell and bring us to the new eternal righteousness and eternal life. Amen.

NINETEENTH SUNDAY AFTER TRINITY.

This sermon, which is not found in the c. edition, was issued in pamphlet form under the title: "A sermon on the ninth chapter of the Gospel of Matthew; The Kingdom of Christ, which consists in the forgiveness of sins; the trying of the spirits; the efficacy of the faith of others; The twofold power on earth to forgive sins. Martin Luther, Wittenberg, 1525." Erl. 14, 190; W. 11, 2281; St. L. 11, 1710.

Text: Mat. 9, 1-8. And he entered into a boat, and crossed over, and came into his own city. And behold, they brought to him a man sick of the palsy, lying on a bed: and Jesus, seeing their faith said unto the sick of the palsy, Son, be of good cheer; thy sins are forgiven. And behold, certain of the scribes said within themselves, This man blasphemeth. And Jesus knowing their thoughts said, Wherefore think ye evil in your hearts? For which is easier to say, Thy sins are forgiven; or to say, Arise, and walk? But that ye may know that the Son of man hath authority on earth to forgive sins (then saith he to the sick of the palsy), Arise, and take up thy bed, and go unto thy house. And he arose, and departed to his house. But when the multitudes saw it, they were afraid, and glorified God, who had given such authority unto men.

CONTENTS: JESUS CURES THE MAN SICK OF THE PALSY; OR THE KINGDOM OF CHRIST, THE FAITH OF OTHERS; AND THE POWER TO FORGIVE SINS.

main on the true road of the kingdom of Christ. 10.

6. What persons belong to this kingdom and who do not. 11.

7. The whole kingdom of Christ consists in two words. 12-14.

* The raging spirit of the world against the Gospel.

 a. The first characteristic of this spirit. 16.

 b. The second characteristic. 17.

 c. With what should Christians comfort themselves in the presence of this spirit. 18.

8. By what is Christ's kingdom maintained and increased. 19f.

 * Of faith and works. 19-21.

 * The whole life of a Christian must be in accord with the Word. 21.

 * What answer should we give to the Papists when they reproach the Protest-

ants, that they perform no miracles. 23.

II. THE FAITH OF OTHERS.

1. Whether children are baptized upon the faith of others or whether they have their own faith. 24-25.

2. The faith of others avails nothing for salvation. 25.

3. How far the faith of others help and to what does it serve. 26.

4. Children must be saved not through the faith of others, but through their own faith. 27.

III. THE POWER TO FORGIVE SINS.

1. The nature of this power. 28.

2. All Christians have this power. 29.

3. How a Christian should make this power to be of benefit to himself. 30-31.

THE SUMMARY OF THIS GOSPEL: 1. The faith of others brings faith to sinners, but it will soon require their own faith; for Christ says to the sick of the palsy: Be of good cheer; that is, only believe, and have a good heart, there is no need or distress.

2. The world and the flesh in their wisdom set themselves against the Gospel. The natural man does not believe that the forgiveness of sins is through Christ.

3. The outward miracle and signs one sees with the eyes, are only signs of the inner healing, and a publishing of the forgiveness of sins.

4. We are certain that we have the forgiveness of sins through Christ. But how are we assured of this? First, from his invitation and promise: for he is true and faithful. Secondly, from his power; for he is God.

1. My friends in Christ, as we hear and enjoy this Gospel every year, I hope you also understand it, and know what it teaches us, and may God grant that the right life may also follow this knowledge! For the greater part of the Gospel we hear only with the ear, and we know it, but do not live according to it, whereas it should be so taught that few words and nothing but life would be the result. But what shall we do for it? We can do no more than preach it and no further raise it and carry it, we must preach and urge it until God comes and gives us his grace to the end that our words be few and that life may spring forth

and grow. The first theme here offered us is the Gospel
when Christ says:

"Son, be of good cheer; thy sins are forgiven."

2. These words show and contain in brief what the kingdom of Christ is, namely, this sweet voice, these motherly
and fatherly words penetrating our inmost soul: "Thy sins
are forgiven." In no other sense are we to view the kingdom of Christ, so far as it is understood, than how we
are to live before God. As you, beloved, well know that
our highest duty is rightly to establish the conscience that
we may know how we stand before God and our neighbor.
Therefore we must also hold fast to these words and become accustomed to the expression: "Son, be of good cheer,
thy sins are forgiven", and like sayings of which the Gospel
is full.

3. From this it follows that the kingdom of Christ is
realized where nothing but comfort and the forgiveness of
sins reign not only in words to proclaim it, which is also
necessary; but also in deed, as we shall see in this example.
For he did not only speak these words into the ear of this
sick man; but he also forgave his sins and comforted him.
This knowledge is proper for us Christians to know. It is
indeed easily and quickly said and heard; but when it comes
to the test the light is early extinguished, and satan soon
leads us astray; as you here observe that the scribes undertake to destroy this knowledge. I have before often said
and will always say, that you should beware and properly
learn the character and nature of the kingdom of Christ.
For you know how reason is inclined in its every movement to fall from faith and from this knowledge to works.
But here you see no works at all, no merit, here there is
neither command nor law; there is nothing more than the
offering of Christ's assistance, his comfort and his grace,
only kindness meets the man sick of the palsy.

4. Therefore, if the kingdom of Christ is to grow, we
must keep out of it with the law, and not be busy with
works; for it is not in harmony with it to say: Go out and
run hither and thither and atone for your sins; you must

observe and do this and that, if you will be free from sin; but directly without any work and law, out of pure grace, your sins are forgiven. Therefore, it is beyond the sphere of the kingdom of Christ to urge the people with the law.

5. But we receive such things only with the ear and on the tongue, and it enters not into the depth of the heart; for sin at all times still hangs about our necks, it clings firmly to us, as St. Paul speaks of this in Romans, 7, 18-19, and Heb. 12, 1. But in death we will experience it. Of this class are at present our fanatics who boast of the Holy Spirit, and pretend they would do better, some of whom are also in our midst, listen to us and contend that it is not enough for us to preach only faith and love. Yea, they say, You must do better and climb much higher. How high then must I climb? You must destroy pictures, you must kill the ungodly, and do whatever they propose. This filth now enters nearly every community where the Gospel has just been planted. These tares of satan will also come to us, as I have often warned you. Take heed that you remain sound in your knowledge, in the true doctrine of Christ, for this knowledge and light is soon lost.

6. Thus I say, my friends, and would beseech you not to esteem that spirit great who proposes to you any kind of work, call it what you may, even if it would raise the dead, which they have not yet been able to do. And how is it that they say: we must kill the godless! Even if Moses commanded it that you must really do it, what sort of Christians are you then? But by this you shall truly experience which spirits are of God, and which are not. For if you give me a work to do, it is not the Holy Spirit who does it; but he goes and first brings me the grace of Christ, and then leads me to works. For thus he speaks: Thy sins are forgiven, be of good cheer, and the like. He does not first insist on works, but first leads up to God through his sweet Word and grace, and does not immediately refer you to do some work; but later you will find works enough to do unto your neighbor.

7. But the fanatics soon torment us with works, and pro-

fess to have a nobler spirit; they urge and insist upon our doing something first of all, and permit faith and love to be overlooked. This of course is not of the Holy Spirit. Christ first takes possession of the conscience, and when it is right in faith toward God, then he also directs us to do works toward our neighbor. But he first highly extols faith and keeps works in the background. This they cannot understand. I would forgive them everything, if they would only not patch and mend their good works, to which they trust their existence, honor and fame. I would not care about their destroying all pictures, and melting cups and bells into one mass; but that they should make a matter of conscience out of it for those who do not destroy pictures, just as though the Holy Spirit or faith were not present unless this work be performed.

8. I say this: Even if it were a work which God at this present hour commanded, I would not so insist upon it and condemn those who do not immediately obey it; and would find him some kind of protection, as that he is yet perhaps weak, and thus spread over him the kingdom of grace. Let us be conscious of the fact that the work among them is directed to God, and not toward our neighbor. They make their works a necessity and say: If you do this, then you are a Christian; if you will not do it, you are no Christian. Where this or that is done there are Christians. And the fame follows their work, that they want to be esteemed better than others. Now you have the true light, therefore be warned. Prove the spirits. We do not wish to prefer ourselves, as these persons do; but we boast in this, that we hear the Word, "Son, be of good cheer, thy sins are forgiven." I know that I have a gracious God; but these spirits cannot do this. Therefore it is a mere devilish apparition that they carry from house to house. In this they lie against the Holy Spirit, and blame the Holy Ghost that he is the father of their cause. And even if the works were good, the forcing and compelling must remain in the background. Let them then keep quiet about setting us an example by their crazy works.

9. The kingdom of Christ consists in finding all our praise and boast in grace. Other works should be free, not to be urged, nor should we wish by them to become Christians, but condescend with them to our neighbor. Thus we should hear this Gospel to hold fast to its expressions so that they may be written in our hearts, that this light, this Word and lamp may truly shine in us, by which we can judge all other doctrines. Thus he says to the man sick with the palsy: "Thy sins are forgiven". These and similar words are to be taken to heart and meditated upon, since they are nothing but pure grace, and no work, by which the conscience is oppressed and forced to do something. Thus, with these words you must protect yourselves against false teachers.

10. We have now sowed a little of the Word, and this the devil cannot stand, for he never sleeps; the worms and the beetles will come and infect it. Yet so it must be, Christ will prove his Word, and examine who has received it and who not. Therefore let us remain on the right road to the kingdom of Christ, and not go about with works and urge and force the works of the law, but only with the words of the Gospel which comfort the conscience: Be happy, be of good cheer, thy sins are forgiven.

11. By this observe how narrow and how wide the kingdom of Christ is. Few there be who so receive the Word that it tastes good to them and judge themselves by it, and who understand what is said by: "Thy sins are forgiven." If we are now in the kingdom of Christ why then does he mention sin? Are sins always there? No one belongs to this kingdom unless his sins are revealed to him by the Gospel, otherwise these words apply to no one: "Thy sins are forgiven." Indeed all hear the Gospel, but it does not enter the hearts of all, for they do not all feel their sins. But the Gospel preaches that everything we have in us is sin. Therefore it also offers comfort; forgiveness of sins is here. If I am to receive forgiveness of sins, I must have knowledge of sin.

12. Forgiveness of sins is nothing more than two words,

in which the whole kingdom of Christ consists. There must
be sins, and if we are conscious of them, we must confess
them; when I have confessed them, forgiveness and grace
are immediately present. Before forgiveness is present
there is nothing but sin. This sin must be confessed that
I may feel and know that all that is in me is blindness;
otherwise forgiveness of sins could not exist where there
is no sin. However, there is no lack of sins to confess, but
the lack is in not feeling and knowing our sins to confess
them; then only forgiveness of them follows. But it is
quite a different thing when God forgives sins, than when
one man forgives another. One man forgives another his
sins in a way that he thinks of them again tomorrow, or
casts them up to him. But when God forgives sins it is
quite a different thing than when man forgives. For God
condemns no more, he banishes all wrath from him, yea, he
no more thinks of the sin, as he himself says in the prophet
Isaiah, 43, 25. Now if this wrath is gone, then hell, the devil,
death and all misfortune that the devil may bring with
him, must also disappear; and instead of wrath God gives
grace, comfort, salvation and everything good that he himself is.

13. Sin is pure unhappiness, forgiveness pure happiness.
The divine majesty is great, great is also that which it forgives. As the man is, so is also his forgiveness. But you
must know in your heart how great these words are in
which you know how to trust, yea, for which you can cheerfully die. But only few rightly receive these words, therefore there are but few true Christians.

14. This then is the kingdom of Christ, and he who
possesses it thus, possesses it in the right way. Here there
is no work, but only the acknowledgment of all our misfortune, and the reception of all the gifts of God. Here
there is nothing but simple comfort, here the words are continually heard: Be joyful, let not your conscience be troubled
because of sin, or because you have not done a great amount
of good; I will forgive you all. Therefore it is not by merit,
but it is a simple gift. This is the Gospel, upon which

faith depends, through which you grasp and keep these
words, so that they may not have been spoken in vain.
For we have no other comfort of which God tells us to
boast than that God says: "Be of good cheer. be comforted;
for I forgive thy sins; and in my forgiveness you can glory
and rejoice." Here then you have reason to boast and rejoice, but not in your own works.

15. This the workrighteous person cannot do, for honor
always follows, as they have said: Honor follows virtue as
the shadow follows the man. If it is the honor of works,
whether man or God has commanded them, it is nothing;
if it is the honor of the works God does in us it is all right,
as Psalm 118, 16 says: "The right hand of Jehovah is
exalted; the right hand of Jehovah doth valiantly." As
though he should say: "In this will I boast and glory, namely, in that he has exalted me out of death, hell and all evil."
Workrighteous people have not this glory, for they have
not the Word; but as the work is, so is the praise, they urge
and compel us to depart from the Word to human work.
But the Holy Spirit urges us from our works to the Word.
The former boast of their works, the latter, where the Holy
Spirit is, rejoice internally in the heart with God, that he
has done this work, and they remain clinging to grace, and
attribute nothing at all to their own works.

16. Thus the scribes do here. When they heard these
words they said among themselves: *"This man blasphemeth."*
For this is the nature of the holy Gospel and the true Word
of God where it is truly believed, that it is blasphemed on
both sides, and the whole world would destroy it; as was
the case in the time of the Apostles, and as our raging
princes now do, who simply wish it were dead, entirely
crushed and destroyed with all those who preach and confess
it. This however is the least persecution.

17. The other persecution is much worse, which takes
place among us as it also did in Apostolic times among the
Apostles. So too our country squires, who enjoy the Gospel
with us, and do not want to be followers of the Pope, but to
be regarded as Christians; they must plunge into it; so furi-

ous they are that they boast of the Gospel, and yet they trust in their works. And here the Holy Spirit must be called the devil, there the beautiful spirit. But we must venture to say: Their cause is not just; then they will say again: Your cause is not right; for the wicked spirit does not rest unless it is praised. We have a Lord of protection, he will successfully accomplish his work.

18. Paul calls all false spirits bold and proud. Yes, in their filth with their protectors they are proud and impudent, otherwise they are the most cowardly villains that can be found. When they are to appear and answer for their conduct, they cannot produce a single answer. Among themselves they are bold, and venture to catch God in his own Word; but when it comes to the test, they simply despair. But the Holy Spirit stands firm, checks their buffeting, makes us bold and courageous, comforts weak consciences and says: "Be of good cheer, thy sins are forgiven." The true spirit is bashful, and becomes bashful in the sight of God, as Christians do who bow before God, honor him and are not proud. But before tyrants the Holy Spirit encourages them so that they fear neither tyrants nor devils, and are not frightened even if they tore their heads from their shoulders. But in God's presence they fear and tremble like a rustling leaf. But, alas, I see the great mass of people are only concerned about continually hearing without understanding what is said, and when the time comes that they should give an answer, they stand like the pipers and can answer nothing. And thus we also go forth to execution. We must endure such assaults and factious spirits and cannot change it. Nevertheless, we may well comfort ourselves with the thought that we have the true foundation, that our cause is right and theirs wrong. This they also know well enough, and for this reason they can never be bold except among themselves, and there they may boast as long as they please.

19. But the kingdom of Christ consists in this and thereby grows, namely, that the conscience be comforted with the Word. What else takes place through works and laws,

all pertains to our neighbor. For I need no works before God, and must only be careful rightly to confess my sins. Then I have forgiveness of sins and am one with God, all which the Holy Spirit works in me. Then I break forth with blessings toward my neighbor, as they did here who brought the man sick with the palsy to the Lord. Those were in the kingdom, or show who are in the kingdom, as the Evangelist says. that the Lord had respect unto their faith. For had they not had any faith, they would not have brought the sick to the Lord. Faith precedes works, works follow faith. Therefore, because they are in the kingdom by faith, they bring in the sick man and thus do the work.

20. On this earth man lives not for the sake of works, in order that they may be profitable to him, for he is not in need of them. But if you do good works in order thereby to obtain and merit something from God, all is lost, and you have already fallen from this kingdom. But since you believe and continue to live you ought to know that you live for this very cause, namely, to carry in the sick man. God does not desire the Christian to live for himself. Yea, cursed is the life that lives for self. For all that one lives after he is a Christian, he lives for others. So these also do who bring in the sick man, they no longer live for themselves, but their lives serve others; yes, with their faith they win for the sick man a faith of his own. For this sick man had at first no faith, but after he heard the Word, Christ instills into him a faith of his own, and awakens him with the Gospel; as he is accustomed to instill faith by the Word.

21. Thus all works should be done, only to the end that we may see how they agree with the service for other people, to bring them to a true faith and lead them to Christ. If I tear down the pictures in churches that men may see a Christian is present, that is of no profit to the people, nor does it preach how to become free from sin; but he only desires praise, which does not lift up the consciences, and only makes the people gape, with ears, eyes and mouths

wide open. It is a contemptible art to demolish pictures. But to know the kingdom of Christ that I or others may be benefited, this is well done. But you will not accomplish this even if you tear down all the churches, but only by hearing the words: Son, be of good cheer, thy sins are forgiven; then by bringing others to God's Word.

22. The Word must be enforced, it must be beaten into men, here I must eat and drink, adorn and clothe myself, not that I may live, but that I may enforce the Word. For where the life of a Christian is not centered in the Word, it is not right. I am required to aid the conscience with the Word. I must give my neighbor meat and drink and do all I can for him in order to reach the chief thing, namely, to encourage the conscience, as they do here, who assist the sick man to recover his bodily health. And although it is a kindness or work to his body, nevertheless they so help him that his soul is also strengthened. Thus I feed the hungry, give the thirsty drink, clothe the naked, and the like. Yet I do this not only that he may eat and drink, but that I may secure the opportunity to tell him the Word, and thus also to bring him to Christ. These works are outside the kingdom, done to those who are not in the kingdom, in order to bring them into the kingdom.

23. Thus the Holy Spirit preaches, but the mad spirit of the separatists only desires to perform great wonders, to see and do miracles and signs. It is miracle enough that people learn by our preaching to know Christ and obtain a joyful conscience. Likewise, that I learned monachism, priestcraft, and everything belonging to popery to be nothing, is for me a great miracle. There is nothing in it when they make the charge that we perform no miracles. Although they do not shine so brightly and our ministers perform no miracles, as the Papists imagine they do, nevertheless, our light is pure and our knowledge correct. We surely preach the Gospel, and this they must of course conscientiously confess before each and every one, whether they desire to do so or not. So you have learned here that the kingdom of Christ and the Gospel are devoted to the end that you

concentrate all your life, whether you be wife, child or husband, that you may be one who brings the sick to Christ, and thus be of assistance to others.

II. THE FAITH OF OTHERS.

24. Now we should also consider a little the faith of others and the power to forgive sins, had we the time. I said before that it is an error to baptize the children into the faith of the church; men preached as though they were baptized without faith. This error enters among us by force at present, for the devil does not sleep. They think infants have no faith. The Pope with his subordinates has hitherto maintained that children have no faith, but are laid into the lap of the Christian church, and were baptized in the faith of universal Christendom. These new fanatics, like the Pope, also say that children have no faith; but that we should wait until they grow up.

25. We say that the faith of others does not assist unto salvation, even if two Christendoms were present. The child must itself believe in Christ. For I have not been born in the place of the child or for the child, nor will I die in its stead, it has a death and birth of its own. If it is to live and become free from death, it must also come to this through faith in Christ. However, we pray for the children as well as for all unbelievers; and preach, pray and labor that the unbelieving and children may also come and believe; for this we also live.

26. So these people here had also faith, but not the man of the palsy. Yet, he must receive it if he is to get well, otherwise their faith would not have helped him. They, however, in their faith prayed Christ to give the man sick of the palsy a faith of his own. So the faith of others assists to the end that I may obtain a faith of my own.

27. Yes, one might say: "How do we know whether children believe or not?" Neither do we know who among adults believe or who do not. If I be baptized as an adult and say: I believe; how can you know whether I believe

or not? How do you know it? How, if I were to lie? No
one else can know it, to this every one is brought by his
own heart and thoughts; if it is right, it is right. The
child cannot stand on my faith, I have scarcely enough
faith for myself. Nor shall I lay it into the lap of Christendom, but into the Word of Christ where he says: "Suffer
the little children to come unto me, for of such is the kingdom of heaven." Mat. 19, 14. Luke 18, 15. And thus I shall
say: "Here, O Christ, I bring a little child to thee, thou
hast commanded me to bring it to thee." Now I have done
my part, Christ will also certainly do his part.

So I do not baptize the child in my own faith or in the
faith of Christendom. But my faith and Christendom bring
the child to baptism, in order that by rightly bringing it
God may give it a faith of its own, that it may believe as I
believe and be preserved in the same Word that Christ has
given me. And I do not baptize the child on that it has no
faith, as the Bohemians think, that when it grows up it
shall then first obtain faith, and speak the Word of God
over the child: Thy sins are forgiven thee; and yet it does
not, as they hold, believe the words. Is not this to charge
the Word of God as being false? Now to sum up: I can of
course by my prayers and faith help another that he may
also believe, but I cannot believe for him.

THE POWER ON EARTH TO FORGIVE SINS.

28. The Pharisees knew very well that to forgive sins
was the work of God, and belonged to him alone. For
this reason they regarded Christ as a blasphemer, who as
a man pretended to forgive sins. The forgiveness of sin
is of two kinds: The first is to drive sin from the heart
and infuse grace into it; this is the work of God alone.
The second kind is the declaration of the forgiveness of
sin; this man can do to his fellowman. But here Christ does
both. He instills the Spirit into the heart and externally
he declares forgiveness with the word, which is a declaration and public preaching of the internal forgiveness.

29. All men who are Christians and have been baptised, have this power. For with this they praise Christ, and the **word** is put into their mouth, so that they may and are able to say, if they wish, and as often as it is necessary: Behold, O Man! God offers thee his grace, forgives thee all thy sins; be comforted, thy sins are forgiven; only believe and thou wilt surely have forgiveness. This word of consolation shall not cease among Christians until the last day: "Thy sins are forgiven, be of good cheer." Such language a Christian always uses and openly declares the forgiveness of sins. For this reason and in this manner a Christian has power to forgive sins.

30. Therefore if I say to you: Thy sins are forgiven, then believe it as surely as though God himself had said it to you. But who could do this if Christ had not descended, had not instructed me and said that we should forgive one another our trespasses? As when he says, John 20, 22-23: "Receive ye the Holy Ghost; whosesoever sins ye remit, they are remitted unto them, and whosesoever sins ye retain, they are retained unto them." And at another place, Mat. 18, 19-20, he says: "If two of you shall agree on earth as touching anything that they shall ask, it shall be done for them of my Father which is in heaven. For where two or three are gathered together in my name, there I am in the midst of them." The word penetrates and performs it.

31. Now if there were no man on earth to forgive sins, and there were only law and works what a weak, and miserable thing a poor troubled conscience would be. But now when God adequately instructs every one, so that he is able to say to others: Thy sins are forgiven thee, wherever thou art; the golden age has arrived. On this account we are to be defiant and boastful against sin, so that we can say to our brother, who is in anxiety and distress on account of his sins: Be of good cheer, my brother, thy sins are forgiven; although I cannot give thee the Holy Ghost and faith, I can yet declare them unto thee; if thou believest, thou hast them. They who thus believe these words, praise and glorify God, even as they do here in the Gospel.

That is, God has given man power to forgive sins, and thus the kingdom of Christ is spread, the conscience is strengthened and comforted. This we do now through the Word. God grant that we may also thus understand it.

NINETEENTH SUNDAY AFTER TRINITY.

Second Sermon. Mat. 9, 1-8.

This sermon appeared instead of the preceding one in the c edition. Luther delivered it on Oct. 3d, 1529, while the Marburg Coloquium was in session. It appeared in print the following year under the title: "A sermon on Christian righteousness, or the forgiveness of sins, Preached at Marburg in Hesse, 1529, Martin Luther, Wittenberg, 1530." On the last page are the words: "Printed at Wittenberg by Hans Weissen, 1530." Erl. 14, 206; W. 11, 2301; St. L. 11, 1724.

CONTENTS: THE RIGHTEOUSNESS OF THE WORLD, AND THE CHRISTIAN, HEAVENLY RIGHTEOUSNESS. OR, JESUS CURES THE PALSIED MAN, AND THE POWER ON EARTH TO FORGIVE SINS.

*How and why the article on the forgiveness of sins should be well learned and faithfully practiced. 1.

I. OF THE WORLDLY RIGHTEOUSNESS AND PIETY.
1. The nature and aim of this righteousness. 2.
2. How God requires this of all persons. 2-3.
3. In what way it can be inculcated in the people. 4.
* Of the Word of God and the Gospel. 5-7.
4. It should not be lightly esteemed. 8.
5. An admonition to exercise ourselves in this righteousness and piety. 9.

II. OF THE CHRISTIAN AND HEAVENLY RIGHTEOUSNESS.
A. This righteousness in itself and its right use.
1. Its nature. 10.
2. This righteousness makes us Christians and is different from work-righteousness. 11.
3. Great art and tact are required to grasp this righteousness well and to use it aright. 12-14.

4. How to use this righteousness properly. 15-20.
5. How and why we should faithfully practice this righteousness, praise and spread it. 21-22.

B. The fountain and foundation of this righteousness.
1. The nature and need of this fountain and foundation. 23.
2. Only Christians grasp this fountain and foundation. 24.
3. How and why it is necessary to know this fountain and foundation. 25.
4. All our righteousness rests upon this fountain and foundation. 27.

C. The means and institutions by which to become partakers of this righteousness.
1. The nature of these institutions and means. 28.
2. How and why God established them. 29.
3. Without them no one can know and obtain righteousness and salvation. 30-31.
* The righteousness as conceived by the world must follow the Christian righteousness. 32.

1. The theme of this Gospel is the great and important article of faith, called "the forgiveness of sins", which, when rightly understood, makes an honest Christian, and gives eternal life. Therefore it is necessary in the Christian Church to teach this article diligently and unceasingly, so that we may learn to understand it clearly and distinctly. For this is the one great and difficult art of a Christian, where he will have enough to learn as long as he lives, so that he need not look for anything new, higher or better.

2. But that we may rightly understand this, we must thoroughly know how to distinguish two powers or kinds of piety. One here upon earth, which God has also ordained and has included under the second table of the ten commandments. This is called the righteousness of the world or of man, and serves to the end that we may live together on earth and enjoy the gifts God has given us. For it is his wish that his present life be kept under proper restraint and passed in peace, quietude and harmony, each one attending to his own affairs and not interfering with the business, property or person of another. For this reason God has also added a special blessing, Lev. 18, 5, "Which if a man do, he shall live in them", that is, whosoever upon earth is honest in the sight of all men shall enjoy life; it shall be well with him, and he shall live long.

3. But if on the other hand man is unwilling to do this, he has ordained that the sword, the gallows, the rack, fire, water, and the like be used, with which to restrain and check those who will not be pious. Where such punishment is not administered and the whole country becomes so utterly bad and perverted, that the officers of the law can no longer restrain, God sends pestilence, famine, war, or other terrible plagues, in order to subvert the land, and destroy the wicked, as has happened to the Jews, the Greeks, the Romans, and others. From this we may learn his will, namely, that such piety be exercised and maintained; and know that he will provide what is necessary; but if such piety is not practiced he will in turn take away and destroy everything.

4. This is in short the sense and the whole substance of this piety on earth. But it is further necessary to urge it and to admonish people that every man diligently, zealously and voluntarily exercise himself in it, and that he be not driven to it by force and punishment. This admonition consists in setting forth God's commandments and in applying them to every station of life on earth, as God has ordered and appointed them. They are to be respected and highly honored; we should find pleasure in them and heartily do what is required in the different spheres of life. When God says, ''Honor thy father and thy mother,'' every child, man-servant, maid-servant, citizen, and the like, should receive the Word with joy, have no greater treasure on earth, and not imagine if he do this he is already halfway or altogether in paradise. And this should be solely done, that every heart may be assured without a doubt and say: Now I know, that such work, life, or position is right and proper and is assuredly well pleasing to God; for I have his Word and command as a sure witness, which never deceives nor fails me.

5. For do not let this be the least grace upon earth, when you have come to this decision in your heart and your conscience rests upon it. We owe this assurance to the blessed Gospel alone, in which we should delight and which we must reverence, even if we receive no other benefit or use from it than this, that it quiets our conscience and positively teaches us how to live and in what relation we stand to God.

In what error and blindness we were aforetime, when not even a spark of such teaching enlightened us and we allowed ourselves to be led in the name of the devil by the whims of every lying preacher; we tried all kinds of works, ran hither and thither, expended and wasted our energies, money and property; here we established masses and altars, there cloisters and brotherhoods, and every one was groping for the way in which he might serve God; yet no one found it, but all remained in darkness. For there was no God who might say: This is pleasing to me, this I have commanded, etc. Yes, our blind guides did nothing less than lose sight of God's word, separated it from good works, and instead of these set up other works everywhere; in addition to this they discarded and despised the positions in life, which God had appointed, as though he knew no better, nor even as well as we, how to manage his affairs.

6. Therefore we must constantly take heed to inculcate this Word of God, which does not burden us with any special, great and difficult works, but refers us to the condition in which we live, that we look for nothing else, but with a cheerful heart remain satisfied in it, and be assured that by such work more is accomplished than if one had established all the cloisters and kept all the orders, although it be the most insignificant domestic work. For hitherto we have been woefully deceived by the fine lustre and pomp of works, hoods, bald pates, coarse apparel, by fasts, wakes, pious looks, playing the devotee, and going barefoot.

Our foolishness consists in laying too much stress upon the show of works and when these do not glitter as something extraordinary we regard them as of no value; and poor fools that we are, we do not see that God has attached and bound this precious treasure, namely his Word, to such common works as filial obedience, external, domestic, or civil affairs, so as to include them in his order and command, which he wishes us to accept, the same as though he himself had appeared from heaven. What would you do if Christ himself with all the angels were visibly to descend, and command you in your home to sweep your house and wash the pans and kettles? How happy you would feel, and would not know how to act for joy, not for the work's sake, but that you knew that thereby you were serving him, who is greater than heaven and earth.

7. If we would only consider this, and by the power of the Word look beyond us, and think that it is not man, but God in heaven who wishes and commands these things, we would run full speed, and in a most faithful and diligent manner rather do these common, insignificant works, as they are regarded, than any others. There is no other reason why this is not done than the simple fact that the works

are separated from the Word, and God's command is not regarded nor respected; we move along in a blind, drowsy manner, and think the doing of the works is all sufficient. Because we regard these works as insignificant, we stare and look around for others, become indolent and fretful, do nothing in love, faithfulness and obedience, have no scruples on account of our negligence, are faithless to our fellowmen, injure or vex them, and thus heap upon ourselves all manner of misery, wrath, and misfortune.

8. This then is one part of our discourse, that this external righteousness be urged both in admonitions and in threatenings, and not be considered as of no importance. For whosoever despises it, despises God and his Word.

9. Therefore let every man look to himself what he is or what he has to do, and what God demands of him, whether it be to rule, to command and order, or on the contrary to obey, serve and labor, that he may attend to the duties of his office with all faithfulness for God's sake. Let him be assured that God has more respect for such faithfulness than for all the work and piety of the monks, who never yet have attained to this outward righteousness; nor are they able to extol all their works and doings as heartily as a child or servant girl performing their duties according to God's command.

O, what a blessed world we would have, if people believed this, and every man remained at his post, always keeping in mind God's will and command. Then there would shower from heaven all kinds of blessings and gifts instead of the many vexations and heart-aches, which we now have, are looking for, and deserve.

10. Above this external piety there is another, which does not belong to this temporal life on earth but which avails only before God and which leads us to the life beyond and keeps us in it. The former piety consists in works, which this present life requires to be done among men, whether they be our superiors or inferiors, our neighbors, or our kindred. It has its reward here upon earth, also ends with this life, and they who do not practice it shorten their

days. But this latter piety moves and soars far above everything that is upon earth, and has nothing to do with works. For how can it have works, since all that this body can perform and that is called works, is already included in the former piety.

This piety is now called the grace of God, or the forgiveness of sins, of which Christ speaks in this and other gospels, and which is not an earthly but heavenly righteousness; it does not come of our work and ability but is the work and gift of God. For that human piety may well shield us against punishment and the hangman, and permit us to enjoy temporal gifts; but it cannot attain for us God's grace and the forgiveness of sin. Therefore, even though we may have this external piety, we must nevertheless have a much higher one, which alone avails before God, frees us from sin and an evil conscience, and leads us out of death into eternal life.

11. This is, furthermore, the only part or article and doctrine, by believing which we become and are called Chirstians, and which separates and divorces us from all other saints on earth; for they all have a different foundation and nature of their saintliness, peculiar exercises, and rigorous life. It separates us also from the works of those holding positions and offices approved by the Word of God, which are indeed much higher and better than all the self-chosen ecclesiasticism of the monks. These also constitute a holy calling, so that they are called pious and deserve praise of all men because they do their duty. But all this makes no one a Christian. He alone is a Christian who receives this article in faith, and is assured that he is in the kingdom of grace, in which Christ protects him, and daily forgives him his sins. But he who looks for something else or wishes to deal otherwise with God, must know that he is no Christian, but is rejected and condemned by God.

12. For this reason the greatest skill and intelligence is needed to grasp and understand this righteousness, and in our hearts and before God rightly to distinguish it from the

above mentioned outward righteousness. For this is, as has been said, the skill and the wisdom of the Christian, but it is so high and great that even all the beloved Apostles could not speak enough of it; and yet it meets the painful misfortune that no art is mastered as soon as this.

There is no greater theme for a preacher than the grace of God and the forgiveness of sin, yet we are such wicked people, that, when we have once heard or read it, we think we know it, are immediately masters and doctors, keep looking for something greater, as though we had done everything, and thus we made new factions and division.

13. I have now been teaching and studying this subject with all diligence for many years (more than any one of those who imagine they know it all), in preaching, writing and reading, yet I cannot boast of having mastered it and am glad that I still remain a pupil with those who are just beginning to learn. For this reason I must admonish and warn all such as want to be Christians, both teachers and pupils, that they guard themselves against such shameful delusion and surfeit, and understand that this subject is most difficult and the greatest art that can be found upon earth; so that even Paul had to confess and say (2 Cor. 9, 15) that it is an unspeakable gift, that is, one which cannot be described among men with words so that they may regard it as highly and dearly as it really is in itself.

14. The reason for this is, that man's understanding cannot get beyond this external piety of works, and cannot comprehend the righteousness of faith; but, the greater and more skillful this understanding is, the more it confines itself to works and rests upon them. It is not possible for man in times of temptation and distress, when his conscience smites him, to cease from groping around for works on which to stand and rest. Then we seek and enumerate the many good deeds, which we would like to do, or have done, and because we find none, the heart begins to doubt and despair. This weakness adheres so firmly to our nature, that even those who have faith and recognize the grace of God, or the forgiveness of sins, cannot overcome it with all their

efforts and exertions, and must daily contend against it. In short it is entirely beyond human knowledge and understanding, ability and power, to ascend above this earthly righteousness, and to transfer oneself into this article of faith; and although one hears much about it and is conversant with it, there continues nevertheless the old delusion and inborn corruption which would bring its own works before God and make them the foundation of salvation. Such is the case, I say, with those who are Christians and fight against this work-righteousness; others, critics and inexperienced souls are even lost in it.

15. Therefore this doctrine, that our piety before God consists entirely in the forgiveness of sins, must be rightly comprehended and firmly maintained. We must therefore get beyond ourselves and ascend higher than our reason, which keeps us in conflict with ourselves and which reminds us both of sin and good works; and we must soar so high as to see neither sin nor good works, but be rooted and grounded in this article and see and know nothing besides. Therefore let grace or forgiveness be pitted not only against sin, but also against good works, and let all human righteousness and holiness be excluded. Thus there are in man two conflicting powers: Externally in this life he is to be pious, do good works, and the like. But if he aims beyond this life and wishes to deal with God, he must know that here neither his sin nor his piety avails anything. And though he may feel his sins which disturb his conscience, and although the law demands good works, he will not listen nor give heed to them, but will boldly reply; If I have sin, Christ has forgiveness; yea, I am seated on a throne to which sin cannot attain.

16. Therefore we are to regard the kingdom of Christ as a large, beautiful arch or vault which is everywhere over us, and covers and protects us against the wrath of God; yea, as a great, extended firmament which pure grace and forgiveness illuminate and so fill the world and all things, that all sin will hardly appear as a spark in comparison with the great, extended sea of light; and although sin may oppress, it can-

not injure, but must disappear and vanish before grace. They
who understand this, may well be called masters, but we
will all have to humble ourselves and not be ashamed to keep
on learning this lesson as long as we live.

17. For wherever our nature succeeds in finding sin, it
tries to make an unbearable burden of it. Satan fans the
spark and blows up a great fire which fills heaven and earth.
Here the leaf must be turned and we must firmly conclude:
If the sin were ever so great or burdensome, this article of
faith is nevertheless much higher, wider and greater, which
has been recommended and established not by man's wisdom, but by him who has comprehended heaven and earth
and holds them in the hollow of his hand. Is. 40, 12. My
sin and piety must remain here on earth as far as they concern my life and conduct. But in heaven above I have
another treasure, greater than either of these; there Christ
is seated and holds me in his arms, covers me with his wings
and overshadows me with his grace.

18. You may say: How is this, since I daily feel sin and
my conscience condemns me and threatens me with God's
wrath? I answer: For this reason, I say, one must understand that the righteousness of a Christian is nothing that
can be named or imagined but the forgiveness of sin, that
is, it is a kingdom of power which deals only with sin and
with such abundant grace as takes away all wrath.

It is called the forgiveness of sin for the reason that we
are truly sinners before God; yes, everything in us is
sin, even though we may have all human righteousness. For
where God speaks of sin, there must be real and great sin;
so also forgiveness is no jest, but real earnestness. When
you, therefore, consider this article you have both. Sin takes
away all your holiness, no matter how pious you are on
earth; again, forgiveness takes away all sin and wrath.
Therefore your sin cannot cast you into hell, nor can your
piety elevate you into heaven.

19. Therefore, when the devil disturbs your conscience,
and tries to bring despair to your heart by saying: "Have
you not learned that one must be pious?" then answer cour-

ageously and say: Yes, you are right; I am a sinner, that I
have known before; for this article, called the forgiveness of
sins, has taught me this long ago. I am to be pious and do
what I can before the world; but before God I am willing to
be a sinner, and to be called nothing else, that this article
may remain true, else there would not be forgiveness or
grace; but it must needs be called a crown of righteousness
and of merits. Therefore, although I feel nothing but many
and great sins, yet they are no longer sins; for I have for
them a precious panacea and drug which takes away the
power and poison of sin and wholly destroys it. It is this
word, "Forgiveness," before which sin disappears like stub-
bles before the fire. Without it no work, suffering, or martyrdom avails against the smallest sin. For without forgiveness sin is and remains pure sin, which condemns us.

20. Therefore only confess this article heartily and boldly
and say: Before the world I may be pious and do everything
that is required, but before God it is only sin according to
this article. Therefore I am a sinner, but a sinner who now
has forgiveness and who sits at the throne where grace rules
supreme, Ps. 116. If this were not so I would be a sinner
like Judas, who saw only his sin, but no forgiveness. But
Christians, no matter how much sin they feel in themselves,
in that word forgiveness see much more abundant grace
presented to them, and poured out over them.

21. Thus learn then to magnify this article and spread it
as far as Christ reaches and rules, that you may elevate it
far above everything in heaven and on earth. For as the
Word soars over all this, so must also faith, which compre-
hends the Word and keeps the heart steadfast in it, overcome
sin, conscience, death and the devil.

22. Consider now what kind of a person a Christian is,
who lords it over death and the devil, and before whom all
sin is as a withered leaf. Now examine yourself and see
how far you have learned this lesson, and whether it is such
an insignificant and easy matter as some inexperienced souls
think. For if you have learned and believed it, all misfortune, death, and the devil will be as nothing. But since

you are still so vexed with sin, and since you are still frightened and in despair on account of death, hell and God's judgment, humble yourself, give honor to the Word and confess that you have never yet understood this matter.

In short let every man examine his own heart, and he will find a false Christian who imagines that he knows all about this subject before he has learned the first principles of it. The words are soon heard, read and repeated, but to carry out the principle in practice and in character, so that it may live within us, and our conscience may be founded upon it and rest in it, is not in the art of man. Therefore I say and admonish, that those who wish to be Christians may always keep it in mind, assimilate it, practice it, and chastise themselves with it, that we may at least have a taste of it, and as James says, 1, 18, be a kind of first fruits of his creatures. For we shall never advance so far in this life as to come to a perfect understanding of it; nor did even the blessed Apostles, full of the Spirit and of faith, advance so far.

23. Thus far I have explained the first part, what Christian righteousness is and in what it consists. But if you ask further, whence it comes, or how it has been brought about or gained, I answer: Jesus Christ, the Son of God, has come from heaven and has been made man, has suffered and died for our sins. This is the cause, the means, and the treasure, through which we obtain the forgiveness of sin and for the sake of which the grace of God is bestowed upon us; for such a treasure does not come to us without means or merit. But since all of us are born in sin and are the enemies of God, we have deserved only eternal wrath and punishment. All that we are and have is condemned, and there is no help or way out of it. For sin is so grievous that no creature can quench it, the wrath so great that no man can appease and conciliate it. Therefore another man must take our place, namely Jesus Christ, God and man, and through his suffering and death make satisfaction for our sins and pay for them. This is the price that has been set, and has been expended for us, by which sin has been quenched and the

wrath of God appeased, the Father has been reconciled and made our friend.

24. Christians alone know this and believe it, and are in this respect different from those of every other faith and worship on earth. For the Jews, Turks, false Christians, and those who would be righteous by works, also boast that God is merciful; and there is no man on earth but knows something of the grace of God, and yet all of them fail to obtain it, or in other words, they do not have the treasure in which it lies and from which it flows. They continue in their blindness and imagine they can acquire it by their works, rigid life, and their own holiness, with which they only make the wrath and displeasure of God the more grievous.

25. Therefore it is necessary that we rightly learn to know this treasure, and seek forgiveness where it may be found; that is, that we thoroughly learn to know, comprehend, and keep the Lord Jesus Christ. For it is ordained that no one shall come into God's presence, find grace, nor obtain forgiveness of the least sin except through Christ. Because you are a sinner, and will always remain one, your conscience is ever present, condemns and threatens you with God's wrath and punishment, so that you cannot see the grace of God.

With reference to the forgiveness of sins let me say, that you will not find anything in your heart with which you can pay them off, nor raise any funds for which God might recognize you and cancel the debt in the ledger. But if you seize Christ as the one who has become your substitute, who has taken your sin upon himself, and who has given himself with all his merit and worthiness for you, no sin can avail anything against you. If I am a sinner, he is holy, and is Lord over sin, death, satan and hell, so that no sin can harm me, because he has been given me as my righteousness and salvation.

26. Therefore we have, indeed, pure grace and forgiveness of all sins, but nowhere except in and through Christ alone, and in him only it must be sought and obtained.

Therefore whoever will come before God with any kind of work, that God shall recognize and regard as meritorious for obtaining grace, will be disappointed and undeceived, yea, instead of grace he will heap wrath upon himself. Thus you see that all other ways and means are condemned as the doctrines of devils; by which men are led and directed to their own works, or to the holiness and merits of others, as for example, of the saints who have led ascetic lives and followed the rules of their orders, and have suffered and expiated a great deal; or as those have done who have comforted people in the throes of death and have admonished them to suffer death willingly for their sins. Whoever dares to offer anything else for sin or to atone for it himself does nothing else than deny the Lord Jesus Christ, yea, disgrace and slander him, as if the blood of Christ were of no more consequence than our repentance and satisfaction, or as if his blood were not sufficient to take away all the sins of the earth.

27. Therefore, would you be freed from your sins, cease to seek works and satisfaction, and to bring them before God; but simply creep under the wings and into the bosom of Christ, as the one who has taken away your sins, and has laid them upon himself. Thus you need not chastise yourself with them, nor have anything to do with them! For he is the Lamb of God, says John 1, 29, which taketh away the sins of the world; and Peter says, Acts 4, 12, There is none other name under heaven, given among men, whereby we must be saved. The reason we are Christians is because we have Christ with all His merit and worthiness, not because of our efforts and works, which indeed make a St. Carthusius, a St. Francis, or an Augustinian monk, an obedient servant and extremist as they are called; but such works can never make a Christian. Behold, this is the second part which belongs to the sermon on this article.

28. The third thought is how and by what means we may appropriate such righteousness, so that we may receive the treasure acquired by Christ. Here also we need to give heed that we take the right way, and not make the mistake, which

certain heretics have made in times past, and many erroneous minds still set forth, who think that God ought to do
something special with them. These imagine that God will
deal separately with each one by some special internal light
and mysterious revelation, and give him the Holy Ghost, as
though there was no need of the written Word or the external sermon. Consequently we are to know that God has
ordained that no one shall come to the knowledge of Christ,
nor obtain the forgiveness acquired by him, nor receive the
Holy Ghost, without the use of external and public means;
but God has embraced this treasure in the oral word or
public ministry, and will not perform his work in a corner
or mysteriously in the heart, but will have it heralded and
distributed openly among the people, even as Christ commands, Mark 16, 15: Go ye into all the world and preach the
Gospel to every creature, etc.

29. He does this in order that we may know how and
where to seek and expect his grace, so that in all Christendom there may be the same custom and order, and not every
man follow his own mind and act according to his own
notions, and so deceive himself and others, which would
certainly happen. As we cannot look into the heart of any
man, each one might boast of having the Holy Ghost and set
forth his own thoughts as divine revelation which God had
inspired and taught him in a special manner; as a result, no
one would know whom or what to believe.

30. Therefore this part also, namely the external word or
preaching, belongs to Christianity as a channel or means
through which we attain unto the forgiveness of sins, or the
righteousness of Christ, with which Christ reveals and offers
us his grace or lays it into our bosom, and without which no
one would ever come to a knowledge of this treasure. For
whence should any man know, or in what man's heart would
it ever come, that Christ, the Son of God, came from heaven
for our sake, died for us, and rose from the dead, acquired
the forgiveness of sins and eternal life, and offers the same
to us, without publicly having it announced and preached?
And although he acquired this treasure for us through his

suffering and death, no one could obtain or receive it, if
Christ did not have it offered, presented, and applied. And
all that he had done and suffered would be to no purpose,
but would be like some great and precious treasure buried
in the earth, which no one could find or make use of.

31. Therefore I have always taught that the oral word
must precede every thing else, must be comprehended with
the ears, if the Holy Ghost is to enter the heart, who through
the Word enlightens it and works faith. Consequently faith
does not come except through the hearing and oral preaching of the Gospel, in which it has its beginning, growth and
strength. For this reason the Word must not be despised,
but held in honor. We must familiarize and acquaint ourselves with it, and constantly practice it, so that it never
ceases to bear fruit; for it can never be understood and
learned too well. Let every man beware of the shameless
fellows who have no more respect for the Word than if it
were unnecessary for faith; or of those who think they
know it all, become tired of it, eventually fall from it, and
retain nothing of faith or of Christ.

32. Behold, here you have all that belongs to this article
of the righteousness of Christ. It consists in the forgiveness
of sins, offered to us through Christ, and received by faith in
and through the Word, purely and simply without any
works on our part. Yet I do not mean that Christians should
not and must not do good works, but that they are not to be
mingled and entwined in the doctrine of faith, and decorated
with the shameless delusion that they avail before God as
righteousness, whereby both the doctrine of works and of
faith are besmirched and destroyed. For everything possible
must be done to keep this article pure, unadulterated and
separate from all our own doings. But after we have this
righteousness by faith, works are to follow and continue here
on earth, so that there may be civil righteousness, and that
both be maintained, each in its proper place, but separate in
their nature and efficacy,—the former before God in faith
over and above all works, the latter works in love to our
neighbor, as we said plainly enough above and always taught.

TWENTIETH SUNDAY AFTER TRINITY.

This sermon does not appear in c edition. It was printed first in the "Two sermons on the festival of all saints," 1523. It is also one of the collection of 12 sermons. Erl. 14, 223; W. 11, 2319; St. L. 11, 1738.

Text: Mat. 22, 1-14. And Jesus answered and spake again in parables unto them, saying, The kingdom of heaven is likened unto a certain king, who made a marriage feast for his son, and sent forth his servants to call them that were bidden to the marriage feast: and they would not come. Again he sent forth other servants, saying, Tell them that are bidden, Behold, I have made ready my dinner; my oxen and my fatlings are killed, and all things are ready: come to the marriage feast. But they made light of it, and went their ways, one to his own farm, another to his merchandise; and the rest laid hold on his servants, and treated them shamefully, and killed them. But the king was wroth; and he sent his armies, and destroyed those murderers, and burned their city. Then saith he to his servants, The wedding is ready, but they that were bidden were not worthy. Go ye therefore unto the partings of the highways, and as many as ye shall find, bid to the marriage feast. And those servants went out into the highways, and gathered together all as many as they found, both bad and good: and the wedding was filled with guests. But when the king came in to behold the guests, he saw there a man who had not on a wedding-garment: and he saith unto him, Friend, how camest thou in hither not having a wedding-garment? And he was speechless. Then the king said to the servants, Bind him hand and foot, and cast him out into the outer darkness; there shall be the weeping and the gnashing of teeth. For many are called, but few chosen.

CONTENTS: THE SPIRITUAL INTERPRETATION OF THE
PARABLE OF THE MARRIAGE FEAST THE KING MADE
FOR HIS SON.

SUMMARY OF THIS GOSPEL: 1. Paul also writes of this
marriage, Eph. 5, 25–27, where he speaks of Christ and his Church,
as of a bride and of a bridegroom.

2. The Jews, who were the despisers and murderers, will in turn
be despised and murdered.

3. Thus disposed are all men by nature, when left to themselves.

4. The heathen were without, that is, the sinners had no place
in this wedding; but later, when the true guests despised the wedding, the heathen were then brought in.

5. The people will be cast out from the marriage feast, who
have only the name of Christ.

6. He has not the wedding garment on who has not faith, by
which alone this marriage feast is made and maintained. Our
first parents lost this garment and were put to shame in their
bareness and nakedness. But faith covers all that we received
from Adam. Therefore Ps. 32, 1 says: "Blessed is he whose transgression is forgiven, whose sin is covered.

PARABLE OF THE KING WHO MADE A MARRIAGE FEAST FOR HIS SON.

1. This Gospel presents to us the parable of the wedding;
therefore we are compelled to understand it differently than
it sounds and appears to the natural ear and eye. Hence
we will give attention to the spiritual meaning of the parable, and then notice how the text has been torn and
perverted.

2. First, the King, who prepared the marriage feast, is
our heavenly Father. The bridegroom is his Son, our Lord

Jesus Christ. The bride is the Christian Church, we and the whole world, in so far as we believe, of which we shall hear later.

3. God first sent out his servants, the Prophets to invite guests to this wedding; they were to bid them, that is, preach, and preach only faith in Christ. But those invited did not come; they were the Jews, to whom the Prophets were sent, they would not hear nor receive those sent to them. At another time he sent other servants, the Apostles and martyrs, to bid us come, and to say to the bidden guests: "Behold, I have made ready my dinner; my oxen and my fatlings are killed, and all things are ready; come to the marriage feast."

4. These words beautifully picture to us and teach how we should make use of the life of the saints; namely, to introduce examples by which the doctrine of the Gospel may be confirmed, so that we may the better, by the aid of such examples and lives, meditate upon Christ, and be nourished by and feast upon him as upon fatlings and well fed oxen. This is the reason he calls them fatlings. Take an example: Paul teaches in Rom. 3, 23f. how the bride is full of sin and must be sprinkled by the blood of Christ alone, or she will continue unclean, that is, she must only believe that the blood of Christ was shed for her sins, and there is no other salvation possible. Then he beautifully introduces the example of Abraham and confirms the doctrine of faith by the faith and life of Abraham, and says, 4, 3: "And Abraham believed God, and it was reckoned unto him for righteousness." That is a true ox, it is properly slain, it nourishes us, so that we become grounded and strengthened in our faith by the example and faith of Abraham. Again, soon after Paul lays before us a fine fatling, when he cites David the Prophet of God and proves from him, that God does not justify us by virtue of our works, but by faith, when he says, Rom. 4, 6-8: "Even as David also pronounceth blessing upon the man, unto whom God reckoneth righteousness apart from works," saying in Ps. 32, 1-2: "Blessed are they whose iniquities are forgiven, and whose sins are covered.

Blessed is the man to whom the Lord will not reckon sin."
Behold, that fattens and nourishes in the true sense, when
we use the example and doctrine of pious saints to confirm
our own doctrine and faith. And this is the true honor that
we can give to the saints. Follow now further in this Gospel:

5. "But they made light of it, and went their ways, one
to his own farm, another to his merchandise; and the rest
laid hold on his servants, and treated them shamefully, and
killed them." These are the three barriers that prevent us
from coming to the marriage feast. The first, or the farm,
signifies our honor; it is a great hindrance that we do not
think of Christ and believe in him; we fear we must suffer
shame and become dishonored, and we do not believe that
God can protect us from shame and preserve us in honor.
The second go to their spheres of business, that is, they fall
with their hearts into their worldly affairs, into avarice, and
when they should cleave to the Word, they worry lest they
perish and their stomachs fail them; they do not trust God
to sustain them. The third class are the worst, they are the
high, wise and prudent, the exalted spirits, they not only
despise but martyr and destroy the servants; in order to
retain their own honor and praise, yea, in order to be something. For the Gospel must condemn their wisdom and
righteousness and curse their presumption. This they cannot suffer; therefore they go ahead and kill the servants
who invited them to the dinner and the marriage feast.
They were the Pharisees and scribes, who put to death both
Christ and his Apostles, as their fathers did the Prophets.
These are much worse than the first and second classes,
who, although they despised and rejected the invitation,
yet then went away and neither condemned nor destroyed
the servants.

6. Further, the Gospel says: "But the king was wroth;
and he sent his armies and destroyed those murderers, and
burned their city." That happened to the Jews through the
Romans under Titus and Vespasian, who burned Jerusalem
to the ground, to its very foundation. However I prefer to
have it understood spiritually, since the whole Gospel is to

be explained spiritually. Hence this came to pass when God totally destroyed and burned to the ground the synagogue at Jerusalem, he entirely abandoned faith, scattered the people hither and thither, so that none remained together and they were robbed both of their priesthood and of their kingdom; so that there is not now a poorer, a more miserable and forsaken people on the earth than the Jews. Such is the end of the despisers of God's Word.

7. It now follows: "Then saith he to his servants, The wedding is ready, but they that were bidden were not worthy." This has also come to pass; for the Jews have not desired to know anything at all of Christ; they put him to death, also the Prophets and Apostles, and from that time to the present they have not been worthy to hear a word concerning Christ.

8. Further: "Then he said to them, Go ye therefore unto the partings of the highways, and as many as ye shall find, bid to the marriage feast." Hence they went out into the highways, namely, to us heathen, and gathered us together from the ends of the world into a congregation, in which are good and bad.

9. Then the King goes in to behold the guests. This will take place on the day of judgment, when the King will let himself be seen.

10. Then he will find one, not only a single person, but a large company not clothed with a wedding garment, that is, with faith. These are pious people, much better than the foregoing; for you must consider them the ones who have heard and understood the Gospel, yet they cleaved to certain works and did not creep entirely into Christ; like the foolish virgins, who had no oil, that is, no faith.

11. To them the King will say: "Bind him hand and foot, and cast him out into the outer darkness," that is, he condemns their good works, that they no longer avail anything; for the hands signify their work, the feet their walk in life, and he will then cast them into the outer darkness.

12. Now, this outer darkness is in contrast with the inner light, since faith alone must see within the heart. There our

light, our reason must be covered and cease, and faith alone lighten us. For if a person will act according to reason and open it, there is nothing but death, hell and sin before his eyes. Reason then considers itself a candidate for death; yet it finds no help in any creature, all is a desert and dark. Therefore reason must be barred out here, or it must despair and surrender itself as a captive to the light of faith alone. This same light then sees that it is God in heaven who is interested in us, who cares for us, upon whom the heart can meditate, who rejects all aid of reason and depends upon no creature; then man will be sustained. Now this is the sense of the words, that those cast thus into outer darkness will be robbed of faith, and thus cast out. Since they do not cleave to God's mercy alone through faith, they must despair and be condemned.

13. Let us now briefly notice what is taught by this marriage feast. First, this marriage feast is a union of the divine nature with the human. And the great love Christ has for us is presented to us in this picture of the wedding feast. For there are many kinds of love, but none is so ardent and fervent as a bride's love, the love a new bride has to her bridegroom, and on the other hand, the bridegroom's love to the bride. True love has no regard for pleasures or presents, or riches, or gold rings and the like; but cares only for the bridegroom. And if he even gave her all he had, she would regard none of his presents, but say: I will have only thee. And if on the other hand he has nothing at all, it makes no difference with her, she will in spite of all that desire him. That is the true nature of the love of a bride. But where one has regard to pleasure, it is harlot-love; she does not care for him, but for the money; therefore such love does not last long.

14. This true bride-love God presented to us in Christ, in that he allowed him to become man for us and be united with our human nature that we might thus perceive and appreciate his good will toward us. Now, as the bride loves her betrothèd, so also does Christ love us; and we on the other hand will love him, if we believe and are the true

bride. And although he gave us even heaven, the wisdom
of all the Prophets, the glory of all the saints and angels,
yet we would not esteem them unless he gave us himself.
The bride can be satisfied by nothing, is insatiable, the only
one thing she wants is the bridegroom himself; as she says
in the Song of Solomon, 2, 16: "My beloved is mine, and I
am his." She cannot rest until she has her beloved himself.
So is Christ also on the other hand disposed toward me: he
will have me only, and besides nothing. And if I gave him
even all I could, it would be of no use to him; he would
have no regard for it, even if I wore all the hoods of all the
monks. He wants my whole heart; for the outward things,
as the outward virtues, are only maid servants, he wants
the wife herself. He demands, that I say from the bottom
of my heart: I am thine. The union and the marriage are
accomplished by faith, so that I rely fully and freely upon
him, that he is mine. If I only have him, what can I desire
more?

15. Now, what do we give to him? An impure bride, a
dirty, old, wrinkled outcast. But he is the eternal wisdom,
the eternal truth, the eternal light, an exceptionally beautiful youth. What does he give us then? Himself, wholly and
completely. He does not cut a piece off for me or give me a
little morsel, but the whole fountain of eternal wisdom,
not a little brooklet. If then I am thus his and he mine, I
have eternal life, righteousness and all that belongs to him.
Therefore I am righteous, saved, and in a sense that neither
death, sin, hell, nor satan can harm me. If he gave me only
a part of his wisdom, righteousness and life, I would say:
That is of no help to me, but I want thee, without thee nothing is real and true. When he gives me his servants, his
Prophets, he gives me only a part and a morsel; the gifts are
only concubines, among whom there is only one who is the
true bride. They are distinguished thus: there are many
souls to whom gifts are made, as, wisdom, love and the like;
but they are not the true brides, for they do not say, Thou
art mine: but they court your purse on the side, for they
love the gifts. But the true bride says: Thee alone will I

have, thou art mine, and not the ring, not the jewel, not the present. The above is all spoken of love.

16. Now, what do we bring to him? Nothing but all our heart-aches, all our misfortunes, sins, misery and lamentations. He is the eternal light, we the eternal darkness; he the life, we death; he righteousness, we sin. This is a marriage that is very unequal. But what does the bridegroom do? He is so fastidious that he will not dwell with his bride until he first adorns her in the highest degree. How is that done? The Apostle Paul teaches that when he says in Tit. 3, 5-6: "He gave his tender body unto death for them and sprinkled them with his holy blood and cleansed them through the washing of regeneration and renewing of the Holy Spirit." He instituted a washing; that washing is baptism, with which he washes her. More than this, he has given to her his Word; in that she believes and through her faith she becomes a bride. The bridegroom comes with all his treasures; but I come with all my sins, with all my misery and heart-griefs. But because this is a marriage and a union, in the sense that they become one flesh, Gen. 2, 24; Mat. 19, 5, and they leave father and mother and cleave to one another, they should embrace each other and not disown one another, although one is even a little sick and awkward; for what concerns one, the other must also bear.

17. Therefore, the bride says, I am thine, thou must have me; then he must at the same time take all my misfortune upon himself. Thus then are my sins eternal righteousness, my death eternal life, my hell heaven; for these two, sin and righteousness, cannot exist together, nor heaven and hell. Are we now to come together the one must consume and melt the other in order that we may be united and become one. Now his righteousness is truly incomparably stronger than my sins, and his life unmeasurably stronger than my death; for he is life itself where all life must be kindled. Therefore my death thus vanishes in his life, my sins in his righteousness and my condemnation in his salvaton. Here my sin is forced between the hammer and the anvil, so that it perishes and vanishes. For now since my sin, my filth is

taken away he must adorn and clothe me with his eternal
righteousness and with all his grace until I become beautiful; for I am his bride. Thus then I appropriate to myself
all that he has, as he takes to himself all that I have; as
the Prophet Ezekiel 16, 6f says: "I passed by thee, and
thou wast naked, and thy breasts were fashioned and were
marriageable; then I spread my skirts over thee and covered
thy nakedness, gave thee my Word and put on thee beautiful
red shoes." Here he relates many kind acts he did for her;
and later he complains in verse 15, how she became a
harlot. He tells us all this, that he clothed us with his
riches and that we of ourselves have nothing. Whoso does
not here lay hold of this as sure, that he has nothing of himself, but only Christ's riches and cannot without doubt say,
Thou art mine, he is not yet a Christian.

18. Now since Christ is mine and I am his: if Satan rages,
I have Christ who is my life; does sin trouble me, I have
Christ who is my righteousness; do hell and perdition attack
me, I have Christ, who is my salvation. Thus, there may
rage within whatever will, if I have Christ, to him I can look
so that nothing can harm me. And this union of the divine
with the human is pointed out in the picture here of the
marriage feast, and the exalted love God has to us, in the
love of the bride.

19. Now the wedding garment is Christ himself, which is
put on by faith, as the Apostle says in Rom. 13, 14: "Put
ye on the Lord Jesus Christ." Then the garment gives forth
a lustre of itself, that is, faith in Christ bears fruit of itself,
namely, love which works through faith in Christ. These
are the good works, that also flash forth from faith, and
entirely gratuitously do they go forth, they are done alone
for the good of our neighbor; otherwise they are heathenish works, if they flow not out of faith; they will later come
to naught and be condemned, and be cast into the outermost
darkness.

20. This is indicated here in the binding of his hands and
feet. The hands, as said, are the works, the feet the manner
of life in which he trusted and failed thus to cling to Christ

alone. For we blame him that he had not on the wedding garment, that is, Christ; therefore he must perish with his works; for they did not sparkle forth from faith, from the garment. Hence will you do good works, then believe first; if you will bear fruit, then be a tree first, later the fruit will follow of itself.

21. The mistake is also readily observed here, by which many have perverted the Gospel in that they say: Although the Pope and his following are wicked, yet we must obey him and acknowledge him as the head of Christendom. Let him do what he may, and yet he cannot err, and although he may not have on the wedding garment, nevertheless he is in the congregation. But they are not so good that one might compare them to the one who had not on the wedding garment. They are the villians and murderers who killed the servants of the King; and even if they were worthy to be compared to him, yet the Gospel in this parable does not teach us to follow them, but to cast them out and protect ourselves against them. For whoever has not on the wedding garment does not belong to the congregation, is filth, like the slime, pus, and ulcers in the body; it is indeed in the body, but it is no part of the healthy body. Counterfeits are among money, but they are not money; chaff is among the wheat, but it is not wheat; so these are among Christians, but they are not Christians. This is sufficient on to-day's Gospel. Let us pray God for grace, that none of us may come to such a precious and glorious marriage feast without a wedding garment.

TWENTIETH SUNDAY AFTER TRINITY.

Second Sermon: Mat. 22, 1-14.

Instead of the preceding sermon the c edition gives the following sermon. Erl. 14, 232; W. 11, 2330; St. L. 11, 1746.

CONTENTS: THE KING'S MARRIAGE FEAST FOR HIS SON AND THE WEDDING GARMENT; OR CONCERNING THE KINGDOM OF CHRIST.

THE KINGDOM OF CHRIST.

1. This Gospel is a very earnest admonition, like to-day's Epistle, to make good use of the time of the Gospel; and a terrible threatening of the awful punishment, that shall pass

upon the secure and proud heads that despise the time of
the kingdom of grace and persecute the preaching of the
Gospel, and upon the false trivial spirits who bear the name
of the Gospel and of Christ for a show and do not mean it
in earnest. And by this Gospel is well painted forth and
made plain what the multitudes are who are called God's
people or the church and possess his Word, and how they
are and act both as to their inner nature and their outer
appearance.

2. First, God builds up his Christendom in a way that he
calls it, and what pertains to its government, the kingdom
of heaven; to signify, that he has called and separated out
of the world a people for himself here upon the earth
through the Word of his Gospel; not to the end that it should
be fitted and organized, like the outer and civil government, with temporal rule, power, possessions, government
and maintenance of outward worldly righteousness, discipline, defence, peace, etc. For all this has already before
been richly ordered, and it was commanded and put into man
to rule in this life as well as he can; although this is also
through sin weakened and spoiled so that it is not as it
should be, and is a poor, miserable, weak government, as
weak and transient as the human body, and is able to go no
farther, where it is at its best, than the stomach, as long as
the stomach performs its functions. But above that God
has arranged and instituted his own divine government,
after he revealed his fathomless grace and gave his Word
to prepare and gather a people, whom he redeemed from
his wrath, eternal death and sin, through which they fell
into such misery, and from which they could not help themselves by any human wisdom, counsel or power, and taught
them to know him aright and to praise and laud him forever.

3. Christ here calls his kingdom the kingdom of heaven,
where he does not rule in a temporal way nor deals with
the things of this life; but he founded and developed an
eternal, imperishable kingdom, which begins on the earth
through faith, and in which we receive and possess those

eternal riches, forgiveness of sins, comfort, strength, renewal
of the Holy Spirit, victory and triumph over the power of
satan, death and hell, and finally eternal life of body and
soul, that is, eternal fellowship and blessedness with God.

4. Such a divine kingdom can be governed, built up, protected, extended and maintained only by means of the external office of the Word and of the Sacraments, through
which the Holy Spirit is powerful and works in the hearts
etc., as I have often said in speaking on this theme.

5. But in the most lovable and comforting way it is pictured to us here by Christ our Lord, in that he himself likens
it to a royal wedding feast; when a bride was given to the
King's son, and all were full of the highest joy and glory, and
many were invited to this marriage feast and its joy. For this
is among all the parables and pictures, by which God presents
the kingdom of Christ to us, a select and beautiful one; that
Christendom or the Christian state is a marriage feast or a
matrimonial union, where God himself selects a church on
the earth for his Son, which he takes to himself as his bride.
God here by our own lives and experiences will make known
and reflect as in a mirror what we have in Christ; and also
by the common state of marriage on earth, in which we were
born and reared and now live, he delivers a daily sermon
and admonition in order that we should remember and consider this great mystery (for so St. Paul calls it in Eph. 5,
32), that the conjugal life of a man and wife, instituted by
God, should be a great, beautiful and wonderful sign, and
a tangible, yet spiritual picture, that points out and explains
something special, excellent and great, hidden to and incon-
ceivable by the human reason, namely, Christ and his church.

6. For this accompanies the marriage state, where it is
worthy of the name and may be called a truly married life,
where man and wife truly live together: firstly true heart-
confidence each in each from both sides, as Solomon in Prov.
31, 11 among other virtues of a pious wife also praises this:
"The heart of her husband trusteth in her;" that is, he
entrusts to her his body and life, money, possessions and
honor. Likewise on the other hand, the heart of the wife

clings to her husband, he is her highest, dearest treasure on earth; for she expects and has in him honor, protection and help in all times of her need. Such a completely harmonious, equal and eternal confidence and affection are not found among other persons and stations in life, for example between master and servant, mistress and maidservant, yea, not even between children and parents. For there the love is not thus alike, strong and perfect to one another, and an eternal union does not endure here as in the marriage state, instituted by God; as the text in Gen. 2, 24 says: "Therefore shall a man leave his father and his mother, and shall cleave unto his wife: and they shall be one flesh."

7. Out of such love and heart confidence follows now also the fellowship in all they have in common with one another or in all that befalls them, good or bad; so that each must accept it as his or her own, and add and impart help to the other with his or her means, and both suffer and enjoy, rejoice and mourn together, according as it may be well or ill with them.

8. This now should be a parable or sign of the great, mysterious and wonderful union of Christ and his church, whose members we all are who believe on him, and as St. Paul says, Eph. 5, 30, of his flesh and bones, as at creation the wife was taken from the man. It must indeed be a great, fathomless and inexpressible love of God to us, that the divine nature unites thus with us and sinks itself into our flesh and blood, so that God's Son truly becomes one flesh and one body with us, and so lovingly receives us that he is not only willing to be our brother, but also our bridegroom, and turns to us and gives us as our own all his divine treasures, wisdom, righteousness, life, strength, power, so that in him we should also be partakers of his divine nature, as St. Peter says in his 2 Epis. 1, 4. And it is his pleasure that we should believe this, so that we may be placed in possession of this honor and of these riches; then we may rejoice and with all assurance take comfort in this Lord, as a bride does in the riches and honor of her betrothed. And thus his Christendom is his wife and empress in heaven and

upon earth, for she is called the bride of God who is Lord over all creatures, and she sits in the highest manner in her glory and power over sin, death, satan, hell, etc.

9. Behold, this he shows us in the every-day picture of the wedding feast or of the married state, where we see the love and faithfulness of pious wedded persons; also in the marriage feast, in the bride and the bridegroom s joy and riches; that we learn to believe this and that we also think that Christ's heart and mind are truly thus disposed to his bride the church; but with far greater love, faithfulness and grace. This he clearly shows us in his Word of the Gospel and by the Holy Spirit, whom he gives to his church; and prepares the glorious, joyful marriage feast, at which he is wedded to his bride and he takes her to himself, and, to speak in our childish and human way, leads his bride to the dance as with fife and drum, and takes her in his arm; again, he honors and adorns her with all his finery, that is with the blotting out and washing away of sins, with righteousness and the gift of the Holy Spirit, and with his light, knowledge, strength and all the gifts which belong to that life. These are different chains, rings, velvet, silk, pearls, treasures and jewels from the earthly ones, which are only a dead picture of those heavenly treasures.

10. Therefore, wherever you see or hear bride and bridegroom, or the joy and beauty of a marriage feast, there open your eyes and heart, and behold what your loving Lord and Savior presents and shows to you, who prepares a glorious, royal marriage feast for you, his beloved bride, a living member if you believe in him. In that is eternal joy, good cheer, singing and springing, eternal ornaments, and all riches and the fulness of everything good.

11. Therefore a hearty confidence in him should grow and increase in thee that he called and chose thee through baptism to his fellowship through his inexpressible hearty love and received thee, to release thee from sin, eternal death and the power of satan, and imparted to thee his body and life, and all that he has; yea, he so completely gave himself to thee, that thou mayest not only glory in what he did for thy

sake and gave to thee, but thou mayest comfortably and joyfully glory in him as being thine. And as a bride relies with hearty confidence upon her bridegroom and holds the heart of the bridegroom as her own heart, so do thou rely from the depth of thy heart upon the love of Christ, and entertain no doubt that he is not otherwise disposed to thee than as thy own heart is.

12. But this is opposed beyond measure in us by our old Adam, our flesh and blood, our blindness and the stiffened hardness of our hearts, which does not permit us to see or believe it; especially if we see and experience in ourselves and in this miserable life other things before our eyes and senses. For reason sees and understands it well that the marriage feast and bridal love are in themselves a lovely and cheerful picture, and it may be taught that Christ is a beautiful, noble, pious and faithful bridegroom, and his church a glorious, blessed bride. But things come to a stop later, when everyone is to believe for himself that he is also of Christ and a member of his body and Christ bears such a heart and love toward him. The reason is that I do not see such excellent glory in myself, but on the contrary my weakness and unworthiness, and feel nothing but sorrow, sadness and all kinds of suffering and even death, the grave, and maggots, which are about to consume me.

13. But in the face of this you should learn to believe the Word Christ himself speaks to you and God commands you to believe, that it is true (unless you wish to give God the lie) regardless of what you feel in your heart. For if you should believe, you must not cleave to what your thoughts and feelings say to you, but to what God's Word says, no matter how little of it you may experience. Therefore, if you are a person who feels his need and misery and desires from the heart to partake of this comfort and love of Christ, then incline your ears and heart hither to Christ, and lay hold of this comforting picture he presents to you, wherewith he shows that he will have himself known and believed by you, that he has in his heart a much warmer love and a more loyal fidelity to you, than any bridegroom to his be-

loved bride. And on the other hand you should have a much heartier and greater confidence and joy in him than any bride has to her bridegroom. So that here you may justly chastise yourself because of your unbelief, and say: Behold, can the bridal love cause such hearty confidence and joy between the bride and the bridegroom, which is still of a low order and transitory? Why do I not rejoice much more over my holy and faithful Savior, Christ, who gave himself for me and to me wholly as my own? Shame on me because of my unbelief, that my heart is not here full of laughter and eternal joy, when I hear and know how he says to me through his Word that he will be my beloved bridegroom. Should I not much rather have here another, a higher joy, and my eyes, thoughts, heart, and whole life cleave more to my beloved Savior, than a bride to her bridegroom, who, if she is a pious and true bride, sees and hears indeed nothing more gladly than her spouse? Yea, even when she does not see him and he is absent from her, her heart cleaves to him, so that she can not but think of him.

14. However, as I said, it is our old Adam, the corrupt nature, that does not allow the heart to lay hold of this knowledge, joy and consolation. Therefore it is and will doubtless continue to be, as St. Paul calls it in Eph. 5, 32, a mystery, a secret, deep, hidden, incomprehensible thing, but yet a something great, excellent and wonderful. Not only to the blind, foolish world, that cannot think or understand anything at all of these high divine things; but also for the beloved apostles and advanced Christians, that herein they have enough to learn and believe, and they themselves are compelled to confess how long they labored with it, preached about it, strove after it, and it is to them still a mystery in this life.

For St. Paul himself often complained that it did not work so powerfully in him, because of his flesh and blood, as it should work if it were as fully understood and apprehended as it should be; for he and other saints would not have been so anxious, sad and terrified, as he often was, and the prophet David also lamented in many Psalms; but their hearts would have soared in pure joy. However, they will be free from all this in the life beyond, where they will see without any covering and dimness to the vision, and be filled with joy and live forever. For the present it remains a mysterious, hidden, spiritual marriage feast, that one does not see with the eyes, nor grasp with the reason; but faith alone is able to grasp it, as faith holds only to the word it hears concerning it, and yet grasps it still very weakly on account of our perverse flesh.

15. For this marriage feast is so totally foreign to reason, that it is terrified when it thinks how great it is. I speak now still of the Christians; for the others do not come to it, they hold it simply as impossible, yea, as mere talk of fools and a fable, when they hear that God becomes man's bridegroom; but the Christians who have commenced to believe it, must be shocked and amazed at its greatness: Dear God, how shall I exalt myself so highly as to boast of being God's bride, and God's Son my bridegroom? How do I, a poor, offensive worm of the dust, come to this honor, which never befell the angels in heaven, that the eternal Majesty condescends so very low into my poor flesh and blood and thoroughly unites himself with me, that he will be one body with me, and yet I am from the sole of my foot to the crown of my head so completely full of filth, leprosy, sin and stench before God; how shall I then be considered the bride of the high, eternal and glorious Majesty and be one body with him?

16. But hear well that God desires it to be so. In Eph. 5, 25-27 he says: I will dress and place before me a bride, who shall be my church, that is glorious, of the glory I myself have and not having spot or wrinkle, but holy and without blemish, etc., just as I am. He does not speak of a bride that he finds in this state, pure, holy, blameless, without spot, etc.; such a bride he should not seek on the earth, but he should have remained among his angels in heaven to find her there. But he revealed himself through his Word to men, surely not for the sake of this life, but that he might be praised forever through her; and therefore he must

have had in mind something greater, to do with and through her. The great mystery is that he did not take upon himself the nature of angels, but united himself with the human nature.

17. Here on the earth he finds nothing but a corrupt, filthy, shameless, condemned bride of satan, that has become faithless to God, her Lord and Creator, and fallen under his eternal wrath and curse. If he is now to secure here a bride or congregation, who, to be sure, must be also pure and holy, otherwise there could be here no union, then he must first and in the highest degree show his love, that he applies his purity and holiness to her sins and condemnation, and thereby cleans and sanctifies her. This he did do, as St. Paul says in Eph. 5, 25-26, in that he gave himself for her and purchased her by his blood to sanctify her for himself, and besides cleansed and washed her by the baptism of water; and he adds a Word which one hears. By means of the same Word and baptism he prepares her to be his loving bride, and praises and claims her to be pure from sin, God's wrath and the power of satan; furthermore does he desire that she esteem herself also as a loving, beautiful, holy, glorious bride of God's Son.

18. Here no one sees how excellent a work is accomplished thus hidden and secretly through God's Word, baptism and our faith; and yet by it the result is accomplished that this company of poor sinful men, who were not worthy to behold God at a distance because of their great filthiness, are made through this bath and washing clean, beautiful and holy, so that they are well pleasing to God as the bride of his beloved Son and as his loving daughter; and this purifying commenced in this life, he develops and continues constantly in her until she is presented to him purer and more beautiful than the light and brightness of the sun.

19. Therefore a Christian must learn to believe this, so that he in the future does not consider himself in the light of his first birth, as he was born from Adam; but as he is called to Christ and baptized into him, and like all Christians

confides in and is united with him; so they should cling to him as to their bridegroom, who through the same washing of regeneration and the renewing of the Holy Ghost, while they are still unclean he continually purifies and adorns them until the day he presents his church to himself, not only without a spot or stain, but also without a wrinkle, very beautiful, sleek and perfect, like fresh youth.

20. Therefore do not be terrified if you feel too entirely unworthy and impure; for if your thoughts are fixed on that you will forget and lose this confidence and trust in Christ. But you must heed the Word Christ speaks to you: Although you are full of sin, death and perdition. yet you have here my righteousness and life, which I apply and give to you. If you are impure and filthy, you have here the washing of baptism and of my Word, through which I wash you and pronounce you clean, and will constantly cleanse you for ever and ever until you shall stand before me and all creatures perfectly beautiful and pure.

21. This he tells us not only through his Word; but in order that we might not complain being left without admonition and preaching, he presents it to us in so many different every-day pictures and parables of wedded love, yea, of the first warmth and fervency between a bride and groom; when we see how both hearts cling to one another and one has joy and pleasure in the other. Here the bride does not fear in the least that her groom will cause her suffering or harm or cast her away; but in hearty affection confides in him and doubts not he will take her into his arms, sit with her at the table, and give her as her own whatever he has. We should in this also truly know Christ's heart, and not allow ourselves to picture him otherwise than we hear and see him both in his own Word and in the parables and signs which present him to us, that we may indeed never dare to complain, except of ourselves and of our old Adam that hinders us in our beautiful joy.

22. For should not man become his own enemy, and only wish that death might soon do away with him, for the reason that he knows not himself and cannot rightly, as he

should, taste and enjoy his great treasure, joy and blessedness? And so perhaps it might be best for us, except that this life with its temptations, cross and sufferings is to be the school in which always and daily we more and more learn to know what he is in us and we in him, and in which therefore we also work for this that we may seize him, even as he ran after us and seized us, in that he fetched and won us for his own with his sweat and blood. Alas, however, that we are too weak, lazy and slow thus to run after him in this life!

23. Behold, such is the glorious royal wedding in this kingdom, which Christ calls the kingdom of heaven, and to which we, all of us, bidden and unbidden, Jews and Gentiles, come by means of the Gospel resounding in all the world, as called by fifes and drums which, after the manner of the Scriptures, are called the voices of the bridegroom and the bride. That is to say, a marriagelike voice or sound and tone, that is a token of the wedding and the joys, and is to announce unto everyone such joy and call us thereunto.

24. But now consider further how this wedding feast fares in the world, and how the world carries itself towards it when it is to become a partaker in this blessed kingdom. We have just heard how hard, on account of their flesh, this is even to Christians, albeit they strive after this kingdom of God and seek their comfort in Christ. But now it is further shown how the other, adverse realm of the devil in the world, as in its empire (as Christ in John 12, 31 calls him a prince of the world, and St. Paul, Eph. 6, 12, the lord of the world), fights against God's kingdom and drives and chases people, lest they accept and hear the joyous, comforting word about this wedding and joy in Christ, but rather, wittingly and knowingly, scorn the same, aye, oppose themselves to it, even though they be called and bidden thereto.

25. This is said especially of the Jewish people, who are the first bidden guests to whom God sent his servants, first the patriarchs and prophets, later also the apostles, causing them to be begged and admonished not to neglect the time of their blessedness and salvation. They, however, not alone

despise this but also fly at the servants of God, who offer them such grace, to beat them to death; nor will they listen or suffer to be told more of this wedding.

These are not common and ordinary people, but the best, wisest and holiest of all, who are occupied with far higher and more needful things than to be persuaded to come to this wedding, to receive good things for nothing, and to be helped into heaven. They know much better for themselves how, by their own precious life, to bring about great works, the law's holiness and God's service. Hereof more is said in the Gospel story of the great supper (Luke 14), concerning those who excuse themselves and would not come.

26. Like unto these are also all such as are by the Gospel called to faith and the knowledge of Christ, but will not hear and accept the same. These are always the greatest and best part of the world, who as we know, wish to be called God's people and the church. They also have to attend to far greater and better things,—how they may keep up their fine and glorious estate and condition, which they call the government and glory of the church. Of that they will not hear, and esteem it an innovation and change of the good and praiseworthy old order, etc. And the more one urges them to obey the Gospel, the less will they listen to it, and the more bitterly do they pursue it, as we always have it before our eyes in the world.

27. Well then, we should therefore honor at his wedding-feast the King and Lord of Glory, and thank him for his abundant grace and the good to which he has called us and of which he makes us worthy, sobeit we judge ourselves worthy of everlasting life, as St. Paul says, Acts 13, 46. And whatever men were to gain thereby, Christ has herewith foretold them. Thus they have themselves experienced and the belief, as it were, has come into their hands, that he has told them no lying story, but that it has proved only too true that the king has sent out his host and slain these murderers the which for now 1,500 years experience has confirmed, namely, that this judgment has not been removed, and that thus finally wrath has come over them and

they shall remain as naught. For he himself shows that it has never yet repented him, in that he thereupon forthwith says to his men: "The wedding is ready, but the guests were not worthy," etc.

28. Which is, also for other scorners and presecutors, a terrible token and example of the final wrath resolved against them and of such punishment wherewith he will altogether make an end also of them, because they would not partake of and enjoy this feast: as has already happened to Greece and Rome, and will likewise happen to our blasphemers and pursuers, unless the day of judgment come between.

29. These then have received their judgment as they would have it. In order, however, that Christ may still get people to his wedding feast, his servants must continually go on with their preaching, and bid and call whomsoever they find, until they fetch so many together that the tables are full, not indeed of the great ones, the holy and mighty men (who were first bidden but would not come). Rather must the poor, the cripples and the halt, as he elsewhere says, rejoice at being allowed to come to this feast—that is, the heathen, who are not numbered among God's people and have nothing whereof they might be proud.

But among this company who are here sitting at table, there is also found a rogue, whom the king, in looking over the guests, speedily recognizes and judges to have no wedding garment, and to have come, not in honor of the wedding, but as disgracing the bridegroom and the lord who has invited him. Now these are such as also permit themselves to be numbered among true Christians, hear the Gospel, are in the outward communion of the right church and make before the people as if they also might be of the Gospel—and still they are not in earnest about it.

30. With this Christ shows who on earth are that community which is called the church, to wit, not those who pursue God's Word and his servants of the Gospel. For these are already wholly excluded and removed by his final judgment, aye, they have spilt their own milk by their public

and self-confessed act of not accepting and suffering this preaching of the Gospel, and should not and cannot among Christians be considered members of the church, because they have not its doctrine and faith. Just as little can one consider professed heathen, Turks and Jews as the church or its members.

Such judgment we must now also pass on our persecutors and blasphemers of the Gospel, as for example the Pope and his following, and entirely separate ourselves from them, as they do not in the least belong to the church of Christ, but are damned by their own judgment; to which they testify by having turned us away as outlaws and outcasts. The church on earth, however, if we speak of the outward community, is a gathering of such as hear, believe and confess the right teaching of the Gospel of Christ, and have with them the Holy Ghost who sanctifies them and works in them by the Word and sacraments. Yet among these some are false Christians and hypocrites, who nevertheless are at one with them in the same doctrine and also hold communion in the sacraments and other outward offices of the church.

31. Aye, such people the Christians must suffer in their gathering and cannot, as men are, avoid it or prevent them from being amongst them, nor can they remove them or turn them out of their gathering. They cannot, indeed, judge and recognize them all, but must bear them and suffer their company, but only till God himself comes with his judgment, so that they become manifest and give themselves away by their wicked life or false belief and spirit of heresy as not being true and honest Christians. Of this St. Paul speaks, 1 Cor. 11, 19: "There must be also heresies among you, that they who are approved may be made manifest among you," and on the other hand also those who are not approved.

32. Thus here the King comes in, himself to behold the guests, and makes manifest him who has not the wedding garment. And now that he has become manifest and is nevertheless, hypocrite that he is, impenitent, obstinate and dumb, he causes him to be bound hand and foot and, that

he may not enjoy the feast, be cast out of the festive gathering, where there is naught but light and joy, into darkness, where there is no comfort nor blessedness, but only
weeping and gnashing of teeth.   This, then, likewise is done
in the church, by which such impenitent sinners, convicted
and overcome, are also openly shown out of the congregation and publicly declared outcasts from God's kingdom.

33. Therefore the Christians, who are the right and dear
guests at this wedding, at all times have this comfort that
the others who do not belong thereto, that is both persecutors
and false brethren, shall not enjoy the same.   For even as
the former, the persecutors, manifest themselves as not being
members of the church, in that they exclude themselves and
go apart; thus the others, who for a time have crept in and
have falsely sought cover under the name and semblance
of true Christians, shall also finally become manifest.   This
also St. Paul says, 1 Tim. 5, 24-25: "Some men's sins are
evident, going before unto judgment; and some men also
they follow after.   In like manner also there are good works
that are evident: and such as are otherwise cannot be hid."

34. And from this it is easy to understand what is meant
by this man's being without a wedding garment, namely,
without the new adornment in which we please God, which
is faith in Christ, and therefore also without truly good
works.   He remains in the old rags and tatters of his own
fleshly conceit, unbelief and security, without penitence and
understanding of his misery.   He does not from his heart
seek comfort in the grace of Christ, nor betters his life by it,
and looks for no more in the Gospel than what his flesh
covets.   For this wedding garment must be the new light of
the heart, kindled in the heart by the knowledge of the
graciousness of this bridegroom and his wedding feast.
Thus the heart will wholly cleave to Christ and, transfused
by such comfort and joy, will so live and do as it knows to
be pleasing unto him, even as a bride towards the bridegroom.

35. This St. Paul calls "putting on the Lord Christ" (Gal.
3, 27; Rom. 13, 14), also "being clothed that we shall not

be found naked" (2 Cor. 5, 3) ; which takes place especially through faith, by which the heart is renewed and purified, and of which thereupon also the fruits—provided it be the true faith—follow and prove themselves. On the other hand, where there is no faith, there also the Holy Ghost is not, nor such fruits as please God. For whosoever does not know Christ through faith and has him not in his heart, he will also care little for God's word, nor think of living according to it; he will remain proud, insolent and headstrong, though outwardly he may, with a false semblance, practice hypocrisy and deceit.

TWENTY-FIRST SUNDAY AFTER TRINITY.

This sermon is found in all the editions of the Church Postil and in five pamphlet editions printed at Wittenberg in 1522, 1523 and 1524. The title of one pamphlet is: "A sermon on the fourth chapter of the Gospel of John. A nobleman whose son was sick at Capernaum, etc. In which is shown how faith once begun should be increased and laid hold of. Martin Luther, 1524, Wittenberg." Perhaps printed first: "The Three Sermons," Mat. 12, "The Sign of Jonah"; John 4, "The Nobleman's Son," and Luke 19, "Palm Sunday. Wittenberg, 1522." Erl. 14, 249; W. 2351; St. L. 11, 1762.

Text: John 4, 46-54. He came therefore again unto Cana of Galilee, where he made the water wine. And there was a certain nobleman, whose son was sick at Capernaum. When he heard that Jesus was come out of Judæa into Galilee, he went unto him, and besought him that he would come down, and heal his son; for he was at the point of death. Jesus therefore said unto him, Except ye see signs and wonders, ye will in no wise believe. The nobleman saith unto him, Sir, come down ere my child die. Jesus saith unto him, Go thy way; thy son liveth. The man believed the word that Jesus spake unto him, and he went his way. And as he was now going down, his servants met him, saying, that his son lived. So he inquired of them the hour when he began to amend. They said therefore unto him, Yesterday at the seventh hour the fever left him. So the father knew that it was at that hour in which Jesus said unto him, Thy son liveth: and himself believed, and his whole house. This is again the second sign that Jesus did, having come out of Judæa into Galilee.

CONTENTS: THE NOBLEMAN'S SON OF CAPERNAUM HEALED. AN EXAMPLE OF FAITH.

*The contents of this Gospel. 1.

I. THE FIRST POINT TO NOTE IN THIS GOSPEL IS, THAT FAITH MAKES THE TREASURES OF CHRIST THE PROPERTY OF ALL BELIEVERS. 2.

II. THE SECOND POINT TO NOTE IS, THE INCREASE OR GROWTH OF FAITH.

1. The foundation and cause of this increase. 3.
2. The nature of this increase. 4-7.
3. The objection raised by this increase, and the answer. 8-10.
4. The increase takes place under many kinds of trials and temptations. 10-12f.
* Where the heart does not stand firm on the Word, it cannot withstand temptation. 13-15.
* Of the knowledge of the law and of Christ. 16.

* The stronger faith is, the weaker is the flesh; and the weaker faith is, the stronger is the flesh. 17.

III. THE THIRD POINT TO NOTE IS, THE SEALING AND CONFIRMATION OF FAITH.
1. The nature of this sealing and confirming. 18-19.
2. This sealing and confirming takes place under many kinds of temptation. 20-21.
* Of the exercise of faith. 22.
* Conclusion. 23.

SUMMARY OF THIS GOSPEL: 1. Here we have an example, in which you see how imperfect faith increases, even when we do not cease to pray.

2. When we are delivered from temptation, our faith is increased, to the end that we may more strongly withstand future temptations and persecutions.

THE NOBLEMAN'S SON HEALED.

1. Today's Gospel pictures to us a remarkable example of faith, for St. John carefully notes at three different times that the nobleman believed, and we may indeed be greatly moved by the fact, and ask, what kind of faith must he have had, that the Evangelist mentioned it so often. We have already learned so much about faith and the Gospel that I think we should rightly understand it. But since it ever occurs again and again, we are obliged to discuss it frequently.

2. In the first place, I have often said that faith through the Gospel fully brings the Lord Jesus with all his riches home to every man; and that one Christian has just as much as another, and the child baptized today has not less than St. Peter and all the saints in heaven. We are all equal and alike in reference to faith, and one person has his treasure just as full and complete as another.

3. Our Gospel lesson speaks further of the increase of faith, and here there is a difference. Although faith fully possesses Christ and all his riches, yet it must nevertheless be continually kept in motion and exercised, so that it may have assurance, and firmly retain its treasures. There is a

difference betweeen having a thing and firmly keeping hold of it, between a strong and a weak faith. Such a great treasuse should be firmly seized and well guarded, so that it may not be easily lost or taken from us. I may have it indeed in its entirety, although I hold it only in a paper sack, but it is not so well preserved as if I had it locked in an iron chest.

4. Therefore we must so live on the earth, not that we think of something different that is better to acquire than what we already possess; but that we strive to lay hold of the treasure more and more firmly and securely from day to day. We have no reason to seek anything more than faith; but here we must see to it how faith may grow and become stronger. Thus we read in the Gospel, that, although the disciples of Christ without doubt believed (for otherwise they had not followed him), yet he often rebuked them on account of their weak faith. They had indeed faith, but when it was put to the test, they let it sink and did not support it. So it is with all Christians; where faith is not continually kept in motion and exercised, it weakens and decreases, so that it must indeed vanish; and yet we do not see nor feel this weakness ourselves, except in times of need and temptation, when unbelief rages too strongly; and yet for that very reason faith must have temptations in which it may battle and grow.

5. Therefore it is not as the idle babblers among the theologians of the schools taught, who make out that we are lazy and careless, by saying: If one have the smallest drop or spark of love and faith, he will be saved. The Scriptures teach that one must increase and progress. True it is that you possess Christ through faith, although you only hold the treasure in a poor cloth; yet you must see to it that you firmly lay hold of him and let no power rob you of him.

6. Consequently this nobleman or officer, whoever he was (I hold he was a courtier of King Herod), was so far in faith that he believed if he could bring Jesus into his home, he would then surely heal his son; for he had heard God's Word or the Gospel of Christ, that he cheerfully helped every person that was brought to him and refused no one his

favor. His faith laid hold of this and that was the reason
he went to Christ. For if his heart had been kept in sus-
pense, so that he had thought: Who knows whether he can
help you or will help you? he would not have gone to him.
Therefore it is certain that he had beforehand so conceived
of Christ and believed that he would help him.

7. The nature and manner of faith are to picture and
mirror the goodness of Christ thus in the heart of man.
Therefore the Epistle to the Hebrews says, in 11, 1: "Faith
is the substance of things hoped for," that is, of something
good, the grace and goodness of God. Now the faith of this
man stood so, that if he had continued in it he would without a doubt have been saved, and the Lord would have had
pleasure in it. However, he dealt severely with him, found
an imperfection in his faith, chastised him and said:
"Except ye see signs and wonders, ye will in no wise believe."

8. How does this agree with what I said before? If faith
and a good confidence in him brought the nobleman to
Christ, how can he then say: Ye will in no wise believe, unless ye see signs? But, as I said, he wishes to show him
that his faith is not yet strong enough; for he still clings
only to the seeing and the experience of the bodily present
Christ. Likewise did Christ chastise the disciples in the
boat, when the storm came and he said to them: "Why are
ye fearful, O ye of little faith?" Mat. 8, 26. As if he were to
say: Where is your faith now? Therefore, however good
and genuine faith may be, it falls back when it comes to a
battle, unless it has been well disciplined and has grown
strong.

9. Therefore you should not imagine it is enough if you
have commenced to believe; but you must diligently watch
that your faith continue firm, or it will vanish; you are to
see how you may retain this treasure you have embraced;
for satan concentrates all his skill and strength on how to
tear it out of your heart. Therefore the growth of your
faith is truly as necessary as its beginning, and indeed more
so; but all is the work of God. The young milk-faith is
sweet and weak; but when long marches are required and

faith is attacked, then God must strengthen it, or it will not
hold the field of battle.

10. Therefore this man would not have been helped by the
faith he had at first; he would have been forced to retreat
had not Christ come and strengthened him. But how did
he strengthen him? The nobleman believed, if he came to
him in his house, he could surely heal his son. Then Christ
gave him a rebuke, a bitter and hard answer: "Except ye
see signs and wonders, ye will in no wise believe." With
these words he gives faith a scornful rebuff that it can
not stand. The poor man was terrified and his faith at once
began to sink and to vanish, therefore he says:

"Sir, come down ere my child die."

11. As if he would say: Yes, you must hasten and come
and yourself be present, or my son will die. Here Christ
now bestows upon him a stronger faith, as God does upon all
whom he strengthens in faith, and raises him thus to a
higher degree or plain that he may become strong and believe in a different way than he did before; and he speaks
thus to the father:

"Go thy way; thy son liveth."

12. Had he thus said to him before that his son would
live he would have been unable to believe; but now he believes when faith springs forth in his heart and begets in
him another faith, so that he becomes a different man. Therefore the Lord adds to his great rebuke great strength. For,
he must now cling to that which he does not see; for he did
not before believe that Christ had such power and influence
that he could heal his son when he did not see him and was
not present with him. It is truly strong faith, that a heart
can believe what it does not see and understand, contrary to
all the senses and reason, and can cling only to God's Word.
Here there is nothing manifest except that he believed,
otherwise he would have received no help. In faith one
must look to nothing but the Word of God. Whoever permits anything else to be pictured in his eyes is already lost.
Faith clings to the naked and pure Word, neither to its

works nor to its merits. If your heart does not thus stand naked, your cause is lost.

13. Let us now take an example of this: When a priest, nun or monk boasts that he has maintained his chastity, said many masses, fasted often, prayed much and the like, and then does not keep in mind God's Word, but his own good works, and builds upon them, so that he thinks God must consequently hear him, then he is lost; for as long as this picture is in the mind, faith cannot be there. Therefore when one is about to die and death is present, and he looks around for a way of escape and for the first step he should take, then satan is at hand and pictures to him how dreadful and horrible death is; and besides he sees hell and God's judgment before his eyes. Then satan is victorious, for there is no help as long as this is before his eyes. If he were wise and pictured nothing else in his heart and continued to cling to the Word of God alone, he would live, for that is a living Word. Therefore, whoever clings to the Word must stand where the living and eternal Word stands.

14. However, this is exceedingly difficult to do; for here you see how hard it was for this nobleman; also, for the Apostles in the Gospel, Mat. 8, 25-26, when they were on the water in a boat and the boat was about to sink and the waves beat into the boat, so that death was before their eyes; then they lost their hold on the Word. Had they firmly believed and said: Here we have the Word of God, here is Christ; where he is, there we are also; there would have been no danger. But since they did not have such faith, they would have had to sink and perish had not Christ come to their help. Just so it was with Peter, when he walked on the sea and came to Christ: so long as he held to the Word, the water had to bear him up; but when he turned his eyes from Christ and he let go the Word he saw the wind blowing and he began to sink.

15. Therefore I said, we must let go of every thing and cling only to the Word; if we have laid hold of that, then let rage and roar the world, death, sin, hell and all misfortune. But if you let go the Word, then you must perish.

This we see also in people who seek temporal nourishment: when they have sufficient, and their house and barn are full, they easily trust in God and say, they have a gracious God; but when they have nothing they begin to doubt, then their faith vanishes; for they picture before their eyes, that there is nothing at hand and not any provision in store, and they know not how they shall exist; thus care and worry drive faith out of the heart. But if they would lay hold of God's Word, they would think thus: My God lives, he assures me he will sustain my life; I will go forth and labor, he will make everything right, as Christ says, Mat. 6, 33: "But seek ye first the kingdom of God and his righteousness; and all these things shall be added unto you." If I retained this Word and would cast the other out of my mind, I would not come into need. But as long as you picture before your eyes your poverty, you cannot believe. This nobleman doubtless had also a picture in his eyes, that he might have thought: He will not grant my request, he will give me a hard answer, will not accompany me home and will cruelly turn me away. Had he fixed his eyes upon such treatment he would have been lost; but since he turned his eyes from such thoughts, Christ later gives him blessed consolation and says: "Go thy way; thy son liveth."

16. This is the nature and way of faith:—thus God deals with us, when he wishes to strengthen us. This is also what St. Paul means in 2 Cor. 3, 18, when he says: "But we all, with unveiled face beholding as in a mirror the glory of the Lord, are transformed into the same image from glory to glory, even as from the Lord the Spirit." The glory of the Lord with Paul is the knowledge of God. Moses also possessed a glory, the knowledge and understanding of the law. When I have a knowledge of the law, I look into his clear countenance and into his pure light. But now we have passed through that and have a higher knowledge of Christ our Lord. Whoever knows him as the man who helps in time of need and gives power to fulfil the law, through whom we have acquired the forgiveness of sins: in that way he mirrors his glory in us. That is, as the rays of the sun are

reflected in the water or in a mirror, so Christ reflects himself and gives forth a lustre from himself in our hearts, in a
way that we are transformed from one degree of glory to
another, so that we daily increase and more clearly know
and understand the Lord. Then we shall be changed and
transformed into the same image, in a way that we all will
be one bread with Christ. This is not accomplished in that
we ourselves do it by virtue of our own power; but God, who
is the Spirit, must do it. For even if the Holy Spirit
began such glory or illumination in us and would later forsake us, then we would be as we were before.

17. Now we ought to be so armed that we do not remain
standing still at the first degree, but continually increase;
therefore the cross, temptation and opposition must come,
by means of which faith will grow and become strong, and
as the glory of faith increases, the mortification of the body
also increases; the stronger faith is, the weaker will the flesh
be, and the smaller the faith, the stronger the flesh, and the
less will the flesh be denied. We are apt to think, if I shall
continually help my neighbor, what will become of me? To
what will I come at last? But if we had mirrored in us
true faith and Christ, we would not doubt that we should
have enough, but remember that God will surely come to
our assistance when the crisis comes. But if we are lost in
such a little tempest, what will we do in the great conflicts of
the soul? See, in this way faith is exercised and increased;
if we go forth, and are to-day as yesterday, to-morrow as
to-day, that is not a Christian life. Now the second thing
for which John praises this man is, that he increased in faith.

18. In the third place, he says: While he was going home,
his servants met him and said to him that his son lived, and
he experienced that his son began to amend in the very
hour that the Lord had said to him, "Thy son liveth;" and
he believed and his whole house. Here the Evangelist says
again that he believed. But, if he had not believed heretofore
why did he come to Christ? This is a more perfect faith,
that was confirmed by the miracle. In this manner our Lord
God deals with us to make us more perfect and raise us

ever to a higher plane of faith. If we pass through this condition, we thus come into the experience and become assured of our faith, as we see here that the nobleman overcomes all difficulties like an iconoclast who tears down pictures and images, receives applause and becomes certain of his cause, in that he has experienced it, and finds that he is helped by faith, and all agree; the time, the miracle and the word with the faith.

19. What then did he now believe? Not that his son had been healed, for this kind of faith is now at an end, the healing has been done, and it is now a thing of the past. He sees before his eyes that his son lives. But out of his experience comes forth another faith, that Christ would in the future continue to help him out of other troubles and whatever dark pictures might rise before him; that is what he believed. If the Lord had said to him: Go and die; he would have replied: Although I do not know whither I shall go or where the inn is, yet since I tried before what faith is, I will again cling to the Word. You helped me once when I could not see nor understand; you will now again help me. Moreover, if Christ had said to him: Leave home and land and your possessions, and come, follow me; he would not have thought: Yes, but how shall I support myself? No doubt the picture would have appeared before his eyes: There is everything in abundance, here is nothing; shall I let go of that, what will I come to? But now he thinks: Although nothing is here, and I see nothing, I will nevertheless cling to the Word, he will surely help me. I tried it before. This is impossible for reason, but faith can do all things.

20. Therefore faith exercises itself in various temptations and every day new temptations arise; for the former experiences do not always return, as one sees here. This nobleman has already made use of the work of faith, that is now past, it will never return again; but he must now try another. Therefore the oftener a person experiences the same temptation, the better it is for him; the more he triumphs over the storm, the firmer he lays hold of Christ,

and becomes skilled so to be ready to bear all that is laid upon him.

21. In like manner it went with the Holy Patriarchs, and thus it always goes with us; so that I believe what has taken place in former times, is of no help to me, but my faith must always turn its attention to things of the future. Therefore, when God called Abraham to depart out of his own country, he did it, and believed it, Gen. 12, 1f. Now when he came into that country, God called him to go into another and later into another. Thus he continually increased in faith, and later he became so assured, and had traced and experienced how God dealt with him, and became such a perfect character that he was willing to offer his own son as a sacrifice to God. From this it follows: Whoever is greatly tried and disciplined in this way, faces death much more willingly.

22. Thus you see how an example of growing faith is here portrayed; it is now clear enough, therefore take it well to heart. Every person has indeed his own experiences in life by which he may exercise his faith, to trust God to help him. Thus he will be able to prove how God helps him, and he can thus make progress and grow in faith. As soon as one experience ends another always begins, so that we may see and grasp the truth that our Lord God is true. If we have the confidence that he will nourish and sustain our bodies, we can also believe that he will save our souls. I have now spoken enough about faith.

23. The other part of this Gospel, on love, every one can easily understand for himself. It is clearly enough set forth and it is not necessary to speak much about how Christ served and helped this nobleman. He had no advantage or gain from it himself, but he did it purely gratuitously out of love. Also you see how the nobleman became a servant of his son. Whatever there is more in this Gospel belongs to its spiritual significance, and its exposition word for word we will commend to the quiet and wise spirits.

TWENTY-FIRST SUNDAY AFTER TRINITY.

Second Sermon: John 4, 46-54.

This sermon is printed in all the editions of the Church Postil and in three pamphlet editions, all of which appeared at Wittenberg in one year, 1526. The title of all three is the same: "A sermon for the 21st Sunday after Pentecost, on the true nature of faith. Of the nature of the wickedness of the devil our adversary. The saying of Paul in 2 Cor. 4, "we have this treasure in earthen vessels' and Mat. 13, 'Faith is like a grain of mustard seed.' Richly explained and adorned with beautiful examples from Moses, St. Peter and others. How faith begins like a blossoming tree. Martin Luther, Wittenberg, 1526." Erl. 14, 261; W. 11, 2365; St. L. 11, 1772.

CONTENTS: OF FAITH IN GENERAL, AND OF THE NOBLE-
MAN IN PARTICULAR.

1. A beautiful example of faith is presented in this Gospel, exhibiting, as it does, the nature and character of faith, namely, that it is to increase and become perfect; and it portrays faith in a way as to show that it is not a quiet and idle, but a living, restless thing, that either retrogrades or advances, lives and moves; and where this does not occur, faith does not exist, but only a lifeless notion of the heart concerning God. For true, living faith, which the Holy Spirit pours into the heart, cannot be inactive. This I say for the purpose that no one may be sure, even if he has attained faith, that he now has everything; with this it shall not stop, for it is not sufficient to begin, but one must constantly grow and increase, and continue learning to know God better.

2. For, on the other hand, it is not the nature and custom of our enemy, the devil, to be idle, as 1 Peter, 5, 8 says: "Be sober, be watchful; your adversary, the devil, as a roaring lion, walketh about, seeking whom he may devour." If then the devil neither sleeps nor rests, it is not right for a Christian to be idle and fold his hands; but he is to consider how he may fortify himself against the power of the devil; for he is not called the prince of this world in vain, John 14, 30, as to-day's Epistle teaches, Eph. 6, 12: "For our wrestling is not against flesh and blood, but against the principalities, against the powers, against the world-rulers of this darkness, against the spiritual hosts of wickedness in the heavenly places." This prince rules the world, howls and rages, is mad and foolish, cannot bear that a Christian progresses; nor is it to be wondered at, for thereby a rupture is made in his kingdom and his net broken. Hence, wherever possible, he hinders the growth and development of the Christian life.

3. When, therefore, the fire of faith is kindled and burns, and the devil feels it and becomes aware of it, he immediately grasps it with all his cunning, for he knows how his

kingdom is endangered by it. Therefore he endeavors with great zeal to protect his kingdom, and exerts himself to retain all under his obedience. Certain it is, therefore, that, when a person begins to believe, temptation and persecution will be sure closely to follow him; and if this does not occur, it is a sign his faith is not true and he has not rightly apprehended the Gospel. For that rogue, the devil, has a sharp vision and easily becomes conscious of the presence of a true Christian. Therefore he exerts himself to entrap him, and surrounds and attacks him on all sides; for he cannot bear that anyone should desert his kingdom.

4. Therefore it is dangerous to live heedlessly, for the devil is likely to take us by surprise. This happens even to the great ones among the saints, who rightly apprehend the Word of God. If they regard themselves as standing securely, this rogue is behind them, strikes them down and wrestles with them until they are vanquished. Behold, what happened to the great men of God, to Moses, to Aaron and to the princes of Judah. They had an excellent faith, when they led the people out of Egypt, and all the people went in faith through the Red Sea, through death, through the wilderness and through many other wonderful experiences, in which they manifested their faith; but at last they came to a point where everything was ruined; they feared that they would have to die of hunger and thirst in the parched wilderness. Is it not a pity that after manifesting their faith in so many great trials, going into and through death, wrestling with and overcoming it, when they regarded themselves at the very best, they should fall, allow themselves to be overcome by their belly and murmur against God, and be so fiercely attacked that they succumb and all be overthrown by satan. Hence no one is secure, unless his faith continues to grow stronger and stronger.

5. Moses, who had such an exceedingly strong faith, also fell; when he was to strike water out of the rock with his rod, he doubted and said to the people, Num. 20, 10: "Hear now, ye rebels; shall we bring ye forth water out of this

rock?" [According to Luther's translation, "Come here, let us see if we can bring forth water out of the rock for you."] The good man, Moses, who had performed so many miracles, is tripped by reason and falls into carnal thoughts, fearing that the unbelief of the people would hinder the great miracle and sign. But he should have adhered firmly to the Word of God and esteemed that higher, greater, stronger and more efficacious than the unbelief of the people; but the good man was so severely tempted that he stumbled and fell.

6. We have similar examples in the New Testament. Peter was strong and confident in faith. When he saw Jesus walking on the water, he said, impelled by his strong faith, Mat. 14, 28: "Lord, bid me come unto thee," and stepped out of the ship into the water. He was confident that the water would bear him. Peter had a remarkable faith and a bold spirit, so that he ventured upon the water and danger, yea, even death, making the venture boldly and daringly by reason of his faith in Christ. But when he thought he was most secure, the wind and storm arose and he forgot the Word and lost faith; he fell, sank into the water and permitted satan to tear faith out of his heart. Where was then his great faith? Faith is a tender, subtle thing, and we so easily make a mistake and are liable to stumble; but the devil is watchful, and unless men exercise watchfulness, he quickly gains his point.

7. How strongly the people were inclined toward Christ! They regarded him as a Prophet, followed him eagerly, defended him with a zeal that even the nobles of the people were amazed and did not dare to lay hands on him. But when he had been seized and bound, and led away and crucified, the people forsook him. Alas! alas! he is no longer a Prophet; no one stands by him, yea, instead they cry out, Luke 23, 21, "Crucify him, crucify him!" and what is still worse, his own Disciples forsake him. Where now was their faith and holiness?

8. So, also, we meet with similar occurrences in our day. At first, when the Gospel was proclaimed, it was a lovely

sermon and all the world desired to become Christian, nobody opposed it.   But when attacks were made on the
monks, priests, and nuns, when the Mass was criticised;
alas! they fell like leaves from the trees.   Afterwards, when
the nobles were also attacked, the Gospel was still more
persecuted and its reception began more and more to abate.
The devil does not rest yet, and hence he stirs up so many
sects and factions.   How many sects have we not already
had? One has taken up the sword, another has attacked the
Sacrament of the Lord's Supper, others that of baptism.   The
devil does not sleep, he will do many more such things, he
looks around and exerts himself to exterminate the pure
doctrine in the Church and will finally, it is feared, bring
it to this, that should one pass through all Germany he
would find no pure pulpit, where the Word of God is
preached as in former days.   He tries with all his might to
prevent the pure doctrine from being taught, for he cannot
endure it.

9.   Escape from the enemy is most difficult.   He lurks
and watches everywhere, and pushes his affairs so hard,
that even the learned fall and the elect stumble, as did Moses,
St. Peter, and the Apostles.   We think we are safe, permit
matters to drift along, no one is concerned for his own
welfare, no one cares for it.   We should pray and call on
God to maintain the Gospel and cause his holy name to be
proclaimed more and more widely; but no one cares, no
one prays for the advancement of the Gospel.   The consequence of this must be, God will overthrow both us and
satan.   Our end will be, he will make us bite the dust, and
through our own rashness and indifference we shall fall
into great misery.

10.   The devil also is able to present to the factious spirits
the idea that they regard themselves as right, like the
Arians who thought their cause was right.   But there was
no one who could decide whether or not their teachings
were orthodox.   The Christian, however, subdues his reason
and does not deceive himself, but in humility says to God:
"Dear Lord, although I feel certain concerning the matter,

yet without thee I cannot maintain it; therefore help me or else I am lost.'' To be sure he may feel certain of it, like Peter on the water, who could not well feel more sure that the water would bear him on; he knew of no more hindrance; but when the storm burst on him he saw wherein he lacked. The heart must have thoroughly grasped this idea that, although we may feel secure concerning a matter and have Scripture for it, and be prepared and fortified in the best possible manner with clear proofs, it is the power, will and might of God that protect us and defend us against the devil, our adversary and most bitter foe.

11. This occurs only, however, when God awakens us and keeps us in his fear, so that we may always be concerned and cry to him: ''O Lord, help us and increase our faith, for without thee we are lost,'' Luke 17, 5. Our hearts should always be in the condition as if we had only begun to believe to-day, and always be so disposed toward the Gospel as if we had never before heard it. We should make a fresh beginning each day. The nature and character of faith is constantly to grow and become stronger. The devil, as has already been said, is not idle, and has no rest. If he is struck down once, he will arise again; if he cannot enter at the front door, he sees to it that he enters at the rear; if he cannot effect an entrance in this way, he breaks in through the roof or digs his way through underneath the doorsill, toiling until he effects an entrance, employing all manner of cunning and schemes. If one way fails, he tries another and perseveres until he succeeds.

12. Over against this, man is a poor, weak creature, as St. Paul says, 2 Cor. 4, 7, ''We have this treasure in earthen vessels.'' The treasure is the Gospel; but I am weaker than the vessel in the potter's hands. An earthen vessel is a weak thing and is easily broken and its contents spilled. Hence the devil, when he notices what a treasure faith is and in what a poor vessel it is kept, rages and storms, and in his wrath says to us: ''I will strike you and shatter your vessel: you have a great treasure, but I will spill it for you; I will give you a blow. If I were permitted, how

soon would I shatter the vessel. You are after all nothing but a little poor and weak vessel of earth.''

13. So God has placed this poor, little vessel among enemies. How soon may it not therefore be destroyed! It may be broken with a club; yea, if a serpent would prick it, it would go to pieces. It would be a small matter for satan suddenly to ruin an entire country. Hence he is angry, because God takes hold of the matter in such a bantering manner and confronts him with a poor little earthen vessel, and yet he is so great a prince and so powerful a lord of the world. I would also be vexed, if I were a strong man and some one were to tickle me with a straw. I would undoubtedly crush the straw in my anger, and would rather be met with spear, sword and complete armor; even as the strong Goliath was vexed because David, without armor, dared to approach him with a staff, 1 Sam. 17, 43. Thus also the devil is angry because God wants to trample him under foot by means of flesh and blood. If a mighty spirit were opposed to him, he would not be so sorely vexed; but it greatly angers him that a poor worm of the dust, a fragile earthen vessel defies him, a weak vessel against a mighty prince. God has placed his treasure, says St. Paul, in a poor, weak vessel; for man is weak, easily aroused to anger, avaricious, arrogant, and weighed down with other imperfections, through which satan easily shatters the earthen vessel; for if God would permit him, he would soon have utterly destroyed the whole vessel. He breaks many an earthen vessel with false doctrine.* Now all this happens, says St. Paul, in order that we may learn our inability to accomplish anything by our own strength, but alone by the power of God. God has, therefore, bid defiance to the devil and said to him: Thou mighty spirit, I will oppose thee with a poor, weak earthen vessel; nevertheless, seize it. This angers the devil exceedingly. Therefore he goes about, as a roaring lion, in

---

* Instead of "the whole vessel" etc. d. has: "Destroy all men just as he ruins many souls through false doctrine."

order to break and shatter to pieces the fragile vessels made of earth.*

14. See what he did with the prophets whom the peasants raised up. Certainly, no one did this but the devil, who desired to shatter the vessels and indeed did shatter many of them, so that faith and the Scriptures fared badly among them.

15. Indeed, more factious spirits shall arise and it shall come to pass that they will not regard Christ as God, nor as the son of a virgin. For the devil is so cunning and skilful that, if one thing is taken from him, he makes use of another. Thus it has been from the beginning, and it will continue to be so in the future. And all this is permitted, in order that we may be on our guard, lift up our eyes to heaven, so that we may know and acknowledge God, and, if we have made a beginning in faith, that God may nourish and protect the same and preserve the vessel by his power. But satan would gladly break this earthen vessel and crush it under his feet. Others, who belong to him, he pushes hither and thither, according to his pleasure, and rejoices in them.—This is intended to serve as an introduction to the Gospel. We will now consider the text in its proper order. The Evangelist says:

"And there was a certain nobleman, whose son was sick at Capernaum."

16. This has occurred to other people also, namely, that they have had sick children; but what is to be particularly noted here, appears in these words:

"When he heard that Jesus was come out of Judea into Galilee, he went unto him, and besought him that he would come down, and heal his son; for he was at the point of death."

17. Here begins the faith that depends on Christ. This Gospel shows that he had faith; for he hears of Christ, how he heals the sick; his heart recognizes Christ, cleaves to him and thinks thus: If he helps all others, he will also help

* Instead of "and said to him" etc. d. has "that he might overthrow him through the greatest weakness of flesh and blood and bring shame upon him. This angers" etc.

me and heal my son. He regarded Christ as the person who can help men, and he expects every benefit from him. This indeed, is the heart of a true Christian, since it leads him to attach himself to Christ. If, however, this nobleman had remained in doubt, he would not have come to Christ, but his heart would have been in the condition to say: "He, indeed, helps others, but who knows if he will help me also;" and he might have left the matter rest at this. But his faith was a living faith, and hence he arose and went to Christ. This was the beginning of faith.

18. Now you shall see how strangely and contrary to expectation Christ met him and how his faith was tried, when he said to him:

"Except ye see signs and wonders, ye will in no wise believe."

19. How are we to understand this? He says, Ye do not believe, and yet ye have faith? Thus the Lord also spoke to Peter, Mat. 14, 31, "O thou of little faith, wherefore didst thou doubt?" Peter was confident and had faith; therefore he ventured out on the water; but when he saw the storm rage, he doubted and sank. So here also: The nobleman had heard reports concerning Christ, that he was helping everybody. He believed this and came to him. But when he heard that Christ refused to come to him, he felt hurt and his faith drooped, and he feared lest Christ would refuse to help him. This was a rebuff and here began the trial of incipient faith; for this was a hard saying, "Except ye see signs and wonders, ye will in no wise believe." This expression was a trial of his faith, and produced a doubt, and caused him to stumble. The devil stood back of him and said: Return to your home, await the result; he will not help you. But the nobleman was not so easily repulsed, but said to the Lord:

"Sir, come down ere my child die."

20. Faith was ready to droop and sink; but the Lord did not forsake him, raised him up and said to him:

"Go thy way; thy son liveth."

21. He must have had a pure faith, or else he would not have asked the Lord to come to his son. What then did he

lack? This: He believed if Christ came to his house, he could heal his son; but unless he were present, he could not effect the cure. His faith was not strong enough to realize that Christ could heal without being present. Hence, his faith had to attain a higher stage. His weak faith was gone, the little earthen vessel was shattered, and he thought his son had to die; but Christ approached, raised him up, placed him on a higher plane of faith, and said to him: "Go thy way; they son liveth." Thus the man advanced from his first faith, when he believed that Christ could heal if he were present, to a higher stage of faith, by reason of which he now believed the mere word of Christ. For if he had not believed the Word, he would not have ceased until the Lord had accompanied him to his house; but he accepted the Word, believed Christ and clung to his word; for the son was at home, and Christ was with the father.

22. The father accepted the word of Christ and said in his heart: My son is ill; but I shall find him well. This was faith over against reason and experience. Reason would have led him to say: When I left my son, he was ill. As you left him, so you shall find him. But faith says the contrary, stands firmly on the Word and drowns itself in it, and does not at all doubt that it shall be as the Word declares: "Go thy way; thy son liveth."

23. This is a pure and strong faith, that requires the individual to cast away all sense, understanding, reason, eyes and heart, and sink himself into one little word and be satisfied with and feel secure in it. Christ says, Thy son liveth, so he says to himself: It is certainly true, I shall find it so. Thus faith does not remain idle or quiet, but progresses and rises higher.

24. So Christ also deals with us and permits us to be tried, in order to strengthen our faith. If at the close of our lives, when our time comes to die, we shall have a spark of such faith, it will be well with us; as Christ said to his disciples in the Gospel, Mat. 17, 20, "If ye have faith as a grain of mustard seed, ye shall say to this mountain, Remove

hence to yonder place; and it shall remove; and nothing shall be impossible to you.'' A mustard seed is very small, but he who has such faith, shall certainly be saved. The truth lies not in the fact that faith is small; but in that the mustard seed remains and is not destroyed by the birds; that the devil cannot tear faith out of our hearts. It does not matter how insignificant faith may be; but the power lies in seeing to it that faith be not overthrown.

25. Peter on the water retained his pure faith as long as he unhesitatingly ventured on the water according to the word of Christ; for that reason the water bore him and he did not sink. Had he remained in this faith, he might have gone hundreds of miles on the water; but as soon as he wavered, he began to sink. So also Moses, who had a strong faith, but fell from it. Therefore, it does not matter whether faith be strong or weak; but that it perseveres, no matter how weak it may be. It may happen that he who has a weak faith, abides in faith; and that he who has a strong faith, doubts and falls. Moses and Peter had great and strong faith, so that Moses by faith led the people of Israel through the midst of the sea and through death, and Peter boldly ventured on the sea; but they both fell, although God raised them up again.* But the thief on the cross laid hold on faith once for all and clung to it.

26. God deals with us in a way so as to put down arrogance, and that we may not become haughty and wanton, but always remain in his fear. For when temptation comes, we are liable to fall into error. We have a beautiful parable of this in the tree which begins to blossom in the spring, and soon spreads out entirely covered with white blossoms; but as soon as rain falls on it many of the blossoms are ruined, and frost utterly destroys many more of them. Afterwards when the fruit begins to appear and any wind happens to arise, much of the young fruit falls to the ground; when the fruit has more fully developed, caterpillars and

---

*Instead of "Moses and Peter" etc. d. has: "Moses also had a great and strong faith, so that he led the people of Israel through the midst of the sea and through death; but afterwards he and his brother fell; although God soon afterwards raised them up again."

worms make their appearance, and they prick and destroy
the fruit to such an extent, that scarcely the twentieth part,
yea, hardly a hundredth part ripens. The same thing happens to the Gospel. At first everybody wants to become a
Christian, it promises to do well and is pleasing to all men:
but as soon as the wind or rain of temptation comes, large
numbers fall away. Afterwards come the sects and factions,
like worms and beetles, which prick and pollute the fruit
of the Gospel, and so much false doctrine is taught, that
only a few remain faithful to the Gospel.

27. This parable is a sign and picture of true faith. Thus,
faith first consists in this, that we may be not secure and presumptuous,* but remain in fear. By the grace of God we
are rich in the Word of God and have been brought out
of deep and great darkness; but we forget the Word, become
weak, continue unconcerned about the matter and have no
taste for it. If, under these conditions false prophets should
break in with their false teachings and even the devil burst
in, and find us idle and the house swept and garnished, he
brings with him seven other spirits, more wicked than himself, and our last state is worse than the first. And even if
this should happen, we are not therefore to despair, but instruct one another, so that we cling to God and pray to
him, saying: "Merciful God, thou hast permitted me to become a Christian, help me to continue to be one and to increase daily in faith. Even if the whole world should fall,
and each one conspire to do evil, and the devil break all
the earthen vessels, yet I will not be turned by it, but by
thy divine help will abide in the Gospel." Each one should
think of the matter, as if he were alone in the world; even as
it will be in death at the end of the world, when no one
will be concerned about others, but each one must be concerned about himself.

28. Thus the faith of this man was most excellent and
noble. He hears the single word, "Thy son liveth." He
believes it and goes home, gives the glory to God, grasps

* Instead of "this parable" etc. d. has: "Therefore we should not
be too certain, although we have made a beginning in faith, nor
deceive ourselves" etc.

the word, clings to it, and does not grope after other things. Hence God also honors him in return, heals his son, lifts him up and increases his faith, does not permit him to remain in doubt and in weakness, but makes him certain and strong in faith, permits him to continue and become stronger. Nor does he wait until the man has returned to his home, but while he is still on the way allows the restoration of his son to be announced to him, permits his servants to meet him on the way, who bring him the joyous tidings, saying, "Thy son liveth." For God cannot delay and remain outside, where there is a true heart, which depends solely on him and clings to his Word, and lets everything else go and looks only to the Word of God. In a case like this, God cannot hide himself, but permits himself to be seen and enters his heart and makes his abode there, as we read in St. John's Gospel, ch. 14, 23. Thus he richly manifested himself to this nobleman, and for this reason, that we might understand the nature of this man's faith, namely, an excellent and true faith, that was produced purely by the Word of God.

29. What is more blessed and joyous than to believe God's Word and cling to it in the face of all temptations, and to shut the eyes to all temptations of the devil, to lay aside sense and understanding, reason and cunning, and unceasingly say in one's heart: "God has spoken, he cannot lie?" Nothing can be more joyful, I say, than such faith. For whatever we ask of God in such faith, we receive more abundantly than we can ever imagine, and God is nearer to us than we can realize. In a word, it all depends upon our belief and trust in him. Therefore, the Evangelist uses so many unnecessary words, as it seems to us, as these:

"The man believed the word that Jesus spake unto him, and he went his way. And as he was now going down, his servants met him, saying, that his son lived. So he inquired of them the hour when he began to amend. They said therefore unto him, Yesterday at the seventh hour the fever left him. So the father knew that it was at that hour in which Jesus said unto him, Thy son liveth."

30. All this means, if we believe and trust in God, we shall know that he will richly give us all things for which we pray. And the Evangelist concludes the Gospel with these words:

"And himself believed and his whole house."

31. Thus his faith had increased, not only that he had risen from a lower to a higher stage of faith, but also that he had caused the members of his household to believe. He did not merely abide in faith, but he had an active faith, which did not lie still and idle in his heart, but broke forth and was exposed to others, and preached Christ to others and praised him before them, telling them how he had come to Christ, received consolation from him and how he had received help through his faith, so that all who were in his house had to believe. For it is the character and nature of faith that it attracts other people, breaks forth and becomes active in love, as St. Paul says, Gal. 5, 6, "Faith working through love" is the thing that avails; for it lives and can neither remain silent, nor inactive, as King David says, Psalm 116, 10, and as St. Paul, referring to believers, says, 2 Cor. 4, 13, "I believed and therefore did I speak." Faith cannot do otherwise, it must break forth and speak; it cannot remain quiet, for it desires to benefit its neighbor. This man had faith for himself; but it did not remain such, but broke forth; for he doubtless preached to his household, telling them how he had come to Christ and received comfort from him; and no doubt they believed his words.

32. Thus we see, if we believe we are to open our mouths and confess the grace God has shown us. This also is the greatest and best work of faith, namely, to inform and teach others in the Word; for as Paul says, Rom. 10, 10, "With the heart, man believeth unto righteousness; and with the mouth, confession is made unto salvation." If one is ashamed of the Word and hides it, it is a sign of a lax faith.

33. Thus we see that Christ makes no distinction between weak and strong faith, and rejects no one; for weak faith is also faith, and if it only continues, it will ever grow stronger-d. He came into the world, to receive the weak,

and to carry and sustain them. If he were as impatient as we are, he would at once say to us: "Depart from me. I will have nothing to do with you; for you do not believe as you ought." Who could receive help from him? But the great art of Christ is to know how to deal gently with the weak, not to knock them about and impatiently drive them away. Even though to-day they may not be strong, it may happen in an hour's time that they grasp the Word more richly than we who regard ourselves as strong.

34. Thus we should teach one another to cling to his Word. For if we abide in his Word, we shall be sufficiently fortified against the devil; for we have a defiance of him in the Word, even though we ourselves are weak. But to the devil, who in an hour's time could break in pieces all earthen vessels, all men would be as a feather, and he could blow them when and where he wished; but this feather shall become heavier for him than heaven and earth. For a Christian has Christ within himself; but Christ is heavier than heaven and earth. This must suffice concerning this Gospel.

35.* We have made a beginning in the attempt to formulate a German Mass. You know that the Mass is the most important external office, that has been instituted for the comfort of true Christians. Therefore I beseech you Christians, that you may pray and supplicate God, that this work may be acceptable to him. You have often heard that no one should teach, unless he knows, that this is the Word of God. Hence nothing should be ordered or arranged unless we know that it is acceptable to God. Nor should we depend on our reason; for unless it begins of its own accord, nothing will come of it. For this reason I have hesitated so long with reference to the German Mass, in order that I might not give any encouragement to the sectarian spirits, who rush into things without thought, and have no regard whether it is God's pleasure or not. But now, since so many people from all countries have requested me, by petitions

* The following words, concerning the newly regulated mass at Wittenberg, are found in the last of the above-mentioned separate publications, at the close of the sermon. Cf. Erl. Ed., 14, 278 f.

and letters, and since the secular government forces me to it, we could not well excuse ourselves and evade the matter, but must regard it as the will of God. If there is anything, therefore, in this work that is human and our own, let it fall and perish, even though it have a grand and fine appearance. But if it is the work of God, it must go forward, even though it appear foolish. Therefore all things that God does, even though not acceptable to any one, must prosper. Therefore, I beseech you to pray the Lord, that, if it is a proper or correct Mass, it may be maintained to his honor and glory.

TWENTY-SECOND SUNDAY AFTER TRINITY.

This sermon is found in all the editions of the Church Postil and in three pamphlet prints, which appeared in 1524, two at Wittenberg and one at Augsburg by S. Otmar. Title: "Sermon on the 23 Sunday after Pentecost." Erl. 14, 279; W. 11, 2383; St. L. 11, 1786.

Text: Mat. 18, 23-35. Therefore is the kingdom of heaven likened unto a certain king, who would make a reckoning with his servants. And when he had begun to reckon, one was brought to him, that owed him ten thousand talents. But forasmuch as he had not wherewith to pay, his lord commanded him to be sold, and his wife, and children, and all that he had, and payment to be made. The servant therefore fell down and worshipped him, saying, Lord, have patience with me, and I will pay thee all. And the lord of that servant, being moved with compassion, released him, and forgave him the debt. But that servant went out, and found one of his fellow-servants, who owed him a hundred shillings: and he laid hold on him, and took him by the throat, saying, Pay what thou owest. So his fellow-servant fell down and besought him, saying, Have patience with me, and I will pay thee. And he would not: but went and cast him into prison, till he should pay that which was due. So when his fellow-servants saw what was done, they were exceeding sorry, and came and told unto their lord all that was done. Then his lord called him unto him, and saith to him, Thou wicked servant, I forgave thee all that debt, because thou besoughtest me: shouldest not thou also have had mercy on thy fellow-servant, even as I had mercy on thee? And his lord was wroth, and delivered him to the tormentors, till he should pay all that was due. So shall also my heavenly Father do unto you, if ye forgive not every one his brother from your hearts.

CONTENTS: THE UNMERCIFUL SERVANT; OR, THE PARA-
BLE OF THE KING WHO RECKONED WITH HIS SERVANTS.

SUMMARY OF THIS GOSPEL: 1. Through the mercy and
grace of God all sins will be forgiven, however great they may be.
But his sins will not be forgiven, who will not forgive his brother,
as Christ has taught us to pray: "Forgive us our debts, as we
also have forgiven our debtors." Mat. 6, 12.

1. This Gospel or parable Christ our Lord spoke in reply
to St. Peter, to whom he had just entrusted the keys to loose
and to bind, Mat. 16, 19, when Peter asked him how often
he should forgive his neighbor, whether seven times were
enough? He answered: "Not seven times, but seventy times
seven," and Christ then related this parable, and with it concludes, that our heavenly Father will do unto us, if we forgive not our neighbor, as this king did unto his servant,

who would not forgive his fellow-servant a very small debt, after he had fogiven him so great a debt.

2. First, before we consider the Gospel itself, let us examine what kind of a rebuke it is, by which this servant's right is denied. For the other servant who owed him a hundred shillings, should according to justice have justly paid him this money. Even the first also had a good right to demand what was his own. If an appeal had been made to the public sentiment, every one would have been compelled to agree with him and say: It is just and right for him to pay what he owes. Why then this procedure, that his lord abolishes his claim, and besides condemns the servant because he demands and executes his right? Answer: It was thus written that we might know that it is altogether a different thing in the eye of God than it is in the eye of the world, and often that which is not right before God, is right and just before the world. For before the world this servant stands an honorable man; but before God he is called a wicked servant, and he is blamed for acting as one who is worthy of eternal condemnation.

3. It is therefore decreed when we deal with God that we must stand free, and let goods, honor, right, wrong, and every thing go that we have; and we will not be excused when we say: I am right, therefore I will not suffer a man to do me wrong, as God requires that we should renounce all our rights and forgive our neighbor. Concerning this, however, our high schools and the learned have preached and taught quite differently, that we are not obliged to give way to another and surrender our rights, but that it is just for every one to secure his dues. This is the first rebuff. Now let us consider this Gospel more fully.

4. We have often said that the Gospel or kingdom of God is nothing else than a state or government, in which there is nothing but forgiveness of sins. And wherever there is a state or government in which sins are not forgiven, no Gospel or kingdom of God is found there. Therefore we must clearly distinguish these two kingdoms from each other, in which sins are rebuked, and sins are forgiven, or in which our

right is demanded, and our right is pardoned. In the kingdom of God, where God rules with the Gospel, there is no demand for right and dues, but all is pure forgiveness, pardon and giving, no anger, no punishment, but all is pure brotherly service and kindness.

5. By this, however, our civil rights are not abolished. For this parable teaches nothing of the kingdom of this world, but only of the kingdom of God. Therefore, whoever is only under the civil government of the world, is far from the kingdom of heaven, for all this still belongs to perdition. As when a prince so rules his people as not to permit anyone to be wronged, and punishes the evil doer, does well and is praised. For thus it is in this government: Pay what thou owest, if not, you will be cast into prison. Such government we must have, but no one will thereby get to heaven, nor will the world be saved by it. But it is necessary for the reason that the world may not become worse, it is only a protection against and a prevention of wickedness. For if it were not for this government, one would devour the other, and no person could protect his life, goods, wife and child. So in order that everything may not go to ruin, God has instituted functions of the sword, by which wickedness may in part be prevented, so that the civil government may secure and maintain peace, and no one may wrong another. Therefore it must be tolerated. And yet as we have said, it has not been established for citizens of heaven, but simply in order that the people may not fall deeper into hell, and make matters worse.

Therefore no one dare boast, who is under the civil government, that he therefore does right before God. Before him, all is yet wrong. For you must come to the point, that you also avoid what the world claims to be right.

6. The aim of this Gospel is to describe to us forgiveness for both parties. First the lord forgives the servant all his debt. Then he demands of him that he also in like manner forgive his fellow-servant and pardon his debt. This God demands, and thus his kingdom shall stand. Hence no one should be so wicked and allow himself to be so angry, as to

be unable to forgive his neighbor. And, as is written, if he would even offend you seventy times seven times, that is, as often as he is able to offend you, you are to let your right and claim go, and freely give him everything. Why so? Because Christ has also done the same for you, in that he began and established a kingdom in which there is nothing but grace, that is to endure forever, that every thing, as often as you sin, may be forgiven; because he has sent forth his Gospel, not to proclaim punishment, but grace alone. Now, because this government stands, you can at all times rise again, however deep and often you fall. For even if you fall, yet this Gospel and mercy-seat remain and stand forever; therefore as soon as you come and rise again, you again have grace. But he requires of you to forgive your neighbor whatever he has done against you, else you will neither be in this gracious kingdom nor enjoy the Gospel, that your sins may be forgiven. This in short is the idea and sense of this Gospel.

7. However, it is here not forgotten who those are who grasp and enjoy the Gospel. For it is indeed a glorious kingdom and a gracious government, because there is preached in it nothing but the forgiveness of sins, though it does not enter every one's heart. Hence there are many rude and vicious people who misuse the Gospel, who live a free life and do as they please, and think no one shall ever rebuke them, because the Gospel preaches nothing but the forgiveness of sins. To those the Gospel is not preached, who thus despise the great treasure and treat it wantonly; for this reason they do not belong to this kingdom, but only to the civil government, where they may be prevented from doing whatever they wish.

8. To whom then is the Gospel preached? To those who feel their distress as this servant does his. Therefore observe, how it is with him? The lord has compassion on his wretchedness, and gives him more than he could desire. But before this is done, the text says that the lord would make a reckoning with his servants; and as he began to reckon this one appeared before him, who owed him ten thousand talents; but as he had not wherewith to pay, his lord commanded him to

be sold, and his wife and children, and all that he had, and payment to be made. This was indeed no cheering sermon, nothing but great earnestness, and the most terrible sentence. Now he becomes so uneasy that he falls down and pleads for grace, and promises more than he has and can pay, and says: "Lord, have patience with me, and I will pay thee all." Here are pictured and set forth those who enjoy the Gospel in its full measure.

9. For thus it is between God and us. When God wishes to reckon with us, he sends forth the preaching of the law, by which we learn to know what we owe. As when God says to the conscience: "Thou shalt have no other gods," but esteem me only as God and love me with all thy heart, and trust in me alone; this is the reckoning and the register, in which is written what we owe, this he takes in hand and reads to us and says: Do you see what you are required to do? You are to féar, love and honor me alone, and trust only in me, and hope in me for the best. But you do the contrary and are my enemy, you do not belive in me, but put your trust in other things. To sum up, you see here you do not keep a single letter of the Law.

10. Now when the conscience hears such things, and the Law thoroughly comes at us, then we see our duty, and that we have not done it, and we perceive that we have not kept a letter of it, and must confess we have not believed or loved God a single moment. What now will the Lord do? When the conscience is thus led captive and confesses that it must be lost, and becomes anxious and fearful, he says: Sell him and all he has, that payment may be made. This is the sentence which immediatetly follows, when the Law reveals sins and says: This thou shouldst do and have done, but thou hast not done it. For punishment follows sin, that payment may be made. For God has not given his Law to the end to allow those to escape who disobey it. It is not sweet nor friendly, but brings with it bitter, horrible punishment, and delivers us to satan, casts us into hell, and leaves us in punishment until we have paid the uttermost farthing. This St. Paul has correctly explained to the Romans, 4, 15:

"For the Law worketh wrath." That is, when it reveals to us that we have done wrong, it brings home to our hearts nothing but his wrath and displeasure. For when the conscience sees it has done wrong, it feels that it is worthy of eternal death; and if punishment would soon follow, it would have to despair. This is meant, when the lord commands this servant to be sold with all he has, because he cannot make payment.

11. What does the servant do now? He foolishly goes to work and thinks he will still pay the debt, falls down and asks the lord to have patience with him. This is the torment of all consciences, when sin comes and smarts deeply until they feel in what a sad state they are before God; then they have no rest, run hither and thither, seek help here and there, to become free from sin, and in their presumption think they can do enough to pay God in full. As we have been taught hitherto; from which also have come so many pilgrimages, charitable foundations, cloisters, masses and other nonsense; so we fasted and scourged ourselves, and became monks and nuns. And all this came because we undertook to begin a life and to do many works of which God should take account and allow himself to be paid by them, and had thought to quiet and put the conscience at peace with God; and so we have acted just like this fool in to-day's lesson.

12. Now a heart that is thus smitten with the Law, and feels its blows and distress, is truly humiliated. Therefore it falls before the Lord and asks for grace, except that it still makes the mistake that it will help itself; for this we cannot root out of our nature. When the conscience feels such misery, it dare promise more than all the angels in heaven are able to do. Here one can easily promise and bind himself to do every thing that may be required of him; for he finds himself at all times thus prepared, that he still hopes to do enough for his sin by means of his good works.

13. Now behold the things men were guilty of heretofore in the world's history, and you will find it so. Then men preached: Give to the church, run into the cloister, estab-

lish many masses, and then your sins will be forgiven. And when they forced our consciences in the confessional, we did everything they imposed upon us, and gave more than they demanded of us. What should the poor people do? They were glad to be helped in this manner; therefore they ran and martyred themselves to get rid of their sins; and yet it did no good whatever, for the conscience remained in doubt as before, so that it did not know on what terms it stood with God; or if it were secure; it became still worse and fell into the presumption, that God had to regard their works. Reason cannot let this alone nor get around it, so as to abandon it.

14. Hence the Lord comes and sympathizes with this distress, because the servant thus lies captive and bound in his sins, and in addition to this is such a fool as to want to help himself, looks for no mercy, knows nothing to say of grace, and feels nothing but sins, which press him heavily, and knows no one to help him. Then his lord has mercy on him and sets him free.

15. Here is represented to us the Gospel and its nature, and how God deals with us. When you are thus held fast in sins and you torment yourself to become free from them, the Gospel comes and says: "No, not so, my dear friend, it will do no good for you to torture and torment yourself to madness; your works accomplish nothing, but God's mercy does it all; he has compassion on your affliction, and sees you a captive in such anguish, struggling in the mire and that cannot help yourself out, he sees that you cannot pay the debt, therefore he forgives you all."

Hence it is nothing but pure mercy. For he forgives you the debt, not because of your works and merit, but because he pities your cries, complaints and humiliation. This means that God has regard for an humble heart, as the Prophet David says in Psalm 51, 19: "The sacrifices of God are a broken spirit, a broken and a contrite heart, O God, thou wilt not despise." Such a heart, he says, is broken and cast down and cannot help itself, and is glad when God gives it a helping hand; this is the best sacrifice before God, and the true way to heaven.

16. Now this follows out of mercy; because God pities our distress, he yields his claims and nullifies them and never says: Sell what you have and make payment. He might well have proceeded and said: You must pay, I have the right to demand it, I will not on your account annul my own right, and no one could have blamed him. Yet, he does not wish to deal with him according to our ideas of right, but changes justice into grace, has mercy on him, and gives him liberty, with wife and child and everything he has, and makes him a present of the debt besides.

This is what God preaches through the Gospel, namely: He who believes, to him not only the debt, but also the punishment shall be remitted. To this no works are to be added; for whoever preaches that through his works one can atone for his debt and punishment, has already denied the Gospel. For the two can not be tolerated together, that God should have mercy, and that you should have any merit. If it is grace, then it is not merit: but if it is merit, then it is justice and no grace. Rom. 11, 6. For if you pay what you owe, he shows you no mercy; but if he shows mercy, you do not pay for what you receive. Therefore we must leave him alone to deal with us, receive from him and believe. This is what to-day's Gospel teaches.

17. Now you see, since this servant is thus humbled through the knowledge of his sins, that the Word ministers very strong comfort to him, when the Lord declares him free, and remits him both the debt and the punishment. By this is indicated that the Gospel does not reach vicious hearts, nor those who walk forth impudently, but only troubled consciences whose sins oppress them, from which they desire to be free; on these God will have mercy and bestow upon them all things.

18. Thus this servant now received the Word, and thereby became God's friend. For if he had not received the Word, it would have done him no good, and forgiveness would have amounted to nothing. Therefore it is not enough that

God has the forgiveness of sins offered to us, and has proclaimed the golden year of the kingdom of grace; but it
must also be grasped and believed. If you believe it, then
you are free from sin, and all is right. Now this is the
first part of a Christian life, taught by this and all the
Gospels, which properly consists in faith, that deals only with
God. Besides it is also indicated that we cannot grasp the
Gospel, unless there be present first a conscience that is
afflicted and miserable because of sin.

19. Now conclude from this that it is nothing but deception that is preached in relation to our works and free will,
and if a different way to blot out sin and obtain grace is
taught, than this Gospel here advocates, namely, that the
divine Majesty looks upon our wretchedness and has mercy
upon us. For the text says clearly, that he presents and
remits to those who have nothing; and thus concludes that
we have nothing wherewith to remunerate God. So you
may have free will as you wish in temporal things, in outward life and character, or in outward piety and virtue, as
man can have in his own strength, yet you hear now that
it is nothing before God. What can free will do here?
There is nothing in it at any rate but struggling and
trembling. Therefore, if you would be free from sin, you
must desist from and despair in all your own works, and
cling to the cross and plead for grace, and then lay hold
of the Gospel by faith.

20. Now follows the second part of this parable, that of
the fellow-servant. We would gladly die every hour for the
sake of our faith. For this servant has enough, he retains
his life and goods, wife and child and has a gracious lord;
so he would be a great fool if he would now go and do
everything he could to obtain a gracious lord. His lord
might then well say, he only mocks me. Therefore, he dare
not add any work, but only receives the grace offered him,
be joyful and thank the Lord, and do unto others as the
Lord did to him.

21. Thus it is now with us. If we believe, then we have
a gracious God, and need no more, and it would indeed

be well for us to die soon. But if we are to live on earth, our life must not be devoted to obtain God's favor by means of our works; for he who does this mocks and blasphemes God. As men hitherto have taught, that we must so long lie at God's ears with our good works, praying, fasting and the like, until we obtain grace. Grace we have already received, not through our works but through God's mercy. If you are to live, you must have something to do and work at, and all this must be devoted to your neighbor, says Christ.

22. But that servant went out. How does he go out? Where has he been within? He had been in faith, but now he goes out through love, by which he is to show himself to the people. For faith leads the people from the people unto God, but love leads out unto the people. Previously he was within, between God and himself alone, for no one can see or vouch for faith, how both work together. Therefore one must needs go out of the eyes of the people, where no one is seen or felt but God; this is transacted alone through faith, and no external work can be added to it. Now he comes out before his neighbor. If he had remained within, he could well have died; but he must come out and live among other people and mingle with them. Here he finds a fellow-servant whom he strikes and beats, and throttles him, demands payment and shows no mercy.

23. This is what we have often said, that we Christians must break forth, and show by our deeds and before the people that we have the true faith. God does not need your works, he has enough in your faith. Yet he wants you to work that you may show thereby your faith to yourself and all the world. For God indeed sees faith, but you and the people do not yet see it, therefore you should devote the works of faith to the benefit of your neighbor. Thus this servant is an example and picture of all those who should serve their neighbor through faith.

24. But what does he do? Just as we who think we believe, and partly do believe, and rejoice that we have heard the Gospel and can say a great deal about it; but no

one wants to follow it in his life. We have brought matters so far, that the doctrine and jugglery of the devil have been partly overthrown, and we now see what is right and what is wrong, that we must deal with God alone through faith, but with our neighbor through our works. But we cannot bring it to pass, that, as to love, one does to another as God has done to him; as we ourselves complain that some of us have become much worse than they were before.

25. As this servant will not forgive his neighbor, but seeks to collect his claim; so we also do and say: I am not in duty bound to give what is my own to another, and yield my rights. If another has offended me, he owes it to me to reconcile me and ask pardon. For thus the world teaches and acts. And here you are right, and no prince or king will compel you to give to another what is your own; but they must permit you to do what you wish with your own. The civil government only compels so far, that you may not do with another's goods what you would, not that you must give your goods to another. This is right before the world, as reason concludes: To every one belongs his own. Therefore, he does not do wrong, who uses his goods as he will, and robs no one of his own.

26. But what says this Gospel? If God also would have acted thus and had maintained his right and said: I act in harmony with justice, when I punish the wicked and take what is my own, who will prevent me? where then would we all be? We would all go to ruin. Therefore, because he has given up his claim on thee, he desires that you too should do likewise. Therefore, also give up your right and think: If God has given me ten thousand pounds, why should I not give my neighbor a hundred shillings?

27. Thus your goods are no longer your own, but your neighbor's. God could indeed have kept his own, for he owed you nothing. Yet he gives himself wholly unto you, becomes your gracious Lord, is kind to you, and serves you with all his goods, and what he has is all yours; why then will you not also do likewise? Hence, if you wish to be in

his kingdom you must do as he does; but if you want to remain in the kingdom of the world, you will not enter his kingdom. Therefore the sentence in Mat. 25, 42, which Christ will speak on the last day belongs to those who are not Christians: "For I was hungry, and ye did not give me to eat; I was thirsty, and ye gave me no drink," and so on.

28. But you say: Do you still insist that God will have no regard for our good works, and on their account will save no one? Answer: He would have them done freely without any thought of remuneration; not that we thereby obtain something, but that we do them to our neighbor, and thereby show that we have the true faith; for what have you then that you gave him and by which you merit anything, that he should have mercy on you and forgive you all things that you have done against him? Or what profit has he by it? Nothing has he, but that you praise and thank him, and do as he has done, that God may be thanked in thee, then you are in his kingdom and have all things that you should have. This is the other part of the Christian life, which is called love, by which one goes out from God to his neighbor.

29. Those who do not prove their faith by their works of love are servants who want others to forgive them, but do not forgive their neighbor, nor yield their rights; hence it will also be with them as with this servant. For when the other servants, who preach the Gospel, see that God has freely given them all things, and they refuse to forgive anyone, they become sad to see such things, and they are pained, that they act so foolishly toward the Gospel, and no one lays hold of it. What do they do then? They can do no more than come before their Lord with their complaint and say: So it goes; you forgive them both the debt and the punishment, and freely give them all things; but we cannot prevail upon them to do to others as you have done to them. This is the complaint. Then God will summon them to appear before him at the last judgment and accuse them of these things and say: When you were hungry, thirsty

and afflicted, I helped you; when you lay in sins I had compassion upon you and forgave the debt; therefore you must also now pay your debt.   There is now no grace nor mercy, nothing but wrath and eternal punishment, no prayers will help from now on, and they become speechless, and are cast into torment until they pay the uttermost farthing.

30. St. Peter said the same of those who heard the Gospel and again fell away. 2 Pet. 2, 21: "For it were better for them, not to have known the way of righteousness, than, after knowing it, to turn back from the holy commandment delivered unto them." Why would it be better? Because, if they turn back it will be twofold worse with them, than it was before they had heard the Gospel; as Christ says in Mat. 12, 45, of the unclean spirit, who takes unto himself seven other spirits worse than himself, comes with them and dwells in the man out of whom they were cast, and the last state of that man becomes worse than the first.

31. Thus it is now with us also, and it will be still more so. So it also was with Rome. There things were in a fine condition in the days of the martyrs. But afterwards they went to ruin, and abominations arose and Antichrist ruled, and the city became so wicked that it could not be worse. The grace of God preached through the Gospel is so great that the people do not grasp it, therefore great and terrible punishment must also follow. Thus we will see just punishment come upon us, inasmuch as we do not obey the Gospel we have and know.

32. For as often as God has afflicted the people with severe punishment, he previously set up a great light; as when he led the Jews out of their country into captivity, he first brought forth the pious king Josiah, who again restored the law in order to reform the people; but when they again fell away, God punished them as they deserved. So also when he wished to overthrow the Egyptians, he sent Moses and Aaron to preach and enlighten them, Ex. 4, 14. Again, when he wished to destroy the world with the flood, he raised up the patriarch Noah, Gen. 6, and 7. But when the people would not believe and only grew worse, terrible

punishment followed. So it was with the five cities; Sodom and Gomorrah with the rest were punished, because they would not hear pious Lot, Gen. 19.

Therefore such terrible punishments will also now come upon those who hear the Gospel and do not receive it. So this servant in the Gospel is cast off, and must pay what he owes. This means, that he must endure the pain and consequences. But he who endures the pain for the debt, will never be saved. For to sin belongs death, and when one dies he dies forever, and there is no more help nor salvation for him. Therefore let us receive these things as a warning; those, however, who are hardened and will not hear, will guard against it.

33. This is an elegant, comfortable Gospel, and is sweet to the afflicted conscience, because it contains nothing but forgiveness of sins. But for stubborn heads and hardened hearts it is a terrible sentence, and particularly so because this servant is not a heathen, but belongs to those under the Gospel, who held the faith. For as the Lord has mercy on him and forgives him what he had done, he must without doubt be a Christian. Hence this is not a punishment for the heathen, neither for the common crowd who hear the Gospel with the external ear, and have it on their tongue, but do not live according to it. Thus we have the sum of this Gospel.

34. What further the sophists are accustomed here to discuss, whether the sins will come back that were once forgiven, I let pass. For they do not know what forgiveness of sin is, and think it is something that sticks in the heart and lies still there, whereas it is the whole kingdom of Christ, which lasts forever without end. For as the sun shines and gives light none the less, although I close my eyes, so this mercy seat or forgiveness of sins stands forever, though I fall. And as I see the sun again as soon as I open my eyes, so I have the forgiveness of sins again when I look up and again come to Christ. Therefore we must not make forgiveness so narrow, as the fools dream. This is said on to-day's Gospel.

TWENTY-THIRD SUNDAY AFTER TRINITY.

This sermon is not found in c edition. Erl. 14, 295; W. 11, 2404; St. L. 11, 1802.

Text: Mat. 22, 15-22. Then went the Pharisees, and took counsel how they might ensnare him in his talk. And they send to him their disciples, with the Herodians, saying, Teacher, we know that thou art true, and teachest the way of God in truth, and carest not for any one: for thou regardest not the person of men. Tell us therefore, What thinkest thou? Is it lawful to give tribute unto Cæsar, or not? But Jesus perceived their wickedness, and said, Why make ye trial of me, ye hypocrites? Show me the tribute money. And they brought him a penny. And he saith unto them, Whose is this image and superscription? They say unto him Cæsar's. Then saith he unto them, Render therefore unto Cæsar the things that are Cæsar's; and unto God the things that are God's. And when they heard it, they marvelled,. and left him, and went away.

CONTENTS: CAESAR AND GOD, OR CHRIST'S ANSWER TO THE QUESTION OF THE PHARISEES, IS IT LAWFUL TO GIVE TRIBUTE UNTO CAESAR?

I. THIS QUESTION AND ANSWER IN DETAIL.

A. The Question.
1. What moved the Pharisees to ask this question. 1.
2. It is a very pointed question, and according to reason well put. 1-4.
3. How it appears from this question that the Jews worried about unnecessary things and neglected the weighty matters. 5.

B. Christ's Answer.
1. His answer is to be considered a masterpiece. 6-7.
2. How this answer is written for our consolation. 8-13.
   * Of the great wisdom and strength of Christians. 8.
   * Human wisdom and power avail nothing against God's Word. 9f.
   * With what a Christian should comfort himself when the Gospel is persecuted. 10-13.

II. THIS QUESTION AND ANSWER IN GENERAL.
1. How to learn from it.
   a. That those who oppose God the most often have the best natural gifts. 14.
   b. The great corruption of human nature. 15f.
   * How and why we should trust no human being. 16-20.
   * Whence the worship of saints originated in the Papacy. 20.
   * What is the greatest perse-

cutor of the Gospel. 21-22.
2. How the civil sword or power is here confirmed.
   * Of the civil authority.
   a. What stand a Christian should take, when the civil authority misuses its office. 23-24.
   b. How a Christian should

conduct himself when the civil government would rob him of the Gospel. 25.
c. What a subject is indebted to give to the government. 26.
d. For what purpose is government ordained. 27.

SUMMARY OF THIS GOSPEL: 1. The flesh continually seeks carnal liberty. Thus the Jews also expected from the Messiah, that he would by force deliver them from the dominion of the Romans. As we in our day rejoice that we have been delivered bodily from the tyranny of the Pope and bishops.

2. Concerning the civil government St. Paul writes to the Romans, 13, 7: "Render to all their dues; tribute to whom tribute is due; custom to whom custom; fear to whom fear; honor to whom honor"; and likewise, render to God, the things that are God's.

3. Here you see the wickedness of human wisdom, what all men are by nature, where they are left to themselves, if they have not the Holy Spirit of faith.

1. In this Gospel there is pictured to us, how high reason and human wisdom agree with the divine wisdom, and how shamelessly they attack even when they wish to be the most prudent; as takes place here among the Pharisees who were the best and the most intelligent people among the Jews, as they also prove themselves to be; yet their wisdom must become foolishness. They could not catch Christ in his sermons nor in his works; and yet they would gladly have had found a reason to put him to death. Therefore they thought to seize him in the most subtle manner, and propounded to him a pointed syllogism, so pointed that human reason could not have devised a more pointed one; and said to him:

"Teacher, we know that thou art true, and teachest the way of God in truth, and carest not for any one: for thou regardest not the person of men. Tell us therefore, What thinkest thou? Is it lawful to give tribute unto Caesar, or not?"

2. They imagined thus: now we will lay hold of him: for he must answer either yes or no. Does he say yes, then we have conquered him; does he say no, then he is also caught. In that they say: "Teacher," they aim to compel him to answer and rightly agree with them; and in that they say, "We know that thou are true," they admonish him of his office.

Where should Christ flee? Every door was closed to him. But he would not escape through the opening they made.

3. Was not this a subtle device? Do they not sufficiently show that they were prudent people? Whichever way their Lord had answered he would have been taken. Yea, did they not act wisely enough in that they brought with them the servants of Herod? and thought, indeed, they would accomplish their end by stratagem, so that he should not escape. They thought thus: Wait, we will now counsel him; does he say no, then the servants of Herod are present and will put him to death as a revolutionist and as one who sets himself against the Roman government. Does he say yes, then he will speak against the independence of the Jewish people, and we will excite the people against him. For the Jews wish to be a free people, and to have their own king, of their own blood, as was promised to them by God through Moses when he wrote in Deuteronomy 17, 15: "Thou shalt surely set him king over thee, whom Jehovah thy God shall choose: one from among thy brethren shalt thou set king over thee; thou mayest not put a foreigner over thee who is not thy brother." And they did not know differently than that the same kingdom should stand until the time of the true king, until the time of Christ; as the patriarch Jacob preached concerning it and said: "The scepter shall not depart from Judah, nor a lawgiver from between his feet, until Shiloh come," Gen. 49, 10. And to this end God also chose especially this people and formed a kingdom from them only for the sake of Christ. They had many other sayings to the end that they should not serve any one, they were the head and not the tail, etc., Deut. 28, 44. This and other like passages moved the Pharisees and scribes among the people and they boasted of it; as is now beaten into the people that the Church cannot err. Therefore they thought thus: Does he say yes, then he blasphemes against God and is worthy of death as a blasphemer of God, and the people will stone him; for God promised and agreed to give this people liberty and they were in all times God's people even in the midst of their captivity.

4. However, at that time as at the present, they had no king and therefore there arose among the people at large a great murmur, faction and insurrection. For this people were educated by the law that they should have a king of their own flesh and blood, as I said; therefore they did not cease to set themselves against foreign kings and rulers until they were destroyed and many consequently suffered death. And this happened frequently; for they were a stiff-necked, rude and hardened people; therefore the Romans, who at the time had the rule and authority over them, protected the country well and they had to divide it into four provinces, and in all places they thoroughly took possession by means of princes and tetrarchs; in order that they, thus divided, might not so soon come together and create revolution, so that they could be better kept in subjection where they wished to rebel against the Roman empire. Hence, Pilot was a governor appointed by Rome in the country of the Jews; Herod a tetrarch of Galiléa, and his brother Philip tetrarch in the region of Iturea and Trachonitis, and Lysanias tetrarch of Abilene, as Luke relates in 3, 1, and all for the purpose to make the Jews subjects of Rome. Hence the Jews became angry, raging and foolish, and especially at the time of Christ when they greatly desired to have their own king.

Consequently the Pharisees now devised this scheme and thought thus: Wait, the Romans desire to have the authority and rule; if he answers no to our question, then the tetrarch is at hand and will behead him; does he say yes, then the people in a mass will rise up against him and we will accomplish our end. They wish thus, as they think, to find cause to put the Lord to death, or forever suppress his doctrine and work among the people.

5. As the Jews now do here so it is everywhere that the principal things are overlooked and we worry ourselves about other unnecessary matters. Thus the Pharisees here take in hand and concern themselves about whether they are free or not, seeing they had in the law and in the Word of God the promise that they should be subject to none other

than to their own king and yet now they are subject to the
Roman emperor. They learned in their Scriptures how they
should honor God and love their neighbor; they let go of
that and concern themselves about other matters. They had
the promise if they did according to the Word and commandment of God they should be a free people. About doing this they did not concern themselves and yet they wished
to be free and have their own king. We act also in the
very same way. We wish to enjoy Christian liberty and imagine if we destroy pictures or are disobedient to the government that we are by virtue of this Christians, and in
this way we overlook faith and love.

6. But what does Christ do when the Pharisees so cun-
ningly lay hold of him? He slays them with their own
words and catches them by means of their own counsel, by
which they thought to catch him, he says neither yes nor no;
as the Evangelist writes and says:

*"But Jesus perceived their wickedness, and said, Why make
ye trial of me, ye hypocrites? Show me the tribute money.
And they brought unto him a denarius. And he saith unto
them, Whose is this image and superscription? They say unto
him, Caesar's."*

7. Here you see the master stroke the Lord uses. He
asks them to hand him the tribute money and inquires
whose image and superscription it bears. Then they answer him Caesar's. He then freely concluded that they
were subject to Caesar, to whom they were obligated to
pay tax and tribute. As if he should say: Have you thus
permitted Caesar to come among you, so that he mints your
money, and his coin is in circulation and favor among you,
then he has triumphed in the game, as if he said: you are
to blame that Caesar is your ruler. What should they do
now in the face of this answer? They marveled and went
away, they thought they would conquer him in a masterly
manner, but their wisdom and shrewdness deceived them.

8. This is written for our consolation, in order that we
who believe in Christ should know that we have a wisdom
that far surpasses all other wisdom; a strength and right-

eousness, which are not to be compared with any human strength or righteousness; for against the Holy Spirit no counsel can prevail. We have the power through Christ to trample sin under our feet and to triumph over death, also a wisdom that surpasses the wisdom of the whole world. If Christ live in us by faith then we possess him who establishes this in us; but it is not experienced except in times of temptation and opposition: therefore if I make use of it then he comes and gives me the power vigorously to press through all difficulties to victory.

9. In like manner we should not worry that our doctrine will fail and be put to shame. For let even all the wise and prudent of the world together rise up against the Word of God; they overlook the joke that they opposed it, that it took place for their sake. It may indeed happen that they may howl and bite and snap against it so that the people think the Gospel will fail; but when they set themselves against it and wish to overthrow it, then it is certain that they are weak, and by the same trick they wished to seize and take Christ, they themselves are finally caught. As we see in this Gospel, and here and there in the writings of Paul and especially in the history of St. Stephen we see how they failed to quote the Scriptures aright, yea, that which they did quote is used against them, for the Jews charged Stephen that he spoke against the temple, Acts 6, 7, and also against God who told them to build the temple, they brought forth passages of Scripture by which they tried to suppress and conquer him; but Stephen, full of the Holy Ghost, showed unto them by one passage of Scripture after another how God did not live in houses made with hands. David wished to build him a house, but he did not desire it. What was the reason? God had lived a long time before David's day among his people; he must indeed be a poor God who needs a house for his dwelling place. And thus by many histories he proves that God does not dwell in houses made by man. What should the Jews do? They have the passage clearly before their eyes, which they

quoted against Stephen, (that he witnessed against them-selves).

10. In like manner must all come to shame and be over-thrown who rise up against this divine wisdom and the Word of God. Consequently no one should fear even if all the wisdom and power of the world oppose the Gospel, yea, even if they plan to suppress it by the shedding of blood; for the more blood is shed, the more Christians there will be. The blood of Christians, as Tertulian says, is the seed from which Christians grow. Satan must be drowned in the blood of Christians, consequently there is no art that can suppress the Gospel by force. It is with the Gospel as with the palmtree, which has the nature and character that it flourishes at the top, and one may laden it as heavy as he wishes; and especially if it be used as a beam or support it does not weaken under any burden, but rises in spite of the burden. Such is also the nature of the Gospel, the more one opposes it the greater it lays hold of us and the more one burdens it, the more it grows.

11. Therefore we should not be afraid of powers. But we should fear our prosperity and good days which cause us more harm than our anguish and persecution; and we should not be afraid in the face of the wisdom and the shrewdness of the world, for they can do us no harm. Yes, the more the wisdom of the world opposes the truth, the purer and clearer does the truth become, consequently the Gospel can experience nothing better than that the world rise up against it with all its force and wisdom; yea, the more my conscience, sin and satan attack me, the stronger does my righteousness become. For the sins which worry me, pain me; then I persevere harder and harder in prayer and in my cry to God; then faith and righteousness become stronger and stronger. This is what St. Paul means when he says in 2 Cor. 12, 9: my power is made perfect in weak-ness. Now since we possess such a treasure that becomes stronger by virtue of trial and opposition we should not fear, but be of good courage and rejoice in tribulation; as St. Paul says to the Romans, Rom. 5, 3: and as the Apostles

did who departed from the presence of the council with great rejoicing, and thanked God that they were counted worthy to suffer dishonor for the Name, Acts 5, 41. If satan were only prudent enough to keep quiet and let the Gospel be preached, he would receive less injury from it; for if the Gospel is not attacked it completely rusts and has no occasion or reason to make its power and influence manifest.

12. Thus we are here still secure, no one attacks us; as a result we always continue just as we were, yea, we become worse. In that certain enemies attack us with the Scriptures, they gain very little. In that they have taken up their pen against us, they accomplish no more than if they blew into the fire; but if they had cast us into the fire or beat our heads, there would indeed be more Christians for our sake.

13. Consequently we have here a consolation, when we are attacked; that Christ is in us and holds the field of victory through us. Christ is so near us that we triumph at all times through him because we abide in Christ. As long as we do not have opposition taking us by the neck, he does nothing; but when we are attacked and conquered, then he is at hand and puts all our enemies to shame.

14. Here we may also learn the lesson that those who are a little more than other people, brighter, stronger, and endowed with special gifts of reason, nature and fortune, who are more artistic, learned and intelligent than others, who indeed are gifted with speech and are talented to lead other people and are able to rule and arrange everything in the best way, they are the most opposed to God and to faith, and trust more in their own strength and reason than in God. For nature, poisoned as it is, leads them to the point that they cannot and will not use their gifts to the best advantage, for the welfare and edification of their neighbor; for they trust in their gifts, and think they will obtain now this, now that, and never remember that they also need God's help and strength to that end. As the Pharisees and scribes do here, who are so certain, as they

think, if they thus lay hold of Christ, they would take him captive, for it is not possible, they say, for him to escape, we have ensnared him whether he says yes, or no.

15. Behold, how cunning and perverse human nature is! Methinks this is well pictured here. Aye, there is nought in man but evil, lying and deceiving, cunning and all manner of mischief. Indeed, in his very nature man is nothing else than a liar, Ps. 116, 11. One may not entrust anything to man. Do not imagine that any one tells you the truth; man lies in whatsoever he speaks. And why? The fountain is evil, that is to say, the heart is not good; therefore also the rivers flowing therefrom cannot be good. Hence does the Lord oftimes call men a generation of vipers and a brood of serpents, Mat. 22, 34. Is not that a beautiful title for man? Just you go and boast of your piety, your strength, or your free will! Before the world indeed one may be fine and pious, shining with holiness; but at bottom nothing will be found but a generation of vipers and a serpent's brood, and that most of all in the worthiest, most estimable, intelligent and wise people. If you peruse the history of the Greeks, Jews and Romans, you will find that the best and wisest rulers, who according to the judgment of men, governed well, have not thought of God, but confided in themselves alone; to God's might they have attributed nothing.

16. From this it follows that the less adroit a person is before the world, the less will he do against God; and those who are ingenious and honored in the world, lie and deceive more than the others, thinking to cover up their deception and malice by deceitful and cunning acts. True it is they may full well conceal it; the Holy Spirit, however, has a keen eye and knows them exceeding well. Therefore Scripture often calls such fellows lions, wolves, bears, swine, and wild beasts, namely, such as rage, eating and devouring everything with their deceit. Hence in the Old Testament the Jews were forbidden to eat some animals, as being unclean—those that are enumerated and others—for no other reason than that it might be thus indicated that

there are some people who are strong, mighty, rich, adroit, learned, intelligent and wise, people that must be shunned and fled from as though they were something unclean; such people as mislead and deceive others by their appearance, their power and wisdom. For people will not consider them as such, nor believe that they are men who plan evil things and dare to carry them out. No man whatever, therefore, is to be trusted or believed. Believe no one: he will mislead you wherever he can. Aye, if indeed you trust any one, you will act against God, not trusting in him. For it is written, Jer. 17, 57: "Cursed be the man that trusteth in man; blessed is the man that trusteth in the Lord."

17. Now someone might object: What is to be done? Must we not have intercourse and dealings one with the other; and how otherwise could human life continue? Surely we must buy and sell and market our goods among the people? If no one should believe and trust the other, all human dealings would come to an end! I answer: It is true one must deal with the other, and one needs the other's help. But that I demand: Whatever you deal about among men, in buying or selling, you are to consider it as something uncertain, which is not to be trusted and believed in. For certain it is, if you trust any man, you are already deceived, for human nature, in itself, cannot but lie and deceive. Everything is uncertain among men, their deeds and words are unstable; that you may well believe.

18. Therefore we are to put all our trust only in the Lord, and say: O Lord, thou art my life, my soul and body, my goods and possessions, and all that is mine. Do thou direct and ordain it all according to thy divine will. In thee do I trust, in thee do I believe. Thou wilt surely not desert me in such a perilous undertaking with such and such a man, whom I do not trust. If thou knowest it to be good for me, then see to it that he be true to me; if thou dost not see that it will help me, then do not let him keep his word. I am content, thy will be done.

19. As soon, however, as you think a purchaser to be an

honest man who will keep his word, and of whom you are certain that he will not deceive you; so soon you have fallen away from God, have prayed to a spectre and put your trust in a liar. Therefore, in dealing with a man, just think in this wise: If he is true, it is good; if not, why then, in God's name, let him be; he cannot do otherwise than lie and deceive. I will leave it all to God; he will make all well.

20. Out of such false and wicked confidence placed in man there has crept into Christianity the abuse of the worship of saints. By this the Christian church, that is, the true assembly of the faithful, have suffered notable decline and damage. What else has saints' worship been but solely a devilish thing? For thus have people reasoned: Such and such a man has been holy; such things has he said and done; therefore we will follow after him, and teach and do likewise. St. Jerome, St. Augustine, and Gregory have done this; therefore it is right, and I will believe it. St. Francis, Benedict, Dominicus, and St. Bernard have lived thus, have done such and such a thing; therefore will I also live thus, and do as they have done. Furthermore, St. Augustine has been saved by such a rule. Alas, what a poor, unstable, miserable thing this is, nought but lies and dreams of man. I should damn St. Augustine and his rule, had he laid it down for the purpose of being saved thereby. So blind and foolish is our reason, that it will accept even a spectre and a fiction, whereas only God's Word is to be accepted in matters of salvation. If, for example, Herod, Pilate, Caiaphas and Hanes preached the Gospel, I should have to accept it And, on the other hand, if those who are considered saints arose and preached lies, about regulations, hoods and gowns, tonsures, ceremonies and other inventions of man, I ought not to accept them. For in such cases not the persons are to be considered, but that which they preach.

21. Now someone might say: See here, would you be wiser than all church fathers and saints, than all bishops and rulers of the whole world? Far be it from me. I do not claim to be wiser than they. But this is true: It is im-

possible for that which is wise, prudent, great, handsome, mighty and powerful before the world to agree with the Word of God. For thus it is ordained by God, that such people must always persecute the Gospel; if they were not such the Gospel would not shine and triumph as it does. The Roman emperors Hadrian, Trojan and Diocletian were the wisest of rulers, and reigned so well that all the world praised their government. Yet they persecuted the Gospel and could not tolerate the truth. Likewise do we read of Jewish kings, Ahaz and others, who governed well, that they despised God's Word and acted contrary to God's will. In our times there have never been emperors, princes, or other people to compare with those. But then it had to come to pass that God put all wisdom of this world to shame through the foolishness of preaching, 1 Cor. 1, 21.

22. All this is shown to us in this Gospel, which, though apparently simple and ordinary, is exceedingly rich and comprises many things. How then does the Lord finally deal with the Pharisees after they had shown him the tribute money, and answered that the image and superscription was Caesar's? The Evangelist tells us that he answered thus:

"Render therefore unto Caesar the things that are Caesars; and unto God the things that are Gods."

23. Although they did not deserve it of the Lord, yet he teaches them the right way. And with these words he also confirms the worldly sword or government. They had hoped he would condemn it and speak against it; he does not do it, however, but praises earthly government and commands to render unto it what is due to it. It is therefore his desire that there should be magistrates, princes and masters, whom we are to obey, be they what they may and what they list; neither should we ask whether they possess and exercise government and authority justly or unjustly. We should only pay heed to that power and authority which is good, for it is ordered and instituted by God, Rom. 13, 1: You are not allowed to upbraid the government, when at

times you are oppressed by princes and tyrants, who abuse the power they have from God: some day they will surely have to answer for it. The abuse of a thing does not make it bad, if it was good in itself. A golden chain is good, and it is not made worse by being worn around a whore's neck; or if someone were to destroy one of my eyes with it, should I therefore blame the chain? Truly nay.

24. Thus one must also bear the authority of the ruler. If he abuses it, I am not therefore to bear him a grudge, nor take revenge of and punish him with my hands. One must obey him solely for God's sake, for he stands in God's stead. Let them impose taxes as intolerable as they may: one must obey them and suffer everything patiently, for God's sake. Whether they do right or not, that will be taken care of in due time. If therefore your possessions, aye, your life and whatsoever you have, be taken from you by those in power, then you are to say: I give it to you willingly, I acknowledge you as my masters, gladly will I be obedient to you. Whether you use the power given to you by God well or ill, that is your affair.

25. But what if they would take the Gospel from us or forbid us to preach it? Then you are to say: The Gospel and Word of God I will not give up to you. This is not within your power, for your rule is a temporal rule, over worldly matters; but the Gospel is a spiritual, heavenly treasure, and therefore your authority does not extend over the Gospel and God's Word. We recognize the emporer as a master of temporal affairs, not of God's Word; this we shall not suffer to be torn from us, for it is the power of God, Rom. 1, 16, against which not even the gates of hell shall prevail.

26. Therefore, the Lord beautifully summarizes these two things, and in one saying distinguishes them from each other: "Render unto Caesar the things that are Caesar's, and unto God the things that are God's." This honor is due to God, that we are to hold him as a true, almighty and wise God, and attribute to him all the good things that can be named. And even if I do not render him this honor, he still keeps it; nothing is added to or subtracted from it. But in

me he is true, almighty and wise, if I consider him as such, and believe him to be such as he proclaims himself. To the emperor, however, and to all in power, are due reverence, taxes, revenue and obedience. God will have the heart; body and possessions are the government's, which is to rule over them in God's stead. This St. Paul says to the Romans in round and clear words, Rom. 13, 1-7: "Let every soul be in subjection to the higher powers: for there is no power but of God; and the powers that be are ordained of God. Therefore he that resisteth the power, withstandeth the ordinance of God: and they that withstand shall receive to themselves judgment. For rulers are not a terror to the good work, but to the evil. And wouldest thou have no fear of the power? do that which is good, and thou shalt have praise from the same: for he is a minister of God to thee for good. But if thou do that which is evil, be afraid; for he beareth not the sword in vain: for he is a minister of God, an avenger for wrath to him that doeth evil. Wherefore ye must needs be in subjection, not only because of the wrath, but also for conscience' sake. Hence for this cause ye pay tribute also; for they are ministers of God's service, attending continually upon this very thing. Render to all their dues: tribute to whom tribute is due; custom to whom custom; fear to whom fear; honor to whom honor."

27. And for this reason also has government been ordained by God, that it may uphold general peace, which thing alone cannot be paid for by all the money in the world. We just noticed a few things in the uprising of the peasant, what damage, misery and woe are caused by rebellion and the breaking of peace. God grant that things do not go further and that we experience no more. Enough is said on this Gospel. Of temporal government we have written a special booklet. Whoever desires to read it may do so. There he will find more on this subject.

TWENTY-THIRD SUNDAY AFTER TRINITY.

Second Sermon: Mat. 22, 15-22.

This sermon is found only in the c edition and in one pamphlet print: "A sermon on Mat. 22. The Tribute Money, Dr. Martin Luther, Wittenberg, 1535." On last page: "Printed at Wittenberg, by Joseph Klug, 1535."

In this as in his other sermons Luther wrote in his copy Bible passages at the beginning and close, also marginal notes to the text, which were edited under the following title by Just von Einem: "The fragments that were left over, or notes of Dr. Martin Luther; which he added to some of his first printed sermons; gathered, and edited as an appendix to the instruction drawn from Luther's writings, how to preach edifyingly and forcibly, edited by John Just von Einem, a servant of the Word of God at Osterweddingen, Duchy of Magdeburg 1729."

For example, the cited passages in the civil government: Rom. 13, 1f.; Col. 1, 18.—Tax, Tribute, Fear, Honor are due the civil government. Christ pays the tribute money. Mat. 17, 24–27.—1 Pet. 2, 17. Erl. 14, 309; W. 11, 2423; St. L. 11, 1816.

CONTENTS: THE COUNSEL OF THE PHARISEES PUT TO NAUGHT.

I. THE COUNSEL OF THE PHARISEES.
1. The foundation and origin of their counsel. 1.
2. The nature of their counsel. 2-3.
3. The character of the people who took this counsel. 3-4.
4. Of the ways and means by which the Pharisees tried to accomplish their counsel and how they were put to shame. 5-6f.
* He who attempts to deceive and mock God, only deceives and mocks himself. 7.
5. How the Pharisees plan the best they can that their counsel should not fail. 8.
II. THEIR COUNSEL PUT TO NAUGHT.
1. How Christ in putting to naught their counsel proves himself to be a true teacher. 9-18.
2. How Christ appears to begin to destroy their counsel in a

childish and foolish manner. 10.
* How and why one should guard against trifling with divine things. 11.
* God acts toward men as they are disposed toward him. 12-13.
3. How Christ here uncovers the trickery of the Pharisees.
A. The uncovering of this trickery in general. 14-15.
B. The disclosing of their trickery in detail.
a. The subtilty of the Pharisees is disclosed in this, that they rob the Emperor. 16-17.
b. In that, they rob God. 18.
c. How this subtilty, that Christ here discloses, is to be found among the Papists. 19f.
* An opinion of the doctrine of the Papists in that they say, one is not obliged to suffer authority over him, but may resist it. 20-25.
4. What use true Christians may

1. This Gospel is in itself plain enough and easy to understand. Its contents are noteworthy, especially because of
Christ's answer to a practical question and its doctrine.
First of all our attention is directed to the intensely wicked,
bitter and venomous persecution of Christ and his Word on
the part of the Jews, who schemed to attack him with
shrewd and deceitful questions. For these villains and base
characters would gladly have put him to death as one who
had wearied them beyond endurance and must be gotten out
of the way, although they could find no cause for impugn-
ing either his doctrine or his life, eagerly as they sought to
do so. They studied all sorts of devices and ways to catch
him in his words and condemn him, which they kept up
until God allowed them to vent their spite and crucify him.
That class of people will obtain what they strive for, even to
their own hurt. They had their time of probation and could
have repented when the Son of God appeared in their midst,
but they flatly refused to accept him, God suffering them to
go their way and fulfil the measure of their sin to its utmost extent in that they murdered him who came to save
them. Their end was destruction and obliteration as a nation. The enemies of the Gospel are no better in our day.
They would put Christ out of the way if they could, and
thus it will be even to the end of time, with the same result.
Amen.

2. See now how they scheme and succeed. The wisest and
most learned leaders assemble, put their heads together and

decide on one of the many shrewd plans by which to cause
Christ's death. Their wise counsel is as follows: If we
weigh and balance the situation we find two ways to seize
and accuse him. First, if he opposes Caesar, he can be
charged with conspiracy; and if he is considered a conspirator we will have him in our control as one guilty, like
a thief and robber, who would despoil the emperor of his
majesty and crown and who is worthy of death, with which
the law punishes such a crime. Should this scheme fail we
can have recourse to another one, namely, to prove him to
be guilty of robbing God, and have him condemned as a
blasphemer. It would be regarded as a still greater crime
to prove that he robs God of the honor due him and mis-
leads the people under the cloak of serving him. For should
he say, We must pay tribute to Caesar and acknowledge him
as our sovereign; he would detract from God, who alone
wants to be this nation's sovereign and who has chosen us
from all races to have no king but him. This also would
condemn him to death. Whichever way therefore he may
answer, he will be caught and fall into our hands. Does he
favor Caesar, he robs God; and if he decides in favor of God
he declares against Caesar and makes himself a conspirator.

3. Such is the counsel of those wiseacres and petty saints
who resolved to lay hold of Christ with all law and authority, as an enemy either of God or of Caesar. Not that they
cared so much either for the one or the other, but in order to
carry their point. They were indeed anxious enough to free
themselves from the yoke of Roman power, causing frequent
insurrections and drawing abundantly deserved executions
upon their own heads, by hundreds and thousands, and
finally suffering entire destruction as a nation.

In like manner they were before God thieves and evil-
doers in that they corrupted his Word and persecuted its
pure doctrine. So entirely submerged in these two vices
were they as to have become doubly worthy of death, before
God and before Caesar; they manifested their wickedness,
moreover, by attempting to catch an innocent man as if

guilty of their own sin, pretending to be most pious saints before God and most loyal subjects of Caesar.

4. The Jews were used to this from time immemorial; they had treated their prophets and many godly teachers in a similar manner, and afterwards did the same to the Apostles, so that it is no wonder if they treat us in the same manner. And what have the Apostles or we either to complain of in particular, since they did not spare their Lord and God? The world cannot do otherwise. It is under the devil's control, revelling in robbery and rebellion, at the same time imputing these crimes to Christians, as if they were sinners above all sinners.

5. And see further how they play their trick and seek to entangle the Lord so that they may not fail in their plans. They do not put the question abruptly, but approach him with a neat introduction of flattery, as though they had the best of intentions and were really in earnest about the matter. They praise and humor him with smooth words; for they think he is human and a preacher like themselves, who thus loves to hear such flattery and praise, and say: You are a true teacher and an upright man, what you say ·and do is right and good, etc., etc. With such praise a young fool might be misled to preach what the people want to hear, as nearly all false prophets do who look for the approval of men rather than that of God. They accept honor, and preach what is paid for; where their pay ends, there also ends their preaching. These were of a kind characterized by Christ when he says of them that they like to be called Rabbi, etc., Mat. 23, 7. Because they are so foolish they think he also likes to be tickled and can be befooled by servile adulations, surrendering himself to their two prongs and their death-thrusts, before he would be aware of any danger.

6. But the saying is true: ''The Lord will have them in derision.'' It is not an uncommon thing for one man to deceive another, but no trickery will avail with Christ. He understands the wiles of men and can entrap them in their own devices. So here; he compels these hypocrites to speak the plain truth, although they have many other things in

their hearts, and thus perfectly puts them to shame. It is indeed true that he teaches the way of God right, and fears nobody, while not one of his enemies speaks from the heart. The lips may utter truth that amounts to nothing but lies. Christ's words are true, however they may twist them. They judge him by themselves and represent him as a disturber of the peace, who would rob Caesar of his tribute money and rally the populace around him in rebellion, while he is afraid to make such declaration in public. That is their design and scheme, but they veil it under the words: "Thou teachest the way of God in truth," praise not to be condemned so far as it goes.

Caiaphas, the high priest, acted in like manner, John 11, 48-50, when he said: "It is expedient for you that one man should die for the people, and that the whole nation perish not. If we let him thus alone, all men will believe on him; and the Romans will come and take away both our place and our nation." That was a true declaration, fitting them, while they dissembled as to their hearts' sentiments. They did not believe that the Romans would come, but were intent on putting Christ out of the way, thinking they would then fare better. And yet it happened to them even as they had prophesied, that Christ had to die for the people, and the Romans did despoil them of their land and nation.

7. That is the lot of those who would deceive and mock God; they mock themselves and come to grief. They seek a teacher of truth, and they find such in him, against their wish, for he hits them on the head with truth in a manner that makes them reel in confusion. They wish to submit a puzzling question to him, not about the law and matters of salvation, but one that is unnecessary and insidious. They pass by the whole Pentateuch and what pertains to God's Word and way of truth, and catch on something calculated to confuse him. Moses has not instructed us about giving tribute, nor had Christ anything to do with that.

8. There, think they, we have him securely as between two spears. Does he say yes, then we accuse him as one who would rob God; who holds heresy, and, as an apostate

Jew, teaches contrary to Moses and the prophets: if, on the other hand, he says nay, we will know what to do, for the servants of Herod are at hand. He must fall into the hands of these tempters or into those of the rabble, in either case he is lost; indeed he must fall into the hands of both and surely die, for there is no escape possible in either yea or nay, represented by the two classes of people, Jew and Gentile. Was not that planned shrewdly enough? Who could escape from such a dilemma with gauntlets on both sides? They themselves would have failed to extricate themselves in a similar predicament.

9. But the wise people met with a wisdom they neither knew of nor looked for; it was divine wisdom. Christ seizes the spear and club in their hands and turns their weapons against themselves, answering neither yea nor nay, but compelling them to give an answer which indicts themselves. There he is the Master as they had greeted him; he proves that he can answer their slippery interrogation by themselves. They are thus obliged to run the gauntlet, and are caught in the net with which they had planned to catch him.

10. As of in a playful mood, Christ has them show him the tribute money to start with, and asks whose stamp and superscription it bears. In that childlike way he may have made the impression that he did not know, or was not able to read, so that they concluded: We have him surely now; he is afraid and wants to dissemble in favor of Caesar, not daring to say a word against him, etc. Instead of that he takes the word from their lips, making them admit that they are caught. They must confess it, and cannot do otherwise than say, It is Caesar's. With that answer he turns the conclusion against them: If the currency and its image is Caesar's, also the superscription, then you have my thanks for saying yea yourselves to the question you put at me. Why need you bother me with a matter that you can settle so readily? This is truly digging a pit for others and falling in yourself; setting a trap and being caught in it.

11. Christ makes use of the same dialectics in answering

others who would impugn his character, and entraps them
where they meant to entrap him. As in Luke 19, 21-22,
where a servant had buried the pound entrusted to him in
a napkin, saying: "I feared thee because thou art an
austere man: thou takest up that which thou layest not
down, and reapest that which thou didst not sow." He
saith unto him: "Out of thine own mouth will I judge thee,
thou wicked servant," etc. That is, be it as thou hast said.
Because thou regardedst me to be an austere man, taking
what I had not laid down, therefore it serves thee right that
thou shouldst be treated in that way, and thy pound be
taken from thee as from one who compels me to be austere
and strict with him. I give this as a caution that people
may learn to take heed and not trifle with holy things. For
men can be deceived, but those who try to deceive God deceive themselves.

12. I have often said that God acts toward man even as
man is disposed; as thou thinkest and believeth concerning
him, such he is to thee. The servant of whom we speak did
not have an austere and severe man for his master; on the
contrary, he was treated kindly and justly; but since he
pictured him that way he must learn how it feels. It is the
same with our belief or disbelief. If our hearts picture him
as gracious or angry, pleasant or harsh, we have him that
way. God is not to be mocked. Those who regard him as
angry toward them will find him so; but whoever can say:
I know that he will be a gracious father to me and forgive
my sins, they will have that experience with him. There
must, however, be no hypocrisy, no dissembling, as if the
lips should say one thing and the heart thinks the opposite.

13. Since, then, these people call him Master and a teacher
of truth, although they do not believe what they say and
simply try to catch and deceive him in his words; he
turns the matter to their discomfiture and gives them an un-
expected proof of what their lips profess. Like as if we
were to regard him wrongfully as an ungracious and angry
God, we would so experience him, for it is, as he says: "Out
of thine own mouth will I judge thee;" again: "By thy

words thou shalt be justified, and by thy words thou shalt be condemned," Mat. 12, 37. That would serve us right and be just. Why dost thou not look him straight in the eyes and judge him as what he is, or believest on him as he reveals himself in his Word, namely, as a teacher and savior of all who are burdened with sin and desire to be godly? If such an ideal does not suit thee and thou formest a different one, thou must take what thou hast provided for thyself.

14. This is the experience these plotters make. Their words pronounce him to be a teacher of truth, yet in their hearts they are false; however, he is a real teacher to them and exposes their knavery and hypocrisy. Christ is a good doctor. Such physicians as clearly understand the disease must be commended; they can help a patient so much better than one who simply experiments on the case. He soon learns what knaves they are; but since they call him Master, as if they would learn of him, they must hear what they do not expect, namely: "If I am a master and teacher of truth I will tell you truly what you see and seek: *You are hypocrites* in my judgment." That put in plain language means: "You are deceitful fellows." They deserve this, first, because they are not pious at all; secondly, because they cover up and decorate their falseness by making a pretence of virtue before the people. "You are double hypocrites; you do not seek the way of God nor the truth, yet you flatter me as teaching such to make yourself appear holy; and because you will not hear the truth that could save you, you must hear truth that shall reveal your hypocrisy and condemn it. For, I am, as you say, a teacher of truth. To some, that signifies life, to others, death and damnation, according as their respective faith and hearts may be. Therefore I tell you plainly and truly what you are inwardly, namely, hypocrites and desperate rogues who are beyond help and advice and who belong to the devil. But those who are godly and would like to be so, to them I say: "Come unto me, all ye that labor and are heavy laden, and I will give you rest," Mat. 11, 28.

15. Behold, thus they find the right teacher of truth, not

to their salvation, however, which they do not seek, but to their condemnation. They are enemies to the truth and do not like to hear such preaching; yet they must hear it, as if from their own lips, answering their question themselves, to their own exposure; as explained above.

16. After this exposure and reproof of their impudence, silencing them with their own answer, the Master continues: "Render unto Caesar the things that are Caesar's; and unto God the things that are God's." Let the child be baptized that its name become known. In other words: "You want to take away from Caesar what is his, and have already taken from God what is God's. You, therefore, are rebels and blasphemers. You take and withhold, and not even question your own dishonesty, nor manifest a purpose to do what is right. That is indeed and rightly called disloyalty, where one refuses to give to Caesar what he can claim as his own.

17. This truth they must hear from this teacher of truth, however much it may displease them to be so sternly rebuked. They hate to be called thieves and robbers, as if they were disposed to despoil the emperor (Caesar) of his authority and belongings and usurp the rights of their superiors under a pretence of justice, for which they deserved punishment in body and estate as twofold rebels. This is the first thought.

18. Secondly. Just as they have been shown to be thieves and robbers toward the state they are similarly guilty of robbing God. They withhold what is God's and even claim to be in the right by so doing. The Phophet Jeremiah, 23, 11, calls those who do not preach God's Word in God's name "profaners," as withholding it from the people for whom it was given; they rob and take, not from God in heaven, but from the people to whom God sent and commanded it to be given, and give them something else instead of it. Thus they profane and rob God, withholding the honor and obedience they owe him. Such fruits they are, these smart saints, who wished to bring Christ in reproach! It is on that account that they must hear the rebukes ad-

ministered to them and be exposed as God-thieves who deserve capital punishment.

19. Let us now pay attention to the hypocrites of our day—those prudish pietists, bishops and the Pope's whole coterie of clerics, who persecute Christ and his followers in that they reject and condemn his Word and the acknowledged truth of the Gospel. Christ rightfully calls them robbers and profaners of God and of Caesar. They are obedient neither to God nor to the true Christian church; neither to the state nor to any constituted authority, but would be lords themselves and live and do as they like, none daring to oppose them. They are disobedient in person, and also assault innocent Christians, devour and kill whom they can and would destroy God's kingdom completely; yet they wish to be well spoken of as being in their right, being obedient, pious and peaceable, and regarding us as heretics and sinners against God and Christendom and against the powers that be, who therefore deserve death. Just like these in the Gospel, who would give neither to God nor to Caesar; pretend to great piety, while they seek to put Christ out of the way as one teaching what is opposed to religion and to patriotism.

20. But how, if the wheel should reverse itself and throw the guilt, which they now heap on us Christians, upon their own heads so that they receive the reward due to the openly condemned rebels and God-thieves, who profane the majesty of both divine and human right? True, neither the Gospel nor Christ himself makes use of physical punishment, yet they should beware lest others come (and I fear very much that such will be the case) who will handle them roughly, teaching them, as others have been taught, that they must cease to persecute Christians. This would be treating them after their own fashion. The Pope, with all his apostles, disciples, lawyers and theologians, teaches: Violence need not be endured, but vim vi repellere licet, that is, open violence may be repelled by force. They say, what Christ teaches, Mat. 5, 39, is not a duty, but simply counsel, and no one is bound by it, namely: "I say unto you, resist not him

that is evil; but whoever smiteth thee on thy right cheek, turn to him the other also,'' etc. Their interpretation of this has the sanction of all high schools, institutions and monasteries; it can be found in all their books, nor do they hesitate to praise and justify it, holding that no one is obliged to take wrong even from the emperor, but that it is right to resist evil and strike back in self-defense, let it hit Caesar or whom it may.

21. It were, therefore, not wrong, according to their own teaching, to resist such insufferable injury by force; and I would not lament so very much if, as a punishment from God, it should come about through some false preacher or rabble leader that such tyrants were killed. For they are intent on disorder; their teachings and doings instigate uprisings and war, while they throw the blame on us who teach righteousness, hold the government in honor and oppose conspiracy by word and deed. They would gladly kill us, and although they fail in their loyalty, they want to be honored and safe-guarded in their mischief so that no harm may befall them. The popes with their followings have taught thus not only, but they also practised it by their acts, opposing kings and emporers as it suited them, despising all authority and trampling the law under their feet, even claiming divine right for their doings. They would do the same now, if they could, boasting that they are in supreme authority and owe allegiance to no ruler.

22. If they should now allow such doctrine to be preached among them, as I myself could do if I were so minded to avenge myself (may God forbid it), or the public would take such teachings from their books and statutes, and a general uprising should follow, whom would they have to blame and who could reason otherwise than that it served them right? Why are they so desperate and perverse that they reproach Christ with his teachings as seditious and blaspheme him who is their Lord, while they themselves are rebels and profaners of God? They disseminate and defend such godless and seditious teachings, and persecute us who preach the pure Gospel, as they well know, and with all

faithful ones resist and preach against disloyalty and disorder. They themselves must acknowledge, if they would
or could do so in their concealed malice, that they owe it to
no other source than to our preaching that they for so long
a time have been and are yet secured against rebellion, for
if it had not been for us they might have had some different
experiences. By their teaching they could not maintain nor
enforce peace, favoring uprisings as it does, and if I could
approve of it I would not trust myself to advocate or at
least wink at any resistence of their adherents in self-protec-
tion by force.

23. But we will neither teach nor allow that Christ's
words are nothing more than counsel; we teach that Christians must suffer wrong, if needs be, and leave vengence to
God. They are to be what the Scriptures call them in Ps.
44, 22, "sheep for the slaughter," who may expect death
every hour of the day. The Papists know full well that they
are safe in our presence; they show their gratitude by persecuting, devouring and murdering us unceasingly, until we
are entirely done for. But may it not also happen that in
so doing they will meet with such as will defend their rights
against them and give them their due so richly deserved,
thus paying for what injury they have done to the Gospel
and to us? Their doom is sealed. For the present we must
suffer, and leave to God how and when he will avenge us.
The punishment they deserve is in God's hand to be meted
out in his own time and manner. Although they pretend to
be afraid of us, we will do them no harm, allowing them to
imitate the Pharisees over against the common people who
adhere to Christ. Others will give them what they fear
from us, as did the Romans to those who opposed and sus-
pected Christ and his adherents, giving them their full reward when they believed themselves secure.

24. That is the way these will fare in time. They are
afraid, though they know that we have attempted nothing
to their hurt, nor de we now do so; we offer them peace and
uphold peace, exhorting and teaching our people and the
public generally to abstain from disloyal acts. We will not

stain our hands with their blood. That is something we do not wish to be guilty of. We glory in our innocence over against them before all the world and will not implicate ourselves in their downfall. But others shall arise who will visit upon them what is written of that class of people in the Bible, as, for instance, in Prov. 10, 24, "The fear of the wicked, it shall come upon him." And as Christ expresses it in Mat. 12, 37: "For by thy words thou shalt be justified." Thou hast complained of disloyalty, disloyalty shall be thy portion. We will then say, Amen, and deo gratias, thanks to God, besides.

25. Let that be said on this text to those who would reproach Christ in order to promote their own reputation and standing, so that they may see and learn what sort of a truth-teacher he is, exposing their lies and falsehood and fastening on them what they like to accuse him of, as being real liars and murderers, or misleaders and rebels; they insist on such a course, but endeavor to throw the suspicion on Christ and his adherents, in spite of the fact that these are and teach the very opposite.

26. But we must keep this Word before our eyes; it is our rule of conduct toward the two kingdoms, God's and Caesar's, so that we may give to each the honor due him as both of divine order and example. That in both there are many who are not godfearing, who abuse the charge and position committed to them, especially toward Christians, persecuting us as disobedient and disloyal, we admit, but it does not disturb us. We must and are willing to suffer this, at the same time we maintain our right to punish them by word of mouth, telling them the truth and hurling back the accusations heaped upon us. In so doing we satisfy justice and fulfil our duty; the rest we commit to God, how and by whom he may want to avenge us.

27. We have said much about the teaching of Christ's answer; for it is the doctrine we insist on, that the two powers or governments, God's and Caesar's, or spiritual and temporal kingdoms, must be kept apart, as Christ does here in a clear and brief declaration, making a distinction

not only, but also illustrating finely how each is to be constituted and administered. When he says, "Render unto Caesar the things that are Caesar's," he refers to the relation of subjects to their rulers; the other part, "Render unto God the things that are God's," is especially intended for such as are in authority.

28. For it is thus ordained of God that subjects must and shall give to their rulers what they need; when he commands them to give, it is implied that these may take; and where we are to give what is due, there we infer that we owe them something, so that the language might be: "to return," rather than simply to render or give. That is something for subjects under civil authority.

29. On the other hand, there are restrictions placed upon rulers that they govern in the same spirit, and not take from their subjects what is not due them; but remember to give and do also what they are in duty bound to do by virtue of their presiding over countries and nations, so that they may grow and prosper. That is why they were elevated by God to their respective positions of honor, not that they sit there simply as place-thieves, and doing what they like.

30. But if that were emphasized it would be found that the world is full of real thieves and rogues, rulers as well as subjects, and the number would indeed be small from the highest to the lowest, who obey and do what is right. Subjects are most generally so disposed as to cheat their ruler and appropriate to their own use what is his, wherever they can, to say nothing about giving cheerfully, hesitating as they may do to admit that. Princes and office-holders wish to have the name of being Christians and obedient subjects of the emperor, yet they do only what suits them and, if they could, they would gladly usurp the places of their superiors.

31. The same is true of the knights who wait upon and assist the princes; if they could do so, they would gladly confiscate everything, strip their chiefs of what they have and trample them under foot; instead they take villages and castles, delight in being called "dear subjects," advise and

govern in their own interests, thus reveling, oppressing and plaguing both lords and subjects, according to their sweet will. By the way, how many princes and office-holders are there now in high positions who could claim that they give to Caesar what is Caesar's? Would not all rather fill their own coffers, bags and pockets? This all can do; but giving to Caesar what belongs to him is difficult to find; taking and stealing from him is much more common.

32. There is a similar state of things in all other situations and offices. Servants deceive and cheat their masters, maids their mistresses, day laborers and mechanics those for whom they work. It is so in daily intercourse, at the market and elsewhere; stealing and robbing, even boldly and openly, is the common practice. In that way things go on among high and low, so that there is no royal residence, no city, no house, that is not full of knaves and thieves. Were the world plagued with this sin only, it were already too much and it deserved to have been destroyed long ago; and yet no one wants to be charged with and punished for theft, the evil-doers would rather claim honor for their misconduct; especially is that the case with the lords of the nobility who strut around in glittering chains. But if they were treated as they deserve they would not be allowed to wear them on the streets, but would be dealt with as those who stole five or six dollars. It is here, as the saying goes, "Little thieves are hung in iron chains; the big public thieves are permitted to walk about with chains of gold."

33. It should not be thus, but everyone respects his estate and position and do as it behooves him. Yea, sayest thou, is it not enough that I take nothing from anybody? Yea, truly; but there are many ways of taking; not only from under the bench where there is nothing that belongs to thee, nor out of the bag or chest of another, but also where thou art unfaithful to thy employer and permittest damage to ensue because of negligence or mischief, rather than in consequence of a mistake. As, for instance, where a citizen or neighbor overcharges another, and the nobleman filches and squeezes. According to the seventh commandment all

such sharp dealing is called stealing and doing wrong; those who practice it are thieves who care nothing for a troubled conscience, and the maxim, "Render unto Caesar the things that are Caesar's," becomes a rare bird. All the world is full of the perversity, "taking from Caesar the things that are Caesar's," from the bottom up; from servant up to knights and princes, so that there is no estate on earth so plagued with thieves and rogues as that of the emperor's and government's.

34. Government must also be told how to act toward its subjects. Those in authority also rob and take what is not theirs, and that on the responsibility of their superiors. As when an emperor or prince goes on, plaguing land and people with unnecessary assessments and other burdens. In that situation thou must also hear thy text. If thou desirest the subjects to put into practice their lesson and be honest with thee, thou must also avoid taking from them what is not thine. For Christ does not say here, Render to Caesar that which he wants and likes, but he assigns limits to him, how far he may reach, that is: "The things that are Caesar's," or what he is rightfully entitled to.

35. Therefore, land, cities, homes, are not to be governed as the one in authority over them may like, as if an employer could treat his employes to suit his notion, contrary to the Lord's justice. Nay, the employe would say, I owe thee what is thine, not what thou mayest desire to have. One might require so much as my head or fist, or he would not pay me wages or food and clothing, and so plunder and plague me as not to leave a rag upon my body. That would be taking the rights from the man-servant, and her property from the maid-servant.

36. So also if a burgomaster, ruler or office-holder should compel and plague the people to serve his whims, that could not be regarded as a lordly right, but would be stealing and doing wrong, just as much as if a fellow-citizen should steal from them. However, there is no position nowadays so insignificant but that its occupant should not desire to have the right and the power to do and command what he pleases,

studying how he may oppress the people and holding that
his authority empowers him to squeeze, drive and torment
everybody as he pleases. Even as is now the case more
especially with the poor clergymen and preachers, so that
there is danger in all estates, especially in the higher ones,
for in them the really great thieves are to be found. A
house-servant may make a householder poor by his dishonesty; but a nobleman can steal what amounts to something,
namely, a whole principality, land and people.

37. Therefore we must tell them how Christ has limited
their prerogatives in this text, so that they may not do what
they might personally wish. It would go entirely too far,
and the Pope's rule would go into effect, they being flogged
by their subjects; but we neither teach nor approve of such
practice. Christ does not say *de facto, sed de jure*, not by
fact, but by right; that is, he teaches what each man must
do, namely, the subjects must give, and the government must
not take more than what is due; but who is to punish where
both parties sin against the law is not stated.

38. Christ does not do, as the Pope teaches that one
should hit back, nor does he allow anyone to avenge himself, neither the employer nor his employee; the infliction
of punishment and judgment he reserves for himself as the
highest Lord and God. "Vengeance is mine," saith God,
Deut. 32, 35. He who does not give heed to this teaching
will experience this judgment. If God does not punish by
the ordinary authorities he will do it by pestilence, war, rev-
olutions and other plagues; for he can punish rulers as well
as their subjects. Therefore both are instructed as to their
duty, and we will abide by his declaration. We must not
and will not coerce anyone by violent measures, but say only
what is right and resist wrong-doing by word of mouth.
Whoever will not mind that, we excommunicate such an one
in accordance with Christ's teaching, telling him that he
belongs to the devil, and let him go. Others may punish
the Pope and his followers who will not abide by the Word
of God, but resort to violence.

39. This is a brief statement as to the first estate or gov-

ernment, both in its higher and its lower functions, to show how far we are away from our true position and how full the world is everywhere of thievery. But these matters are worst of all, if one is to expound this passage (Render to God what is God's) and speak of the God-thieves in the spiritual government of Christendom, in which I and the likes of me are. For as high as heaven is above the earth so dangerous and difficult is this office in comparison with secular or imperial positions which, indeed, are also dangerous where their occupants do not call upon God for help to discharge their duties properly and without injury to their subjects. But if unfaithful ministers or preachers get into their office they will be, not thieves of bread, meat or clothing, wherewith the body is nourished and with which jurists busy themselves, who teach nothing further than what ministers to the belly and try to check that class of stealing; but those who occupy the office that is to give the bread of eternal life to souls and, instead, cause them everlasting thirst, hunger and nakedness, taking away the word by which man is nourished from death to life, such are not simply belly-thieves, but thieves of God and of the heavenly kingdom.

40. Such now is the Pope with his bishops and all their retinue, who do not preach to the people, rather preventing them from receiving God's Word and what it gives and affords; doing their very best in mischief when they forbid and hinder the sacrament to be administered under both forms, as Christ instituted it, and they well know, in sheer violence and blasphemous thirst; they cannot rightly be called anything else than sacrilegious, public thieves of God, robbers of his Word and sacrament.

41. There are among us also some who so plague and press the poor pastors with hunger and care that they cannot do their work properly; some also lowering their calling so as to reach out for the heavenly things and at the same time hanker after carnal goods, as the cliques of Pope and priest also do, who are charged with spiritual matters, but do not preach them nor suffer it to be done. They practise the two kinds of robbery and deserve all the more severe pun-

ishment.   Yet the world is just as full of this miserable dishonesty as of the secular sort, and they are thieves through and through, from top to bottom, from the least to the greatest.

42. But how will it be in the end when the final judgment shall take place?   What does it mean that God must continue to call and preach: "Do render both to God and to Caesar," but all in vain, and should thus be mocked and his Word trampled under foot?   Are we not to expect that at last there should rain upon the world a flood with thunder, lightning and hellfire?   It cannot and must not be otherwise, because the trespass against God's and Caesar's right continues so boldly and so eagerly and turns the single into a double robbery, ever defending its course and resisting its punishment.   God will and can not suffer that forever. I would that he might take us and ours away in mercy so that we be spared the coming calamity!   Wickedness is so very great, and so manifold in the whole world, that it exceeds the leaves on the trees and the blades of grass upon the earth in number.   May God preserve and deliver us from this distress, and grant grace that we may hold to his Word in earnestness and be delivered from such evil!   Amen.

THE TWENTY-FOURTH SUNDAY AFTER TRINITY.

This sermon is not found in the c. edition. Erl. 14, 331; W. 11, 2447; St. L. 11, 1834.

Text: Mat. 9, 18-26. While he spake these things unto them, behold, there came a ruler, and worshipped him, saying, My daughter is even now dead: but come and lay thy hand upon her, and she shall live. And Jesus arose, and followed him, and so did his disciples. And behold, a woman, who had an issue of blood twelve years, came behind him, and touched the border of his garment: for she said within herself, If I do but touch his garment, I shall be made whole. But Jesus turning and seeing her said, Daughter, be of good cheer; thy faith hath made thee whole. And the woman was made whole from that hour. And when Jesus came into the ruler's house, and saw the flute-players, and the crowd making a tumult, he said, Give place: for the damsel is not dead, but sleepeth. And they laughed him to scorn. But when the crowd was put forth, he entered in, and took her by the hand; and the damsel arose. And the fame hereof went forth into all that land.

CONTENTS: THE GOSPEL AND CHRIST, OR JAIRUS' DAUGH-
TER RAISED AND THE WOMAN WITH AN ISSUE OF
BLOOD HEALED.

grace and goodness of Christ. 17.

II. OF THE GOSPEL AND CHRIST IN DETAIL.

A. How we find this painted forth in the woman with the issue of blood, and:
1. In that, when she heard Christ preached, she formed a sure hope that he would help her. 18-19.
2. In that the woman had not merited the help of Christ and she regarded herself unworthy. 19.
* Of the true preparation for the grace and goodness of Christ. 20.
3. In that she spent all she had on physicians and still received no help. 21-26.
* Of workrighteous teachings and teachers; also of the ordinances of the Papists.
  a. They only distress the afflicted conscience more. 21-23.
  b. The doctrine of workrighteousness is a cause of the

many orders and institutions. 23.
  c. Workrighteousness teachers are dangerous physicians. 24.
  d. How and why the doctrines and institutions of the workrighteousness of the Papists are not to be encouraged. 25-26.
4. In that the woman turned to Christ. 27-29.
* We are Christians, not through works but through grace. 29-30.
5. In that the woman received from Christ absolution. 31-32.
* Works do not make us Christians, but only prove that we are Christians. 32-33.

B. How we find this pictured in the daughter of Jairus.
1. The first part of this picture. 34.
2. The second part. 35f.
* How and why satan and the world persecute the Gospel so hard. 36-37.
* Conclusion of this exposition. 38.

SUMMARY OF THIS GOSPEL: 1. Christ came into the world to take away sin.

2. Worldly wisdom and human righteousness mock the work of Christ.

3. The faith of this woman is praised who touched the fringe of the Savior's garment; concerning this read what Mark writes in his fifth chapter.

THE SPRITUAL INTERPRETATION: By the little daughter of the ruler of this synagogue of the Jews is to be understood Judaism; by the woman, heathenism, both of whom Christ helps. Mark took special pains to add that the little daughter was twelve years old and that the woman had the issue of blood also twelve years. Also that the damsel was healthy and strong and went about jumping and rejoicing, while the woman was lying ill. But when the woman was healed the damsel lay down and died. This signifies that the Jews delighted and rejoiced in God and his law, while the heathen remained in sin without God, and were not permitted to mingle among the Jews, Acts 10. Now since Christ came and desired to help the heathen and the whole world, the damsel, or the synagogue, begins to die, despises the proffered grace of God through Christ; but the woman meanwhile recovers her health, that is, the heathen obtain grace, which the Jews rejected; yet, at last Christ raises the damsel from the dead, which signifies that not all the Jews are lost, but many will return through the preaching of the Gospel and through faith in Christ. Rom. 11. The substance, therefore, of the spiritual interpretation is: Christ goes and will raise from the dead the synagogue of the Jews; then the heathen nations came in his way and mingle with them; concerning this there is much here and there in the writings of Paul and the prophets.

1. Dear friends, you know that the Gospel is nothing else than a sermon about one person who is called Christ. And although there are many other books written here and there, and many sermons preached by many different persons, both about the heathen and the Christians, yea, also about the mother of God, St. Peter, angels and many of the saints; yet they are not Gospels, for this alone is the true Gospel which sets before us Christ, and teaches the good things we may hope from him.

2. Of course there is also at times something in the Gospel on John the Baptist, Mary and the Apostles, but this is not properly the Gospel, for they are taken into consideration so as more perfectly to indicate whence Christ came and what his office is. So Luke relates the history of John the Baptist from the beginning, his conception and birth; and that of the Virgin Mary, all which is written not for their sake, but only for the sake of the one person Christ, so that everything written in the Gospel concerns this person Christ alone. In St. Paul's Epistles there is nothing written about the saints, all there is about Christ alone. The Evangelists describe what miracles and wonders Christ performed; but they write of no work that John or Mary did; but only what Christ did, how he helped the people in body and soul, and how the people clung to him.

3. For God has decreed it is his will that all should cling to the one man Christ, to hope in him and hold fast to him if they would be saved. Thus they know nothing of any one aside from Christ, who alone has been presented unto us by God as our mercy-seat, as St. Paul writes, Rom. 3, 25. Hitherto one has clung to this saint, another to that, one has had Mary, another Saint Barbara, and there have been manifold sects and orders. But no one cared anything for Christ except for the name. We have had many mediators, all of whom we abandoned and held only to Christ. Therefore St. Paul says in Rom. 1, 2, that the Gospel was

promised by God through the prophets concerning his Son. And he insists upon it so very strongly, that nothing avails in the Gospel except the one only person, Jesus Christ. He who knows this may well thank God, that he knows where to place his comfort, help and confidence, and he will then despise and cast away all sermons about other persons.

4. For this reason the Lord is pictured to us in to-day's Gospel, mingling among the people, drawing all the world unto himself by his friendliness and comforting doctrine so that they may cling to him with their hearts, depend upon his goodness, and hope to receive from him both spiritual and temporal treasures. Nor do you see him take anything from those he heals and helps; yea, he receives nothing from them but scorn and mockery, as we shall hear. Good deeds proceed from him, but he receives mockery and scorn in return.

5. Now this is preached and submitted to the whole world, that they may learn to know this man aright, and to know how to become Christians, not how to become good and innocent. Other doctrines outside of the Gospel, like the books of the heathen masters, insist that the people should through them become good; again, the legends of the saints especially insist that the people are to live as the saints lived. To make good people does not belong to the Gospel, for it only makes Christians. It takes much more to be a Christian than to be pious. A person can easily be pious, but not a Christian. A Christian knows nothing to say about his piety, for he finds in himself nothing good or pious. If he is to be pious, he must look for a different piety, a piety in some one else.

6. To this end Christ is presented to us as an inexhaustible fountain, who at all times overflows with pure goodness and grace. And for such goodness and kindness he accepts nothing, except that the good people, who acknowledge such kindness and grace, thank him for it, praise and love him, although others despise him for it. This is what he reaps from it. So one is not called a Christian because he does much, but because he receives something from

Christ, draws from him and lets Christ only give to him.
If one no longer receives anything from Christ, he is no
longer a Christian, so that the name Christian continues to
be based only on receiving, and not on giving and doing,
and he receives nothing from any one except from Christ
alone. If you look at what you do, you have already lost
the Christian name. It is indeed true, that we are to do
good works, help, advise and give to others; but no one
is called a Christian by reason of that, nor is he on that
account a Christian.

7. Therefore, if you wish to consider the word in its true
meaning, you must identify a Christian by the fact that he
only receives something from Christ, and has Christ within
him; for this is what the word properly means. Just as
a person is called "white," because of his white color, black
because of his dark color, large because of his size. So also
one is called a "Christian" because of Christ, who dwells
in him and from whom he receives his blessings. So, if one
is called a Christian because of Christ, he is certainly then
not called a Christian because of his works. From this it
also follows that no one is called a Christian by reason of
his good works. If this be true, as it undoubtedly is, then
it must follow that our orders and sects do not belong
under the Christian name, and they do not develop Christians.

8. Therefore they are deceivers, who preach or teach in
the church, and occupy themselves with commandments,
works and statutes, that accomplish nothing. Although
they pretend to be Christians, nevertheless they still, under
this name, attempt to burden and torment us with their
commands and works. By reason of my works I may well
be called one who fasts, one who prays, or a pilgrim, but
not a Christian. If you were to weave all your works together, and add to them all the works of others, you would
still not have Christ, and from these things you could not
be called a Christian. Christ is something different and
higher than law and the commandments of men. He is
the Son of God, who is ready alone to give and not to

receive. If I am so wise as to take what he offers, I
have him, and if I have him I am then justly called a
Christian. Thus you have the distinction as to what a
Christian is and what Christ is.

9. Now this Gospel teaches us that Christ is the greatest
and highest person, renowned in all the world, not in order
to terrify the people, but to pour out all earthly and
heavenly gifts, so that all men may depend upon and trust
in him, and continually receive from him alone what they
need. If sin terrifies my conscience and preachers of the
law come and want to help me with their works, they will
accomplish nothing. Christ alone can help here and no
one else. Yea, the others only make it worse, even if they
were Peter or Paul, or even Mary, the mother of God herself.
Christ alone can do this, being ordained of God to the end
that he should send forth the good news in which is proclaimed how my sins are to be forgiven gratuitously, without any work or merit on my part, only and simply out of
pure grace through faith in this Christ. If now I accept
what is preached I have a comfort that my sins are forgiven
me before God and before the world. If I at heart hold
fast to this, then I am a Christian, and for this I thank
God through Christ, who at all times gives me his Holy
Spirit and grace, that sin may not harm me either here or
at the day of judgment.

10. If I fear death and do not like to die, I find in this
Christ a comfort and medicine, so that I care nothing for
death. If terrified at the anger of God, I have here a
Mediator. Many a one runs into the desert or puts on gar-
ments of coarse hair, and thinks he will force God not to be
angry with him; but it will amount to nothing; whoever has
not this Christ, on him the wrath of God remaineth forever,
for it is so decreed. John 3, 36.

11. Therefore, whoever would have a joyful conscience
that does not fear sin, death, hell, nor the wrath of God,
dare not reject this Mediator, Christ. For he is the fountain that overflows with grace, that gives temporal and eternal life. Only open thy heart and hold it forth and you

will receive all. He gushes and flows forth, and can do nothing else but only give, flow and gush forth, if you can only believe it. You justly deserve that people should call you a Christian, when you are called a Christian by virtue of what you receive from Christ; if not, and you want to give him so much, you are no Christian. This is the rich precious word which St. Paul praises so highly, and can never sufficiently praise, that he so graciously gives us his Son, to pour out his grace over all who receive it. Rom. 3, 24 and 8, 32; Gal. 3, 25.

12. From this it further follows, when a Christian does good works and shows love to his neighbor, that he does not thereby become a Christian or pious, but before this is done he must have been a Christian and pious. He indeed does good works, but his good works do not make him a Christian. The tree brings or yields good fruit, but the fruit does not make the tree good. So also here, no one becomes a Christian through his works, but through **Christ.**

13. From this you understand what kind of people Christians are, and what their kingdom is, namely, that they are a multitude that cling to Christ, and have one Spirit and the same gifts with him. And through this all Christians are equal, and no one has any more of Christ than another; St. Peter is no more than the thief on the cross; Mary the mother of God is no more than the sinner, Mary Magdalene. In external acts and works, of course, there is a difference among them, for the Virgin Mary had a greater work to do than Mary Magdalene, St. Peter a greater work than the thief on the cross. This is the case when we reckon according to works; but by virtue of our works we are not Christians. The Virgin Mary is not a Christian on account of her great work that she bore in her body Christ, such a costly and inexpressible treasure, as Christ himeslf said to the woman, Luke 11, 27-28, who cried aloud among the people to the Lord: "Blessed is the body that bore thee, and the breasts which thou hast sucked." "Yes, blessed are they," said he, "who hear the Word of God and keep it." Here you see he exalts believers above his mother. For Chris-

tians are called Christians because they believe in Christ.
Virgin and mother are two very beautiful names, but they are
nothing in comparison to the name of believers or Christians.
Again, St. Paul is so proud, that in his Epistle to the Galatians, 2, 6, he gives the office of the great and high apostles
a reputation which amounts to little before God, except as it
brings a blessing and is of service to others.

14. Therefore we are all alike through faith in Christ.
Although St. Peter has a stronger faith than I, it is still
the same faith in Christ. For his Father offers his Son
Christ to the promisouous crowd, and whoever receives him,
gets the whole Christ, whether in weakness or in strength,
it makes no difference. The woman in this Gospel who had
been sick for a long time lays hold of Christ as well as Mary
the Virgin, his mother did. Therefore Christians have the
same Spirit, one is as high-born as another, St. Peter must
call me his brother, and I can also call him my brother.
Yea, Christ receives us unto himself and holds us as his
brothers, as after his resurrection he said to Mary Magdalene: "Go unto my brethren and tell them, I ascend unto
my Father and to your Father, to my God and to your God."
John 20, 17. And St. Paul calls Christ the first-born among
many brethren, Rom. 8, 29. Of this he speaks very beautifully in his First Epistle to the Corinthians, 8, 9-12, where
he speaks of weak brethren thus: "But take heed lest
by any means this liberty of yours become a stumbling-
block to the weak. For if a man see thee who hast knowledge sitting at meat in an idol's temple, will not his conscience, if he is weak, be emboldened to eat things sacrificed
to idols? For through thy knowledge he that is weak per-
isheth, the brother for whose sake Christ died. And thus,
sinning against the brethren, and wounding their conscience when it is weak, ye sin against Christ."

15. The summary of this entire Gospel is, that we learn
to know Christ aright, and not only that we have the mere
name, but know that we have all things from him. If we
are Christians we have all things, and God is our Father,
and we are lords of all things in heaven and on earth; this

no work of ours can bring to pass, be it as great and costly as it may. Now you see how far they are from the Christian name, who live under the dominion of the Pope. The Gospel preaches nothing but the one person, Christ; not even Mary, much less the Pope or any work, be it as costly as it can. It must offer Christ alone and no one else, whom God the Father has sent among us, only that we should draw all from him, and wait for his grace and goodness.

16. Now when they preach to you Christ as a judge, how he is to appear on the judgment day, and how you should do many good works that he may reward you for them, and you agree to this, then he will indeed be a judge to you and not a Savior. And if he be thus presented to you as people are accustomed to paint his mother showing him her breasts, this is actually to preach the devil and not Christ, who only gives but receives nothing. It is indeed true, when you have received from him, then good works will follow of themselves, without force or demand; and this is represented to us very beautifully in to-day's Gospel.

17. For here, you see, Christ preaches the Gospel to the people. Now preaching is no insignificant work, for here he does us a great service, in that he becomes our teacher and instructs us, how we may come to the knowledge of himself. This is a part of his great grace and kindness. While he is here on earth he does not cease to teach, so that we may receive him as our Savior and Redeemer; afterwards he follows us with his good works which he manifests everywhere to everyone as he needs. You find no one in the Gospel who ever asked anything of the Lord, whose help was denied and not given. As many as came to him, blind, deaf, lame, palsied and dropsical, he received and helped all as they desired, and healed them from all diseases, as Luke 6, 19 says: "And all the multitude sought to touch him; for power came forth from him, and healed them all."

PART II.—OF THE GOSPEL AND CHRIST IN DETAIL.

18. Thus he does also to this woman. The woman hears

him preach, and perceives he is a good, indulgent man, who
appears friendly toward all the world; then she also began
to cleave to him and take courage to think, because he cast
none away from him, she too was welcomed to enjoy his
friendship and goodness.   Therefore she lets all the Apostles
go, and casts her heart's trust and confidence only on the
Lord, and says to herself:

"If I do but touch his garment, I shall be made whole."

19. Only see what a heart the woman had.   Hers is indeed
a noble, great faith and confidence.   She did not think otherwise in her heart than that he would certainly help her, if
she only touched his garment with her hand, and yet she is
not so bold as to approach him openly.   She regards herself
as unworthy to speak to him or look at him; for she knows
that she deserved nothing, and never did anything for the
Lord.   Therefore she so plans as to approach him from behind, falls down at his feet and merely touches the hem of
his garment.   There is nothing but mere awkwardness and
unworthiness here.   Who had merited that the Lord should
permit the Gospel to be preached to these people?   There is
no preparation, no work; yet the poor woman is there and
hopes to obtain great things from the Lord, that he would
release her from her sickness.   She had had an issue of blood
for about twelve successive years.   How could she earn
anything under such circumstances, or how could she because of her disease be worthy of anything?   Of course she
was worthy, but only to receive and not to give; for at that
time she was not able to give the least thing.

20. And this is the true preparation for the grace and
goodness of Christ, that I feel my need of it.   And then it
harmonizes beautifully, that the two meet together, the rich
and the poor, Christ and the sinner.   Yet it is a great art,
to persuade people that they are poor and in need of grace.
It is a difficult matter, nor does the devil permit it to be
done, but always diverts the people to their good works,
that they may under no circumstances receive the idea that
they stand in need of the grace and mercy of Christ.

21. The text says the wretched woman had the issue of

blood for twelve years, and to cure it, had spent all her living upon physicians. And the more she spent for this purpose, the worse she became. Luke and Mark both especially refer to this, and show thereby that, the more the law and works are preached, the worse it becomes among us, and we receive nothing from it but one harm and injury after another. The conscience can never be quieted by our good works. When one sin is expelled from the conscience, another soon enters, yea, the medicine and the work often make a sin, where otherwise there is none, until we come to Christ; as this woman here who had been sick so long and would never have received help, had she never come to Christ, from whom she received her health without any work whatever; she gives him nothing, and only receives from him, and allows him to give.

22. So it goes with all sermons that do not preach Christ, and it is here indicated that we must constantly employ the Word, and always exercise ourselves in the Word without intermission, for such men we still find at all times, who have like anxious and troubled consciences. For this woman signifies all poor consciences who have an issue of blood, that is, they feel their sins. And the issue of blood flows continually and cannot cease. For flesh and blood does nothing but what they wish. Now when feeling gets the upperhand, the wretched people go to work and want to help themselves; then one does this, the other that, and none as yet has accomplished anything.

23. Hence many orders and institutions have arisen because men have conjured up so many works that all of them can scarcely be named. What was the cause of all this? Nothing but the conscience tormented with sin, that has so exercised and harrassed us, that we thought thereby to redeem our souls and be free from all sins. But Christ was not in it, because we only wished to give without receiving. Therefore it has ever become worse with us, as with this woman, whom all the physicians endeavored to heal, but she never found one able to help her. Thus too we have believed all the physicians; if any one came who had accomplished some

little work we welcomed him. Dear Lord, we were anxious to be well, were anxious to have a joyful conscience, and were anxious to be free from sin.

24. The physicians are the preachers of the law and the lords over Christians. If one were very anxious to be free from sin, what did they do to him? They gave him medicine, from which he only became weaker and sicker. This we have seen and in part also felt a great deal, how, to our great and real injury, the people sought to be good by means of their own works, and thereby deliver themselves from sin. But it did no good, we only became more and more discouraged by sin and death, so that there were no more discouraged people to be found on earth than just the priests, the monks, the nuns, and those who go about with their good works. If one had a boil, then the druggists had to work, there was a drugging, a going and running as though the soul would immediately pass away; thus they were afraid and discouraged. And no one fears the last judgment so keenly as just these very spiritual people. This they also beautifully show, when they so treat of works that **they** always add one work to the other, and never constantly trust in any single work; and the more they do the worse they become, the more discouraged and unbelieving they become, and it is with them just as with this woman.

25. It is quite a beautiful parable, and is well adapted for our benefit. We have not only spent our temporal goods for this purpose, but we have also risked our lives with fasting, with castigation, and with other unbearable burdens, so that some become insane over it, and lose all their natural strength and finally lose their souls in the bargain. I have also been one of these and have been caught deeper in this drugstore than many others. I could not so quickly come to the point, to cast to the winds the law of the Pope. It was a bitter and difficult task for me to eat meat on Friday, and conclude that the law and order of the Pope amounted to nothing. God help us, how difficult it was for me, before I dared to do it! Therefore one should become free from this in his conscience, and despise the traditions of the Pope,

to do which he must indeed have a strong, firm foundation in faith; if he has this not, he will think several itmes before he takes the risk.

26. And as it was with this woman, who spent all her living upon the physicians, and even then was not made whole, yea, only became worse, so it is with us. Here all our works, cares and labors are lost. Here all our human obedience and all our orders fall to the ground, and all we spent in that line was wholly lost. Now we see the laws and traditions of the Pope and the bishops are nothing, before which we trembled and feared. All this helped us just as much as it did this poor woman, who spent all her goods and possessions, yes, and also risked her life to this end. O, what medicine and treatment this woman had to use! How tried, weak and sick she often became from them! Yea, if she could have become well, she would have devoured the whole drugstore. But all availed nothing, she had to bear her sickness for twelve long years.

27. But how was the poor woman at last helped? As soon as she approached the man called Christ and placed her hope and comfort in him, she became well. But who directed her to this man? Of course the physicians did not. For when our pastors preach Christ, the affairs of the Pope and all his traditions are overthrown. Who then told her? She heard it from some one who also had been healed, and that not by the physicians. He without doubt told her there was one who is called Jesus, who is a friendly, gracious man, helps everyone, and allows no one to go from his presence unassisted, and that he is sent from God just for the purpose of helping everyone. And many had told her who received help from him. So that they also brought her to him. As the woman heard these things she abandoned the physicians and went to Christ.

28. And so it takes place to-day. Christ is not preached, but only mere human works: do this, and do that. And in spite of this the knowledge of Christ enters among the people, what we are to expect of him, and that he alone must do everything, without our works and merit. When we hear

this voice we follow him, and obey his Word, and let the physicians go for good, and care no longer for the preachers of the law or of works, nor inquire about their commandments and traditions, but we go with all the desire of our heart to this man, called Christ, and say: Yes, indeed, from this man we must receive it without any merit, yea, how foolish I acted, that I ventured so much for it! May God bless thee, my dear Pope! May God bless you, my dear bishops, monks and priests, I shall never need your medicine again, your work and merit, your commandments and traditions, you have martyred me too long with these things. I have found one who gives me all things freely, that I in time past had to buy from you with piles of money. He gives it to me without work or merit, whereas I before had to risk my body, strength, health and life for it. Good night and farewell! I will never come to you again.

29. Thus one becomes a Christian, not by the decretals of the Pope, or by means of works and human traditions, but by the grace and kindness of Christ. Now whoever has a troubled, distressed conscience, fears sin and is terrified at death, or otherwise experiences no good in himself, let him come hither to this man and confess what ails him, call upon him, and he will most certainly help. "Pour out your heart before him; God is a refuge for us," Ps. 62. 8; 50, 15, and say to him: Behold, here is an empty vessel that needs to be filled. Fill it, O Lord! I am weak in faith, strengthen me; I am cold in love, warm me and make me burn, that my love may flow out to my neighbor. I have not a firm, strong faith, at times I doubt, and cannot wholly trust in God! Alas, Lord, help me, increase in me my faith and trust. I have locked up the treasure of all my goods in thee. I am poor, thou art rich, and hast mercy on the poor, I am a sinner, and thou art righteous. In me is the river of sin; in thee is all fulness and righteousness.

30. If you once learn this, the laws of the Pope cannot take thee captive. From his laws and commands you receive nothing, but like this woman you spend everything you have, your body and goods, and at last your soul besides. And

then you will say: I desire him from whom I can receive something, not him to whom I must give.

31. The other Gospels write thus of this woman: When she became well Jesus felt that a power had gone out of him, and turned to the people and asked: "Who is it that touched me? And then the Disciples answered: "Master, the multitudes press thee and crush thee;" but the Lord was not satisfied with this, and replied: "Some one did touch me; for I perceived that power had gone forth from me," Mark. 5, 25; Luke 8, 46; I know that some one has received something from me. The Lord did all this because this woman's faith was acceptable to him, which he desired to make known to all people. For he desires nothing more than that a man trust and believe in him. It was also done for the sake of the ruler, to confirm his faith by this miracle and transaction. Therefore Mark writes thus: As the woman saw that the Lord knew it, she feared and trembled and came and cast herself at the feet of the Lord and told him all in truth that was done to her by him. Then the Lord goes to work and absolves her and says to her: "Daughter, thy faith hath made thee whole; go in peace, and be whole of thy plague."

32. Are not these friendly words? What joy must not this woman have experienced, as she permitted another to show her a kindness? This joy and peace all receive, who look to this man for help. Now where this joy is there its works must immediately follow, which prove this joy. So the peace and joy in this woman had to become manifest. For as soon as she received the good deed from the Lord, she confessed it before all the people, and was not ashamed to have it told that she received something from him, and yet gave nothing for it. This work and thanksgiving, however, God desires from us, namely, that we confess and proclaim his kindness, grace and good deeds before all men, so that others may also come and receive his benefits as this woman did. Thus my Christian life urges me to do good to others, as God has done to me through Christ, only that thus Christ may become known; but thereby I do not become a Christian. Just as

this woman is not made whole by her knowledge, for she was well before all her work and knowledge. But after she becomes well she confesses Christ, and praises him, only for the good of others, and goes and does good works, one after the other. Thus we, too, live, if we are only Christians, in order that one may serve the others wherever we can. Hence, as this woman became well before she did all her works, so we Christians must also become whole before we can do any good works.

CONCERNING THE DAUGHTER OF THE RULER.

34. As the Gospel is represented in this woman, so it is also represented to us in the daughter of the ruler. This ruler of the Synagogue whom Mark calls Jairus, had a strong faith and confidence in the Lord that he would raise his deceased daughter to life. For had he not had such a disposition of heart toward him, he would not have come to him, and requested a thing of him which was by nature impossible. Therefore in this he shows his faith. When now the Lord observed the faith in him, he could not but do his will, and immediately arose and went with him. During his journey the history of this woman takes place, who had been sick for twelve years, as we have heard.

35. And when Jesus came into the ruler's house, and saw the flute-players and the crowd making a tumult, who were there in compliance with the law of Moses, and blew with horns and trumpets, as in our country the bells are rung, to call the people together; he commanded the people and the flute-players to give place and said: "The damsel is not dead, but sleepeth." And they laughed him to scorn.

This means that, when the preaching of the Word goes forth thus, that Christ is the man who helps and our works will not do it, then the world cannot avoid it, it must laugh and scorn, and be offended (1 Cor. 1, 23), for it is not acceptable to the world that Christ should help us. As the people do here, who said without doubt: Alas, this is a grand master or doctor, what shall he help? for he does not know what it is to sleep or enter the grave.

36. In the world the Gospel must have the reputation of being a foolish sermon, despised and scorned; for the devil cannot hear that this preaching is honored in the world, for it brings no advantage to his kingdom, this he feels, of course, and hence he attacks it with all cunning, so that he may hinder it and cause it to be worthless among his own followers, whose hearts he has entirely blinded and possessed, that the light of the Gospel may not shine for them, as St. Paul says in 2 Cor. 4, 4. For it is impossible that the preaching of Christ should not produce some fruit. It will not be preached in vain, Is. 55, 11; although there be but few who receive it, it matters not.

37. As satan feels it is a loss to him, and that the preaching of the Word is directed against his kingdom, he has no rest, he persecutes, despises and attacks it on all sides, as he at present rages and storms in all the world. For the preaching of Christ overthrows everything pleasing to the devil and the world, and what the world regards as the most holy and costly. For the world paints for itself a god who accepts our good works, and is pleased with the mass, vigils, foundations, rosaries, caps, pates, hempen ropes, and what more be the works of fools with which the Pope is employed. Now when one comes and brings the Gospel, and preaches against this nonsense of the Pope, and he is obliged to do, and says: It is nothing, it is deception, it is opposed to Christ and the Scriptures; he must suffer himself to be called a heretic and a worthless fellow, a perverter of the people, and then they quite grandly assert: Do you want to rule the whole world? do you think you are the wisest? Our forbears also were not fools. Many holy, pious people have done these works and preached of them, should you first come to destroy all? This must not be! Then the raging and storming time begins, with persecution and death, and the devil will claim he is right, let it go as it may.

38. This is enough on to-day's Gospel for the present. Mark well, that you learn from the Gospels that all things are to be found in the one person who is called Christ. And remember, too, that a Christian receives his name alone from

Christ. I do not say this in vain, for I know what it costs to keep it, in temptation and in the battle of life. Let us call upon God for grace, that we may take this in earnest, and grasp it with our hearts. Amen.

TWENTY-FOURTH SUNDAY AFTER TRINITY.

Second Sermon.—Matthew 9, 18-26.

This sermon is given instead of the preceding one in edition c. A part of it, §§ 33–39, is in the little book, "Etliche Trostschriften etc." Title: "The daughter of the ruler of the synagogue raised from the dead, Mat. 9." Erl. 14. 349; W. 11, 2468; St. L. 11, 1850.

CONTENTS: TWO EXAMPLES OF FAITH, AND CHRIST'S CALL FROM THE DEAD.

I. TWO EXAMPLES OF FAITH.

1. This narrative is more fully and faithfully presented by the other Evangelists, Mark and Luke, and is a rich and beautiful Gospel, both in its doctrine and consolation, for it teaches the correct knowledge of the divine will in spiritual wisdom and understanding, (as may be noted in the Epistle for to-day) and affords consolation and strength under the cross and amid suffering. Let us note a few of its lessons.

2. First, the Lord is here represented surrounded by the people, as a kind and affable man, as St. Paul in Tit. 3, 4, says, that through him the grace and love of God have been made manifest, through which he shows himself willing and ready to help and serve all men, and also renders help to those who in true faith seek it from him.

3. But they are people who are in misery, trouble, sorrow and distress. He will be with them and permit himself to be found by them; for with such, his Word and work can be made effective. But his Word and miracles are useless and lost among the carnally secure, the mighty, the rich and prosperous, because they are not capable of receiving his grace and favors, for they are already satisfied and satiated, and seek comfort and happiness in other things or even in themselves. In order to receive the grace and benefits of Christ, men must realize they have no comfort and help in any creature, and that they experience nothing but trouble and sorrow; and it is true as the Church sings in Luke 1, 53: "The hungry he hath filled with good things; and the rich he hath sent empty away."

4. From this you see how graciously and paternally God manifests himself toward us, since he comes to us so closely through his beloved Son and seeks the poor and miserable, in order to pour out his grace upon all, who are willing to receive it; because he sent his Son to us, in order to be with us and dwell among us, as St. John, 1, 14, says, and take care of us as his own flesh and blood. He assumed the same poverty and misery, so that he might deliver us from our misery, that is, from sin and death. Therefore, he also desires that we seek and expect such help from him through faith, as he says in John 6, 40: "For this is the will of my Father, that every one that beholdeth the Son and believeth on him, should have eternal life."

5. This is the knowledge which Christians require and through which alone they become Christians and children of God, as Isaiah, 53, 11, says: "By his knowledge shall my righteous servant justify many," and John 1, 12: "To them gave he the right to become children of God, even to them that believe on his name." For whatever else can be taught, done, or comprehended, however great, beautiful, praiseworthy, valuable or holy it may appear, cannot make Christians of people, that is, persons who have obtained forgiveness of sins and a gracious God, unless they know and by faith lay hold of the Savior, the Son of God, who came into the world that by the shedding of his blood he might take away our sins and reconcile us to God.

6. This doctrine and knowledge of the Gospel should be cherished and lauded by the whole world, because it alone publishes this true and joyous consolation, that God has had mercy on poor, unworthy and miserable sinners, and does not wish to impute unto them their sins, but out of pure grace forgives them. No other doctrine or sermon on earth can save or give the same, as the whole world, Jews, Gentiles and Turks, must acknowledge.

7. Therefore, no person can of himself reach that point where he is before God free from horrible unbelief, and a condemned conscience, is able with a true heart to call upon God, and knows for a certainty that God will hear him, except alone through this knowledge of Christ, whom God himself has appointed as his Mediator and publicly testified that he will be gracious, hear and bless all who call upon

him through Christ. Hence those only are Christians who render true service to God and can comfort themselves in the joyful assurance, that the true God is their God and that he will be with them and help them; whereas all others, who do not know Christ, are truly without God and cannot call upon him with true hearts, nor be comforted, but must perish before God in eternal and terrible doubt and destruction.

8. This Gospel presents two beautiful examples both of the help of Christ and of faith which clings to and finds comfort in Christ, and obtains help from him. First, that is a beautiful faith of the ruler of the synagogue, which leads him to Christ in his distress, at the time when his daughter was lying at the point of death and when he could only say that she must die before he could return home; for he says: "My daughter is even now dead," and when all men had given up the hope and thought that help could be secured for her. Yet he did not despair, but, while the rest of his household despaired, wept and lamented, and could think of nothing except how to lay out the dead body and arrange it for the flute-players and others, he went to Christ in the firm confidence that if he brought him to his daughter, she would be restored to life. He believed Christ was the one who could help not only to restore and maintain health as long as body and soul were still united, but that he could also restore life after body and soul had been separated by death. This was certainly at the time a remarkable example of faith, since nothing like it had ever before been heard or seen, unless perhaps the miracle of the raising of the widow's son to life, Luke 7, 11 sq., had occurred before and the report of it had reached his ears. Nor was it a greater mark of faith that he could without a doubt conclude in his heart that Christ would restore his daughter to life; for if he would have doubted and followed the human thoughts of reason, he would certainly not have gone to Christ, but would have thought that he had delayed too long; or that although Christ had restored some one else to life, it would not necessarily follow that his daughter should also be re-

stored to life, since so many sons and daughters of parents were daily dying, none of whom were being restored to life.

9. This is the virtue of the right kind of faith, which was also, shortly afterwards, praised in the woman who had an issue of blood, namely, that it clings steadfastly to Christ, grasps and holds fast to the Word heard from him, does not inquire or look to that which the human mind may suggest, nor to what other people believe or do; but straightway concludes, with reference to the reports concerning Christ, that he is the one who can help in time of need; who has helped others and therefore will help now. Such a heart and faith truly find Christ and receive according to their faith.

10. In the second place, his faith concerning the Person of Christ was of such a character (which was indeed a great spiritual knowledge) that he rightly regarded him as the true Messiah sent by God, not such as the great mass of the Jews, especially the scribes, thought that he would come publicly before the people as a great and mighty lord and king with great pomp and show, so that everybody would regard and receive him as the one sent to them from God and in addition expected that he would deliver them from bodily slavery under the foreign dominion of the Roman Emperor and establish them as the mighty rulers of the world. On the contrary, overagainst such dreams and Jewish notions, he regarded him as the true Lord and Messiah, although he was not thus regarded and received by his own people, the Jews, who was sent from God, not to confer temporal power, possessions, honor and freedom, but to help in those things and necessities where no man can help, namely, to redeem us from the peril of death and the power of the devil, yea, to turn death into life and confer life. He must not be regarded as a mere man, but as that one who truly has in himself divine and eternal power and authority over all creatures, because he belives that he holds in his hands power over life and death, that is, that he truly is the Son of God, as the Scriptures declare.

11. The other example of faith deserves no less praise,

namely, that of the poor woman who had an issue of blood twelve years, on account of which she suffered in her body and lost all her strength, and because of this she had long despaired of receiving human help and comfort. She came to Christ, as she had heard of him, and could come to him in the certain and undoubted confidence that he could help her in her great need, and with the heartfelt assurance that he was so good and gracious as to help her and not let her go away unaided. Of this she was so certain and confident that her heart was free from care and grief, although she had reason to doubt. She was concerned only with the thought of how she would be able to get to Christ, wondering and thinking: "Ah! If I could but touch the hem of his garment." Then she firmly and confidently concluded in her heart, "I shall be made whole." But she did not know how to reach him, because she saw the crowd was so great and she, a poor, sick woman, could not well break through such a crowd of people. Besides, the law did not permit her to come among the people; yet her faith and desire urged her not to desist, but to press through the crowd until she came behind him and touched his garment.

12. Behold here, how her faith overcame two obstacles. First, her faith was so strong that she believed she could obtain help, if only she could touch his garment. She did not deem it necessary to come to him and with many words present her complaint and pray that he would have mercy on her and help her, nor did others pray for her; but she sought only to reach him and touch him, for she thought, if only she could do this, she would receive help. She neither doubted his power, nor his willingness to help. Hence she did not deem it necessary to do more, in order to secure his help, than to touch merely the fringe of his outer garment. Therefore she did not deem it necessary that she should come before him to be touched by him; yea, she did not regard herself worthy to be addressed by him; nor was her heart so full of confidence that, notwithstanding this, she lacked courage to come into his presence, and hence was neither seen nor heard by him. But she was satisfied simply

to come up behind him, secretly and unnoticed by the crowd, and did not doubt as to the help she expected to receive. Nor did her faith deceive her, for as soon as she touched the hem of his garment, the fountain of blood was stopped.

13. Now, that a poor, simple woman should be able to see and know that this man's help and power were such that it was not necessary to speak to him at length, but that he was able to see in secret, even though he should not publicly show that he knows anything of our necessities or wished to help us, must be the result of a great and extraordinary illumination of the Spirit and the knowledge of faith. Accordingly, her faith produced such an assurance in her, that all doubt was removed, and she realized that if she could only reach him with even the most insignificant means, she would be helped. This, indeed, means a strong faith that this man must possess divine, almighty power and authority, that he can see and understand the secret thoughts and desires of the heart, although not a word is spoken; and that he can prove his work and help, although she sees and feels nothing externally except the words we heard him utter, which produced faith in her heart.

14. She desired nothing besides this Word, nor did she ask for more than merely to touch his garment, which she used as an external means and sign to gain the desired help. Likewise, we need nothing more in our lives and in the kingdom of faith than the external Word and Sacraments, in which he permits himself to be touched and seized as if by his garment.

15. Hence you may see what faith, which clings to the Person of Christ is and does, namely, a heart that regards him as the Lord and Savior, the Son of God, through whom God reveals himself and bestows upon us his grace, assuring us that through him and for his sake, he will hear and help us. This is the true spiritual and heartfelt worship of God, where the heart has to do with Christ and prays in his name, even though not a single word may be uttered aloud, and gives the honor due him, regards him as the true Savior, who can hear and know the secret desires of the heart and

manifest his power and help, although he does not permit himself to be externally touched or approached, according to our thoughts.

16. The other master-piece of her faith is, that she is able to overcome the feeling of her own unworthiness and roll from her heart the heavy stone, which weighed her down so heavily, and yet makes her so diffident that she dare not publicly approach Christ like other persons. The judgment passed upon her by the law was that, as an unclean woman, she was not allowed to associate with other people. For, in Levit. 15, 19 we read that a woman like her shall be regarded unclean as long as she has the issue of blood; and that whatever she has on or about her, shall be unclean; and that whoever touches her or whatever she touches, shall be unclean. This proved no small distress to her, not only by reason of her malady and bodily uncleanness, but especially because she recognized and felt in it the punishment of God, imposed upon her before all people, and which separated her from the congregation of God's people. This continued for twelve long years, during which time she had tried all kinds of remedies with many physicians and yet was not helped by any, but grew worse continually, so that she was compelled to conclude that God had punished her with special severity because of her sins and would not help her. She was now forced to despair of human aid and thought she had to die of her disease and punishment.

17. It was, therefore, not without a struggle and conflict that she maintained her faith in that which she sought in Christ; for she could not help but think: Behold, I am an unclean woman, punished of God, and every one knows me. If I appear before this Lord, every one and even he himself may simply condemn my boldness and impudence for coming into his presence and I may receive more wrath and severer punishment from God instead of mercy, and be forced to confess that I had been served rightly if he casted me from him in his anger. This trial and struggle show also that, as the text says, after she had been discovered, she was terrified and trembled, even though she had received the

desired help; and yet she was filled with fear, lest he would speak harshly to her and censure her, because she had not been afraid to come to him and secretly steal the desired help.

18. But her faith, which clearly set before her the good and gracious heart of Christ, broke through all these barriers; besides, her great need, yea, even her despair compelled her to become impudent before God and, regardless of the prohibition and judgment of the law, her own shame urged her to conclude: This Savior must be laid hold of, in spite of what the law, her own heart and all the world, yea, what even he himself may say. Here is the man who can help and who is also a good, gracious and faithful Savior. On the other hand, I am a poor, miserable woman, who needs his help. He will certainly not become other than he is, because of me, nor permit his grace and help to fail me. Let his will be done in me; it will be better for me that I should be covered with shame, than the injury I would receive if I should fail to seek the help which I may be able to receive from him. She fixed her heart on the idea that if she could only touch this man, her need would be removed and the desired help received; and she would afterwards speak with Moses and the law, so that she might remain uncondemned by him, etc.

19. Behold, that is a beautiful faith, which realizes its unworthiness and yet does not permit itself to be hindered on this account to place its confidence in Christ, nor to doubt his grace and help, but breaks through the law and everything that frightens it away from him; yea, if the whole world would attempt to hinder and thwart, yet it does not think of leaving this man until it has laid hold on him. Therefore it presses through all barriers and attains what it seeks in Christ, and immediately experiences the power and work of Christ, even before he begins to speak. For it cannot apply to Christ in vain, even as Christ himself testifies, when he says: "Thy faith hath made thee whole."

20. Besides, faith like this is so pleasing to Christ that he

does not wish it to remain concealed in her and that the power and work made effective by it should remain a secret, but what is in her heart must be published to everybody so that her faith may be praised before the whole world and be strengthened in her. Therefore, turning and looking around, he asked and desired to know who touched him; for he felt that power had gone forth from him. When she found she had to be discovered, she became afraid and began to tremble; for a heart filled with the great and implicit trust which she had in him, and yet also with humility and the knowledge of her unworthiness, must regard itself guilty, because she had gone contrary to Moses and because she realized he might justly be angry with her, because she could be so bold and impudent as to press through the crowd to him. And hence in the midst of the work, after she had already been healed and her heart was filled with joy, her faith had to contend with fear and terror, and yet only to enjoy all the more consolation and joy in Christ. For Christ does not wish faith to remain concealed in the heart, but desires it to be publicly confessed, so that the glory of God may thereby be praised and others also be spurred on to believe.

21. Therefore, when this woman was in fear and danger, lest she should be disgraced before all and be condemned according to the law, yea, even she herself be compelled to make a public confession, Christ began to confirm her faith, to say she had done well in disregarding Moses and the law, that is, the judgment passed upon her unworthiness; and now he publicly shows the same disregard, will have her un-accused and uncondemned, yea, esteems her faith so highly that he ascribes to it alone the power and efficacy that helped her, just as if he had done nothing in the matter. In like manner, he was accustomed to speak at other times, as to the ruler, Mat. 8, 13, "As thou hast believed, so be it done unto thee," and again to the Canaanite woman, Mat. 15, 28, "Be it done unto thee, even as thou wilt."

22. We should learn from this woman to realize the power of faith, and in our temptations and conflicts to call for

help. For, as I have already stated, it is through such faith that we become Christians, and a distinction is shown between us and all other people on the earth, the Turks, heathen and Jews. For we must know that it is one thing to be a good man, perform many and great deeds, live a good, honorable and virtuous life, but quite another thing to be a Christian. For in that which concerns our lives and work we often receive great praise and honor before men, even from Jews and Turks, as many great and excellent men have been highly praised in pagan histories for their uprightness and virtue. Again, there have been many among the Jews, as Gamaliel, Paul before his conversion, Nicodemus and others (as this poor woman), who have with all zeal lived according to the law, so that in their external life before the world, they surpassed many true Christians.

23. But even here a difference as great as between heaven and earth must be noted between Christians and others. A Christian is one who has a different kind of light in his heart, that is faith, which truly knows and lays hold on God and truly worships him. Through the Word of God he knows and realizes his own unworthiness and receives the true fear of God; and again finds comfort in his faith, believes and trusts he has obtained forgiveness of sin and redemption in Christ, the Son of God, and for his sake is acceptable to God and elected to eternal life; and in all his need, when he feels his own weakness, or is tempted, can find refuge in God, appeal to him and expect his help; and he knows he shall be heard.

24. No other person than a Christian has this faith and assurance, be he Jew, Turk, Papist, or whatever he may be called, no matter how pious and good his life may be, or how much he may pride himself that he worships and serves God and hopes for eternal life; for the service, worship and life of such persons still lack two great things, which prevent them from being acceptable to God: first, they do not have the true God, that is, do not know him as he has revealed himself and will be known, towit, as the Father of our Lord Jesus Christ, his Son. Hence they walk in blind-

ness and miss God, because they seek him according to their own notions and apart from Christ, and are deprived of the knowledge of the true Divine Being.

25. Secondly, they lack the possibility of the true and assured knowledge of the will of God, because they do not have the Gospel. Hence, they cannot be certain that God will assuredly hear them, and must always remain in doubt whether or not God will hear them and interest himself in their behalf. Accordingly their appeals and prayers can be nothing more than mere vain and useless thoughts and babblings, through which the heart finds no consolation in God, nor expect anything from him, but rather flee from him and are therefore truly without God, and use the name of God in vain.

26. But the Christian's prayer consists in this that he prays to the true God, namely, the Father of our Lord Jesus Christ, who has revealed himself to men through his Word; and besides he has the certain confidence and assurance against all doubt that God will be gracious to him and hear his prayer for the sake of Christ, his beloved Son.

27. This is the beautiful example of the woman. Now we turn to the daughter of the ruler of the Synagogue. But here, too, faith must contend and be strengthened; for although, as we have already heard, he had an excellent faith, yet it could scarcely have been maintained, had it not been strengthened. For, while Christ was still speaking with the woman, Mark 5, 35-36 and Luke 8, 49, say a message was brought, stating the man's daughter had died, and requesting him not to trouble the Master. This meant all would amount to nothing, since they had delayed too long; hence he should leave the matter and think only of how to bury his child.

28. This must have been a severe blow to the ruler's faith. But the fact that the woman had just been healed, must have prevented his faith from failing, and indeed strengthened it to resist the doubts concerning his daughter. And Christ himself is present to comfort and strengthen him against this stumbling-block, in order to show that he is un-

willing that even such weak faith should be injured in any way, but be established and strengthened; and in view of this he admonishes and encourages all persons by saying: "Doubt not, only believe, etc." This he said in order to see how highly he was pleased with the faith that clings to him, and that he was ready to guard against its being overcome; as he spoke to the Apostles, and especially to Peter, who fell so easily, "I have prayed for thee, that thy faith fail not."

29. Now when Christ came to the house, this man's faith had to receive another blow; for there they saw and heard nothing but the tumult, weeping and wailing, and the blowing of trumpets (which they used at the death of their friends, as we do bells). All this cries in his heart that nothing was left but death, and his faith had nothing on which to lay hold against despair, except the word which Christ spoke against the tumult and lamentations: "The child is not dead, but sleepeth," on account of which he was mocked and laughed at as a fool; for they all saw and knew that the maid was dead, and that there was no breath nor spark of life in her. They could not but think: See, our master or ruler must be mad or silly to bring this fool here, who tries to convince us that the maid is not dead, when every one can clearly see she lies stiff in death, a dead corpse, ready to be placed under ground.

30. They had come together at the synagogue, as at a common gathering-place, as we do at our churches, where on the Sabbath the Word of God was taught, because throughout the whole country there was neither church nor temple, except at Jerusalem. And this ruler of the synagogue occupied the same position among them that our pastors occupy, and others occupied the place of assistants or readers, who read Moses or preached, circumcised the children and instructed the young, and visited the sick and sorrowing to comfort them. These had to be together in the synagogue and testified concerning this work of Christ, even with their mocking and scornful laughter, namely, that the maiden had certainly died and been raised from the

dead. The ruler therefore, before he could experience the work of Christ, was compelled, in the face of this offence and mockery, to cling to the one word of Christ and with him be regarded as a fool and in his folly learn this spiritual wisdom that death is not death to Christ, but only a sleep.

PART II. CHRIST'S CALL FROM THE DEAD.

31. Let us learn from this to become fools with Christ and this ruler and teacher, in order that we may understand these words. Although this man's words may be despised by the world and be regarded as foolishness, yet they are very precious, for in them there certainly lies hid the highest wisdom of heaven and earth. For this passage, as a general expression, teaches you that your death in Christ is nothing more than a mere sleep, so that you may be able to look through and beyond the horrible sight and frightful larva of death and the grave, yea, apprehend the same truth of death, if only you hear these words in faith and accept them as true in Christ.

32. Here we have nothing to do with ox-eyes, or even man's eyes, but with the eyes with which Christ sees, and with the ears with which Christ hears, yea, a mind and heart like Christ himself has. A swine, when it sees the dead body of a man lying before it, can only conclude that it is a carcass like any other dead body, which is devoured by birds or animals, or is decomposed. So also a person without faith neither sees nor understands more, and in this respect cannot be distinguished from the brute, except in so far as he carries his head upright, while that of the brute is turned to the ground; for his thoughts can reach only as far as this life is concerned. Therefore, it is not to be wondered at that the mind should affect such so-called wisdom as this: "How can a person be said to sleep when he no longer has either breath or life, is buried under ground and is in process of decomposition?" On the other hand, he whc desires to learn how to perceive and understand God's kingdom, power and work, must shut his mind and understanding, purify his eyes, cleanse his ears, and see and hear what Christ says in this matter, and how it is in his sight apart from this life, where our understanding, mind and thought cannot reach.

33. In this passage you hear that Christ says that to him the dying of a person is not death, but a sleep, yea, from his point of view none of those who have lived and died before our time are dead, but are all alive, as those we see standing before us; for he has concluded that all shall live, yea, he holds their lives in his hands. For you must here clearly distinguish between the thoughts and actions of Christ, and the views, thoughts and understanding of the world, as I have said before, so that you may not remain in the blind and brutish thought and opinion concerning the dead and putrifying body, but rather perceive that this is the Lord of all creatures, whether to us they be dead or alive, and that all life comes from him and is maintained in and by him, so that if he would not maintain life no one could live a single moment.

34. Besides the regular daily maintenance of life, he must maintain it without our will and help when we sleep, a condition in which man has no control over his mind and life, and does not know how he falls asleep and wakes again. Therefore it is not difficult for Christ, in the hour when body and soul are separated, to hold in his hand the soul and spirit of man, even though we ourselves neither feel nor see anything, yea, even though the body be entirely consumed. For, since he can preserve the breath of life and spirit, apart from the body, so he can again bring the body together out of dust and ashes. This he has proved in this and similar examples, when he restored to life with one word those who had truly died and whose body and soul had been separated. Hence we must conclude that he holds in his hand the life of those who have died; for if this power did not belong to him, he could not restore life.

35. In the second place, you must not calculate how far life and death are apart, or how many years may pass while the body is wasting in the grave, and how one after another

dies, but endeavor to grasp the thought of Christ with reference to the conditions apart from this time and hour. For he does not calculate time by tens, hundreds or thousands of years, nor measure the years consecutively, the one preceding, the other following, as we must do in this life; but he grasps everything in a moment, the beginning, middle and end of the whole human race and of all time. And what we regard and measure according to time, as by a long drawn out rule, all this he sees as at a glance, and thus both the death and life of the last as well as of the first man are to him as only a moment of time.

36. Thus we should learn to view our death in the right light, so that we need not become alarmed on account of it, as unbelief does; because in Christ it is indeed not death, but a fine, sweet and brief sleep, which brings us release from this vale of tears, from sin and from the fear and extremity of real death and from all the misfortunes of this life, and we shall be secure and without care, rest sweetly and gently for a brief moment, as on a sofa, until the time when he shall call and awaken us together with all his dear children to his eternal glory and joy. For since we call it a sleep, we know that we shall not remain in it, but be again awakened and live, and that the time during which we sleep, shall seem no longer than if we had just fallen asleep. Hence, we shall censure ourselves that we were surprised or alarmed at such a sleep in the hour of death, and suddenly come alive out of the grave and from decomposition, and entirely well, fresh, with a pure, clear, glorified life, meet our Lord and Savior Jesus Christ in the clouds.

37. Therefore we should entrust and commend to our true Savior and Redeemer ourselves, body, soul and life, with all confidence and joy, just as we must commend to him our life without care in our bodily sleep and rest, assured that we shall not lose it, but be truly and carefully preserved in his hand, maintained and again restored. Here you see, as he shows in reality, how easy it is for him to awaken men from the dead and restore them to life, as he came to the

maiden, took her by the hand, as some one else might do
to awaken one from sleep, and with a word called, "Maid,
arise!" and the maiden suddenly arose, as if she had been
awakened from sleep. We see here neither sleep nor death,
but wakefulness and freshness, even as Lazarus came forth
from his tomb.

38. Behold, this Word of Christ is not a matter of laughter and foolishness to faith (as to others among the prudent
and the saints according to the law, who nevertheless remain in fear and terror of death, have to do with their
thouhts about death and works), but of great wisdom, by
which death and all the images of death are swallowed up,
and in their place true comfort, joy and life are obtained.
The act and experience must assuredly follow this Word
of Christ and faith in his Word cannot fail. Let this
be regarded as a master-piece and a wonderful work of
alchemy or a science, which indeed does not turn copper and
lead into gold, but turns death into sleep, your grave into a
soft sofa, the time from the death of Abel until the last day
into a brief hour, a work which no creature has nor can attempt except through faith in Christ. If you can believe
this, that is, let the Word of Christ be true and not a lie, you
have already overcome both death and the sting of death,
and in their place have obtained sweet rest.

39. Scripture everywhere affords such consolation, which
speaks of the death of the saints, as if they fell asleep and
were gathered to their fathers, that is, had overcome death
through this faith and comfort in Christ, and awaited the
resurrection, together with the saints who preceded them
in death. Therefore the early Christians (undoubtedly
from the Apostles or their disciples) followed the custom of
bringing their dead to honorable burial and wherever possible interred them in separate places, which they called, not
places of burial or grave-yards, but *coemeteria*, sleeping-
chambers, *dormitoria*, houses of sleep, names which have remained in use until our time; and we Germans from ancient
times call such places of burial God's acres, as St. Paul, 1
Cor. 15, 44, says: "It is sown a natural body;" for what

we now call church-yards were not at first places of burial. This is the teaching and comfort of this Gospel lesson.

40. Further, we are shown here, as in a painting, both in the woman with the bloody flux and in the maiden, the result of attempting to govern conscience by means of the law, without a knowledge of Christ. There are two classes of people: One class consists of the sick, poor. timid consciences, who feel their secret need and sins, as well as the judgment and curse of the law, that is, that they are under the wrath of God, desire earnestly to be freed from it, seek help and counsel from many physicians, expend all their possessions, body and life, and yet receive no help, neither improvement nor comfort, but continually grow worse; until they at last give up in despair and resign themselves to death; finally Christ comes to them with his Gospel. Many good-hearted people have hitherto experienced this under the Papacy, who earnestly strove to become pious, did everything as they were directed and taught, and yet gained from it only terrified and timid consciences, and on account of the fear and horror of death and of the judgment day, would gladly have ended their lives. This is the result of all teaching at its best, apart from the knowledge of Christ.

41. The other class, like the daughter of the ruler, are those who are without the law, whether they be Jews or Gentiles, that is, are free and live securely, do not feel the terrors of the law, think they are prosperous and safe until they are suddenly struck down and die, as St. Paul. speaking of himself, Rom. 7, 11, says that he lived without the law, but afterwards through the law sin became alive and slew him.

42. Since both the woman and the daughter were delivered from their need and from death, there is no counsel or help other than that which acknowledges Christ and hears the truly comforting, living voice of the Gospel, which has the power to abolish sin and death, and to give to the conscience everlasting comfort, joy and life, wherever these are accepted in true faith. And here the doctrine is clearly set forth, that we are justified and saved, without our merit,

gratuitously, alone through faith, and so are delivered from sin and death. The poor woman brought nothing to Christ, except her great unworthiness, so that she had to be ashamed of it, yea, was fillled with fear and terror when forced to make herself known. There was even far less personal merit or worthiness in the ruler's daughter, because she lay there in death and was altogether without life and action. In a word, we must confess that in ourselves we have nothing, nor are able to live or do anything to please or to bring us favor and life, unless his pure grace be conferred upon us.

43. But after we have received forgiveness of sin, consolation and life, let us begin to teach and do good works. Just as the woman, after she had been healed, and the maiden, after she had been restored to life, did good and living deeds. Thus we too have power in Christ to live according to the will of God, and know that our lives and works begun in Christ are acceptable to him. Whatever else might be said here, how Christ performs his works and wonders in his Church, in which are seen the fruits of faith, though secretly and obscurely, as in both these instances of the woman and the maiden, so that the world was not allowed to see them, would make our present discussion too lengthy.

TWENTY-FIFTH SUNDAY AFTER TRINITY.

This sermon is found in all editions of the Church Postil and in two pamphlet prints, both issued at Wittenberg in 1525, under the title: "A sermon on the Jewish kingdom and the end of the world, Mat. 24, preached on the last Sunday after Pentecost, Martin Luther, Wittenberg." At the end: "Printed at Wittenberg by Hans Lufft, 1525."

This sermon is also printed along with the sermon on the Gospel for the 10th Sunday after Trinity, on the Destruction of Jerusalem, which appeared in three editions during 1525. Erl. 14, 368; W. 11, 2493; St. L. 11, 1868; and Standard English Luther, 13 vol. 315 p.

Text: Mat. 24, 15-28. When therefore, ye see the abomination of desolation, which was spoken of through Daniel the prophet, standing in the holy place (let him that readeth understand), then let them that are in Judæa flee unto the mountains: let him that is on the housetop not go down to take out the things that are in his house: and let him that is in the field not return back to take his cloak. But woe unto them that are with child and to them that give suck in those days! And pray ye that your flight be not in the winter, neither on a sabbath: for then shall be great tribulation, such as hath not been from the beginning of the world until now, no, nor ever shall be. And except those days had been shortened, no flesh would have been saved: but for the elect's sake those days shall be shortened. Then if any man shall say unto you, Lo, here is the Christ, or, Here; believe it not. For there shall arise false Christs, and false prophets, and shall show great signs and wonders; so as to lead astray, if possible, even the elect. Behold, I have told you beforehand. If therefore they shall say unto you, Behold, he is in the wilderness; go not forth: Behold, he is in the inner chambers; believe it not. For as the lightning cometh forth from the east, and is seen even unto the west; so shall be the coming of the Son of man. Wheresoever the carcase is, there will the eagles be gathered together.

CONTENTS: THE DESTRUCTION OF THE KINGDOM OF
THE JEWS, THE ABOMINATION OF DESOLATION, AND
THE END OF THE WORLD.

1. In this chapter there is a description of the end of two
kingdoms; of the kingdom of the Jews, and also of the kingdom of the world. But the two Evangelists, Matthew and
Mark, unite the two·and do not follow the order as Luke did,
for they have nothing more in view than to relate and give
the words of Christ, and are not concerned about what was
said either before or after. But Luke takes special
pains to write clearly and in the true order, and relates
this discourse twice; first briefly in the 19th chapter, where
he speaks of the destruction of the Jews at Jerusalem; afterwards in the 21st chapter he speaks of both, one following
the other.

2. Notice therefore that Matthew unites the two and at
the same time conceives the end, both of the Jewish nation
and of the world. He therefore cooks both into one soup.
But if you want to understand it, you must separate and put
each by itself, that which really treats of the Jews, and that

which relates to the whole world. This we wish to do now.

3. Notice, first, how Christ prophecies in this chapter concerning the final destruction of the Jewish nation, which the Jews did not at all believe, even though they had been clearly told through great signs and words, the promises of God which he made to the fathers, like unto which had happened to no other people upon the earth. For this reason they strongly insisted and depended upon it, thought it will continue forever, as they think even at the present time; that their kingdom is not destroyed but has only disbanded a little and shall be re-established. They cannot get it out of their minds that they are not completely ruined.

4. For this reason God announced besides his miracles with clear and plain prophesies that their kingdom shall have an end and that God had abolished the external reign of the law, meats, offerings, etc., and would establish another which shall endure forever, as the angel announced to the virgin concerning Christ, as recorded in Luke 1, 33. "And he shall reign over the house of Jacob forever; and of his kingdom there shall be no end."

5. Among the various passages which treat of the end of Judaism there is especially one that is introduced by Christ, namely: the prophet Daniel, 9, 25 f., speaks of the terrible abomination, standing where he ought not, when he says concerning the Jewish nation, "Know therefore and discern, that from the going forth of the commandment to restore and to build Jerusalem unto the annointed one the Prince, shall be seven weeks, and three-score and two weeks," that makes together seventy weeks or 490 years, "And after the three-score and two weeks, shall the annointed one be cut off, and shall have nothing: and the people of the Prince that shall come shall destroy the city and the sanctuary; and the end thereof shall be with a flood, and even unto the end shall be war; desolations are determined. And he shall make a firm covenant with many for one week: and in the midst of the week he shall cause the sacrifice and the oblation to cease; and upon the wing of abominations shall come one that maketh desolate; and even unto the full

end, and that determined, shall wrath be poured out upon the desolate.''

6. The Prophet Daniel desired to know the definite time when this should come to pass, but he could not learn it, and although the angel pointed out a definite time, it was nevertheless too dark for the prophet to understand, hence he said before: But at last, at the last time, you shall see everything, that is, your prophecy, that is to be revealed to you, shall transpire at the end of time. For when Christ sent out the Gospel through the ministry of himself and of the Apostles, it lasted three or three and a half years, that it almost amounts to the calculation of Daniel, namely the 490 years. Hence he also says, Christ shall take a half a week, in which the daily offerings shall cease; that is, the priesthood and reign of the Jews shall have an end; which all took place in the three and a half years in which Christ preached, and was almost completed in four years after Christ, in which the Gospel prospered the most, especially in Palestine through the Apostles (that when they opened their mouth, the Holy Ghost fell as it were, from heaven, as we see in the Acts of the Apostles), so that a whole week, or seven years, established the covenant, as Daniel says; that is, the Gospel was preached to the Jews, of which we spoke before. Now, when the time came that a new message or sermon began, there must also begin a new kingdom, that is, where Christ rules spiritually in our hearts through the Word and faith. If this is now to continue, then the other must be set aside and has no more authority and must cease. This is the part of the prophecy of the phophets, which Christ is explaining.

7. The other treats of the abomination of desolation. Here Christ now says, When ye shall see this one standing in the temple, then take heed (he wants to say) for that is a sure sign from Daniel's prophecy that his kingdom is now at an end; and do not let yourselves be deceived because the Jews and weak Christians think that it shall never be destroyed.

8. But the abomination of which Daniel writes is that the Emperor Cajus, as history tells, had put his image in the

temple at Jerusalem as an idol, for the people to worship, after everything there had been destroyed. For the Scriptures call idolatry really an abomination, because God abhors and abominates it, inasmuch as he is the enemy of no sin so much as of this. The others he does truly punish, but he does not cast the people away if they repent, as he says in Psalm 89, 31-34: "If they break my statutes, and keep not my commandments; then will I visit their transgression with the rod, and their iniquity with stripes. But my loving kindness will I not utterly take from him, nor suffer my faithfulness to fail. My covenant will I not break, nor alter the thing that is gone out of my lips." But this sin, called idolatry, which is really unbelief and denial of God, which he cannot at all endure, condemns man completely. For where this remains in the heart of man, so that he teaches and believes correctly, indicates that our works are nothing, and that we shall be acceptable to God and serve him aright alone through faith, then there will be a truly godly character; there light and truth abide. Although along side of faith there runs a sense of the weakness of the flesh. It is not an abomination before God, but only a daily sin that God will punish unto repentance; yet he keeps the people, spares them and forgives them, when the people turn to him and learn to acknowledge his goodness. On the other hand, where this faith and doctrine do not exist, everything is lost; for it is impossible for man not to establish for himself a false worship and choose his own opinion and work, and worship it, so that he really denies God and his Word, and God is entirely turned aside; so that his grace cannot operate. Such abomination is generally the most beautiful and the greatest holiness in the eyes of the world, which outwardly appears in beautiful works and customs; but inwardly is full of filthiness, as we can see at the present day in our orders and church services where they are at their best. However there are again some Christians who are not like these in their works and ways; but are truly holy before God.

9. Now Christ says, when the abomination, that is, this idol,

shall stand in the temple, the kingdom shall finally be made desolate and destroyed, so that it can never be rebuilt again, as Luke expresses it clearly in these words, 21, 20f: "But when ye see Jerusalem compassed with armies, then know that our desolation is at hand. Then let them that are in Judea flee unto the mountains; and let them that are in the midst of her depart out; and let not them that are in the country enter therein. For these are days of vengeance, that all things which are written may be fulfilled." And further, "Woe unto them that are with child and to them that give suck in those days! And pray ye that your flight may be not in the winter, neither on a Sabbath: for then shall be great tribulation, such as had not been from the beginning of the world until now, no, nor ever shall be."

10. All this pertains still to the Jewish nation. For if this should come upon us at the end of the world, then would we, according to the text, have to be in the land of Judea, because he really points to that country. It is also true, when he says that no greater calamity has been or can be upon the earth than was at the time of the destruction of Jerusalem; as we see in history, how unmercifully they were slaughtered and even killed one another, cast themselves into the fire, and permitted themselves to kill one another. Yea, the famine was so great that they ate the strings of cross-bows and even their own children. It was so shameful and abominable that like pity and distress shall never be heard again.

11. But they themselves wanted it, hence God permitted them to be thus blighted and destroyed. He would gladly have had mercy upon them and preserved them, but they brought themselves to such distress with their stiff-necked-ness, that they killed and consumed one another; that as they began it, all such murder and bloodshed had to increase. Thus the death of Christ and of all the prophets is most abominably avenged on them, and that without ceasing, they raged against the Word of God, and persecuted and drove away the Apostles, as St. Paul says in Thess. 2, 15-16, that the wrath of God finally came upon them.

12. When such fearful wrath and abominable plagues are at hand, says Christ, then flee wherever ye are able to flee; for these words, "Then flee unto the mountains, he that is in Judea, and he that is upon the housetop," etc.; then; "He who is in the field," etc., are all written or spoken symbolically, as if to say, hasten quickly away; the sooner the better, and let no one find or overtake you. This also came to pass. After the Jews had been sufficiently warned by many signs, that they should submit themselves to the Romans, and they would not; then the disciples and apostles fled away and followed this saying of Christ, they left everything behind that was in Judea and never returned to take anything.

13. "And pray ye," he says further, "that your flight be not in the winter, neither on a Sabbath;" that is, see to it that you flee at the right time, that you be not overtaken. For he did not want to perform a miracle and keep them safely in the midst of the enemy, although he could have done so; for he had determined that everything that was there should be completely destroyed together; therefore all as one mass were only fit for destruction. If there were indeed a great multitude at Jerusalem according to the record, a million and a hundred thousand men were melted together, as many as were in the city. Therefore Jesus admonishes the disciples that they should not postpone their flight to the Sabbath, when they did not dare to journey; nor to the winter, when it would be cold; but that they should depart, the sooner the better; that if they hesitate, an inconvenient time to flee would come.

14. Thus far Jesus speaks concerning the Jews. Now I have said before that Matthew and Mark unite these two ends together. Therefore it is difficult to discriminate, and yet we must discriminate between the two. Therefore notice that what had been said up to the present, all referred to the Jews; but now he weaves both together, breaks off abruptly, does not concern himself about the order in which the passages were spoken by Christ, and how they are connected with and follow one another; but leaves it to the

Evangelist Luke, yet he wants to say that it shall be thus at the last day, and says:

"And except those days had been shortened, no flesh would have been saved; but for the elect's sake those days shall be shortened."

15. This refers to both parts and the meaning is, that the distress shall not endure long, for the sake of the godly; for the war against the Jews did not last quite two years, when peace was declared. But since all this has reference also to the end of the world, we wish to apply these passages concerning the Jews also to ourselves, so that we do justice to the Evangelist.

16. That a war shall come again as came upon the Jews, I do not expect, because the text says: There shall be such tribulation as shall never be again, as we also read and see; but another punishment shall come upon us; as that was a temporal war, so at the end of the world will a spiritual war come over the ungodly, who will be in the same condition as the Jews. Thus they will agree with one another: as that calamity came upon Jerusalem according to God's ordering and everything was ground to powder; so abominable, and even worse, shall it be before the last day, when he shall come and make an end of the whole world.

17. For when Christ ascended into heaven, he established his kingdom not only in Judea, but extended it into all the world by means of the Gospel, which is being preached and heard everywhere. But we are doing just like the Jews, we deny and persecute the Word of God, kill the Christians who confess and preach this Gospel, as at the first the Romans, and afterwards to the present day, the Pope, bishops, princes, monks and priests do. This has now been done, for more than five hundred years, and no one was allowed to preach the Word of God, unless they repeated from the pulpit the text of the Gospel for a mere show, and afterwards brought out of it or put into it the mere doctrines of men. If anyone opposed it, they rose against him with fire and sword and suppressed it. And it avails nothing, how they are warned and frightened by words and signs; they still stand

in their pride, storm and rage against it as lunatics, so that God will ever have sufficient reason to destroy them finally and eternally at the last day.

18. Therefore this passage in Daniel concerning the abomination applies also to us. For we also have indeed a real abomination or desolation sitting in a holy place, namely: in Christendom and in the consciences of men, where God alone should sit and reign, of which Daniel speaks in very clear words in the 8th and 9th chapters. For this is the real pure doctrine, if we preach that we are redeemed by Christ from sin, death, satan and all misfortune, and are planted in the kingdom of God through the Word and faith and thereby are made free from all law, and that no man, whoever he be, can enter into the kingdom of God through the works of the law nor be made free from sin. Where this is preached and believed, there Christ reigns spiritually in the heart without a medium; there is the Holy Spirit with all the treasures and fullness of the riches of God.

19. But what is the Pope doing? He is sitting not in the natural temple or God's house, but in the spiritual, in the new and living temple of which Paul says: "If any man destroyeth the temple of God, him shall God destroy; for the temple of God is holy, which temple ye are," 1 Cor. 3, 16-17. In all times many devils and heretics have tried to sit here, and all who are preaching against the true doctrine: If you want to be saved, then simply join this or that society and order, and do this or that work. They draw away the people from faith to works, although they are using the words, Christ is the Lord, but in truth deny him, for they do not say a single word that he forgives sins alone through grace, and redeems from death and hell, but they say: Through this order, through these works, we must do penance for sin, and atone for it in order to obtain grace, which is as much as to say: Christ did not accomplish it, he is not the Savior; his suffering and death cannot help, for if your works can accomplish it, then Christ cannot accomplish it only through his blood and death, or the other must be in vain. If you insist upon your works, then you drive out

Christ; you deny and put to shame his precious blood and him with it; then he cannot reign in your heart through his Word, work and spirit, but my work is my idol whom I let sit in my heart and reign.

20. Thus you see whether the Pope is not the greatest arch-abomination of all abominations, to whom Christ and Daniel refer; and the true Antichrist, of whom it is written that he sitteth in the temple of God, among the people, where Christ is named and where his kingdom, spirit, baptism, Word and faith should be: because he interferes with the office and kingdom of Christ by his fanaticism of the spiritual rites of Christ, wants to rule over the consciences and govern with his propositions and works. And he can in truth be called an "abomination of desolation," who is only destroying and laying waste everything, for as has been said: Christ and my works cannot abide together; if the one stands, the other must go down and be destroyed; wherefore the Pope has made desolate the kingdom of Christ, as far as his diocese reaches, and all who join him have denied Christ.

21. St. Paul prophesied all this, when in 2 Thess. 2, 3-4, he calls him: "The man of sin and the son of perdition, he that opposeth and exalteth himself against all that is called God or that is worshipped; so that he sitteth in the temple of God, setting himself forth as God." But that the Papists want to turn this passage from themselves and say: Christ and Paul are speaking of the temple of Jerusalem, that Antichrist shall sit and rule there, amounts to nothing. For Christ says here, that Jerusalem together with the temple shall have an end, and after its destruction it shall never be rebuilt. Therefore since Paul is pointing to the time after the Jewish kingdom, and the destruction of the material temple, it cannot be understood otherwise than of the new spiritual temple, which as he says himself, we are. There, Paul says, the Pope shall sit and be honored, not above God, but above everything that is called God, for the name of God does indeed remain the highest honor, therefore he cannot exalt himself above the true God, but above that which is called God and is worshipped; that is, he is exalted against

his preaching and honor, higher than the true God, as is apparent in that so many princes and the world are clinging to him and regard his command higher and greater than the command of God. If any man eats meat contrary to his command or goes out of the impure calling of the priest, monk, or nun, into married life, as God has commanded, or according to the institution of Christ takes the sacrament in both forms; that is the greatest sin. They regarded it much less than stealing, adultery and all open vice against the command of God, and no one is even allowed to punish them for it. Yea, that they themselves defame the Word of God, persecute and kill the Christians, they esteem as the highest service of God, as it is also the highest service they can do for their god, the Pope. Is not this exalting and honoring Anti-christ against God, so that if anyone speaks or does anything against this, if he gets into their hands, he must immediately die? I think now that enough has been pictured forth and explained concerning this abomination.

22. Now it is high time for him to run and flee, who is able to flee; let everything he has behind and depart; the sooner the better; not with his feet but with his heart, in such a way that he will be rid of the abomination and enter the kingdom of Christ through faith. But to do this reason and a keen insight are needed rightly to discern the abomination. It cannot be seen in any way better than when we compare it to Christ who teaches, as stated above, that we are reconciled to God, and are saved through his blood. But the Pope ascribes this power to our works. Thus you ever see that to be saved through works and not to be saved through works (to believe on Christ as our justification before God) are contrary to each other. If you then want to remain with Christ, you must flee from the Pope and let him go.

23. This is now the abomination of desolation that has reigned until our time; but is now revealed through the grace of God, but will never be destroyed by emperor or worldly power. It must all be higher than that material destruction, since that was such a great tribulation, that there never can be a greater physically. Therefore did God

reserve the destruction of this abomination for himslf, as Paul says in 2 Thess, 2, 8: "Whom the Lord Jesus shall slay with the breath of his mouth, and bring to nought by the manifestation of his coming." Although they themselves fear evil from worldly power and insurrection, yet this shall not be so well with them. For they are not worthy of such mild punishment, and God will not grant unto them that they be destroyed through man, but will do it himself without means, through his Word. Inasmuch as it has now made a beginning and the kingdom is destroyed even to the extent that it avails nothing, nor can take captive the conscience of those who know the Gospel. However hostile the Pope rages against the Gospel; he must nevertheless fall at the feet of princes and seek help from them. Hence his power is weakened and broken by means of the Gospel; but his final destruction is reserved unto the last day. Therefore it must continue in part until Christ at his coming shall destroy and grind to powder all together from heaven.

24. But as at that time among the Jews, the days were shortened, as Christ said, so must now also the days be shortened for the elect's sake; for we see that the government of the Pope has had opposition and has declined during the last hundred years, without, at the Council of Constance where Huss was burned at the stake, having frightened everybody that he was held as God; but the truth came finally to light, so that now it is very much despised and can endure but a little longer; hence we notice, as I said before, that our text refers not only to the Jews but also to our abomination, the Pope's kingdom. Now Christ says further:

"Then if any man shall say unto you, Lo, here is the Christ, or, Here; believe it not."

25. From this passage we should indeed know and understand how to conquer the Pope and his rebel horde, who abolish the kingdom of Christ, and bind the Christian life to external and visible things, as they also publicly declare: Where the Pope is, there is the Christian church. They want to lead us to the point that we should find, feel and touch it in person or state, or in a manner that is wholly external.

Thus they do in all their cloisters and institutions. Therefore they say: If you enter this calling, eat, clothe yourself,
pray and fast so and so, then you will atone for your sins
and be saved. Heretofore Christ pictured this beautifully to
us, and pointed to all these cloisters, callings and works, by
which they wish to help the soul, and warns us to be careful
of them, and not to permit ourselves to be drawn from the
foundation upon which we stand; that we cannot become
Christians through any such thing; but are redeemed from
all evil alone through his blood and are planted into his
kingdom, if we believe. He thus takes from our eyes all
temporal and external things, casts to the ground with one
word all doctrines that do not proclaim faith in its purity,
and all life that is not regulated according to the right doctrine of faith. In short, he adds: "If anyone says, here or
there is Christ," believe it not. which means: Beware
of everything that leads you to works, for it surely deceives
and separates you from me.

*"For there shall arise false Christs, and false prophets, and
shall show great signs and wonders; so as to lead astray, if
possible, even the elect."*

26. These are admirable, earnest and fearful words, that
these preachers of works must force this truth into the people with such a show and emphasis that even the saints who
stand in faith cannot protect themselves against it, but are
led astray thereby, as has been the case. For the dear
fathers, Augustine, I think Jerome also, likewise St. Bernard,
Gregory, Francis, Dominicus and many others, although they
were godly men, have all erred here, as I have often re-
marked in other places. For this error, that the Christian
life was bound to external things, was early introduced and
they with others were swept into it, and it went so far that
they were led into it by their outward conduct, as we see in
the books of St. Bernard, how poorly he writes when he answered anyone on the questions of their monastic life; but
when he writes freely out of his own soul, he preaches so
elegantly that it is a pleasure for him, as Augustine, Jerome,
Cyprian, the great and noble martyr, and many others ex-

perienced. But when any question was laid before them concerning the law and external regulations, whether we should understand it so, or so, then they immediately stumbled and fell, so that little was needed to mislead them. Still the followers of the Pope use this as the greatest argument against us. They say, should so many holy people and teachers have erred, and should God have forsaken the world so completely? They do not see that this becomes to them a stumbling-block to cause their fall.

27. What shall we now answer them? The passage lies clearly before us. This we must believe and let it stand; we cannot get away from it, even though the holy angels in heaven were against it, for should not Christ be holier and his Word amount to more than their word? For he never at any time says: Lord of the many or of the great multitude, but of the small number, of the elect, that they should stumble, so that they would almost be led astray, and he warns us that we should not cling to this, when we see that they cling to external things. Had they then not erred, Christ could not have been right when he proclaimed it. Now if all the saints should come and bid me believe in the Pope, I would not do it, but say: Even though you are of the elect, Christ nevertheless has said that there should be abominable and dangerous times: that you also must err. Therefore we must cling alone to the Scriptures and to the Word of God, which say he is not here nor there. Where he is, there I shall be. He will not be there where my work or calling is. Now whoever teaches me otherwise deceives me; therefore I still insist that nothing avails that they propose, as for example: The holy fathers and teachers thought so, lived so, hence we also must think and live in like manner; but this avails: Christ taught and thought so, therefore we must also think the same, for he is authority, above all the saints.

"Behold, I have told you beforehand. If therefore they shall say unto you, Behold, he is in the wilderness; go not forth: Behold, he is in the inner chambers, believe it not."

28. At the time of the holy fathers, Anthony and others,

shortly after the Apostles, the fallacy already arose, of
which Christ is speaking here, although Anthony strove
against it, that everybody was running to the wilderness by
the thousands, and it gained such favor that later Jerome
and Augustine almost worshipped custom, and did not know
how sufficiently to praise it. Now when we look at it in the
right light, this text powerfully opposes that movement,
and there were also among them many heretics and
many condemned persons, and although there were godly
people among them who escaped the deception, nevertheless
the example was dangerous and cannot be commended. Also
St. Francis was a holy man, but his example and the order
he established we are not to follow. But this no one, not
even the saints, has recognized; so deeply and with such
great display has it taken root. The Christian life is not
confined to the wilderness, but moves freely in public society as Christ and the Apostles lived, that we come before
and among the world, preach and admonish openly, to bring
the people to Christ; but the people who run to the wilderness, do not want to remain in the world where they must
suffer so much. They choose for themselves their own strict
life, want thereby to be better Christians than others, as also
the cloisters do, which are designated by Christ as the
"chambers." Christ closes now and says:

*"For as the lightning cometh forth from the east, and is seen
even unto the west; so shall be the coming of the Son of man."*

29. By this Christ wishes to say: Only do not believe
them, when they want to bind Christ to this or that, and
try to lead you from faith to works. I warn you not to fall
from the pure faith, for you know not it what hour I will
come. When anyone neglects his looking for me, then I will
come as suddenly as the lightning flashes from heaven.
When anyone clings not to him by faith, he is lost. Therefore see to it, that that day does not come upon you un-
awares. Remain steadfast in the faith, so that if you be indolent and sleep, satan may not tare you from your faith.
But these words here follow each other in disorder. For as
I said, Matthew gives these passages all in a heap and not in

order. Therefore it does not agree exactly with the words which follow here:

"Wheresoever the carcass is, there will the eagles be gathered together."

30. That is, you need not ask where the place is, where Christ shall come. I am where I wish to be, hence we will meet each other, as we say: "Wheresoever the carcase is, there will the eagles be gathered together." For as the eagle does not paint for himself the place to which it will fly, but wherever the carcase is, there they will be gathered together; thus mine own will also find me. Where I am, there shall my elect also be. This is the text concerning the end of the Jews and of the world: to which Matthew now unites the passages concerning the signs of the last day, all which Luke separates clearly. This will belong to another occasion and is elsewhere fully discussed.

Note. Some on the last Sunday of the year preach on the Gospel of John 6, where Christ feeds the multitudes with five loaves and two fishes, which is explained in the Winter Postil during Lent.—God be praised forever.

TWENTY-SIXTH SUNDAY AFTER TRINITY.

This sermon is found only in the c. edition. Erl. 14, 375; W. 11, 2515; St. L. 11, 1884.

Text: Mat. 25, 31-46. But when the Son of man shall come in his glory, and all the angels with him, then shall he sit on the throne of his glory: and before him shall be gathered all the nations: and he shall separate them one from another, as the shepherd separateth the sheep from the goats; and he shall set the sheep on his right hand, but the goats on the left. Then shall the King say unto them on his right hand, Come, ye blessed of my Father, inherit the kingdom prepared for you from the foundation of the world: for I was hungry, and ye gave me to eat; I was thirsty, and ye gave me drink; I was a stranger, and ye took me in; naked, and ye clothed me; I was sick, and ye visited me; I was in prison, and ye came unto me. Then shall the righteous answer him, saying, Lord, when saw we thee hungry, and fed thee? or athirst, and gave thee drink? And when saw we thee a stranger, and took thee in? or naked, and clothed thee? And when saw we thee sick, or in prison, and came unto thee? And the King shall answer and say unto them, Verily I say unto you, Inasmuch as ye did it unto one of these my brethren, even these least, ye did it unto me. Then shall he say also unto them on the left hand, Depart from me, ye cursed, into the eternal fire which is prepared for the devil and his angels: for I was hungry, and ye did not give me to eat; I was thirsty, and ye gave me no drink; I was a stranger, and ye took me not in; naked, and ye clothed me not; sick, and in prison, and ye visited me not. Then shall they also answer, saying, Lord, when saw we thee hungry, or athirst, or a stranger, or naked, or sick, or in prison, and did not minister unto thee? Then shall he answer them, saying, Verily I say unto you, Inasmuch as ye did it not unto one of these least, ye did it not unto me.

And these shall go away into eternal punishment: but the righteous into eternal life.

CONTENTS: CHRIST'S RETURN TO JUDGE THE CHRISTIANS
AND THE GODLESS.

1. The words of this Gospel are in themselves clear and lucid. They have been given both for the comfort and encouragement of believing Christians, and for the warning and terror of others, if perchance, they might be of help to them. While most lessons almost exclusively teach and inculcate faith, this one treats only of the works, which Christ will examine at the last day, that it may be seen that he wishes them to be remembered and performed by those who wish to be Christians and be found in his kingdom.

2. And Christ himself gives this admonition here in the strongest terms that can be given, both in the consoling promise of a glorious, eternal reward, and in the most ter-

rible threatenings of eternal wrath and punishment upon all
who despise the admonition; so that whoever is not moved
and aroused by these words can certainly never be moved by
anything. For Christ says, he will himself come visibly in
his majesty, at the last day, with all the angels, and that he
will transplant all who have believed in him and have
exercised love toward his followers, into his father's kingdom of eternal glory all who believe in him and love his
saints; and that he will also cast into hell forever all who
live not as Christians, and who separate themselves from
him and all his saints.

3. Now, had it not been told us we should be inquisitive
beyond measure to know what would happen on the last day,
and what Jesus would say and do on that day. Here we are
now told, and have set before us first of all, death, which no
one can escape; but after that the day of judgment. Then it
shall come to pass that Christ will bring together by means
of the resurrection all who have ever lived upon earth; and
at the same time he will descend in great inexpressible
majesty, sitting upon the throne of judgment, with all the
heavenly host hovering around him; and all the good and
bad will appear, so that we shall all stand exposed before
him, and no one will be able to conceal himself.

4. The appearance of this glory and majesty will immediately become a great terror and pain to the condemned,
as we read in to-day's Epistle lesson, lest they shall suffer
punishment, even eternal destruction from the face of the
Lord and from the glory of his might, when he shall come to
be glorified in his saints, 2 Thess. 1, 9-10. For even if there
were no more than a single angel present, there would not
remain in his presence one fickle, wicked conscience, were it
possible to escape, any more than a thief and a rascal can
bear to come before a human judge. If he could escape, he
would much prefer it, if only for the purpose that he might
escape public disgrace, to say nothing of his being compelled
to hear the judgment passed upon him.

What a terrible sight this will be, when the ungodly
shall see not only all God's angels and creatures, but also the

Judge in his divine majesty, and shall hear the verdict of eternal destruction and hell fire pronounced upon them forever! This ought surely to be a strong, powerful admonition for us to live as Christians, so that we may stand in honor and without fear at the right hand of this majestic Lord, where there will be no fear nor terror, but pure comfort and everlasting joy.

5. For he will then, as he says here himself, immediately separate the goats from the sheep. And this will take place publicly in the presence of all angels, men, and creatures, and before the whole rabble of an ungodly world, that it may be seen who have been pious, honest Christians, as well as who have been false hypocrites. This separation cannot take place in the world until that day, not even in the assembly that constitutes the Christian Church. The good and the bad must remain together in this world, as the parable of the wedding guests says, Mat. 22, 10; or as Christ himself had to tolerate Judas among his Apostles. Christians are even now grieved that they must remain here in the midst of a crooked, perverse, ungodly people, which is the kingdom of Satan, Phil. 2, 15.

6. While they have their sufferings here upon earth, they will have also their comfort on the coming day of judgment, when Christ will separate them from the other flock, so that after that day no false, ungodly men, nor death, nor devil can ever touch them or offend them.

7. Then he will pronounce the verdict in the very words in which he has already prepared it and set it forth, and he will certainly not change it. And the words are peculiar in this that he makes them depend upon the deeds and works here mentioned, which they have or have not done, and which are the basis and cause of his judgment. And all these words set forth at length the works which have been done as well as those which have been neglected. And all this shall happen in the twinkling of an eye, when the hearts of all men shall be revealed before all creatures; and as it is preached here, so there all will be forthwith executed.

8. You may ask why Christ there especially examine

works called deeds of mercy, or the neglect of such works? Six different kinds are mentioned in the text, although many more might be given; yet were one to judge critically in the matter, there are no more works than those implied in the fifth commandment: Thou shalt not kill; in which we are commanded in general, as Christ himself explains it, not to be angry with our neighbor, but to be kind to him and ready to serve and assist him, supply his wants in times of need, whether in hunger, thirst, nakedness, suffering, imprisonment, sickness or other troubles, and to do this even to those who may have given us occasion for anger or for unmerciful acts, and thus do not appear to be worthy of our love and benevolence. For that is a poor virtue which does good only to those we love, or from whom we hope to receive kindness and thanks in return.

But one might, as has been said, add to those works of mercy many more from other commandments; for example from the sixth, that one is to assist his neighbor, to protect his wife, children and domestics, and to keep them under proper restraint and in honor; also from the seventh, eighth and last commandments, that is, to help save and maintain the goods and property, house, home and good report of his neighbor; also to help protect and defend the poor, the oppressed and the down-trodden.

9. Now Christ says also in Mat. 12, 36, that men must give an account on the day of judgment not only of the transgressions of these commandments, but also of every idle word they have spoken. Then where shall the works of the first table, the greatest commandment, as right teaching, faith, prayer, hearing and preaching of God's Word, and the like, find their place? Why does he pronounce such a harsh and severe judgment only upon those who have omitted to do the works of the fifth commandment? Because these works appear almost the same as those which the heathen do. For the Turks do more works of this kind and boast more of them than we who are called Christians. Among them each one regards his neighbor as his brother and shares with him whatever he has. Nay, they regard it the greatest unfaith-

fulness and most shameful vice not to share bread with a neighbor in times of hunger. Why does he so highly extol these works which shine so brightly also among the Turks and among the heathen? Certainly he does not mean to say that those also who are not Christians merit eternal life by reason of such works?

10. For Christ himself shows that he is speaking of the works of believing Christians, when he says: "I was hungry and ye gave me to eat," etc.; "what ye have done unto the least of these my brethren ye have done unto me." For there is no doubt that he who performs such works of mercy to Christians, must himself be a Christian and a believer; but he who does not believe in Christ, will certainly never be so kind toward a Christian, much less toward Christ, so that for his sake he would show mercy to the poor, and needy; therefore he will refer to these works at the judgment, and accordingly pronounce the verdict to both parties, to those who have done, and those who have not done these works, as a public testimony of the fruits of their faith or of their unbelief.

11. It seems as though he meant hereby to show that many Christians, after receiving the preaching of the Gospel, of the forgiveness of sins and grace through Christ, become even worse than the heathen. For he also says in Mat. 19, 30, "Many that are first shall be last; and the last shall be first." Thus it will also be at the end of the world; those who should be honest Christians, because they heard the Gospel, are much worse and more unmerciful than they were before, as we see too many examples of this even now.

Aforetime when we were to do good works under the seduction and false worship of the Papacy, every one was ready and willing; a prince, for example, or a city, could give more alms and a greater endowment than now all the kings and emperors are able to give. But now all the world seems to be learning nothing else than how to estimate values, to rake and scrape, to rob and steal by lying, deceiving, usury, overcharging, overrating, and the like; and every man treats his neighbor, not as though he were his friend, much less as his brother in Christ, but as his mortal enemy, and as though he intended to snatch all things to himself and begrudge everything to others.

12. This goes on daily, is constantly increasing, is a very common practice and custom. among all classes of people, among princes, the nobility, burghers, peasants, in all courts, cities, villages, yes in almost every home. Tell me, what city is now so strong and pious as to be able to raise an amount sufficient to support a schoolmaster or a preacher? Yes, if we did not already have the liberal alms and endowments of our forefathers, the Gospel would long ago have disappeared in the cities on account of the burghers, and in the country because of the nobility and peasants, and poor preachers would have nothing to eat nor to drink. For we do not love to give, but would rather take even by force what others have given and endowed. Therefore it is no credit to us that a single pulpit or school is still maintained. Yea, how many there are among the great, the powerful, and the rich, especially in the Papacy, who would like to see nothing better than all preachers, schools, and arts exterminated.

13. Such are the thanks to the blessed Gospel, by which men have been freed from the bondage and plagues of the Pope, that they must become so shamefully wicked in these last times. They are now no more unmerciful. no more in a human, but in a satanic way; they are not satisfied with being allowed to enjoy the Gospel, and grow fat by robbing and stealing the revenues of the church, but they must also be scheming with all their power how they may completely starve out the Gospel. One can easily count upon his fingers, what they who enjoy the Gospel are doing and giving here and elsewhere; and, were it only for us now living, there would long since have been no preacher or student from whom our children and descendants might know what we had taught and believed.

14. In short, what do you think Christ will say on that day, seated on his judgment throne, to such unmerciful Christianity? "Dear sir, listen, you have also pretended to

be a Christian and boasted of the Gospel; did you not also hear this sermon, that I myself preached, in which I told you what my verdict and decision would be: 'Depart from me, ye cursed?' I was hungry and thirsty, naked and sick, poor and in prison, and ye gave me no meat, no drink, clothed me not, took me not in, and visited me not. Why have ye neglected this, and have been more shameless and unmerciful toward your own brethren than the Turk or heathen?''

Will you excuse yourself by pleading: "Lord, when saw we thee hungry or thirsty?" etc. Then he will answer you again through your own conscience: Dear sir, were there no people who preached to you; or perhaps poor students who should have at the time been studying and learning God's Word, or were there no poor, persecuted Christians whom you ought to have fed, clothed and visited?

15. We ought really to be ashamed of ourselves, having had the example of parents, ancestors, lords and kings, princes and others, who gave so liberally and charitably, even in profusion, to churches, ministers, schools, endowments, hospitals and the like; and by such liberal giving neither they nor their descendants were made poorer. What would they have done, had they had the light of the Gospel, that is given unto us? How did the Apostles and their followers in the beginning bring all they had for their poor widows, or for those who had nothing, or who were banished and persecuted, in order that no one among them might suffer for the necessities of life! In this way poor Christians should at all times support one another. Otherwise, as I have said, the Gospel, the pulpit, churches and schools would already be completely exterminated, no matter how much the rest of the world did.

Were it not for the grace of God, by which he gives us here and there a pious prince, or godly government, which preserves the fragments still left, that all may not be destroyed by the graspers and vultures, thieves and robbers; were it not for this grace, I say, the poor pastors and preachers would not only be starved, but also murdered. Nor are

there now any other poor people than those who serve, or
are being trained to serve the church; and these can obtain
no suport elsewhere, and must leave their poor wives and
children die of hunger because of an indifferent world; on
the other hand the world is full of useless, unfaithful,
wicked fellows among day-laborers, lazy mechanics, servants,
maids, and idle, greedy beggars, who everywhere by lying,
deceiving, robbing and stealing, take away the hard-earned
bread and butter from those who are really poor, and yet go
unpunished in the midst of their wantonness and insolence.

16. This I say, that we may see how Christ will upbraid
the false liars and hypocrites among Christians, on the day
of judgment, and having convicted them before all creatures
will condemn them, because they have done none of the
works which even the heathen do to their fellows; who did
much more in their false and erroneous religion, and would
have done it even more willingly had they known better.

17. Since now this terrible condemnation is justly pronounced over those who neglected these works, what will
happen to those who have not only neglected the same, have
given nothing to the poor Christians, nor served them; but
robbed them of what they had, drove them to hunger, thirst
and nakedness, furthermore persecuted, scattered, impris-
oned, and murdered them? These are so unutterably wicked,
so utterly condemned to the bottomless pit with the devil and
his angels, that Christ will not think or speak of them. But
he will assuredly not forget these robbers, tyrants, and
bloodhounds any more than he will forget or pass over un-
rewarded those who have suffered hunger thirst, nakedness,
persecution and the like, especially for his and his Word's
sake. He will not forget those to whom mercy has been
shown, even though he speaks only to those who have shown
mercy and have lent their aid; for he highly and nobly commends them, when he says. "Inasmuch as ye did it unto one
of these my brethren, even these least, ye did it unto me."

18. On account of this judgment fear and trembling might
well seize our great spiritual prelates, as they call themselves, the popes, cardinals, bishops, canons, priests, and the

whole diabolical rabble of the anti-christian crowd at Rome, and everywhere, in their monasteries and brothels, if they were not altogether hardened and deliberately given to Satan, body and soul. They think and act as though they were especially appointed to snatch to themselves every thing that belongs to the poor church, and in their own wantonness to consume, spend, waste, squander, in dissipation, gambling and debauchery, in the most shameful and scandalous maner, whatever has been given for the maintenance of students, schools and the poor people. They mock God and man, 2 Pet. 2, 13; yea, they publicly murder innocent, pious people.

19. Yea, woe, another and eternal woe, to them and to all who side with them. For it had been better for them, had they never been born, as Christ says of Judas. Therefore they ought rather to wish that their mothers had drowned them in their first bath, or that they had never come forth from the womb, than that one of them should have become pope or cardinal or a popish priest. For they are nothing else than merely desperate and select ones, not highway robbers, but public country-thieves, who take, not the goods of the mighty and the powerful that really have something, but of the poor and wretched, of the parish-churches, schools, and hospitals, whose morsels are snatched from their teeth, and whose drink is torn from their mouths, so that they are unable to maintain life.

20. Therefore let every man beware of the Pope, the bishops, and the priesthood, as he would beware of those who have already been condemned alive to the abyss of perdition. Truly Paul did not prophesy in vain, 2 Tim. 3, 1, that in the last days perilous times shall come. Yet all the world moves along indifferently and gives no heed to this terrible judgment that has already been decided against such unmerciful robbers, thieves, and murderers of poor Christians, but especially against those who pretend to be Christians, who after having received grace slide back again, and like a dog eat their own vomit, or as the swine wallow in their own

filth, 2 Pet. 2, 20-22, and thus, having been first, become last before anyone is aware of it.

21. The second reason why Christ especially mentions these works of mercy and their omission, from the fifth commandment, is, that he wishes to remind us, who have been called to be Christians, have received mercy through our Lord, have been redeemed from the wrath of God and the guilt of the fifth commandment and from eternal death, and on the contrary have a gracious God, who is good to us in time and in eternity, to remind us, I say, to look upon all this and regard it as having been done not only for our salvation but also for an example. For, since he has shown us such mercy as to save us, we are also to act toward our neighbor in a manner as not to transgress against the fifth fifth commandment, which especially demands love and mercy.

And we are not to do these things simply because of the commandment and of the threatening of judgment, but for the sake of the example of the excellent and great goodness God has shown. For this example cannot be without blessed results, as God's work of redemption is not without power and good fruit. Although most people become worse from having heard the Gospel, there must nevertheless be some who rightly understand it and remain faithful to it; for he says that he will separate them into two flocks; therefore there must also be pious ones who have kept this commandment.

22. Therefore see to it that you are among those who are kind and merciful here upon earth for Christ's sake, or who even suffer for his sake, then you may joyfully await the last day, and need not be afraid of the judgment; for he has already selected you and placed you among those who shall stand at his right hand.

23. For we, who are Christians, should hope for the coming of this judgment and desire it with our whole heart; as we pray for it in the words: Thy kingdom come, thy will be done, deliver us from evil; so that we may also hear the glad and welcome words: Come, ye blessed, into the king-

dom of my Father. This is the verdict we await; for this reason we are Christians, and just for the sake of this hope we are so severely oppressed, first by Satan and by our own flesh, which would not have us believe this and rejoice over it; then by the tyranny and enmity of the world. For we must constantly see and hear the maliciousness which Satan and the world practice against the Gospel. There is so much misery upon earth that we ought to be tired of this life and cry aloud: Come, dear Lord, and deliver us.

24. For there are certainly souls who are joyfully and with a good conscience awaiting the judgement of Christ; for they are in the rank and fellowship of those who believe in Christ, and who show fruits of faith through charity and beneficence toward the poor, or through patience in suffering with them. For, as I have said, he who does not have faith will not do works of mercy to Christians, but he who does them, will do them because he believes that he has a faithful Savior and Redeemer in Christ, who has reconciled him to God. Therefore he must have also a kind, loving heart toward his neighbors, even toward his enemies, and serve them in every time of need. Yea, he endures also, as I have just said, those things which come upon him from the world and the devil on account of his faith.

Whosoever is thus minded, I say, let him be joyful and of good courage; for he has already the blessed and joyful verdict: Come, thou blessed one, for thou hast also been one of the least of my brethren, who hast thyself suffered hunger and thirst, or who hast served the other hungry and thirsty ones, and hast shown mercy, as I have done.

25. Behold, therefore, the separation of the sheep and goats is already made in this life, so that every one can experience it internally and must indicate and show it also externally. For they who have not faith will surely do none of these things · they will neither comfort themselves with the grace of Christ, nor think of exercising mercy; they pass by the Word of God and their neighbor, as though they neither saw nor heard anything; they do not care to know

that there is a Lord whom they are to serve and who will demand such service from them. For if they would consider that they must die, and appear before this judgment seat, they would not at the time defraud any one of a farthing. But, on the contrary, they think best to turn their eyes away from death and to keep the heart from thinking of it.

26. The world is so blind and hardened, that it can see before its eyes the great mass of men of all kinds who have passed away, and who are daily passing away, but is unwilling to behold it with seeing eyes, and to heed it, but continues securely and gaily in its wickedness. Furthermore, when it hears of the terrible judgment and condemnation that shall come upon it, it gives no heed to the consolation and example offered through Christ, but practices all kinds of unmercifulness; strives to hear and will have nothing else than the terrible, irrevocable verdict pronounced upon it from the judgment seat of Christ, and immediately after be cast from his presence into eternal hell-fire.

27. Wherefore he who may yet be converted and is ready to listen, will have enough, both to frighten and warn him, and to animate and persuade him to accommodate himself to the Word and example of Christ, while there is time and opportunity, so that he need not hear with the world this dreadful judgment, but may have joy and comfort in mercy with all Christians. Nor did Christ spare his Apostles, but earnestly admonished them, when he said in Luke 21, 34-36: "Take heed to yourselves, lest haply your hearts be overcharged with surfeiting, and drunkenness, and cares of this life," which, he shows, will be most prevalent at the end of the world, " and that day come on you suddenly as a snare; but watch ye at every season, making supplication, that ye may prevail to escape all these things that shall come to pass, and to stand before the Son of man," etc.

28. Notice, however, as I said, that he wishes to distinguish the good works of the Christians from the works of the Turks and the heathen. For he speaks of the works done unto him, of which both parties claim to be ignorant,

the wicked excusing themselves, because they had not seen him, etc. But herewith he has most beautifully explained the fifth commandment, that it means, he who fulfills it can be none else than a believing Christian, who did it unto Christ. Thus the woman who annointed his head and feet, Mat. 26, 10-13, fulfilled this commandment and is praised by him when he says: "She has wrought a good work upon me. For ye have the poor always with you, and if ye wish ye can always do good unto them, but me ye have not always. Verily I say unto you, wheresoever this Gospel shall be preached in the whole world, that also which this woman hath done shall be spoken of for a memorial of her." Again in Mat. 10, 42: "And whosoever shall give to drink unto one of these little ones, who believe in me, a cup of cold water, he shall in no wise lose his reward."

29. We should therefore impress the fact upon our hearts and consider that it is a great and fine thing to do good to a Christian; but on the contrary also, what it is to do evil to him, as I said of the Pope, the bishops, the tyrants, and feudal nobility, who take from the feet of Christ what they have not given him the food, the drink, the lodging and the support of the poor, who are poor for Christ's sake, because they are not in the position, as ministers, sextons and school masters, to rule the world; nor are they able to engage in any other business in which they might gain a livelihood; for then they would also have been made the partakers of power and would receive enough. But since they have no part in the government, the world gives them nothing for their services. As they receive nothing for God's nor Christ's sake, they can have nothing, and must leave behind them poor, wretched widows and orphans.

30. Those in other positions and offices, who have plenty in all respects, do not wish and cannot attend to the duties and the services of the church, neither do they know how. And when ministers and pastors engage in worldly trades and pursuits, they step outside of their proper calling. Therefore they must be supported, if they are to have anything to eat, from beggary, of which Christ here speaks; but

he makes it so precious that whosoever gives meat or drink to the least of his members on earth, he recognizes the same as though it had been done and given to himself. Do we wish then to be Christians, and expect from Christ the honor to be praised and rewarded in the presence of all creatures, we must, indeed, cheerfully and gratuitously give to those who are to perform the duties of their office gratuitously, because they can have no share in secular matters. This we are to do in order to escape the curse and wrath that will come upon those who would not have mercy on their poor brethren, who had to suffer hunger, thirst, misery, and imprisonment in the world in order to bring us to Christ.

31. But how does it happen that the righteous do not recognize and know that they have done their works unto Christ? They say: Lord, when saw we thee hungry, or athirst, etc.? The reason is, that to give something to a poor minister, chaplain, teacher, sexton is regarded as a matter altogether of too small significance to be so precious in the sight of God. Yea, the world looks upon it as so much money thrown away. Yet will any one say that the world would be so much richer, were there no pupils, schools, hospitals? Or that it is on their account any poorer, unless it were entirely heathen, or it were, as heretofore, compelled to give enough for the devil's sake, and allow itself to be flayed to the bone by those who have cheated it of body and soul. In short, the churches and schools receive the very least from the world; yet it is jealous, complains bitterly, and makes a great cry about what they already have, although it gives nothing, and claims to make much better use of its means, when at other times it gives a hundred times as much to shameless, dissolute villains and jugglers; it soon forgets of how much it allows brother Guy to be robbed, and then even it takes a beating in the bargain. It never enters the brain of the world to think and believe that this means to give to Christ; nor is it easy for us to see it ourselves.

32. But Christ is able to speak and judge rightly in this matter, and he knows how much depends upon it. For it is truly impossible to bring up the young in the kingdom of

God in any other way than by means of schools; nor is it possible to maintain the Word of God without pulpits. Where these are allowed to fall into disuse, there will be a second Sodom and Gomorrah, which will fare as those of old, who despised the Word of God, and would not listen to nor endure pious Lot. Thus also Ezekiel, 16, 48-50, prophesies of Jerusalem: "As I live, saith the Lord Jehovah, Sodom thy sister hath not done, she nor her daughters, as thou hast done, thou and thy daughters. Behold, this was the iniquity of thy sister Sodom: pride, fulness of bread, and prosperous ease was in her and in her daughters, neither did she strengthen the hand of the poor and needy. And they were haughty, and committed abomination before me; therefore I took them away as I saw good," etc.

33. The same conditions now exist everywhere. Every peasant, burgher, nobleman is simply gathering dollars, waits and saves, eats and drinks, is insolent and mischievous as though God were nothing at all. No one cares for the despised Jesus in his poverty; nay, he is even tread under foot, until all obedience, discipline and honor are destroyed among us, as they were in Sodom and Gomorrah, and matters become so bad, as to become unbearable, because all admonition and preaching seem to be of no avail.

34. Right unwillingly do I prophesy; for I have often experienced how it came true; but the same conditions, alas, prevail now everywhere; and I fear and must almost resign myself that Germany may have the same experience as Sodom and Jerusalem, and will be a thing of the past; it will either be destroyed by the Turks or it will crumble by its own hand, unless the last day overtake it soon. For the present conditions are altogether unbearable and so exceedingly bad that they cannot become worse; and if there be still a God, he cannot thus let matters go on unpunished.

35. And now the world will not take heed, nor recognize that it must die and stand before God in judgment, but it rages against recognized truth. Let us give heed and take it to heart, that the wrath of God may not also sweep us away. For what else would God need to do to that end, than let

loose both the Turks and Satan against us. The Turk would be compelled to cease doing what he has done and is still doing, were we not so hardened in blindness and impenitence, and so completely ripe for judgment. The reason is that we rage so blasphemously against God's Word and his proffered help, and then in addition make our boast against the Turk.

36. And I hold that, if we Lutherans, as they call us, were only dead, the whole world would immediately cry, *"Victory,"* as though they had already devoured every single Turk. But it shall happen to them also that a hundred shall be slain by one Turk. And when the cry of murder is once heard, how unmercifully the Turks will cut in pieces all people, men, women, and children. Then shall we also begin to cry and lament. It shall come to pass that we shall do as did the Jews, put Christ out of the way. When he has been crucified, we shall be able to take care of the Turk, as Squire Caiaphas and the Jews took care of the Romans; thus the younkers at Jerusalem thought, if they could only put the prophet Jeremiah out of the way, they would surely be safe from the king of Babylon. What happened? After they had cast Jeremiah into the dungeon, the king came and led them all into captivity.

Thus I can also see that God has spun a web over Germany as it is determined to be guilty in the same manner of wilful blindness, defiance, wickedness, contempt, and ungratefulness in opposing the precious Gospel. It is determined to be guilty of foolishness before God, for which it will have to pay dearly. May God preserve us, and grant us and our little flock that we may escape this terrible wrath, and be found among those who honor and serve our dear Christ, and await the judgment at his right hand joyously and blissfully. Amen.

TO THE READER: If it should happen that another Sunday after Trinity should follow the 26th, which is very seldom the case, then it might be well to use the last preceding Epistle and Gospel for the 27th Sunday after Trinity, and on the Sunday preceding the 27th take the following text for the Epistle and the Gospel: Epistle, 2 Peter 3, 3; Gospel, Matthew 24, 37-51.